PITT

LATIN AMERICAN SERIES

UNSETTLING STATECRAFT

Democracy and Neoliberalism in the Central Andes

Catherine M. Conaghan
and James M. Malloy

UNIVERSITY OF PITTSBURGH PRESS

PITTSBURGH AND LONDON

Published by the University of Pittsburgh Press, Pittsburgh, Pa. 15260

Eurospan, London
Manufactured in the United States of America
Printed on acid-free paper

Library of Congress Cataloging-in-Publication Data

Conaghan, Catherine M.
Unsettling statecraft : Democracy and neoliberalism in the central Andes / Catherine M. Conaghan and James M. Malloy.
p. cm.—(Pitt Latin American series)
Includes bibliographical references and index.
ISBN 0-8229-3786-7.—ISBN 0-8229-5532-6 (pbk.)
1. Bolivia—Economic conditions—1982- 2. Ecuador—Economic conditions—1972- 3. Peru—Economic conditions—1968- 4. Bolivia—Politics and government—1982- 5. Ecuador—Politics and government—1984- 6. Peru—Politics and government—1980- I. Malloy, James M. II. Title. III. Series.
HC182.C52 1994
320.98′09048—dc20 94-25328

A CIP catalogue record for this book is available from the British Library

CONTENTS

List of Tables and Figures vi

List of Acronyms vii

Acknowledgments xi

1. Introduction: Explaining Statecraft 3
2. Losing Control: Business-Government Relations in Historical Perspective 22
3. Statism and Military Rule 47
4. The Antistatist Revival and Regime Transition 70
5. Crisis, Elections, and Neoliberal Coalitions 99
6. Theory Into Practice: From Antistatism to Neoliberal Experiments 138
7. Some Things Fall Apart, Some Don't: Exhaustion and Survival of Neoliberal Experiments 162
8. Conclusion: Tocqueville's Fears 203
9. Epilogue: Unfinished Stories 225

Appendix 235

Notes 237

Bibliography 269

Index 295

LIST OF TABLES AND FIGURES

Figure

1. Public Sector Investment and Consumption in Bolivia, Ecuador, and Peru, 1970–78 52

Tables

1. Chronology of Transition in Ecuador 91
2. Chronology of Transition in Peru 92
3. Chronology of Transition in Bolivia 93
4. Peru: Selected Economic Indicators, 1973–83 103
5. Bolivia: Selected Economic Indicators, 1980–85 109
6. Ecuador: Selected Economic Indicators, 1979–84 113
7. Collective Protests in Bolivia, 1970–85 123
8. Summary of Initial Economic Programs 140

LIST OF ACRONYMS

ADEX	Asociación de Exportadores
ADN	Acción Democrática Nacionalista
AIMB	Asociación Industrial de Mineros de Bolivia
ANMM	Asociación Nacional de Mineros Medianos
ANDE	Asociación Nacional de Empresarios
AP	Acción Popular
APRA	Alianza Popular Revolucionaria Americana
BAB	Banco Agrícola de Bolivia
BCR	Banco Central de Reserva
CADE	Conferencia Anual de Ejecutivos
CAEM	Centro de Altos Estudios Militares
CAO	Cámara Agropecuaria del Oriente
CBF	Corporación Boliviana de Fomento
CENDES	Centro de Desarrollo Industrial
CEPAL	Comisión Económica para América Latina (in English: ECLA, Economic Commission for Latin America)
CEPB	Confederación de Empresarios Privados de Bolivia
CEPE	Corporación Estatal Petrolera Ecuatoriana
CERTEX	Certificado de Reintegro Tributario a la Exportación
CFN	Corporación Financiera Nacional

CFP	Concentración de Fuerzas Populares
CGTP	Confederación General de Trabajadores del Peru
CNA	Confederación Nacional Agraria
CNI	Cámara Nacional de Industrias
CNT	Confederación Nacional de Trabajadores
COAP	Comité de Asesoramiento de la Presidencia
COB	Central Obrera Boliviana
COFADENA	Corporación de las Fuerzas Armadas de Desarrollo Nacional
COMIBOL	Corporación Minera de Bolivia
CONACI	Confederación Nacional de Comunidades Industriales
CONAL	Consejo Nacional Legislativo
CONAPOL	Consejo Nacional Político
CONEPLAN	Consejo Nacional de Economía y Planeamiento
CONFIEP	Confederación Nacional de Instituciones Empresariales Privadas
CTE	Confederación de Trabajadores del Ecuador
CTRP	Confederación de Trabajadores de la Revolución Peruana
DINE	Dirección de Industrias de Ejército
DP	Democracia Popular
ECLA	*See* CEPAL
ESAN	Escuela Superior de Administración de Empresas
FADI	Frente Amplio de Izquierda
FEDEXPOR	Federación Ecuatoriana de Industrias Exportadores
FRA	Frente Radical Alfarista
FRI	Frente Revolucionario de Izquierda
FRN	Frente de Reconstrucción Nacional
FSB	Falange Socialista Boliviana
FSE	Fondo Social de Emergencia
FUT	Frente Unitario de Trabajadores
ID	Izquierda Democrática
IESS	Instituto de Estudios Económicos y Sociales
ILD	Instituto Libertad y Democracia

IMF	International Monetary Fund
IPAE	Instituto Peruano de Administración de Empresas
IPC	International Petroleum Company
IU	Izquierda Unida
JUNAPLA	Junta Nacional de Planificación y Coordinación Económica
MBL	Movimiento Bolivia Libre
MIR	Movimiento de la Izquierda Revolucionaria
MNR	Movimiento Nacionalista Revolucionario
MNRH	Movimiento Nacionalista Revolucionario Histórico
MPD	Movimiento Popular Democrático
NPE	Nueva política económica
OAS	Organization of American States
OPIC	Overseas Private Investment Corporation
PCB	Partido Comunista de Bolivia
PCE	Partido Conservador Ecuatoriano
PDC	Partido Demócrata Cristiano
PLR	Partido Liberal Radical
PNR	Partido Nacionalista Revolucionario
PPC	Partido Popular Cristiano
PRA	Partido Revolucionario Auténtico
PS	Partido Socialista
PSC	Partido Social Cristiano
PUR	Partido Unidad Republicana
SI	Sociedad de Industrias
SINAMOS	Sistema Nacional de Apoyo a la Movilización Social
SNA	Sociedad Nacional Agraria
SNI	Sociedad Nacional de Industrias
SNM	Sociedad Nacional de Minería
TGC	Tribunal de Garantías Constitucionales
UCS	Unión Cívica Solidaridad

UDP	Unión Democrática Popular
UEPP	Unión de Empresarios Privados del Peru
USAID	U.S. Agency for International Development
YPFB	Yacimientos Petrolíferos Fiscales Bolivianos

ACKNOWLEDGMENTS

THE KINDNESS OF strangers and the generosity of old friends made this book possible. We respectfully thank the individuals and the institutions that contributed so much to the project.

Luis Abugattás (better known as Chipi) was an original partner in the project. Unfortunately, other professional pursuits made it impossible for him to continue the research with us. Nonetheless, his insights provided an important point of departure for the study—and his expansive sense of humor buoyed us through the early days in Lima. He is a valued friend and continues to be an astute analyst of Peruvian political economy. Through Chipi, we found an institutional home in Peru at the Centro de Investigación of the Universidad del Pacífico where Carlos Amat y León, colleagues, and staff made us feel welcome.

A generous grant from the Howard Heinz Endowment provided the funds for the bulk of the field research. Supplemental funds were subsequently provided by the Advisory Research Council of Queen's University and the University of Pittsburgh. A 1986 faculty fellowship from the Helen Kellogg Institute of the University of Notre Dame allowed Conaghan to begin assembling some of the preliminary findings. A 1989–90 research grant from the Social Sciences and Humanities Research Council of Canada made it possible for her to spend a year in residence at the University of Pittsburgh. In the same year, a faculty leave for Malloy was supported by the Center for International Studies and the Center for Latin American Studies at the University of Pittsburgh. The Latin American Program of the Woodrow Wilson Center in Washington, D.C., provided a venue for a discussion of our findings in a seminar in September 1990. Final revisions were completed while Conaghan was in residence at the Center of International Studies of Princeton University in 1992–93.

At various junctures in the development of this project, we drew on the intellectual support and counsel of an eclectic group of scholars and policy makers: Eduardo Gamarra, Osvaldo Hurtado, Jorge Lazarte, Jorge León, Cynthia McClintock, Harold Mah, John Martz, Juan Antonio Morales, Joan Nelson, Guillermo O'Donnell, Jorge Parodi, Guido Pennano, José Luís Roca, Antonio Sánchez de Lozada, Gonzalo Sánchez de Lozada, and Walter Spurrier. We were also lucky to count on able research assistance from Ernesto Cabrera, Brooke Harlowe, Kwasi Ofori-Yeboah, Carlos Parodi, Orlando Pérez, Maximo Torero, and Demetrio Vavoulis. The support staff at our respective universities were amazingly kind and competent, especially Evelyn McCaugherty at Queen's, Mary Ann Kaper and Marsha Tsouris at Pitt.

Our greatest debt is to the people who told us their stories, our informants in politics and business, most of whom appear as anonymous sources in the text. They carved time out of their hectic schedules. They shocked us with their frankness. They sometimes exasperated, frequently challenged, and always energized us. Many of our informants will profoundly disagree with our interpretations, but we could not have developed our arguments without them. We remember the cigarette smoke, the endless coffee, the moments of revelation, and the privilege of looking back at history with the personalities who made it.

Everyone associated with this book at the University of Pittsburgh has been extraordinarily helpful. We thank Lilya Lorrin, Catherine Marshall, Kathy McLaughlin, and our skillful editor, Pippa Letsky. Marilyn Banting lent her considerable editorial skills to compiling the index.

We conclude with a hearty welcome to the newest members of our respective clans: Sean Patrick Conaghan, Marc Joseph and Maximilian James Malloy—and a final note of gratitude to our families and friends who lived this project with us. You're the best.

UNSETTLING STATECRAFT

CHAPTER 1

Introduction: Explaining Statecraft

No single word was used more than *crisis* to describe the state of Latin America in the 1980s. The imagery of crisis quickly became a cliché invoked by politicians, journalists, technocrats, and academics in their discussions of the interconnected problems of the region. Recession, hyperinflation, the debt burden, political uncertainty, and ungovernability were collapsed into the catchall notion of *la crisis*—it captured the multiple anxieties of the decade.

Two profound problems of statecraft were at the heart of Latin America's crisis in the 1980s. First there was the economic dimension. The familiar problem of managing the economy was rendered even more onerous by a convergence of phenomena that brought economic growth to a halt. Drastic decreases in export earnings and slowed domestic investment joined with a credit crunch in the international financial system. Starting with Mexico's 1982 moratorium on its debt obligations, international creditors refused new lending and demanded payment from Latin American debtor countries. Along with the demands of private creditors, international multilateral agencies such as the International Monetary Fund (IMF) urged Latin American debtors to use the crisis conjuncture to turn away from state intervention and reshape their respective economies along market-oriented lines. It was a complete reversal of the international environment that had prevailed in the 1970s, when an overabundance of foreign credit was used to fuel public and private spending. Instead, domestic policy makers in Latin America found themselves under increasing pressures to impose austerity programs and to scale down the state's role in the economy. Local capitalists joined in the calls for a readjustment in state-market relations.

Economic austerity is never a popular formula among political leaders or the public. The problems involved in carrying out austerity measures in these systems were further complicated by tasks of political construction. Across the region, the economic crisis of the 1980s coincided with the demise of authoritarian military regimes and with political democratization. After a decade marked by authoritarianism, political arrangements were to be restructured around the principles of competition, participation, and representation. Constitutions were engineered to define new rules for political behavior, elections were convened to choose political leaders, and civil liberties were enshrined again as the bases for public life. For lower-middle-class groups, peasants, and urban workers, democratization held out the hope that their demands could be channeled and resolved through new institutional structures.

However welcome the transition from authoritarianism, the political opening came at a time when economic choices for Latin America seemed to be narrowing. In the absence of foreign credit, a renewal of investment and economic growth implied that capital accumulation would have to be fueled by constraining popular consumption or by imposing some costs on at least some segments of the business community. The logic of democracy, however, promised a responsiveness to the concrete material claims of a broad range of groups in society. The economic constraints of the crisis seemed to demand the imposition of costs on some groups while the democratic arrangements structured an opening of the decision-making process to group demands. In many countries, the tensions involved in combining a commitment to democracy with effective economic management became evident in the 1980s; policy makers were often forced to opt for one direction or another, and the costs of both options were high. In countries where governments opted for orthodox approaches to the economic crisis, democratic arrangements were degraded by repression and the enforced exclusion of some groups from policy deliberations. In other cases where economic managers chose the more politically palatable heterodox programs, the economies fell into intense hyperinflation.

The difficulty of combining mass-based democracy with effective economic management of a market economy in crisis is not a new problem for Latin America; nor is it a problem unknown to advanced capitalist democracies. In his path-breaking work of the 1970s, Guillermo O'Donnell argued that the authoritarian military regimes of the Southern Cone countries were responses to bottlenecks in the process of capital accumulation in those countries; many of the bottlenecks were generated by militant labor movements and the left operating in open political systems.[1] Authoritarianism in the 1970s in Argentina, Uruguay, and Chile emerged as the political solution, to eliminate these bottlenecks through outright repression. At roughly the same time, there was an outpouring of literature devoted to the fiscal crisis of advanced capitalist systems and the inbuilt inflationary tendencies in democratic welfare states. At the base of these discussions lay a fundamental concern about the future of democracy, capitalism, and economic growth. Conservatives pondered whether democratic systems would be overloaded with the demands of citizens, and they worried about the fiscal implications of overloaded governments.[2] Analysts on the left wondered whether capitalism could survive if democratic systems could not fulfill their legitimation functions by maintaining social welfare spending.[3]

These recent experiences of both Latin America and the advanced capitalist democracies pose intriguing theoretical and empirical questions for political scientists, some of which were broadly delineated by Charles Lindblom.[4] How do different countries reconcile democratic controls with market controls in their political-economic systems? How does the relative balance between public and private controls shift, especially in crisis circumstances? Who are the key actors in such boundary shifts? What are the implications of shifts for the character of political regimes? Are there situations in which a shift toward market controls can only be accomplished through authoritarian methods?

Our study focuses on these important questions and examines them within the settings of three Latin American republics—Bolivia, Ecuador, and Peru. All three of these Central Andean nations wrestled with problems of democratic political development and crisis-ridden economic management in the 1980s. All three countries were subjected to civilian-led policy experiments aimed at shifting state-market relations through neoliberal economic management. These neoliberal programs included an initial package of economic-stabilization measures (currency devaluations, removal of price controls, reduction or removal of consumer subsidies, for example) with long-term policies to retract the role of the state from the marketplace (trade liberalization, liberalization of laws governing foreign investment, removal of protective labor laws, for example).[5] These neoliberal experiments took place during the presidencies of Fernando Belaúnde (1980–85) in Peru and León Febres Cordero (1984–88) in Ecuador. Of the three countries, the most draconian neoliberal experiment was enacted in Bolivia under the administration of President Víctor Paz Estenssoro (1985–89). The results of these three attempts were mixed, at best. The Paz Estenssoro government was the most successful in terms of affecting a restructuring of state-market relations. In contrast, the Febres Cordero and Belaúnde projects lapsed into incoherence and were eventually abandoned by the presidents and the subsequently elected governments.

The rest of this book tells the stories of these neoliberal projects. We trace the intellectual and political origins of the neoliberal experiments, their relationships to the processes of regime change, and the factors that affected their implementation. To anticipate our conclusions, we will show how the emergence of neoliberal policy positions inside the domestic business community in these countries converged with the push to restore civilian governments. Business groups supported democratization as the means to escape from the uncertainty that reigned during the military governments of the 1970s. Domestic capitalists

believed they would occupy a "privileged position" within the policy-making apparatus of the new democratic regimes. From that position, they believed they would be able to engineer more freedom and opportunities for themselves and a more subsidiary role for the state. Thus, democracy and neoliberal economic management were to converge to produce a recasting of state-market relations.

The political transition to civilian-led regimes (in 1979 in Ecuador, 1980 in Peru, and 1982 in Bolivia) did not, however, resolve the issues of influence and authority to the complete satisfaction of domestic business elites. Businessmen found themselves battling with their own conservative governments on how to define the role of the private sector in economic policy making and the market. Economic technocrats favoring orthodoxy sometimes clashed with the business community over the precise contours and sequencing of neoliberal measures. While espousing probusiness sentiments, conservative politicians often had personal or electoral agendas at odds with the implementation of a neoliberal model. Different sectoral interests among domestic capitalists divided business with respect to specific policies. Within this context, presidents and economic technocrats sought to shield themselves from interest group politics.

In addition to the squabbles with business, conservative governments also faced pockets of resistance to orthodox policies from unions, social movements, contending political parties, and bureaucrats inside the state apparatus, and response to this resistance varied across the different cases. Popular resistance met with doses of official repression, and legislative opposition was either ignored outright or tranquilized with political pacts. What emerged was neither clear-cut democracy nor authoritarianism, but an unsettled regime type and an unsettling style of policy making. Elections were used to rotate leaders, but the democratic structures housed a decidedly non-democratic-style of decision making inside the executive branch. The institutionalization of civil liberties lagged, and the representative functions of legislative bodies were downgraded.

This is, of course, a mere summary of the common threads of the different cases. We approach the three countries as "most similar case" comparisons.[6] We argue that these three countries share commonalities in their historical trajectory and that their similar political dynamics gave birth to equivalent regimes in the 1980s. At the same time, our analysis highlights differences among the three countries that account for the different outcomes of their respective neoliberal experiments. Before turning to the detailed discussion of these cases, however, we begin by looking at recent contributions to the study of comparative economic policy making and how these works have informed our own approach.

Explaining Policy Making: A Comparative Historical Approach

Much of the debate on the role of the state in the 1970s focused on the idea of its "relative autonomy." Based in Marx's discussion of the state in *The Eighteenth Brumaire,* the idea was vigorously put forth in the numerous works of Nicos Poulantzas. Poulantzas argued that relative autonomy—that is, the ability of a state to act against the immediate interests of capitalists in order to assure the long-term functioning of the capitalist system as a whole—was a permanent structural feature of the state in capitalist systems. For Poulantzas, relative autonomy was the product of two phenomena: (1) the formal separation of the state from market actors in the legal-juridical framework; and (2) the lack of consensus and the tensions within the bourgeoisie that render it incapable of functioning as a cohesive ruling class. Under these conditions, according to Poulantzas, the state takes up the task of acting as the guarantor of the capitalist order—a task that sometimes compels state managers to enact policies that run against the short-term interests of fractions of capital in order to maintain the conditions for the reproduction of capitalism itself. Thus, the relative autonomy of the capitalist state is born.[7]

Poulantzas's position sparked fiery interchanges on the left and was challenged by scholars, most notably Ralph Miliband, who raised objections to the notion of relative autonomy. His empirically based analysis depicted the state as being permeable to dominant-class interests and public policies as being directly responsive to those interests.[8]

By the early 1980s, the debate over relative autonomy had waned as scholars acknowledged the limitations of any general theory concerning the capitalist state. Theda Skocpol voiced the scholarly disillusionment with abstract discussions of relative autonomy, and she insisted that the state's capacity to make policy independently of societal interests could only be understood as a product of specific historical circumstances.[9] A shift began toward more focused historical studies of the policy-making process, especially among North American analysts. Among the notable contributors to this new political economy were Peter Hall, Peter Gourevitch, Peter Katzenstein, David Vogel, John Zysman, along with Theda Skocpol and her collaborators Margaret Weir and Kenneth Finegold.[10]

One of the special concerns of this political economy literature was to explain the differences in the levels and modes of state intervention into the market in advanced capitalist economic systems, particularly as adjustments emerged in the wake of crisis situations such as the Great Depression. These studies examined how economic and social policies in advanced capitalist democracies emerged out of the interactions of institutional structures and actors inside the state (for example, bureaucratic agencies, the executive branch, and individual agents such as economists, and so on) and societally based groups (for example, business, labor, reform-minded middle-class professionals, and so on) operating through interest group, union, or party organizations. While these analysts differ in the emphasis they give to certain variables in explaining specific policy outcomes, there is a remarkable similarity in the way they approach the policy-making process and the methods they use to study it.

The positions of business and labor—and the relationships between them—

figure prominently in all these analyses of economic and social policy. The struggles between business and labor over economic surplus and authority relations have been the central conflict in advanced capitalist systems; these conflicts are mediated by the state and have been at the core of public policies. Both business and labor actively seek to shape policy outcomes in a variety of ways in democratic systems—by exercising their power in the market (through labor or ''investment'' strikes), by influencing parties and electoral outcomes, and by interest group lobbying.

Peter Gourevitch argues that business and labor, in their efforts to influence policy, become part of larger ''social coalitions'' that may include other groups (farmers, middle-class professionals, and so on).[11] These coalitions can become embedded in political parties. They may also be linked with state institutions through the development of close relationships between interest groups and segments of the state bureaucracy, forming what Katzenstein refers to as ''policy networks.''[12]

These coalitions are important not only because they may exert short-term influence over policies, but because they can constitute the foundational pillars of political regimes. Katzenstein argues that the modus vivendi established between business and labor in Austria was the basis for ''democratic corporatism''—a regime type that combines liberal democracy with the participation of organized interest groups in institutional economic policy making.[13]

Adam Przeworski's work on the postwar ''class compromise'' also points to the foundational impact of business-labor relations on the character of a political regime. He argues that the business-labor agreement on Keynesian economic policies laid the basis for democratic capitalism. In a consensus forged by social democratic parties, organized labor dropped its challenge to the capitalist economic system in exchange for participation in democratic political institutions and for state interventions to smooth out the business cycle.[14]

In this historical political-economy literature, state institutions are neither functionalist ''black boxes'' that neutrally process societal demands nor are they simply a ''committee for managing the whole affairs of the bourgeoisie.'' Institutions inside the state (governmental branches and their specialized agencies) and their ''managers'' (elected politicians, technocrats, and administrators) are seen as responsive to societal demands; but they are also portrayed as playing a key role in structuring those demands and the configuration of social coalitions. So (as Skocpol argues, for example), politicians in the Democratic party in the United States saw an opportunity for electoral gain by melding together policies to serve a number of constituencies, giving birth to the heterogenous New Deal coalition of the 1930s.[15]

Notwithstanding the innovative powers of politicians and technocrats, however, state managers face serious constraints in policy formulation and implementation. Structural variables or specific conjunctures can generate a variety of constraints. Economic strategies, for example, may be limited by the structure of state institutions and the policy predispositions that reign inside those structures. Hall argues that Keynesian policies were adopted slowly in Britain because entrenched civil servants inside the Treasury ministry were deeply attached to orthodox economic formulas. In contrast, Skocpol and Weir maintain that the administrative structure in Sweden facilitated the adoption of Keynesian policies.[16]

Market structures can exert similar limiting effects on choices of economic policy. John Zysman argues that the characteristics of a country's financial system fundamentally affects a government's capacity to adjust industrial policies.[17] Other constraints on policy emanate from a country's position inside the global economic system. Katzenstein and Gourevitch emphasize that small countries with open economies are especially vulnerable to sharp changes in international markets: policy makers in small countries are forced to consider exogenous events to a much greater extent than are policy makers in countries with large domestic markets.[18]

Lest these views of the policy-making process sound overly pluralist so far, it should be noted that these writers do grapple with the issue of business's privileged position in democratic capitalist systems. In *Politics and Markets,* Charles Lindblom put forth the argument that business groups exert disproportionate influence over public policy both because they hold a strategic position in the market (and can affect economic performance by investment decisions) and also because their economic resources can be wielded to affect the political process through campaign finance, interest group lobbying, and so on. Rather than seeing "privileged position" as a static characteristic of democratic capitalist systems, however, a number of political economy writers focus on how business influence shifts over time in accordance with changing political-economic circumstances.

Finegold and Skocpol see the New Deal reforms as an example of how business hegemony over economic policy wanes during crisis periods. In the calamitous collapse of the market during the 1930s, American capitalists lost much of their ability to veto reformist public policies through market behavior. At the same time, the failure of proposed business "cures" for the crisis stripped business elites of their claims to leadership and ideological hegemony over the political agenda. Under these conditions, the power of business to shape public policy declined vis-à-vis other societal groups. Skocpol's examination of the New Deal reforms demonstrates how normal business domination over policy making (described by Lindblom) can be interrupted by crisis conditions that change political and economic behavior.

David Vogel's interpretation of U.S. history goes even further in challenging the notion of any permanent privileged position for business elites in the policy process. In a complex economy like that of the United States, Vogel sees little evidence that business en masse has successfully employed the ''investment strike'' to turn around government policy.[19] Regarding the centrality of economic crisis in undermining business domination, Vogel argues that the increased regulation of corporations and their loss of control over the political agenda in the 1960s and 1970s was due to the rise of liberal consumer advocacy groups. It is the political rather than the economic weakness of business that explains the recent growth of government regulation. For Vogel, the shifts in the political power of business are related to changes in the bourgeoisie's level of class consciousness and organizational capacity. These factors, in turn, are closely tied to the character and behavior of mass challengers and state managers.

Along with shared themes, what binds these authors together is a methodological insistence that policy making can only be understood in reference to historically specific structures in state and society. Simply put, these writers see each participant in the process as historically conditioned—that is, each actor brings to the process not just a set of material interests, but ways of conceiving those interests and expressing those interests in ideology and through organizations. So, for example, the interests of industrial capitalists in regard to macroeconomic policy cannot simply be deduced by an observer on the basis of the structural position of these capitalists inside the economy. Rather, the policy position favored by industrialists and their capacity to influence the process is shaped by their ideological predispositions, their previous experiences with policies, the ways in which their interest groups put forth policy positions, and the ties between interest associations and the state bureaucracy. In short, a comprehensive explanation of the policy process necessarily entails what John Zysman calls ''a kind of political archaeology.''[20] That is, the story of any policy process must take into account how each actor has come to arrive at the process, the resources they bring to bear on it, and the perceptual and experiential baggage they bring with them. Like societal actors, state institutions also have historical legacies that must be taken into account in explaining the varying directions that policy makers take in responding to similar problems.

This emphasis on the historical specificities of each national trajectory came as a welcome antidote to grand generalizations about the nature and function of the capitalist state. Rather than depicting the state or business as a unitary actor, these analysts disaggregate their categories to show how conflict inside the ranks of state institutions and among societal actors can affect policy outcomes. The contribution of these historical case studies is that they capture the fluidity of the policy process—the making and unmaking of policy is shown as highly contingent on concrete political struggles among power contenders that include classes and their organizations, bureaucratic agencies, technocratic cadres, and politicians and their parties.

As the following chapters will show, we have chosen to approach policy making in the same vein, viewing it as an indeterminate yet historically conditioned process. We believe such an approach opens the doors to understanding why and how certain choices were made within the extraordinary political and economic environment of the 1980s.

Policy Making in Latin America: Recent Concerns

Much of the analysis of Latin American economic policy in the 1970s was marked by a tendency to view policy as an attempt by the state to resolve problems in a way that catered to the long-term interests of the capitalist class. The heavy structuralist bent in economic policy analyses was understandable. It reflected the intellectual impact of debates on the left (for example, Poulantzas versus Miliband). It was also an approach that lent itself to the difficult research environment of the 1970s. Especially in the Southern Cone, for example, the highly repressive character of the military dictatorships made direct research on any sensitive topic virtually impossible.[21] Decision making was inaccessible to the general public and observers, so analysts tended to ''read'' policies as evidence of which societal groups were influential on the basis of whose ''objective'' interests appeared to be served.

The political decompression and the regionwide debt crisis of the 1980s substantially changed the research terrain. Economic policy making was no longer hidden inside the murky environment of military authoritarianism. At the same time, the new conjuncture expanded the range of questions open to political economists. The new civilian-led governments faced a common set of economic problems tied to the debt issue, but countries generated a wide variety of policy responses. The responses ranged from short-term austerity, to more ambitious neoliberal projects, to complicated ''heterodox shock'' programs like those undertaken in Brazil and Argentina in the mid-1980s. Along with substantial cross-national variations in policy responses, drastic policy shifts occurred within countries. Such changes were not always tied to changeovers of governments with elections; in some instances, governments dramatically reversed their own economic policies or fell into ad hoc improvisations. Latin America in the 1980s became an extraordinary laboratory of economic policy experimentation yielding a wide range of results.

To date, much of the recent scholarly work on Latin American economic policy is focused on two issues: (1) evaluating the economic performance of military versus democratic governments; and (2) explaining variations in policy responses to the debt crisis, especially the differing capacities of governments to enact the stabilization programs that are a component of IMF conditions.[22] In regard to the first issue, empirical studies have provided fairly conclusive evidence that military governments of the 1970s did not fare substantially better than civilian governments in inducing economic growth. Work by Jonathan Hartlyn and Samuel Morley along with that of John Sheahan shows that repressive government is not the sine qua non of economic growth. Nor, as Karen Remmer demonstrates, were authoritarian regimes substantially more effective in implementing IMF stabilization programs.[23] These findings are important from both a political and a scholarly point of view. They debunk the myth of the efficiency of authoritarian military governments; at the same time, they demonstrate that regime type, as a broad category, reveals little about economic performance or state capacities.[24]

With this important point established, the analytic focus turned to dissecting the components of regimes by examining specific actors in policy making—much in the vein of the comparative-case-studies approach used by Gourevitch, Katzenstein, and so on. Robert Kaufman, for example, emphasizes how domestic coalitions affect the capacity of governments to undertake stabilization programs.[25] Similarly, Jeffry Frieden's analysis of debt crisis stresses two determinants of country policy responses: (1) the character of business-labor relations; and (2) the structure of sectoral cleavages within the business community. In cases where countries pursued neoliberal models, Frieden argues that class conflict was high; as a result, investors with interests in fixed domestic assets were willing to tolerate some losses in exchange for the "disciplining" of labor by the market model. The net winners were investors with liquid assets who reaped the benefits of market liberalization.[26]

Technocrats and administrative structures also figure prominently in the analysis of the application of stabilization programs. In his review of several Third World cases, Stephan Haggard argues strenuously that the imposition of an IMF-style stabilization program requires a cadre of prostabilizing technocrats who form the domestic core of a transnational coalition including actors such as the IMF.[27] Along with technocrats, analysts have also looked at administrative structures, electoral cycles, and the constraints posed by the international financial community in the determination of the policy paths taken by Latin America in the 1980s.[28]

At a minimum, then, the diverse policy experiences of Latin America in the 1980s offers a rich set of comparative cases that allow us to reexamine many of the same basic questions posed by the political economists of advanced capitalism. How do social coalitions form around specific policy options? How are policy networks created and dissipated? What role do politicians and technocrats play in articulating and mediating social interests?

At the same time, the Latin American experiences suggest other questions, somewhat different from those posed in reference to advanced capitalist cases. How does policy making take place in situations marked by extraordinarily high levels of political and economic uncertainty? In the contemporary policy-making worlds of Western Europe described by Katzenstein et al., actors operate within an environment in which the parameters of the politicoeconomic game are fairly fixed. The reigning uncertainty regards the specific outcomes of the policy process (Will business face more regulations or less? Will lower-class groups receive more social welfare benefits or less?). In contrast, the uncertainty that permeated policy making in Latin America in the 1980s was multidimensional. Democratization and regime transition took place in the absence of any real class compromise, Keynesian or otherwise. The absence of a social pact on the distribution of material rewards was coupled with disagreements as to the parameters and operation of the new democratic regimes. Economic policy making was marked not simply by conflicts over the content of policies; it involved a deeper struggle over both the procedures, mechanisms, and style of governmental decision making and also the whole tenor of state-society relations. The tasks of economic management became interwoven with the problems of regime transition and of consolidation. The nature of politics and the character of the state itself were part of the stakes of the conflicts over economic policy in Latin America in the 1980s.

The process of making policy under conditions of extreme uncertainty and stress affected the development of newly forming democratic regimes in the 1980s, just as the tentative character of the new political arrangements created a special set of parameters for economic policy makers. Political scientists are just beginning to explore the relationships between crisis-ridden economic management and regime evolution in Latin America. Scholars concerned with the question of regime change in Latin America have tended to focus attention almost exclusively on how the modes of the political transition affect the prospects for future democratic development. This has led to something of a fixation on the political transition itself, without further consideration of how the catastrophic economic conditions prevailing in the posttransition period are affecting regime development.[29]

Several recent works are suggestive of how regime development is being affected by the task of managing crisis-ridden economies. Lourdes de Sola's analysis of Brazil and the analyses of Argentina by Guillermo O'Donnell, William Smith, and Juan Carlos Torre point to commonalities in the way governments have operated throughout the 1980s.[30] They argue that new civilian governments strove to maintain economic policy making as a sphere insulated from direct societal pressures, so as to allow maximum autonomy to the economic team. But the creation of this autonomous sphere inside the context of a democratic regime had its drawbacks, leaving economic policy without a support coalition in society and leaving governments in a legitimacy crisis when economic programs failed.[31]

Our study of Bolivia, Ecuador, and Peru looks at the relationships between regime making and economic policy making. These connections are central to

the political future of Latin America. Moreover, Latin America's experience in the 1980s may be instructive for other countries, particularly Eastern European nations, as they proceed down a similar path of political change and economic restructuring.[32]

Concepts and Assumptions

Because political scientists still routinely disagree on the use of many of the basic concepts of the discipline, we take a brief detour here to clarify our use of language in the text. This definitional exercise also exposes some of our basic assumptions on how to approach the study of economic policy making.

It is important to note the distinctions in our use of the notions of state, regime, and government. In our study, we view the state and civil society as sites wherein groups mobilize, to become players in the policy-making process. State and society are always interdependent realms; neither site is autonomous, in any real sense, although at any given moment actors based in one or another site can have the upper hand in shaping policy outcomes. From this perspective, we see no point in focusing on the issue of relative autonomy of the state. The problem with the relative autonomy approach is that it pulls the state out of the manifold of societal relations and looks at ''the state'' as a free-standing entity with definable boundary conditions. The discussion often degenerates then into an exercise in anthropomorphism, endowing the state with an independent will and the capacity to act. In our view, the state acts only through groups of human beings (fiduciary agents) who have the capacity to act in the name of the state either because they are authorized to do so by rules or because of their de facto appropriation of the symbols of the state (or some mixture of both).

In an effort to avoid the temptations of anthropomorphism, we prefer to emphasize the concepts of statecraft and governance. *Statecraft* is broadly defined as the elaboration of procedural rules and public policies by agents empowered to act in the name of the state, which mandates and regulates the basic relationships among actors in the state, civil society, and market. *Governance* is used more narrowly to refer to the capacity of governments to resolve problems through the formulation and implementation of public policies. In our study, the two major problems of statecraft in the Central Andes of the 1980s were the elaboration of new ''democratic'' rules for politics and the effective management of economies under extreme duress.

In explaining how these problems of statecraft have been resolved, we focus on the capacity of actors who occupy institutional positions inside governments and the capacity of actors in civil society to set a public agenda—that is, to define, launch, and sustain rules and policies. This capacity, which is a form of socially produced power, can be concentrated or dispersed. This capacity may be disproportionately lodged in sites within the state or civil society, or can be mixed in both. Finally, when all or the bulk of the capacity is lodged in the state apparatus, it might be concentrated in one segment (the executive branch) or divided across component parts (legislative assemblies, courts, the military, and so on).

Rule-making and policy-making powers are always subject to temporal shifts; one of the tasks in the analysis of statecraft is to locate where these powers are lodged at specific points in time and to chart how and why the capacity moves over time. To be sustained over time, rules and policies become encased in institutional structures, which themselves become part of the process of power concentration and dispersion. Institutional structures not only reflect how these power capacities are organized at any point in time but also shape how capacity is to be distributed in the future.

The distribution of rule-making and policy-making capacities among actors is critical in determining the nature of political regimes. There are at least three defining dimensions of a political regime. First, a regime is characterized by its formal expression through a constitution or other legal instruments. The procedures laid out in the formal framework of a regime stipulate the routes through which individuals and groups are linked to the governing process.

Second, a regime is further defined by its informal rules of the game. In addition to the formal rules laid out in laws, there are the de facto procedures and political practices that both reflect and affect the distribution of political power. The formal and informal characteristics of a regime do not necessarily share a single uniform logic. Max Weber pointed to the rational-legal basis of the political institutions in contemporary western regimes. But these rational-legal principles reflected in the formal political sphere frequently coexist with clientelism in informal behind-the-scenes political behavior. As we show in subsequent chapters, the rational-legal rules of a regime are frequently in conflict with the remnants of clientelism and patrimonial political practices.

Third, in addition to their formal and informal rules, political regimes can be distinguished by their coalitional bases in society. Groups in society provide the foundational basis for a regime, undergirding it and drawing benefits from it. Changes in the structure of support coalitions can fundamentally affect the character of a regime. The coalition that originally provides the social foundations of support for a regime is not necessarily coterminous with the specific coalitions that dominate policy at any given point in time. Policy coalitions may be a subset within the larger support coalition. Thus, the analysis of political regimes involves tracking developments and relationships across these three dimensions—the formal rule structure, the informal political practices, and the societal bases.

Finally, government refers to the individuals that make binding decisions in the name of the state. One of the functions of the formal rules of any regime is to stipulate under which conditions individuals have the authority to make such binding statements. Rules may construe government as the sum total of actions taken by executive, legislative, and judicial branches. But in certain issue areas (especially economic policy making), the "government" may be reduced to an extremely small circle of decision makers that control strategically central bureaucracies (for example, the Central Bank, the Ministry of Finance, and so on). Thus, it may be important to distinguish between the government as a whole and "the government" that manages the economy.

In our three cases, the struggle to acquire and maintain control over the agenda in economic policy has taken place among three (sometimes overlapping) sets of actors: the domestic capitalist class, the political class, and a cadre of technocratic elites who manage the policy-making bureaucracies inside the executive branch of government.

The domestic capitalist class in each country is defined by its ownership of a major portion of fixed and liquid assets in the private sector of the economy. It is a synonym for what other authors have referred to as the "grand bourgeoisie" or the "dominant class"—that is, capitalists at the commanding heights of their respective market economies who control and organize production and labor processes in modern financial, industrial, and commercial enterprises.[33] In terms of their organization as market actors, these capitalists frequently operate through economic groups—multicompany firms under the control of family and friendship cliques.[34] While such groups have domestic origins, some of their operations may be closely tied to international capital through joint ventures, loans, or transfers of technology agreements. In addition to their power to influence economic policy through their market behavior, domestic capitalists project themselves in the policy process through sectoral interest group associations and national peak associations. (It is important to note that we are excluding informal sector entrepreneurs from our discussion of the domestic capitalist class.) To avoid repetition, the terms *business elites, business community, private sector,* and *businessmen* are used interchangeably throughout the text to denote domestic capitalists.[35]

The political class is composed of professional politicians; their primary concern is office seeking and their primary institutional vehicle is political parties. Like politicians, technocratic elites are also interested in office holding, but their claims to authority are based on their claims to special technical expertise (usually formal training in the field of economics or management). Technocrats rely on ties and connections to politicians to gain positions inside the bureaucracies charged with economic policy making; these ties are often, but not always, forged through political parties and interest groups.

Both the political class and the state technocrats are drawn mainly from urban middle and upper classes. This means that many of these individuals are dependent primarily on salaries for their income. As we shall see, the type of economic development that has taken place in these countries has limited the outlets for middle-class employment. Middle-class groups came to view the public sector as a primary source of employment and status. This employment-generating and clientele-maintaining function of the government can complicate the implementation of economic policies.

Readers will note that organized labor and other lower-class groups do not figure as primary actors in our analyses of the cases. That is because these groups were systematically marginalized from significant participation in economic policy making; indeed, this exclusion was part of the political agenda of neoliberalism. Organized labor was unable to project a coherent alternative model to neoliberalism. Labor and other lower-class groups were relegated to a largely reactive role; they vigorously protested austerity programs but were unsuccessful in staving off neoliberal experimentation. As such, labor occupies the wings of our analysis while capitalists, technocrats, and politicians hold center stage.

Incomplete Nation States, Heterogenous Capitalisms:
The Central Andes as Most Similar Cases

Shared structural problems and historical experiences make Bolivia, Ecuador, and Peru well suited for a most similar case approach to studying economic policy making. The differences in each country's politicoeconomic trajectory are delineated in subsequent chapters. For now, we conclude with observations on those commonalities in economic and political development that pushed these countries down similar paths—most recently to regime transition and neoliberalism in the 1980s.

Bolivia, Ecuador, and Peru are classified by the World Bank as lower-middle-income countries. This classification positions them a rung above the poorest countries in the world, such as those in sub-Saharan Africa. Within continental South America, however, these three countries consistently rank among the poorest, along with Paraguay and Guyana. Bolivia, with a population of approximately 7.1 million in the late 1980s, had a per capita GDP of U.S.$724. Ecuador fared a bit better, with a per capita GDP of $1,477 and a population of 10.3 million. Peru, the most populated of the three countries at 21.2 million, registered a per capita GDP of $1,503. These figures contrast with the per capita GDP figures of larger countries such as Brazil or Argentina, which register over $2,000.[36]

But Bolivia, Ecuador, and Peru are joined by more than their relative impoverishment vis-à-vis the larger countries of Latin America. Bolivia, Ecuador, and Peru are countries linked by geography and by a history that predates the Conquest of the Americas.[37] The Andean mountain range cuts its way through all three countries (thus, our reference throughout the book to the three countries as the Central Andes), creating a physical landscape that is both beautiful and treacherous. Portions of the three countries, along with the northern part of Chile, were joined in the multi-ethnic Incan Empire until its collapse in 1532. The territories were subsequently governed by the Spanish as part of the Viceroyalty of Peru. Under colonialism, economic life in the Andes was restructured to subsidize Spain. Mining and metal exporting were the axes of the new economy while agriculture was organized to serve the demands of the new urban centers. Coerced labor, in the mines and on large estates, became a fact of life for the Indians who survived the epidemic diseases that came with the Conquest. Capitalist and precapitalist modes of production were blended together from the start of the region's incorporation into the world market.

Independence movements in the nineteenth century brought an end to colonial rule and the territories split into three separate republics. Peru and Bolivia were founded in 1824 and 1825, respectively, while Ecuador became a sovereign nation after the breakup of the Gran Colombia union in 1830. Independence, however, did nothing to change the place of these countries in the international division of labor. Like the rest of Latin America, the three republics continued as outward-oriented economies. In all three countries, export activities were organized around enclaves. In Bolivia and Peru, the enclaves produced metals for exports; in Ecuador, tropical agricultural products were the primary exports.

This type of outward-oriented growth organized around enclaves produced imbalances and heterogeneity in the economic structures of the three countries. The development of capitalism remained incomplete. Precapitalist relations of production continued, especially in the haciendas that produced for domestic consumption. The coexistence of modern capitalist enterprises in the export sector and traditional neofeudal agriculture produced what the UN Economic Commission for Latin America (ECLA) referred to as economies marked by "structural heterogeneity."

In addition to the structural heterogeneity of these economies, the societies were marked by deep racial, cultural, and regional cleavages. The large indigenous population was not simply exploited as part of the laboring classes but was subject to racial and cultural indignities practiced by white and mestizo society. Persistent racism added fuel to the fires of class conflict in all three countries. Indian revolts punctuate the history of these countries. Indian resistance to white rule, however, was complicated by tribal and linguistic differences within the indigenous population.

Regional conflicts also plagued the republics. In Ecuador, political and economic rivalries between the elites of Quito and Guayaquil became a permanent feature of national life. In Bolivia, a similar conflict developed between highlanders from the altiplano city of La Paz and notables from the eastern city of Santa Cruz. Intense rivalries between Arequipa merchants and elites from Lima also marked Peruvian politics in the nineteenth century.

The result of this heterogenous economic development and multiple social cleavages was that, in the early twentieth century, these countries developed as partial nations, incomplete states, and unfinished capitalist systems. The creation of a common national identity, the construction of a strong state structure, and the elaboration of a dynamic and encompassing domestic market was not realized in the nineteenth century.

Throughout the twentieth century, Andean governments continued to struggle with the task of forging a modern political economy. True to Alexander Gerschenkron's observation that late capitalist development entails a heightened role for the government, the state apparatus in the Andean countries expanded with the drive for economic growth.[38] The process began in the 1920s with the creation of public financial institutions that gave the government a greater role in economic management. State expansion accelerated in the 1950s and 1960s as governments channeled new resources and incentives to the private sector and even launched public enterprises.

The growth of the government's role in spearheading the drive for economic development reflected the weaknesses of the domestic capitalist classes in these countries. The old oligarchies that dominated the scene until the 1930s were a fusion of exporters, merchants, and traditional landholding groups. They did not, on the whole, constitute a dynamic risk-taking entrepreneurial class. These oligarchic groups were acutely dependent on the central government for the unconditional benefits they extracted from it; as such, they forged political arrangements that allowed them to exercise plutocratic control until the 1920s (see chapter 2).

The economic crisis that began in the 1920s and deepened into the worldwide depression of the 1930s severely disrupted the operation of these export-dependent economies and enfeebled the oligarchies that lorded over them. From that time, the capacity to dictate the public agenda began to shift away from the old elites and toward new elites, growing from a new political class and an embryonic technocratic strata. Linked to the dependent middle class, these new elites began to articulate ideologies and economic programs that assigned a leading role in economic development to the state. They envisioned an economic modernization that involved the eradication of antiquated agrarian structures, the creation of a domestic market, and import-substitution industrialization. The first calls for reforms came from populist politicians in the 1930s and 1940s; they were followed in the 1950s by similar calls from technocrats and politicians who were highly influenced by the structuralist economic doctrines proposed by Raúl Prebisch and the United Nations' ECLA.

The economic development models articulated by modernizing politicians and technocrats did not exclude domestic capitalists. On the contrary, the developmentalist formula put forth by ECLA and U.S. mission technocrats in the 1950s and 1960s was built on the notion that the state should foster the develop-

ment of a dynamic entrepreneurial class. Existing business elites, however, were less sanguine about the role they were being assigned by politicians and technocrats—and they frequently objected to the calls for deep structural reforms in the economy. Domestic capitalists had a practical understanding of how ''their'' capitalism should work, which was at odds with the theoretically derived versions of capitalist development put forth by political-technocratic elites.

The progressive attenuation of the links between the oligarchy and the state set the stage for chronic political instability as the old elites jockeyed to stave off the challenge posed by populism and developmentalism. It was a long conflict, which they ultimately lost. The political crisis engendered by the collapse of the oligarchical system was eventually resolved by an extended stay of the military in power in the 1970s.

While there were important differences in the kinds of military government each country experienced in the 1970s, all three shared one common characteristic. All these military governments accelerated state involvement in the economy. The heightened state involvement included the use of public resources aimed at recomposing and restructuring the local business class. The restructured bourgeoisie that emerged in the 1970s was melded together from traditional economic groups and newer maverick capitalists who were able to take advantage of government incentives. The refurbishing of the Andean dominant classes in the 1970s took place at the behest of military governments who were able to take advantage of the favorable financial climate of the period to channel resources to domestic business.

The economic invigoration of the bourgeoisie was not, however, accompanied with the restitution of the previous relationships of the ancien régime in which economic elites enjoyed a near stranglehold over the government and policy making. As we show in chapter 3, the military regimes were at best a mixed blessing for the domestic bourgeoisie. Business elites benefited from many of the economic policies of the period, but they resented the government's increasing attempts at regulation and its occupation of the available economic space through public enterprises. At the same time, access to and influence over the policymaking process was problematic. The military did not set up formal channels through which business interest groups could participate in key decisions concerning the economy.

These frustrations led the domestic bourgeoisie to search for a political alternative to military authoritarianism and for an economic model that embodied their normative vision of capitalism. That search culminated in the transition to civilian rule and the eventual imposition of neoliberal economic programs in the 1980s. In chapters 4 and 5, we show how this process involved the development of an antistatist consensus inside the business community and the ways it was expressed through interest groups, parties, and electoral activism.

In all three countries, however, democratization and neoliberalism did not live up to the expectations of domestic capitalists. While domestic capitalists had rallied with rightist politicians around antistatism and democratization, they discovered that civilian governments did not necessarily produce the policies or the access they desired. Once again, their aspirations for local capitalism diverged with the more theoretically driven prescriptions offered up by domestic technocrats and the IMF. Nor did right-wing politicians prove more pliable than orthodox technocrats; politicians, once in office, were driven by political logics, that is, the quest to survive in office, influence future elections, or carve out their niche in history.

For a variety of reasons, then, politicians and technocrats sought to insulate themselves from direct societal pressures, including those from below and those from the domestic business community. In chapter 6, we chronicle the launching of the policy experiments and the devices used by policy makers to mitigate societal pressures.

Initiating policy is often easier than sustaining policy over the long term, and in chapter 7 we examine the factors that account for the ultimate collapse of the neoliberal experiments in Peru and Ecuador. Juxtaposed to these failures is the case of Bolivia where the Machiavellian political management, exercised within a special set of circumstances, created a foundation to sustain the economic experiment.

While the actual policy outcomes differed across the three countries, the dynamics of the policy-making process were remarkably similar. In chapter 8, we conclude with reflections on how the organization of economic policy making endangers the prospects for future democratic political development. Indeed, the Andean cases may indicate that Latin America is heading toward its own peculiar brand of what Alexis de Tocqueville long ago labeled democratic despotism.

CHAPTER 2

Losing Control: Business-Government Relations in Historical Perspective

IN BOLIVIA, ECUADOR, and Peru, the transition to civilian rule in the 1980s signified an important realignment in relations between the private sector and public authority. In all three countries, the domestic bourgeoisie emerged as a key protagonist in the process of political transition. As we show in later chapters, democracy came to be regarded by business elites as a means to secure steady access to policy makers and to guarantee more predictability and probusiness postures in economic policy. After years of economic experimentation or incoherence under the military governments of the 1970s, domestic capitalists were ready to accept the risks inherent in democratic politics, betting that their privileged position in the system would insure a good measure of control over economic policy.[1]

The bourgeoisie's recent turn toward democracy is the latest installment in a long historical process that involved a progressive loss of elite control over government and economic policy. The 1920s initiated the eclipse of oligarchic politics all over Latin America. The breakdown of the exclusionary politics practiced by commercial and landholding elites occurred in the face of changes in the international market and domestic class structure. A deterioration in international prices for Latin American commodities brought financial troubles for the dominant classes—and led to the demise of the liberal policy coalition that had dominated economic policy making. This economic decline combined with the emergence of new political contenders, especially leaders representing new lower-class urban groups. Financial distress and lower-class contestation loosened the political grip of dominant groups and forced readjustments in their relationship to the state along with important restructurings in the economic composition of the class. In short, a progressive attenuation in the linkages between the dominant class and the state apparatus occurred in all three countries.

This is not to say that the state emerged as an actor exhibiting high degrees of "relative autonomy"—that is, a capacity to implement policies against dominant-class interests. Rather, the old oligarchic political system characterized by the direct occupation of the government by economic elites gave way to a more confused and uncertain set of relations. Dominant groups did not relinquish control of the state in this period inasmuch as they clumsily struggled to remain astride an increasingly complex set of political institutions and a less intimidated society. Repression and the co-optation of populist leaders were frequently used to stem the new challenge from below. Substantive reformism, however, was never championed by economic elites in these countries as a response to lower-class demands. In contrast to the Southern Cone countries where economic elites were pushed into an acceptance of at least some of the claims made by populist movements, there was no such grudging toleration by upper classes in the Central Andes. Indeed, what is striking about the behavior of dominant classes in all three countries was their tenacious rejection of reformism as a political strategy.

The remainder of this chapter provides a comparative overview of oligarchic politics and its breakdown. The purpose of this discussion is to chart the changing nature of business-government relations in the twentieth century—specifically, the demise of the liberal policy coalition that directed economic policy and the erosion of business's capacity to organize politics, monopolize policy-making positions, and dominate the discourse on economic policy.

Liberal Coalitions and State Making

The debate over free trade in the nineteenth century had far-reaching implications for political development everywhere. In Europe and in North and South America, businessmen and party leaders argued the pros and cons of opening their respective economies to unrestricted trade and investment. The resolution of the debate and its consequences, however, differed significantly between countries. In Great Britain, for example, the victory of the liberal coalition reflected the strength of an expansive entrepreneurial class—a set of business elites with global interests who were willing to democratize the political system in exchange for lower-class support for their trade policies. Economic liberalism in Britain was part of a package of change that included a more egalitarian approach to politics. Germany, on the other hand, was the site of a completely different resolution in which conservative industrial and agricultural elites combined in an alliance favoring protectionism and the continued subordination of labor.[2]

In the Central Andes, another dark version of the liberal coalition emerged in the wake of the continental independence. Rather than acting as a catalyst for sustained economic development and democratization, Andean liberal coalitions in the latter half of the nineteenth century secured their countries' dependent status in the world economy and left intact the racially stratified social order bequeathed by Spanish colonialism. Free-trade policies were detached from progressive change in the social and political realms.[3]

The crippled character of liberalism can be traced to the peculiarities in the makeup of its support coalition. Exporters in mining and agriculture were the most adamant supporters of free-trade policies in Bolivia, Ecuador, and Peru. While favoring exporting interests, the switch to free trade did not involve a massive disruption of the economic activities of other segments of the upper class. Traditional landholders firmly entrenched in precapitalist forms of agricultural production in the hacienda system were not displaced by the introduction of free trade. On the contrary, many of them benefited from the enactment of liberal reforms that dismantled communal landholding and forced the sale of village tracts to individuals. The result was the persistence (and in many locales, the expansion) of the hacienda system in all three countries—a brutal institution that left a seigneurial stamp on cultural and social life. At the upper levels of society, a fusion of new commercial and traditional landed elites took place. Intermarriage and the diversification of investments forged a privileged strata that shared a common identity as members of the propertied classes. They built a collective social life that revolved around elite clubs, conspicuous consumption, and an adherence to European culture. These groups developed a Euro-centric lifestyle that denigrated and denied a place to local indigenous culture. Racism became a core component of dominant ideology and a chronic obstacle in the formation of a shared national identity.[4]

The rise of liberal coalitions based in these commercial landholding groups overlapped with the process of state making in all three countries. Thus, the construction of the modern state was profoundly affected by the inclination of the coalition to direct public policy completely in its own interests. In the absence of mass political participation or an independent state bureaucracy, these interests were translated into policy in an unmediated fashion. Exporters turned into presidents, and economic policies responded directly to imperatives of the export trade.

The result was the development of a state that was partial in its construction and captive to dominant economic interests. The term *government* became synonymous with the domination of export barons and their upper-class allies. At the same time, the vast indigenous majority was excluded from citizenship. But the liberalism adopted by dominant groups did not mean they favored a minimalist state. Both new commercial groups and traditional landholders demanded government intervention in the provision of the physical infrastructure they needed and the continued subordination of labor. Dominant groups looked to the state as a source of collusive quasi-rents—that is, resources derived from government-granted monopolies, licenses, and so on. In an environment where there were few opportunities for increasing profits through Schumpeterian innovations, entrepreneurs came to depend on such a close collaboration with the government to extract "favors" in the process of capital accumulation.[5]

In Bolivia. In Bolivia, silver production was the economic base that gave life to a mine-owning oligarchy centered in the city of Sucre. Starting in the mid-nineteenth century, the group flourished until the collapse of world silver prices in the 1890s. These elites combined mine owning with investments in landholding and banking. Policies that opened the economy to foreign trade and investment were initiated by the government of Mariano Melgarejo (1864–1871) in the 1860s and subsequent caudillo presidents. The Sucre oligarchy's control over the state was institutionalized through the Conservative party. It successfully placed mine owners into the presidency between 1884 and 1899. This direct control over the central government was crucial to the fortunes of the Sucre elite. It allowed them to direct fiscal resources into the construction of railroads, which they desperately needed to lower production costs.

Changes in the international market set in motion the decline of the Sucre oligarchy. The result was a recomposition in the Bolivian dominant class and an important adjustment in its association with the state. The collapse of silver prices in the 1890s was followed by a quick expansion in world demand for tin, a metal abundant in Bolivian mines. The rapid increase in demand required a swift reallocation of resources from silver to tin; it was a change that Sucre mine owners found difficult, given their investment in fixed assets. This opened the way for foreign capital and a new set of entrepreneurs to take advantage of the opportunities in tin mining. The tin boom led to an extreme concentration of economic power in the hands of three tin barons who developed strong links to foreign capital: Simón Patiño, Carlos Aramayo, and Mauricio Hoschild. By 1920, Patiño alone controlled 50 percent of the Bolivian tin industry.

In contrast to the silver oligarchy, however, the tin magnates eschewed political office for themselves. Instead, they delegated political management to a new stratum of politicians composed of lawyers and other professionals who insured favorable policies toward the tin industry. This new arrangement coincided with the rise of the Liberal party and its control over the central government until 1920. The political absenteeism of the tin barons mimicked their relationship to economic production. As their enterprises and fortunes grew, these investors turned into absentee capitalists: foreign technicians managed the mines while their owners lived abroad; profits were expatriated to support the luxurious lifestyles of the tin elite or for reinvestment elsewhere.[6]

In Peru. Liberal economic doctrine was embraced by Peruvian elites in the 1850s, laying the foundation for the important interplay of foreign and domestic capital in Peru's subsequent economic growth.[7] British merchants along with domestic investors shared in the wealth generated by the export of guano in the 1850s. So did the central government; the sale of concessions to exploit guano was a boon to public coffers and facilitated an ambitious program of public works. The decline of the guano trade and the War of the Pacific (1879–1883) was a blow to the government's treasury as well as to the capitalists whose lands and mines were devastated by the invasion of Chilean forces. The government's attempt to solve its debt problems after the war resulted in the notorious Grace Contract, which, by conceding the railway system, opened up Peru to extensive control by foreign investors.

The Peruvian upper class directed a more diversified range of economic activities than its Bolivian counterpart. Commercial agriculture as well as mining played an important part in the Peruvian economy. The resurgence of export-led growth in the 1890s consolidated the agro-export bourgeoisie who controlled the sugar and cotton plantations of the northern coast, and then extended some investment into industry. The economic ascendance of agro-exporters, however, did not eclipse the power of other important groups of regional elites such as those in mining and sheep raising in the central and southern highlands. The enduring importance of these regional groups and foreign enclaves limited the reach and authority of the central government apparatus. Indeed, the weakness of the national state was demonstrated in its reliance on local bosses *(gamonales)* to maintain order in the countryside.

The height of political domination by the agro-export bourgeoisie came during the period known as the Aristocratic Republic (1895–1919). During this period, the two major political parties—the Partido Civilista and the Partido Demócrata—were organized as oligarchic clubs through which economic elites vied for public office. With economic liberalism entrenched as the ideology of the upper class, clashes over economic policy during the period were minimal. Instead, oligarchic politics during the Aristocratic Republic revolved around the securing of political and administrative positions for elite factions.[8]

In Ecuador. Ecuador's Liberal Revolution in 1895 established the hold of its coastal agro-export bourgeoisie over the state. The political takeover by Guayaquil's export elites corresponded with their rising economic importance. Increasing demand in the world market for Ecuadorean cocoa was the basis for the expansion of production and commercial activities by the "cocoa kings" of the coast. By the turn of the century, Ecuador was the world's largest single producer of cocoa, solidifying the economic power of the oligarchy that controlled the trade. As in Bolivia and Peru, the ascent of exporters did not imply any fundamental uprooting of the traditional landholding class. Even after the Liberal Revolution, this segment of the upper class continued to function as an important pillar of the class structure and a contender for political power.

The banking system created a symbiosis between government and dominant groups in Ecuador. This relationship was rooted in the chronic fiscal crisis of the central government. Throughout the nineteenth and early twentieth century, the Ecuadorean government resorted to heavy internal borrowing from private commercial banks to finance its operations. The government used its legal power over licenses and its power to recognize private banknotes as legal tender as the means to force banks into making such loans. Thus, dominant-class groups and the central government came to rely on each other heavily in the nexus of the banking system. The growth of the economic power of agro-export elites and their takeover of the government in 1895 consolidated the hold of this group over the financial system.[9] (This merging of the government and banking system under the political control of agro-exporters was given the name *bancocracia*.)

Liberal Coalitions, Weak States. The nation states that developed in the nineteenth century and that were taken over by these plutocratic liberal coalitions were "weak" states. Their weakness was rooted in their subordinate relationships with both external and internal actors. Peru's and Bolivia's losses in the War of the Pacific with Chile demonstrated the states' incapacity to maintain territorial integrity, and the war had serious financial repercussions for the economic elites. In all three countries, the central government had little capacity to impose policies on dominant groups in civil society.[10] Regionally based elites, particularly hacendados, retained their authority and control over the indigenous labor force even after the triumph of liberalism. At the same time, the central government was highly dependent on the performance of the export sector for its financing. In Peru, the state's dependence on the mining export sector allowed for a deep penetration of the economy by foreign investors. State revenues, along with the wealth of the exporters themselves, ebbed and flowed with the fluctuations of commodities prices in the world market, creating chronic fiscal uncertainty for central governments and chronic anxiety for domestic capitalists.

Although the weak state structure was a product of their own making, it was both a blessing and a curse for the dominant groups. It helped create the conditions for capitalist development; but it was also a dependent capital-accumulation process, which left governments and capitalists vulnerable to changes in the international market and limited the bounds of future capitalist development. For the emergent bourgeoisie, opportunities for economic diversification through industrialization were constricted by the small size of the internal market. Chronic fiscal problems made the state a less effective guarantor of order, at both the elite and the mass levels. For dominant groups, control over the machinery of government was both an economic and a political imperative. Elite competition for control over public office frequently spilled over the confines of elections and institutions; violence and instability remained a part of political life.[11]

For the masses, the oligarchically controlled state structure was the executor of "the occupation"—an entity that, along with the white dominant class, extracted surplus while denying the masses even symbolic status inside the nation state. The exclusionary character of the political system precluded the construction of hegemony in the Gramscian sense. Repression and the cultural degradation of the majority, not consent, formed the basis of these systems. The record of chronic Indian rebellions and resistance is evidence of the absence of hegemony and of the explosive character of rural relations in the face of hacienda expansion.[12]

Thus, the intimate ties that developed between economic elites and the government were central to the dependent capitalist development taking place in these systems; but in the long run they enfeebled both dominant groups and government. By the 1920s, the liabilities of the oligarchic system and export-driven growth became all too clear, as financial crisis and political challenges called these models into question. Collapsing commodities prices in the 1920s and the Great Depression of the 1930s initiated a growing estrangement of business elites and central governments.

Fiscal Crisis and the Kemmerer Coalitions

The worldwide economic collapse of the 1930s reshaped business-government relations in capitalist economies across the globe. Suddenly, business elites found themselves cast as the villains responsible for the calamity. The Great Depression generated a crisis of confidence; it called into question both the competence of capitalists as market actors and also their capacity to provide policy solutions to mitigate against the ravages of the business cycle. The 1930s saw a reduction in the political power of big business and its predominance in policy-making circles in Western Europe and North America.[13] New groups, especially labor, demanded and achieved a greater voice in the direction of economic policy.

Out of this conjuncture of the 1930s sprang the foundations of the postwar Keynesian class compromise in the advanced capitalist systems. The compromise entailed a fundamental reshaping of the relations between the state and capitalists and labor.[14] Business accepted labor's demand for material improvements, economic security, and greater political participation, in exchange for the deradicalization of labor movements and parties and their acceptance of capitalism. Central governments, in turn, took on new functions, mediating business-labor relations and intervening directly in the economy to manage the business cycle.

Domestic capitalists in the Central Andes were also subject to important changes in their relationships to public authority, which began with an emergency in state finances in the 1920s and continued in the 1930s as the effects of the depression spread across the region. Yet, the resolution of the economic and political crisis of the period took a very different form from that of the Keynesian class compromise in advanced capitalist systems. Andean capitalists coped with the economic stress of the period in a variety of ways, which ran the gamut from orthodox initiatives at the end of the 1920s to heterodox improvisations in the 1930s and 1940s. On the political level, elites fitfully adapted to the emergence of populist movements with intermittent repression and the co-optation of populist leaders. A full incorporation of lower classes into these political systems did not occur. There was no institutionalization of populism in the style of Peronism or Mexico's all-embracing ruling party. Neither was there a social-democratic class compromise. While economically privileged groups were losing their capacity to lord over the political system, their spasmodic attempts to restore the status quo ante slowed the decay of the ancien régime.

Deep fiscal problems began to undermine the operation of the oligarchical state in the 1920s. In all three countries, the export booms of the late nineteenth and early twentieth centuries were associated with increasing levels of government expenditures. These expenditures underwrote a variety of ventures—the construction of a new physical infrastructure of railways and highways, the creation of public sector employment for new urban groups, and the expansion of the military. Export elites generally favored such public spending, especially on transportation facilities. But the same elites assiduously guarded their profit margins and resisted tax increases by the central government to finance the expenditures. The response by the liberal coalitions in power was to engage in chronic deficit spending and public indebtedness. In Peru and Bolivia, governments turned to foreign borrowing to cover their operating costs and interest payments. In Ecuador, the government resorted to domestic private banks. With limited scope to raise revenues inside their domestic economies, access to foreign credit and the health of the export sector became the source of ersatz solvency.

The unraveling of this system of debt-fed public spending came first in Ecuador. The spread of plant disease on cocoa plantations in the early 1920s coincided with a downturn in world prices for the product. The result was a disastrous decline in production and revenues generated by the trade. The initial response of the coastal liberals who controlled the central government was to pass on the costs of the export sector to other groups through currency devaluations. At the same time, private banks continued the practice of excessive monetary emissions. The ensuing inflation deepened the fissures inside dominant-class ranks and fed popular discontent among lower-class urban groups. Popular dissatisfaction exploded in the Guayaquil general strike of 1922; the army was ordered to quell the disturbance and hundreds of workers were killed.[15]

The liberal coalition in Ecuador was finally displaced by the Revolución Juliana in 1925. Liberal president Gonzalo Córdova was overthrown in a coup staged by young military officers. They were backed by a heterogenous alliance of highland landowners, incipient industrialists, and middle- and lower-class groups.

The modernization of the state was a primary goal of Julianista officers. The Revolución Juliana marked a pivotal moment in state-society relations in Ecuador. The reforms sponsored by the Julianista governments were the first concerted attempt at creating a neutral state—one with more regulatory capacity vis-à-vis dominant groups. The revolution also reflected the growth of reformist currents inside the armed forces, a phenomenon that would considerably complicate the relationship between dominant classes and the state from that point forward.

Despite their political defeat, agro-export and financial groups in Guayaquil did share in the broader consensus among elites on the need to rationalize the operations of the central government. As part of the Julianista program of modernization, the Ayora government invited an entourage of specialists led by Princeton economist Edwin Kemmerer to advise on fiscal and monetary reforms in 1927. Thus, the liberal coalition gave way to the short-lived Kemmererian coalition of the late 1920s.[16]

The Kemmerer mission recommended a sweeping package of policy reforms and important institutional changes. The policies included fiscal austerity, comprehensive tax reforms, exchange rate stabilization, the adoption of the gold standard, and new regulations on the banking system. But of even greater significance in the long run were the institutional innovations suggested by Kemmerer and enacted by the Ayora government. The institutional restructuring included the creation of a central bank, a comptroller's office, and a superintendency of banks. The purpose of these institutions was to enhance the regulatory role of the state. Initially, U.S. advisors were named to head these agencies.

A similar ''Kemmerization'' of institutions took place in Bolivia and Peru. After concluding his mission in Ecuador, Kemmerer moved on to Bolivia in March 1927 at the invitation of President Hernando Siles Reyes. Kemmerer recommended a revamping of the government's Bank of the Bolivian Nation along the lines of a central bank, the creation of a comptroller's office, and the development of a more powerful customs collection agency. In Peru, Kemmerer-style reforms were enacted during the wildly pro–United States dictatorship of Augusto Leguía (1919–30) with advice from American advisors and investors.

In all three countries, the acceptance of the Kemmerer reforms on the part of domestic elites was motivated by their desire to assure a continued flow of foreign credit. For Latin American countries of the 1920s, Kemmerer's seal of approval was the rough equivalent of today's agreement with the IMF; it was a sign of good standing in financial circles and facilitated the extension of credit by U.S. lenders. And like IMF agreements, the Kemmerer missions entailed the extension of the influence of foreign advisors and investors.[17]

Kemmerer-inspired policies were largely scrapped by the early 1930s as support among economic elites and central governments faded. Nonetheless, the changes in the bureaucratic machinery and the style of economic policy making that were part of the Kemmerer reforms were an important benchmark in the evolution of business-government relations. New bureaucratic structures were created expressly to insulate economic decision making from the direct purview of business elites and clientele-oriented politicians. The thrust of the reforms was to construct, inside the executive branch, a new technocratic realm that could direct capitalist economy with more autonomy than had been accorded by the old institutional structures of the oligarchic system. The enactment of the reforms themselves was a prototype of technocratic policy making structured to minimize interference by pressure groups. In all three countries, presidents forced the adoption of the measures with little public discussion. Strong executives stood squarely behind the move to create more technocratically directed economic policy making.

The Collapse of Orthodoxy: Populism and Spontaneous Keynesianism

Fiscal crisis was not the only dilemma eating away at the old system of oligarchical politics. The commodities boom and government expansion had engendered important structural changes in Andean society by the 1920s. Modifications in the class structure made civil society more complex and restive. As economic growth ground to a halt, new middle- and working-class groups turned to new forms of collective action to redress their economic and political grievances.

The most dramatic demographic and occupational shift in the early part of the century took place in Peru. From 1920 to 1931, the population of the capital city of Lima grew by 68 percent to exceed 300,000 inhabitants; much of this growth was based in rural migration. This dizzying population expansion was accompanied by an increase in the size of both working- and middle-class groups. Public employment, for example, increased by 491 percent during the Leguía administration. According to Steve Stein, the 1920s saw the "massification" of Lima. It was a period in which "the working classes had grown from their position as a mere component in the urban scene to domination of that scene demographically and socially."[18]

Bolivia and Ecuador also underwent "massification" in the 1920s. In 1920 in Bolivia, La Paz registered a population of 115,000, which included white-collar government employees and a skeletal working class. In Ecuador, the port city of Guayaquil, as the commercial center of the cocoa trade, was the major site of urban growth. Urbanization, commercial expansion, and some limited industrialization gave life to new social groups across the Andes by the 1920s. Left-wing parties, trade union organizations, and populist movements were part of the effervescence of the urban scene in this period.

The response of dominant elites to the new collective presence of these groups was by no means uniform either across countries or inside them. At times, the masses were viewed as instruments that could be used in power struggles among different elite groups. In other situations, they were viewed as fundamental threats and were severely repressed. In Peru, for example, fissures inside the ruling Civilista party led some politicians to try to mobilize lower-class groups on their own behalf. Civilista president Guillermo Billinghurst (1912–14) was the first to make explicit appeals to Lima's working class. Virulent anti-oligarchic diatribes were also used by the Leguía administration to rally popular support and to silence elite opposition.

Similarly, in Ecuador and Bolivia, politicians began to cast an instrumental eye toward lower-class groups, seeing them as a way to expand their own power. In 1931, Ecuador's conservative landowners organized the Compactación Obrera, a group that functioned as shock troops when electoral disputes spilled over into the streets.[19] In Bolivia, the Republican administrations of Bautista Saavedra (1921–25) and Hernando Siles Reyes (1926–30) tried to create new links to the labor and the student movements, respectively.

It is important to note both the effects and the limitations posed by the opening of politics to the masses. The opening was a recognition of the masses *(el pueblo)* as important street players in the new spectacle of urban politics. The masses marched, sang, rallied; but they were still not recognized as citizens with clearly established rights. In all three countries, restrictions on the franchise remained in place and severely reduced the size of the national electorate. Rafael Quintero estimates, for example, that the Ecuadorean electorate in the 1930s never exceeded more than 5 percent of the total population.[20] But although the entrée of the popular classes into political life remained circumscribed, the new presence of the masses nonetheless constituted a vital modification of the political game. For the first time, a ground opened that allowed for popular-class organization and new political discourse. Among the most important challengers to elite authority were populist leaders and movements.

In Peru. Lower classes in Peru rallied around two populist leaders in the 1930s: Luis Alberto Sánchez Cerro and Víctor Raúl Haya de la Torre. Both gained popularity as part of the opposition to the dictatorship of Augusto Leguía. Sánchez Cerro, a mestizo army colonel, led the coup against Leguía and assumed the presidency in 1930. In the 1920s, Haya de la Torre gained notoriety as a university leader and labor advocate. In 1922, while exiled by Leguía, Haya de la Torre founded what was to become Peru's most important political party, the Alianza Popular Revolucionaria Americana (APRA).

Elites supported the move against Leguía, but the old guard of the Aristocratic Republic was initially dismayed by the style and tone of the Sánchez Cerro presidency (although it later became reconciled to the government as the lesser evil). Mainstream Civilista politicians were given important positions in the Sánchez Cerro cabinet, and the same elite provided financial assistance to his subsequent campaign. Thus, the Sánchez Cerro administration was rapidly penetrated by dominant economic groups. Sánchez Cerro's appeals to the masses were demagogic, paternalist, and punctuated by right-wing nationalism. Economic policy was given an orthodox spin with a visit from Edwin Kemmerer in 1931 at the urging of business elites.

Haya de la Torre's APRA party was clearly a more radical contestation of the existing order in the wake of the elite co-optation of Sánchez Cerro. The APRA program invoked anti-imperialism and called for an incorporation of the indigenous majority into national life. The substance of APRA as well as its militant style was distasteful to the supporters of the Aristocratic Republic. The political violence triggered by the assassination of Sánchez Cerro by an *aprista* cemented the enmity of the dominant-class groups and the military for APRA, and the party suffered severe persecution from 1933 to 1945.

In Ecuador. The dominant class co-optation of populism in Ecuador began in the 1930s and proved to be an enduring feature of political life through the 1960s. As the historical work of Rafael Quintero shows, the traditional landholding class of the sierra backed the 1933 candidacy of the anti-oligarchic orator José María Velasco Ibarra. They provided financial support for his campaign and mobilized voters on his behalf in the highland regions under their control. Like Sánchez Cerro, Velasco was fundamentally conservative and virulently anticommunist; he certainly did not incorporate redistributive promises into his popular rhetorical package. From the beginning, and throughout his long political career that spanned five presidencies, Velasco Ibarra was closely linked to the traditional parties and the dominant-class backers. Ecuador's short spurt of reformism in the 1930s was authored not by Velasco but by the military. In 1937–38, a military government under Colonel Alberto Enríquez granted legal recognition to trade unions, struck down restrictions on left-wing parties, and proposed tighter regulations on foreign investment. The reformist thrust was completely reversed in the subsequent return of civilian rule under Liberal party president Carlos Arroyo del Río (1940–44).

In Bolivia. The most serious breach in the capacity of economic elites to retain political power in the 1930s occurred in Bolivia.[21] The economic dislocations caused by the depression and the loss of the Chaco War with Paraguay (1932–35) fed widespread political alienation and aspirations for change among lower-class groups and young veterans of the war. The result was the development of reformist and left-wing currents inside the military and civil society. The military socialism practiced by the administrations of Colonel David Toro (1936–37) and

Germán Busch (1937–39) reflected these new tendencies. Mild social reforms, the nationalization of the United States–controlled oil industry, and new regulations over the tin industry were some of the policies adopted by the military socialists. Opposition by the tin mine owners finally toppled the Busch government. His overthrow was followed by an attempt of the traditional elite parties to reestablish their predominance: in 1939 they created a new united front called La Concordancia and used it to dominate the government of General Enrique Peñaranda (1940–43). Meanwhile middle-class reformers regrouped and founded the populist Movimiento Nacionalista Revolucionario (MNR) in 1941.

Liberalization and Retrenchment. The Bolivian Concordancia is illustrative of the repeated efforts of dominant groups and traditional parties to backtrack from the process of political opening; experimental moments of liberalization and democratization were cut short and followed by a reassertion of elite control through force and fraudulent elections. All three countries underwent such retrenchment after brief episodes in which democratic fronts came to power in the 1940s. In Peru, a democratic alliance that incorporated APRA won the elections of 1945 and brought José Luis Bustamante y Rivero to the presidency. In 1944, the Alianza Democrática, composed of socialist, communist, and conservative forces, came together under the leadership of Velasco Ibarra to overthrow the dictatorship of Arroyo del Río in Ecuador. The Bolivian left joined with the right in 1946 to overthrow the government of General Gualberto Villaroe. These fronts were viable because of the favorable international climate for democracy in the postwar period and because local dominant classes were eager to incorporate their countries into the new international order.[22] The fronts collapsed, however, as the heterogenous groups that composed them clashed and as elites regrouped to hold the line against increasing popular demands directed toward the fronts.

Across all three cases, the Great Depression inaugurated a notable reduction in the capacity of dominant groups to maintain unilateral control over the central governments and to dictate policy outcomes. The exporting groups that had dominated politics since the 1880s reeled from the precipitous declines in commodities prices on the world market. The financial debility of the export bourgeoisie was matched by the fiscal crisis of their state. The contraction of the export sector and the financial crunch sent shock waves through the local economy—bringing unemployment and considerable public discontent.

In this crisis, the central government became the focus of attention for all groups in civil society seeking relief. In Ecuador and Bolivia, that relief came in the form of an improvised Keynesian adaptation of economic policy. Kemmerer's orthodoxies were abandoned in the 1930s as governments responded with a variety of countercyclical measures to appease both elites and masses. The Bolivian and Ecuadorean governments jettisoned the gold standard, suspended payments on the foreign debt, and turned to deficit spending to finance continued expenditures on infrastructure. Peru abandoned the gold standard and debt payments. But, according to Rosemary Thorp and Geoffrey Bertram, Peru's economy was somewhat less affected by the depression; the export bourgeoisie that backed the Benavides dictatorship (1933–39) continued to endorse fiscal austerity. Thus, Peru's turn toward expansionary policies was somewhat slower; public spending accelerated during the subsequent government of Manuel Prado (1939–45) and José Luis Bustamante y Rivero (1945–48).[23]

But the spontaneous Keynesian reaction of Andean governments in the 1930s and 1940s did not reflect the development of a coherent new policy coalition, nor did it involve a new compromise with labor. Liberal policies were discredited—at least temporarily—by the depression; still, no stable consensus on a future economic model came from the ranks of business groups, nor had a powerful technocratic corps emerged inside the public bureaucracy to spearhead such a consensus. The Keynesianism of the 1930s and 1940s was an ad hoc response to dominant-class disillusionment with liberal formulas and the demands of subordinate urban groups for compensation in the crisis.

Liberalism and Developmentalism: Postwar Peru and Ecuador

The economic recovery of the export sector in Peru and Ecuador was sparked by the effects of World War II on international trade. Attentive to the shifts in the international market, Peruvian exporters responded to the expanded demand for cotton, sugar, and minerals, as did their Ecuadorean counterparts who dealt in rice and other agricultural exports. Postwar reconstruction and the outbreak of the Korean War maintained the buoyancy of the agricultural and mineral commodities market through the late 1940s and early 1950s.

The export revival was accompanied by a resurgence of the political power of traditional exporting groups. They resurrected liberal economic tenets, but with enough pragmatism to allow the state to perform promotional and infrastructural duties for the export sector. In Ecuador, government credit and road-building projects under the presidency of Galo Plaza Lasso (1948–52) subsidized the reorientation of the export sector into banana production.[24] In Peru, the northern cotton and sugar agro-exporters were the direct beneficiaries of massive irrigation projects launched under the government of Manuel Odría (1948–56). Domestic capitalists, including exporters, increasingly recognized the need for state intervention to promote further capitalist modernization and growth. Laissez-faire liberalism as a set of abstract principles continued to be at odds with a reality where domestic capitalists were dependent on selective state intervention on their behalf.

As economic liberalism waned, the intellectual and experiential foundations

for an alternative model of development were already in place. By the 1950s, Latin America could look back on its own experience with ad hoc Keynesianism and view it as a fully elaborated economic doctrine whose principles were being adopted by the advanced industrial nations. At the same time, Latin American economists came under the influence of the ECLA school of thought. Led by Argentine economist Raúl Prebisch, the United Nations' ECLA forcefully argued that state-promoted industrialization was the only way for Latin America to es-

cape its underdevelopment, which was rooted in the deteriorating terms of trade for its primary products. These ideas were widely disseminated by ECLA technocrats in missions throughout Latin America.

Local and international advocates of this developmentalist school *(desarrollismo)* began to be heard in Ecuador and Peru in the 1950s. Developmentalism was not an entirely new phenomenon, either in its policy prescriptions or in terms of the social makeup of groups that advocated it. Developmentalism drew support from middle and lower classes, as had earlier populism, and incorporated many of the same positions (for example, national control over natural resources, industrialization). But in the 1950s, support for developmentalism was strengthened by the growth of a modernizing technocratic stratum inside the public bureau-

cracy and the military. Moreover, domestic capitalists with interests in diversifying their portfolios also supported the development of a coherent industrial policy. Notwithstanding its growing presence, however, the developmentalist coalition remained weak and poorly articulated in party organizations and interest groups in the 1950s.

With the developmentalist coalition still inchoate, the exporters in both countries were able to retain a high degree of influence over the political regimes and economic-policy-making process in the 1950s. Many of the old mechanisms of elite control over the political sphere remained in place. In Peru, the overthrow of Bustamante y Rivero in 1948 ushered in an eight-year dictatorship of Manuel Odría (1948–56). Odría reinstated laissez-faire economic policies that worked to favor exporting interests. The subsequent election of Manuel Prado in 1956, based on an alliance *(convivencia)* struck between APRA and the remnants of the Civilista party, continued with pro-export policies designed by finance minister Pedro Beltrán; but some initial steps toward industrial promotion did take place. Prado enacted a comprehensive industrial law in 1956 and raised tariff protection for domestic industry.

Ecuador's postwar boom in banana export converged with the "democratic parenthesis" of 1948–62—a tranquil rotation of the presidency within a circle of politicians drawn from the ranks of the traditional parties.[25] Like Peru, some measures were taken in this period to promote industrialization. The Social Christian government of Camilo Ponce (1956–60) enacted the Industrial Development

Law; Ponce also founded the national planning bureau, the Junta Nacional de Planificación y Coordinación Económica (JUNAPLA), an entity that became an important transmission belt for ECLA doctrine.

After repeated clashes with forces on the side of developmentalism, the dissolution of the old liberal coalition in Ecuador and Peru was completed in the 1960s. Changes in the international environment played an important role in shifting the balance in favor of the developmentalists. The United States–sponsored Alliance for Progress aid program, launched during the Kennedy administration, stressed the need for moderate structural reforms in Latin America as the way to stave off the development of communist guerrilla movements.[26] The reformist discourse emanating from U.S. foreign policy makers helped to undercut the antireformist stance of traditional oligarchic groups and added clout to the position of the developmentalists. At the same time, a new wave of economic crisis in the export sectors and popular mobilization weakened export elites and called into question their traditional formulas for managing the political economy.

In Peru. By the early 1960s in Peru, the performance of the agricultural and mineral export sectors waned, in part because of production bottlenecks and uncertainties in the investment climate. Local capitalists had largely deserted the mining sector in the 1950s while foreign ownership expanded; U.S. multinational corporations were important investors in the mining sector, but they were disinclined to make the new investments necessary to exploit any new deposits. Growth was stifled in the agro-export sector because the government was unable to invest in the vast irrigation projects required for expansion.[27] These difficulties drained domestic capital out of agro-export activities and channeled resources into real estate, finance, and industrial and commercial activities. The decline in the export sector and the decreasing level of foreign investment by the mid-1960s had contributed to budgetary and balance-of-payments problems for the central government. In addition to contributing to the dynamic of the economic crisis in the 1960s, the exit from the export sector by domestic capitalists reduced the constituency for traditional liberalism. As business interests became more diverse, the consensus on liberal economics faded.

The political challenge in what remained of Peru's oligarchic ancien régime came from all quarters. In the party system, Acción Popular (AP) laid claim to the reformist discourse once championed by APRA. Founded in 1956 by Fernando Belaúnde Terry, AP rallied followers around a platform of agrarian reform and increased state investment in housing, education, and infrastructure building. Christian Democratic and Socialist parties were also founded in the wake of APRA's co-optation during the convivencia. Demands for substantive structural change also emanated from popular movements. Massive peasant mobilization in the La Convención valley of Cuzco in the early 1960s was followed by the outbreak of guerrilla movements by the mid-1960s.[28]

But perhaps the pivotal element in shifting the coalitional structure came from changes within the armed forces. The Peruvian military was progressively professionalized in the postwar period. Part of this professionalization involved a new type of training for officers at the Centro de Altos Estudios Militares (CAEM). Beginning in the 1950s, the CAEM developed an analysis of society that pinpointed foreign investors and the local oligarchy as the primary authors of Peruvian underdevelopment. This strong reformist current inside the military was reinforced in the 1960s by the appearance of guerrilla movements and counterinsurgency doctrines. Peruvian officers began to look at structural changes such as agrarian reform as the way to undercut popular support for guerrilla movements. Groups within the armed forces increasingly identified themselves with the aspirations of middle-class reformers and technocrats and less with traditional elites. This reformist faction surfaced in the brief military government of 1962–63. The armed forces turned the government back to civilians in an election that made Fernando Belaúnde president.[29]

The clash between the old liberal groups and the new developmentalist-oriented groups occupied center stage throughout the tumultuous five years of the Belaúnde administration; it resulted in a stalemate that was finally resolved by a military intervention in 1968 and the imposition of a developmentalist model by the armed forces. The stalemate was played out in chronic executive-legislative conflicts.[30] The Congress, under the control of an antireform alliance of APRA and conservative parties, repeatedly vetoed Belaúnde's proposals for tax and agrarian reforms. The intense conflict was a product of the intransigence of the old oligarchic players and the inability of groups with developmentalist aspirations to pull together to defeat them.

In Ecuador. As in Peru, the developmentalist project in Ecuador suffered from the weak and disaggregated state of the civilian groups that supported it. With restrictions on the franchise still in place, the traditional parties (Conservative, Liberal, Velasquista) and their offshoots (Social Christian, National Revolutionary, Institutional Democratic) were able to maintain their dominant position in electoral politics through the presidential election of 1968. There were contending voices from the center (such as the Christian Democratic party founded by dissident students in 1964) and leftist parties, but they remained electorally marginal. In Guayaquil a new populist party, the Concentración de Fuerzas Populares (CFP), was in place; but it was more oriented to making deals with the traditional parties and maintaining local clientele than it was to promoting an alternative model of economic development. Electorally concentrated in Guayaquil, the CFP did not become a voice for reform at the national level.[31] Meanwhile, popular mobilization around such issues as land reform was more limited than in Peru. Peasants did push for agrarian reform, but the movement did not assume the dimensions of the Peruvian mobilization.

Of the forces pushing the developmentalist line in Ecuador, the most potent lobby was the technocratic stratum inside the state bureaucracy. From its inception, the planning bureau JUNAPLA was directly influenced by ECLA doctrine. Personnel from ECLA wrote the first empirical analysis of the Ecuadorean economy in 1953. Shortly thereafter, ECLA functionaries worked as consultants on the preliminary development plan of 1958. The plan strongly advocated a phasing out of Ecuador's traditional export-led model in favor of growth in the internal market.[32] The creation of JUNAPLA was followed by the development of other agencies concerned with industrial development. The Centro de Desarrollo Industrial (CENDES) was formed in 1960 to undertake feasibility studies for industrial projects; in 1965, the Corporación Financiera Nacional (CFN) was founded for the purpose of investing in targeted industry. Slowly, a developmentalist lobby was coalescing inside the state apparatus.[33]

As in Peru, however, the critical breakthrough of developmentalism came through military intervention. Like their counterparts in Peru, Ecuadorean military officers were increasingly influenced by developmentalist doctrines. John Fitch's study of the Ecuadorean military notes the steady increase in the number of officers espousing ideas of the developmentalist school from the 1950s through the 1960s.[34] The military's first attempt to act on these ideas came in 1963. After deposing President Carlos Julio Arosemena, the new military government moved to implement the tax- and agrarian-reform proposals pushed by JUNAPLA and the U.S. Agency for International Development (USAID). An across-the-board mobilization by business groups forced the military to retreat from the reforms. The armed forces handed power back to the traditional parties in 1966. An interim presidency under Clemente Yerovi of the Liberal party was followed by Congress's selection of Otto Arosemena to serve as president in 1967 and a direct presidential election of Velasco Ibarra in 1969. Velasco subsequently established a dictatorship in 1970 when he ordered a shutdown of Congress. In 1972, however, the military reasserted itself in a coup and resurrected the developmentalist model.

The period from 1966 to 1972 was an attempt by the traditional parties and dominant economic elites to return to oligarchic politics as usual. But the economic stagnation of the agro-export sector of the 1960s, especially the decline in the banana trade, only seemed to verify the developmentalist argument that structural changes in the organization of the economy were necessary. Indeed, many agro-exporters began to diversify into industrial investments as a hedge against price fluctuations in the commodities markets and in order to take advantage of the incentives being offered by the state. Likewise, a significant segment of the traditional landholding class were either making the transition to modern capital-intensive ranching and dairy farming or moving their capital out of agriculture altogether.[35] As in the Peruvian case, important modifications in the structural position of the traditional economic elites of Ecuador took place in the 1960s. We shall discuss these modifications later. For now, let us simply note that dominant-class interests became more heterogenous and complicated by the move into new economic activities. The old interests that bound together the classic liberal coalition were fading as the political pressures for a new economic model intensified.

The Bolivian Revolution: Rupturing and Restructuring Relations

The gradual dissipation of the liberal coalitions in Ecuador and Peru stands in sharp contrast to the dramatic shattering of oligarchic power by a revolutionary movement in Bolivia in 1952, when the populist MNR seized power, backed by a massive uprising of peasants and mine workers. The seizure occurred in response to the attempt by the armed forces to deny the presidency to the leader of the MNR, Víctor Paz Estenssoro, in the wake of his electoral victory in 1952.

With mobilized and militant lower classes rallying around the MNR government, President Víctor Paz Estenssoro enacted policies that stripped the last vestiges of power from the traditional tin and landholding elites. The sweeping reforms of 1952–56 were successful in striking the final blow. Universal suffrage was enacted. Tin mines were nationalized and reorganized into a state-owned enterprise under workers' management, the Corporación Minera de Bolivia (COMIBOL). The trade union confederation, the Central Obrera Boliviana (COB), was given control over three key cabinet positions as part of the *co-gobierno* agreement struck with the MNR. The government legalized the peasants' seizure of hacienda lands through a comprehensive agrarian reform law. The armed forces, which had often functioned as the repressive arm of the old elite, was purged and reorganized.[36]

As in other social revolutions, the victory of popular forces in 1952 was facilitated by the enfeebled state of dominant groups. The traditional elites in mining and agriculture had already deserted the scene, no longer productive economic actors. The tin industry had been progressively decapitalized since the 1930s: given the steady decrease in the assay of ore in Bolivian deposits, massive new investments would have been required to maintain production levels. For a variety of reasons, the tin magnates chose not to make such investments. At the same time, a continuing lack of *latifundistas'* investment in agriculture, within the context of population growth, led to increasing levels of food imports.[37] In short, the traditional oligarchy's abdication of its economic role was already well advanced on the eve of 1952.

The revolutionary triumvirate of peasants, workers, and the MNR agreed on the need to eliminate the last vestiges of the traditional elite. But once that goal was accomplished, the coalition divided, unable to agree on the kind of economic model to be pursued. On one side of the divide stood the mainline MNR and its middle-class constituency, which favored a capitalist modernization of the Bolivian economy to be led by the state. On the other side stood the labor left organized in the COB, which advocated a more radical state-socialist model of development. The conflict was eventually resolved on the side of the state-capitalist model. The turn began in 1956 under Paz's successor to the presidency, Hernán Siles Zuazo. The COB was pushed out of the cabinet. Siles imposed an IMF–mandated economic stabilization program and dismantled workers' control in the mining sector. Economic stabilization was the quid pro quo for the renewal of U.S. foreign aid. The MNR's move to subordinate the labor left continued when Paz Estenssoro returned to the presidency in 1960. Both the Siles and the Paz governments actively sought U.S. funds to underwrite development projects. Indeed foreign aid was a pivotal component of central government revenues. In the period from 1957 to 1961, USAID provided funds that accounted for between 25 and 32 percent of the Bolivian budget.[38]

The thrust of the state-capitalist model pushed by Paz and pursued by succeeding military governments in the 1960s was to use public sector investment to modernize the Bolivian economy and to encourage the development of a stratum of private entrepreneurs. The eastern city of Santa Cruz was targeted as a new pole of economic growth. The idea of targeting Santa Cruz as part of a government-led program of economic modernization had circulated prior to the MNR's seizure of power. In 1942, a U.S. economic mission, headed by Merwin Bohan, presented the Bolivian government with a report that recommended substantial public sector investment in infrastructure and import-substitution industrialization. Along with this investment, the Bohan Mission urged Bolivians to modernize and expand agricultural production, particularly in the Santa Cruz region. UN advisors that came to Bolivia in the early 1950s also urged that the state take an activist role in the economy.[39]

Not all of Bolivia's foreign economic advisors in this period concurred with the state-centric model. In 1956 a U.S. operations mission, headed by ex–World Bank staffer Cornelius Zondag, argued strenuously in favor of a free-market model. The 1956 stabilization program was authored as a step toward such a model. George Jackson Eder, the U.S. economist who served as the primary architect of the 1956 stabilization, was an avowed monetarist who was adamant in his advocacy of fiscal austerity and economic deregulation.[40] While the Siles government did undertake Eder's short-term stabilization measures, there was no move to deeper structural reforms.

The MNR and the subsequent military government of the 1960s remained committed to state-centric economics and the notion of a *marcha hacia al oriente* (march to the east) to build up the Santa Cruz region. The central government used credit programs to build a new agro-entrepreneurial stratum in Santa Cruz. Between 1955 and 1973, the government's Banco Agrícola de Bolivia (BAB) directed 40 percent of its credit solely to the department of Santa Cruz, most of which went to farmers with medium- or large-sized farms.[41]

The final rupture of traditional business-government relations in 1952 set the stage for a reshaping of Bolivian capitalism. After the short interlude of radicalism from 1952 through 1956, the MNR embarked on strategy to revitalize the private sector, albeit under the tutelage of an ever more aggressive public sector. Along with the emergence of a new private sector came renewed income inequalities and a retreat from the egalitarian ideals of 1952.[42]

The Structural Position of Business

By the end of the 1960s, businessmen in the Central Andes were adjusting to changes in the political and economic environment. It is important to keep in mind the structural characteristics and economic interests of this business elite, and let us consider a few of these characteristics before we examine the political behavior of the business elites in the following chapters.

First, even as economic modernization and diversification proceeded, business elites still constituted only a small sliver of the population in the three countries. Alejandro Portes estimated the size of the dominant class (defined as proprietors of large modern firms in manufacturing, mining, and agro-industry) in 1970 as .8 percent of the economically active population (EAP) in Ecuador and as .4 percent in Peru. The Bolivian dominant class was estimated as 1.3 percent of the EAP for the same year. Even if we include members of what Portes calls the bureaucratic-technical class (middle-level managers without ownership interests in private and public sector firms), the size of the business community and its allied personnel remains small. Portes estimates the size of the combined dominant and bureaucratic-technical strata in 1970 as 5.7 percent of the EAP in Bolivia, 4.7 percent in Ecuador, and 7 percent in Peru.[43]

The size of the working class employed in the formal sector of the economy was also relatively modest, accounting for 3.3 percent of the EAP in Bolivia and 10 percent in Ecuador. Given its larger manufacturing sector, Peru had a more substantial formal proletariat in the early 1970s, estimated as 27.6 percent of the EAP. In all three countries, the overwhelming majority of the EAP in the early 1970s was part of the ''informal proletariat''—that is, either self-employed laborers or those who worked in activities neither governed by contractual relations nor subject to state regulation. In short, the informal sector of the economy encompassed a wide range of activities from street vending to artisan production to transient labor in construction or manufacturing. Portes estimated the size of the informal proletariat in 1970 as 86.2 percent of the EAP in Bolivia, 73.3 percent in Ecuador, and 69.5 percent in Peru.

Business elites in the Central Andes stood at the apex of a social pyramid in which a vast majority of the population were trapped in occupations in subsistence agriculture or low-income economic activities, most of which fell outside the "modern" sector of the economy. The economic growth that took place in the post–World War II period did nothing to offset the highly unequal distribution of income that had characterized these economies since the colonial period. On the contrary, studies of income distribution in Latin America indicate that an acceleration in income concentration occurred in the post–World War II period.[44] The available data on the Central Andes confirm a high degree of income concentration in the 1960s and 1970s. In 1970 in Ecuador, for example, the top decile among economically active people appropriated 51.5 percent of the national income; in 1962 in Peru, the top decile accrued 45.2 percent of the national wealth.[45] As Alejandro Portes argues, it is reasonable to assume that the top-income decile corresponds to membership in the dominant and bureaucratic-technical strata, while informal workers cluster in the lower-income deciles. Thus, we can conclude that, like the traditional oligarchies, modern business elites constituted a small circle of individuals with a disproportionate share of the national wealth at their disposal.

The leading strata of the private sector were organized around "economic groups"—that is, multifirm conglomerates directly owned and managed by a single family or interconnected family and friendship networks.[46] Unlike advanced capitalist systems, the ownership and the management of modern firms were not separated. The holdings of economic groups spanned a variety of economic activities but typically included bank ownership. The presence of these groups did not constitute a break with past traditions among the economically privileged in these societies. Families of the nineteenth-century oligarchies also spread their investments across more than one business. The portfolio diversification that had occurred in the 1950s and 1960s was, however, indicative of a new configuration of opportunities and incentives in these economies. Particularly in Ecuador and Peru, industrialization opened up new areas of investment for the economic groups.

In Ecuador. In Ecuador, the economic growth generated by the surge in agricultural exports in the 1940s and 1950s helped to expand the internal market and opened up investment opportunities in industry. In Guayaquil, leading exporters and importers were at the forefront of such investment. Among the most notable was Luis Noboa, a major banana exporter whose fortune gave birth to the Supergroup Noboa, a conglomerate that by the 1980s was comprised of sixty-nine firms in everything from banking to candy making.[47]

In the sierra, traditional landholding families and merchants also began to shift investments into dairies, ranching, manufacturing, real estate, and construction. Not all businessmen in Ecuador were uniformly enthusiastic about the change. Importers occasionally challenged the government's promotion of industrial projects, but for the most part failed in their efforts to block import-substitution industrialization.

The process of portfolio diversification by economic groups in Ecuador intensified during the 1970s. Responding to market conditions and government subsidies, Guayaquil groups undertook investments in the semiprocessing of coffee and cocoa for export. Serrano businessmen responded to the new opportunities in industry stemming from the Andean Pact arrangements and the expansion of the internal market. Multinational corporations (MNCs) also played a role in the industrialization process, often entering into joint venture arrangements with domestic economic groups. This portfolio diversification went hand in hand with a heavy concentration of assets and profits in the firms owned by these economic groups. In a number of productive sectors, a few large firms dominated the field in the mid-1970s. In the industrial sector, three firms or fewer captured 50 percent or more of the sales in all but five product categories.[48]

In Peru. The post–World War II period in Peru also brought important economic shifts, namely the eclipse of agriculture as the dominant productive sector. In Peru, however, foreign capital played an even more pervasive role in the production shift than in Ecuador. By 1968, three-quarters of the mining, a third of the fishing industry, and half the manufacturing firms were under the direct control of foreign capital. The predominant role of foreign capital in Peru was the product of a close collaboration between foreign capital and domestic economic groups. As in Ecuador, economic groups joined with MNCs in joint ventures but also frequently resigned their entrepreneurial function to MNCs in favor of acting as financial or political intermediaries for them.

As in Ecuador, economic diversification in Peru resulted in oligopoly and an extreme concentration of asset holding. In 1968, two hundred manufacturing firms accounted for 80 percent of all assets in the sector and 65 percent of all sales. Over half these elite firms were owned by foreign firms, while the remainder was in the hands of a small number of economic groups.[49]

In Bolivia. The most drastic restructuring of the dominant class took place in Bolivia as a result of the 1952 revolution. Once the radical phase of the revolution concluded in 1956, the MNR and the subsequent military government of General René Barrientos (1966–69) facilitated the rise of a revamped dominant class. During the Barrientos government, a new stratum of "medium miners" formed and became the core of a new set of economic groups centered in La Paz. Among the most important groups were those formed around the firms COMSUR and Emusa S.A., controlled respectively by the Sánchez de Lozada and the Mercado families.[50]

In the eastern departments of Santa Cruz and the Beni, new economic groups developed around agricultural, agro-industrial and commercial ventures. Founded in 1966, the Banco de Santa Cruz became the financial hub that interconnected virtually all the economic groups of Santa Cruz and aided in the portfolio diversification of the groups.[51]

Unlike Peru and Ecuador, economic groups in Bolivia did not show much investment interest in manufacturing apart from the agro-industrial ventures in Santa Cruz. Bolivian industrial development lagged significantly behind those of Ecuador and Peru. Some notable family fortunes were derived from ventures in basic industries such as food processing, textiles, and breweries in Cochabamba, Santa Cruz, and La Paz, but for the most part industry remained marginal in the portfolio diversification of Bolivian economic groups. Susan Eckstein and Frances Hagopian report that manufacturing enterprises constituted the leading firm in only two of the fifteen economic groups they studied in the late 1970s.[52]

Government Incentives. Of critical importance to the whole process of portfolio diversification among economic groups were the incentives provided by the governments of the different countries in order to foment such shifts in investments. Tax breaks, cheap credit, and other subsidies to the private sectors encouraged the process of diversification. In all three countries, new laws enshrined the principle of massive subsidies to the private sector. In Peru, the Industrial Promotion Law enacted in 1959 by the departing Odría administration created a tapestry of tax exemptions for manufacturing industries. This law took its place alongside the Mining Law of 1950 and the Petroleum Law of 1952, which also provided depreciation and depletion allowances and tax exemptions for investors. In Ecuador, the Industrial Development Law of 1957 followed by amendments in the 1960s created a liberal system of tax exemptions for industries. In Bolivia, the MNR's original investment law of 1960 was bolstered by the Barrientos government in 1965 to extend tax exemptions to investors.

As we shall see in the next chapter, public efforts to encourage new private sector investment continued during the military governments of the 1970s. In Ecuador and Bolivia, the military governments channeled millions of dollars in credit to investors in their plans to pump up the private sector. So in all three countries, the emergence of a more modern and diversified private sector owed much to the cues and the real material rewards offered by governments. As much as businessmen would later complain about statism, they were in fact the creatures of state intervention and developmentalist policies.

From Privilege to "Privileged Position"

The 1930s ended the oligarchy's near proprietary relationship with the state. The exercise of domination by economic elites grew considerably more complicated with the appearance of new social forces—populist movements, leftist parties, trade unions, and a more independent-minded military and public bureaucracy. Politics after the 1930s was a volatile arena in which dominant groups were forced to contend with new competitors for power. The liberal coalition continued to try to shape economic policy even as reformist military governments and populist movements put forth alternative economic models. While the attrition of the liberal coalition was already under way, its hold was eventually broken by force: military interventions in Peru and Ecuador and a social revolution in Bolivian signaled the end of oligarchic politics and the liberal economic model.

In this chapter we have described how traditional economic elites were forced to relinquish an increasingly outmoded and ineffective set of controls they had exercised over the market and the political system. The termination of the old system did not, however, put an end to the dominance of the economically privileged in these societies. Instead, the new political powers accrued by technocrats and military officers were used to promote a recomposition and modernization of the dominant class as an economic force. By the end of the 1960s, a more heterogenous and sophisticated business elite was emerging as a result of changing market conditions and public policies. The new challenge for the revamped business elite of the 1970s and 1980s would be to forge and maintain their privileged position within these rapidly changing political-economic systems.

CHAPTER 3

Statism and Military Rule

THE BRAZILIAN COUP of 1964 was the first in a series of military interventions that changed the face of Latin American politics. Along with Brazil, countries that succumbed to military rule over the next decade included Argentina, Bolivia, Peru, Ecuador, Chile, and Uruguay. Military involvement in politics, of course, was not a new experience for the continent; the history of every country had been punctuated by periods of military government. But the ambition, scope, and durability of the regimes were new aspects of the military rule of the 1960s and 1970s. These governments were not in the traditional caretaker mode; these were military governments with a mission.

Without losing sight of the profound differences in the public policies pursued by the different military regimes, we can see that all the military rulers of this period shared a desire to use their power to make fundamental social and economic changes. As many analysts of the period point out, the purposivenesss of these governments sets them apart from most of their predecessors. A number of scholars point to the new mentality, or style, that animated the military regimes of this period. Alfred Stepan's work on the ''new professionalism'' within the Brazilian military highlights the ideological concerns at work in the 1964 intervention. Guillermo O'Donnell's landmark work on bureaucratic authoritarianism points to the military as part of a new social coalition bent on disciplining society and resolving the economic crisis brought on by faltering import-substitution industrialization.[1]

The military regimes of the 1970s shared at least three important traits. First, the military regimes were (at least in their initial phases) committed to reforming or transforming extant political and economic structures. This commitment reflected heightened ideological concerns within the military. Second, the governments were for the most part organized around the military as institution rather than personalist leadership. Third, military governments relied heavily on the participation of civilian technocratic elites, particularly in reference to economic policy. While the economic policies pursued by these allied military and civilian technocrats varied considerably from country to country, all the military governments set their sights on developing some sort of market or mixed economy in which a local national bourgeoisie would play a crucial role.

The new military regimes of this period were animated by the conviction that civilian politicians had failed in their responsibility to bring about economic modernization and development. This failure, in turn, left countries vulnerable to revolutionary political movement driven by ''perverse'' foreign ideologies such as communism. From the perspective of the military, competent economic management was an important component of national security. Preexisting democratic regimes were seen as incapable of producing the concentrated decision-making power (that is, the power to formulate and implement) necessary to sustain a long-term economic development strategy. The source of this problem lay, in part, in the ability of diverse societal interests to interfere with coherent policy making as they lobbied to extract particular benefits or to veto change. This view foreshadowed the critiques of ''rent-seeking'' behavior that would later become the stock-in-trade of neoliberal policy makers. Class conflicts between capital and labor were also seen as deleterious to the forging of a national will. The political landscape, as seen by the military, was filled by immobilized governmental structures and a selfish (perhaps perverted) civil society.

As the sole institution devoted to defending the national interest, one military after another asserted its right and duty to take over government, so as to endow that government with the capacity to act decisively and to impose long-term policies. Along with defining new development strategies, the military regimes seized the opportunity to restructure the relationship between public authority and groups in civil society and redefine the manner in which labor and capital would relate to each other. The objective of the new statecraft practiced by the military was to reconcentrate power in the executive. This power would be used to deploy public policies that were to reflect a technocratically informed pursuit of the ''national interest,'' above the particular interests pressed by groups in civil society. The task of the new executive-focused government was to script the strategy of national interests while groups in civil society were to perform the roles assigned to them in the drama.

There was a wide variation in the particular economic strategies adopted by the military regimes, of course. Whereas the Southern Cone military regimes embarked directly on neoliberal experiments, the Central Andean military regimes followed paths marked by heightened state involvement in economic management. The new statism introduced some policies that directly benefited some segments of the domestic business community, but it also generated sore spots in business-government relations, which eventually culminated in political challenges to statism and militarism. (We describe the business sector's mobilization against the statist model and relationship to the process of political transition in chapter 4.)

Our aim in this chapter is to examine the principal components of the statist projects put forth by the Andean military in the 1970s and to highlight the issues that were the source of significant business-government tensions in this period. Understanding the experience of this period is crucial to an understanding of why and how domestic business groups began their turn toward neoliberalism and democracy.

The Dimensions of Statism

The military regimes that dominated the Central Andes in the 1970s might appear at first glance to have had little in common. In Peru, the military regime—headed in its first phase by General Juan Velasco Alvarado (1968–75)—drew much international attention with its nationalist rhetoric and its broad agenda of progressive structural reforms. In Ecuador, mimicking the reformist discourse of its neighbor, the military regime—initially led by General Guillermo Rodríguez Lara—fell far short of Peru's structural reforms. In Bolivia, in stark contrast to left-leaning regimes in Peru and Ecuador, General Hugo Banzer mounted a military government notable for its antireformist stance. The ideological distance and policy differences separating these three governments might make any most similar case comparisons seem a long stretch. Yet, what binds these three experiences together was the commitment of the military executives to the idea of activist government—that is, that a state, refurbished by the military, would not only set the framework for the economic activity of private actors but would also play a principal role in leading the process of economic development. This *estatismo* distinguishes the Andean experience from the military experiments of the Southern Cone. In the Southern Cone, the state was strengthened by the military, but for different ends. The repressive dimension of the state was enhanced in order to force society to accept a radical application of market principles.

The decision made by the Central Andean military regimes to pursue economic development through an activist state did not constitute a radical departure from the policy directions of the 1960s. There were elements of continuity between the policies set out in previous administrations and those pursued by the military. In this regard, the Central Andean cases parallel that of Brazil where the military government deepened rather than reversed the developmentalist policies established in previous civilian administrations.[2] Traditional economic liberalism was already waning in the 1960s in Ecuador and Peru (see chapter 2); and it had already been dealt a fatal blow in Bolivia in 1952.

The 1952 revolution in Bolivia moved the government to accept new functions in production, regulation, and consumption. With the nationalization of the mines and the creation of COMIBOL, the natural resource industry fell firmly within the grip of public enterprises. The government takeover of Standard Oil concessions in 1936 had already created the state-run petroleum company Yacimientos Petrolíferos Fiscales Bolivianos (YPFB). Public investment in industry and agriculture was expanded through the Corporación Boliviana de Fomento (CBF). Created to fund highway and agricultural projects in 1943, the CBF had its mandate expanded after 1952 to include a wide variety of investments including cement plants, sugar mills, and dairies. Along with this direct investment by the state in productive activities, the Industrial Development Bank was founded in 1962 to channel credit to manufacturing. The Industrial Development Bank was part of a comprehensive public banking system that also financed ventures in mining and agriculture.

In addition to the direct investment functions assumed by public enterprises, the Paz Estenssoro government of 1960–64 inaugurated the first comprehensive effort toward economic planning. In 1961, the National Secretariat of Planning and Coordination issued its first major development blueprint, the ten-year plan of 1962–71.[3] Although the plan was never really put into operation, it was indicative of the belief that the government had an obligation to set out and direct the economy toward specific goals.

This growing concern with active state management of the economy was also at work in Ecuador and Peru. The Ecuadorean planning agency, JUNAPLA, was organized in the mid-1950s and issued its first development plan in 1958 with the aid of ECLA advisors. Peru's planning office was organized during the interim military government of 1962–63.

In contrast to Bolivia, however, Ecuador and Peru lagged in the development of a public enterprise sector; the movement toward a more activist state in the two countries was visible, but still incremental in the 1960s. In Ecuador the creation of the Centro de Desarrollo Industrial (CENDES) in 1960 and the Corporación Financiera Nacional (CFN) in 1965 reflected the government's interest in engineering new public-private partnerships, rather than assuming sole responsibility for productive ventures. CENDES was charged with working with the private sector on feasibility studies for new investments while the CFN provided seed capital to new industries. In Peru, governmental expansion in the 1960s was most evident during the Belaúnde administration, which brought sharp spending increases on high-profile public works projects. Public investment as a percentage of total government expenditures increased from 1.8 to 24.6 percent between 1960 and 1964. Expenditures aimed at economic promotion (that is, public works aid to production or new investments in productive ventures), surged from 6.3 to 17 percent of the overall budget between 1960 and 1964. Foreign advisors from the Organization of American States (OAS) and ECLA favored aggressive public spending and urged on the Belaúnde administration despite the more orthodox views that prevailed in the Central Bank.[4]

In all three countries, then, the role of the state in the economy had already been expanding, albeit in varying degrees and forms, prior to the coups that brought Generals Banzer, Velasco, and Rodríguez Lara to power. Previous military administrations had played an important role in facilitating this expansion. In Ecuador, the military government of 1963–66 put forth a reformist agenda that included an assertion of the government's right to redistribute property through agrarian reform. Similarly, in Peru, the interim military government in 1962–63 made a commitment to implementing Alliance for Progress initiatives in tax and agrarian reform. In Bolivia, prior to Banzer's coup in 1971, the military had headed several different administrations that swerved from probusiness and antilabor policies under General René Barrientos to a left populist agenda under Generals Ovando and Torres. Even as these military administrations swung from antipopulist to populist positions, the Bolivian military never retreated from the heavily statist public philosophy already laid down by the previous MNR governments.

The growth of government under the military regimes of Banzer, Velasco, and Rodríguez Lara was both quantitative and qualitative. The military governments took on new roles and intensified activities in already established spheres. A new regulatory thrust was evident in the agrarian reform policy in Ecuador and Peru. The Peruvians were the most radical in their assertion of the state's authority to abridge property rights. A substantial agrarian reform, which restructured ownership in the agro-export sector, was followed by the Industry Community Law, which was designed to force firms into sharing ownership and management with workers. The Banzer government in Bolivia did not engage in this sort of radical regulation, but it did share in the regional enthusiasm for indicative economic planning. All three governments fortified planning agencies and used them to formulate high-profile economic development plans that outlined a substantial role for public sector agencies.[5]

Quantitative measures confirm growing governmental activity in the economies during the 1970s. Figure 1 shows the trends in each country. Public sector investment and consumption during the Banzer years in Bolivia rose from 20 to 25 percent of GDP between 1974 and 1978. Under Rodríguez Lara in Ecuador, the public sector's contribution to GDP rose from 16 to 23 percent between 1972 and 1976. Peru's public sector accounted for 14 percent of GDP in 1970; by 1975, the figure stood at 20 percent. Within this pattern of overall growth, however, there were some differences in the investment and consumption components of public sector growth. Peru led the pack in public sector consumption, which averaged 13.1 percent of GDP between 1970 and 1978; Bolivia and Ecuador averaged 12 percent. Public sector investment as a percentage of GDP was at its

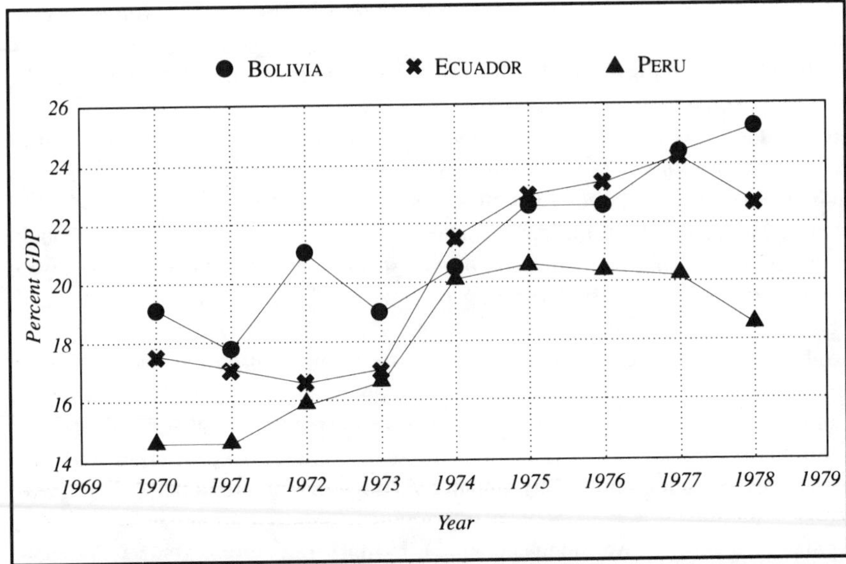

Figure 1. *Public Sector Investment and Consumption (as percentage of GDP) in Bolivia, Ecuador, and Peru, 1970–78*

highest level in Bolivia at 9 percent; Ecuador and Peru lagged behind at 8 percent and 5 percent respectively.[6]

The heightened presence of government in the Central Andes had visible physical manifestations; new offices filled with new bureaucrats opened in Lima, Quito, and La Paz to house new governmental entities. Between 1971 and 1977, the Banzer government created 24 new government bodies, bringing the number of public institutions in Bolivia to a total of 199. From 1971 to 1975, Bolivia's public employment grew at an annual rate of 9.9 percent, a rate three times greater than the growth of the labor force. In 1975, a total of 153,000 persons were employed by the central government and public enterprises in Bolivia, comprising 6.7 percent of the labor force.[7]

In Peru, an expansion in the number of public institutions and employees took place under Velasco. New ministries (of housing, food, commerce) were founded to administer the government's new social and economic programs. Even more notable was the growth in the public enterprise sector. By 1975, Peru had fifty public enterprises playing a substantial role in the economy. According to E. V. K. Fitzgerald, public enterprises accounted for one-half of all productive investment in Peru and produced almost all exports. The number of Peruvian public employees nearly doubled (from 332,000 to 619,000) between 1970 and 1975. That signified an increase of from 15 to 24 percent in the public sector share of nonagricultural employment. By 1975, 13 percent of the economically active population in Peru was located in public sector jobs.[8]

Ecuador underwent the same pattern of public sector expansion. Government bailouts of failing firms created new public enterprises in the airline, utilities, and cement-production industries. The army itself created a firm to produce its own supplies, the Dirección de Industrias de Ejército (DINE). The number of public servants in Ecuador increased from 61,000 to 109,187 between 1970 and 1976.[9]

Military rule in the first half of the decade produced big, activist government.

Statism and the Military Mentality

The statist orientation of the armed forces was not founded in the ascendance of any single ideology, nor did it entail a rigid commitment to any single set of public policies. Diverse intellectual and social forces fed the currents of *estatismo* in the Central Andes. In Bolivia and Peru, the doctrines of the populist parties, MNR and APRA, were heavily statist. Foreign advisors, particularly those from ECLA, reinforced the notion that development required an active state role in promotion, production, and regulation. By the end of the 1960s, economic liberalism had few defenders. Like the rest of society, the military became convinced that the state should take a proactive role in modernizing and developing the economy.

This predisposition toward state activism fitted together neatly with other elements in the new belief system developing within the military during this period. As Alfred Stepan and others argue, the professionalization of the military and the emergence of national security doctrine in the 1960s laid the basis for a redefinition of the role of the military in politics. In this redefinition, the military cast itself as the principal agent of political change and the author of a new model of governance.

The military governments of the 1970s shared the view that civilian politicians had failed in their responsibilities to lead the nation and effectively manage the economy. Politicians, along with groups in civil society, were seen by the military as selfish and corrupt. The armed forces in Peru and Ecuador framed their coups (in 1968 and 1972 respectively) as a response to the incompetence of the political class. The Banzer government in Bolivia reached the same conclusion in 1974. After three years of trying to govern in coalition with the MNR and the Falange Socialista Boliviana (FSB), General Banzer terminated the relationship with an auto-coup (an executive-led coup) and declared military-led political reorganization aimed at creating a new Bolivia.

The military forces in all three countries saw military rule as the best solution to political impasse and economic stagnation, because the armed forces provided both the technical skills and organizational capacity to lead. Military officers saw themselves at the helm of an institution uniquely positioned to serve the national interest, over and above the self-serving interests represented by parties, classes, or interest groups. These beliefs—and the desire of the military to be the agent of change—were expressed clearly in the declaration issued by the Ecuadorean junta in the wake of the February 1972 coup:

> the constant failures of [civilian] governments, the absence of the people from the centers of decision-making, the administrative inefficiency and immorality, the incapacity and insincerity of the political parties, and fundamentally, the economic structure, have contributed to the existence of an unjust and backward society . . . [that] has dangerously weakened national security. . . . Faced with this situation, the armed forces, in accordance with their responsibility for the survival of the Ecuadorian state, have assumed power, without leaders or caudillos, but as an institution, to implant a new national political doctrine, which will make possible the execution of the substantial transformations of the socioeconomic and legal order that the present chaotic state of the Republic demands.[10]

The tutelary orientation of the military forces toward state and society was embodied in the way they organized governments and policy making after the coups. In all three countries, the military governed with the advice and backing of a stratum of civilian technocrats. While the military rooted their authority to rule in their unique custodial relationship to the nation, civilian technocrats sought to legitimize their role because of their technical capacity to interpret esoteric bodies of knowledge (economics, sociology, for example). The ideology and professional training of these technocrats help explain, in part, the distinctive policies adopted by each of the three military governments.

Notwithstanding their individually distinctive policy colorations, the three military governments shared a top-down technocratically driven model of governance. The model was based on a belief in the superior ability of military and civilian technocrats to interpret and define the national interest and to impose that definition, if necessary, on the unruly and selfish interests of civil society and the traditional political class. At the heart of this approach to statecraft lay a deep suspicion of politics as a process of clashing societal interests.

To varying degrees, these military regimes rejected pluralism and eschewed classic liberal notions concerning representation. Instead, they gravitated toward a more monistic model of governance in which military and civilian technocrats would control how the representation of societal interests was organized. All three regimes made some attempt to restructure societal interests and to delimit their role in the policy-making process. This forced restructuring of relations among societal actors and between society and government was seen as a key to overcoming divisive class conflict and political stalemate.

The military's desire to recast civil society included a reprogramming of the behavior of economic elites and revolved around the idea of unfettering a national bourgeoisie. This concern was especially marked in Peru and Ecuador where the reformist military governments defined import-substitution industrialization as a top priority. In line with ECLA and dependency analysis, military and civilian technocrats believed that economic development was stymied by the continued dominance of traditional export and landholding oligarchies. The reformist technocrats in both governments believed that, through a combination of structural reform and financial incentives, a new national bourgeoisie could be unleashed—a class dedicated to industrial development. This national bourgeoisie would, in turn, act as an ally and partner to the nationalist developmentalist state.

Given the extremely small size of the Bolivian market, the Banzer government did not place a heavy emphasis on industrialization in its economic planning. Nonetheless, it did project an important role for a modernizing and diversified private sector. In all three countries, the military's economic plans were predicated on the idea of a complementarity in the relationships between the public and the private sector. The presumption was that a nationalist capitalist class would respond to incentives laid out by government and would invest in targeted economic activities.

The idea that the military regimes were acting as midwives at the birth of a national bourgeoisie was echoed in subsequent analyses of the regimes, particularly by writers on the left. In one of the earliest and most influential works on the Peruvian regime, Aníbal Quijano put forth the argument that the structural reforms authored by the Peruvian military were aimed at strengthening the dependent bourgeoisie. Numerous works on Ecuador characterized the Rodríguez Lara government in a similar fashion, that is, as a champion of the emerging industrial bourgeoisie.[11]

Yet, business elites did not themselves regard these governments as unqualified friends. On the contrary, business elites suffered a variety of experiences under the military governments, and their perceptions of that experience differed from those proposed by leftist writers. For businessmen, the benefits of state-led economic growth came with costs—some material, some political, some psychological, some ideological.

The Benefits of Statism: What Business Liked

Before examining the sources of the estrangement between business elites and the statist military governments, it is important to take note of the benefits that accrued to business during the military interregnum of the 1970s. Even as they chafed under some aspects of military rule, many businessmen directly benefited from government policies.

In Ecuador. The installation of the reformist Rodríguez Lara government coincided with a substantial rise in world oil prices and Ecuador's entry into the world market as an important new oil exporter.[12] The result was a fiscal windfall for the central government. By pursuing a nationalistic oil policy, the new military government was able to extract a significant portion of the oil wealth through taxes, royalties, and the strategic use of the state oil company, the Corporación Estatal Petrolera Ecuatoriana (CEPE).

The thrust of many of the economic policies pursued by the Rodríguez Lara government was to transfer a significant share of resources to the private sector, particularly to investors in large-scale industry. The transfer was realized through a variety of policy instruments. The state banking system (which included the Central Bank, the Development Bank, and the National Finance Corporation) became one of the vehicles for the transfer by providing loans at fixed charges that then translated into negative interest rates. Moreover, the banking system favored large-scale borrowers. Investors in large modern industries, for example, absorbed 98 percent of all credit to industry. In agriculture, 80 percent of all credit went to the large-scale farmers.[13]

The maintenance of a fixed exchange rate and the resultant overvaluation of the sucre was another boon to business, especially to those in industry and importing. Manufacturing industries were the major consumers of foreign exchange because of their high-level dependence on imported inputs and capital goods.[14] This was combined with the elaborate fabric of tax exemptions and tax deductions on imports contained in the Industrial Development Law. These incentives produced industrial expansion in the 1970s based on the development of oversized capital-intensive plants.

To compensate partially for the overvaluated exchange rate, the government extended tax reductions to exporters. Those involved in "nontraditional" exports also received further incentives in the form of tax credit certificates. Such tax breaks were important in the takeoff of the cocoa-processing industry, a focal point of investment for Guayaquil's major economic groups in the 1970s.[15]

In short, the government was using a portion of its new oil revenues to significantly reduce the tax burdens on the private sector. At the same time, business benefited from government price controls on utility rates, fuel, and basic foodstuffs. Low fuel and electricity rates lowered production costs while controlled low food prices reduced employers' wage bills. Jorge Marshall-Silva estimated the cost of these subsidies—combined with the effect of cheap imports from exchange rate appreciation—as increasing from 2.5 to 8.2 percent of GDP between 1973 and 1975.[16]

Without a doubt, the military government of Rodríguez Lara administered a set of policies that was highly favorable to big business, with preferential treatment for industry. Such policies continued under the subsequent military triumvirate of Admiral Alfredo Poveda Burbano (1976–79) and the civilian government of Jaime Roldós (1979–81). In the case of Ecuador, oil revenues opened the door to unfettering the bourgeoisie through a concerted policy of subsidizing private production and accumulation.

In Bolivia. As in Ecuador, favorable developments in external markets generated the financial resources that underwrote a variety of probusiness policies under the Banzer dictatorship in Bolivia. Substantial increases in world market prices for Bolivia's natural resource exports—petroleum and tin—laid the basis for the economic miracle of the Banzer years. Prices for Bolivia's exports rose by 30 percent in 1973, then doubled in 1974. The price increases for mineral exports were matched by a boom in agricultural exports from the Santa Cruz region. Bolivia's economic expansion was reflected in the annual GDP growth rate, which averaged 5.7 percent between 1971 and 1976.[17]

Public enterprise profits from the export boom were drained off by the central government. At the same time, the Banzer government seized on opportunities in the flush international credit market to contract huge foreign loans. The Banzer government directed a substantial portion of these new financial resources to subsidizing the private sector. In 1975, private sector borrowers received three-quarters of all credit disbursed by the state banking system.[18]

As in Ecuador, the state banking system was a key mechanism in the transfer of public resources to private hands through lending at concessionary interest  rates. One of the most important subsidies to the private sector was realized through the Banco Agrícola de Bolivia (BAB), the state agricultural bank. Over half of all agricultural credit in Bolivia was channeled through the BAB. Between 1972 and 1977, the Santa Cruz region received 66 percent of all BAB credit. Among the biggest recipients of BAB credit were large cotton growers, who accounted for half of all agricultural credit distributed by the BAB in this period. Along with cotton growers, investors in sugar, soybeans, and cattle ranching were preferred recipients of BAB credit. A lax collection policy on these loans, authorized by the Banzer government, made for an outright giveaway of the money. The Santa Cruz region registered the highest rate of delinquent loans in the country. By 1975, half of the BAB's portfolio was in arrears; by 1979, the BAB was bankrupt. It was rescued by a $41 million bailout from the central government.[19]

While agro-business elites reaped the benefits from Banzer's credit policies, importers were favored by a fixed exchange rate that overvalued the peso. The overvalued currency helped fuel an increase in the import of consumer durables. Increased public spending and an expanding government bureaucracy also contributed to the increasing demand for imports. The construction industry and the urban real estate market surged, along with public spending. Preferential tariffs protected local industries while exemptions on capital goods and intermediate inputs helped them reduce costs.

As several economists have argued, Bolivia's ''economic miracle'' under the

Banzer government was built on a unique and transitory set of circumstances.[20] A short-term improvement in Bolivia's trade position and the easy credit accessibility in international financial markets heated up the economy, but the boom revolved around increased consumption rather than production. Many of the concessionary loans extended to businessmen and Banzer's political clients were never used for productive purposes—they were used for conspicuous consumption or capital flight. The overvalued exchange rate encouraged such flight.

Another dimension of the Banzer regime's pro–private sector orientation was its hard-line position toward organized labor and other popular organizations. It was in this policy sphere that the Banzer government came closest to mimicking the behavior of the bureaucratic-authoritarian regimes of the Southern Cone. General Banzer had seized power in 1971 as part of a right-wing effort to crush the left-labor forces, which had gained political prominence during the successive military governments of Generals Ovando and Torres. Labor, left, and university leaders were the immediate targets of repression after the coup. Both the COB and the Asamblea Popular—the shadow parliament organized by leftist groups in 1970—were banned. As in the Southern Cone, political exclusion of labor went hand in hand with a policy of wage compression. Price increases were combined with wage controls. Popular attempts at resistance were met with force. A peasant protest against food price increases in January 1974 ended in the Massacre of Toalata in which over a hundred peasants died in clashes with the army.

Banzer embarked on a more systematic policy to dismantle the labor movement after his auto-coup in November 1974. As part of a plan to create a "new Bolivia," all civilian organizations were subject to government control through the appointment of "intervenors." This attempt to control labor organizations by supplanting its leadership ultimately failed, but the Banzer government did not relinquish its antilabor stance. Between 1976 and 1978, government troops were used to occupy mines and textile plants in response to labor disputes. The repressive labor policies were welcomed by business elites and enhanced the image of political stability that the Banzer government wanted to project to international lenders. After what they considered the chaos of the 1969–71 period, businessmen were ready to support the military's efforts to roll back organized labor and crack down on the left.[21]

In Peru Of the three cases under consideration here, the most troubled set of business-government relations emerged in Peru under the "nationalist revolutionary" government of General Juan Velasco Alvarado. The severity of the conflicts should not, however, obscure the benefits that some segments of the business community enjoyed as a result of Velasco's policy packages. A number of economic groups seized on the opportunities opened up by reform policies to diversify their portfolios in manufacturing, commerce, and finance. Other economic groups, particularly the more traditional families anchored in agro-export, fared less well and fell apart in the wake of Velasco's agrarian reform.[22]

Restructuring and restricting the role of foreign capital in the Peruvian economy was a top priority after 1968. Economic nationalism was an important component of what Stepan refers to as the "core programmatic consensus," which had developed in the armed forces prior to the coup.[23] The nationalist economic orientation became immediately evident after the coup. One of the first decrees of the new military government was the expropriation of the holdings of the International Petroleum Company (IPC), a U.S. firm with which Peru had long-standing tax disputes. That was followed by takeovers of other notable multinational operations including ITT Corporation (1969), Chase Manhattan Bank (1970), Cerro de Pasco Corporation (1974), and Marcona Mining (1975).

A network of public enterprises was created to take the place of foreign capital in strategic sectors of the economy. Because public enterprises were concentrated in basic industry and natural resources, they did not crowd out domestic capital. On the contrary, the logic was that state enterprises would complement private sector growth while restrictions on foreign direct investment would open up the most lucrative pockets of the economy to domestic investors. The Velasco government became a militant advocate for stringent regulations within the regional common market organization, the Andean Pact. Fellow pact members (Venezuela, Ecuador, Colombia, Bolivia, and Chile) joined Peru as the original signatories of Decision 24, a regional code governing foreign investment that was contained in the pact's 1970 Cartagena Agreement. With industrialization defined as a top priority, the Peruvian government set out further incentives for the private sector to invest in industry in the 1970 Industry Law, which provided tax relief to investors in targeted sectors—heavy industry, capital goods, wage goods, and industrial inputs. The state banking system provided generous credit to these sectors. As in Ecuador and Bolivia, high tariff levels were used to insure local industry an advantage over foreign imports.[24]

Unhappiness with the government's track record of expropriations and uneasiness about the future investment climate led several multinationals to preemptively sell off their operations to domestic economic groups. The reforms that most directly benefited economic groups were the new laws aimed at the "Peruvianization" of banking. New regulations limited foreign banks to a maximum of 20 percent share-holding in banks; this forced a number of foreign banks to sell to domestic investors.

Despite the reformist thrust of the Velasco government, tax reform never figured in the agenda. Corporations were not subjected to new taxes; companies continued to register robust profits during this period.[25] Increased government spending was financed initially by favorable prices for Peruvian exports; that was followed by an influx of international loans after 1972. As in Ecuador and Bo-

livia, the military government in Peru opted for foreign debt to underwrite its state capitalist development model. The Peruvian debt soared from over one billion to over five billion dollars between 1970 and 1976; the debt service ratio doubled from 13 to 26 percent.[26]

On the whole, Peruvian capitalists were unenthusiastic about the Velasquista-style state capitalism. They did not plunge into new productive investments as a result of the reforms. Instead, capitalists remained wary and, according to Fitzgerald, "a large slice of private sector profits were clearly being used for elite consumption and capital flight."[27] The net effect of the reforms on capitalists was to force a recomposition in the sectoral interests of capital, most importantly forcing economic groups out of traditional export industries. Perhaps the foremost example of an adroit adaptation by an economic group to the changing circumstances was that of the Grupo Romero. The group's agricultural estates were confiscated in the agrarian reform, yet the group was able to use the compensatory agrarian reform bonds it received to finance a major industrial project. With substantial state credit, the Grupo Romero founded Textil Piura, a cotton mill. In addition to this new venture, the Grupo Romero also bought out a cotton-oil complex from the departing U.S. multinational Anderson-Clayton.[28]

Undoubtedly, domestic businessmen were forced to operate within a more complicated environment during the Velasco government. Nonetheless, the climate was not so hostile as to preclude healthy profits for those businessmen ready to take advantage of new incentives. In all three countries, military rule in the early 1970s coincided with economic expansion, increased public spending, and a rise in levels of domestic consumption. Businessmen benefited from the military's drive to pump up these economies. At the same time, they were increasingly troubled by what they perceived as an ever more intrusive government and a remote style of decision making.

What Business Disliked: Ideas and Policies

Conflicts between business and government can be seen along three intersecting planes. First, clashes occurred as the result of policies that imposed direct material costs on the business community, or some subsector within it. Second, there were broader confrontations over ideological principles or precedents set by policies. Finally, discord erupted over the question of access and representation in the policy-making process. In short, there were multiple sore spots in relations between the public and private sectors during the life of these military governments. At varying levels of intensity, business interest group leaders raised questions not only about the substance and philosophy of public policy under the military, but about the style in which that policy was made.

In Peru. The most vociferous disagreements on policies and public philosophy took place in Peru, where the government's agenda of structural reforms was most ambitious. Having declared his government ''neither capitalist nor communist,'' Velasco sought to stake out the territory between the two systems. Part of this territory included the assertion of the state's authority to abridge property rights. Two important reforms embodied this assertion: the 1969 Agrarian Reform Law and the 1970 Industrial Community Law. True to its commitment to eliminate the traditional agro-export oligarchy, in June 1969, the government decreed an expropriation of the agrarian estates of northern Peru and placed them in the hands of workers' cooperatives.[29]

For a variety of reasons, business interest groups outside agriculture remained relatively unalarmed about agrarian reform—a position many businessmen later regretted, for the precedent set by the agrarian reform was subsequently extended into state intervention into the ownership of industrial firms. In 1970, the government issued its Industrial Community Law. The law required industrial firms with more than six workers, or with an annual income of $25,000, to allocate 15 percent of its pretax income to purchasing its own stock to turn over to the firm's *comunidad industrial* (or CI), composed of its workers. The annual transfer of shares was to continue until the CI owned 50 percent of the firm's stocks. Along with the stock, the CI was to hold one seat on the firm's board of directors, with its representation increasing as its stockholding rose.[30] In theory, the Industrial Community Law regulations laid the basis for the eventual workers' management of firms.

The CIs represented a radical restructuring of the business environment. Not only did the CI assert the government's right to amend property rights, but it mandated a gradual realigning of authority relations within the firm through CI representation on the board of directors. The reform had a substantial redistributive edge: along with requiring a firm to transfer 15 percent of its annual income through shares, it mandated that an additional 10 percent of the firm's income be distributed directly to workers.

This wave of regulation was coupled with efforts to build support among labor and lower-class groups. On the labor side, the government sought to weaken APRA's traditional hold over labor by legalizing new trade unions. The communist Confederación General de Trabajadores del Perú (CGTP) and the Christian democratic Confederación Nacional de Trabajadores (CNT) were officially recognized in 1971, and the CGTP picked up substantial new membership. In 1972, the government created its own official trade union, the Confederación de Trabajadores de la Revolución Peruana (CTRP). At the same time, the government moved to create its own popular organization in order to contain lower-class energies and direct them into support for the structural reforms. Unveiled in 1971, the Sistema Nacional de Apoyo a la Movilización Social (SINAMOS) was an umbrella organization with a broad mandate to encourage popular participation. Among the organizations under the SINAMOS umbrella were agrarian cooperatives, industrial communities, and the urban squatter settlement associations.[31]

By 1972, Peruvian businessmen were looking out over a confusing landscape. Although the government depicted domestic capitalists as important participants in economic development along with the public sector, nothing had been done to promote a climate of confidence among investors. Velasco's incubation of popular organization was disturbing. The nationalization of foreign firms, agrarian reform, and the Industrial Community Law raised serious concerns about the long-term security of private investment of any sort. Velasco's July 1971 announcement of a new form of property—social property—only added to investors' fears that the private sector might be on its way to extinction in revolutionary Peru. The social property sector was conceived as a state-funded network of cooperative enterprises under workers' management. It was billed as the first step toward "Peruvian socialism." With notions like social property circulating among the regime's top policy makers, many businessmen believed that Velasco was "more communist than capitalist."[32]

In Ecuador Similar types of concerns—uneasiness about property rights, and fears about the government's coddling of trade unions—surfaced during the Rodríguez Lara interregnum in Ecuador. Although the Rodríguez Lara government attempted a milder set of structural reforms than those of its Peruvian counterpart, the reform agenda met with even less success in Ecuador. This reflected, in part, the strength of the business lobby in Ecuador in contrast to the fractured state of the business community during Velasco. Despite business's ultimate success in turning back reforms, the proposals put forth by the Rodríguez Lara government set off a string of controversies.

Ecuador's 1973 Agrarian Reform Law affirmed the state's right to take over agricultural property in cases in which land was not being put to productive use. In practice, this formulation allowed for many legal loopholes, which landholders used to evade expropriation. Still, the principle was roundly negated by all business interest groups. Other regulatory proposals evoked similar reactions. In 1974, Marco Antonio Guzmán, director of the Superintendencia de Compañías, spearheaded an effort to force companies to disclose financial information on ownership to the government with the hope that such disclosures would encourage more firms to "go public" by selling shares. This mild proposal to "democratize capital" fell far short of the CI law in Peru, which forced owners to sell stock to workers. To Ecuadorean businessmen, however, it looked like the first step to more substantial government intervention in firms and was roundly resisted as such.

The radical antiregulatory stance struck by Ecuadorean businessmen even extended to measures regulating foreign investors. Like Peru, the Ecuadorean government under Rodríguez Lara was an enthusiastic participant in the Andean Pact and a signatory to the regulations on foreign capital contained in Decision

24. But rather than seeing restrictions on foreign investment as a boon, domestic capitalists in Ecuador were virtually unanimous in their opposition to Decision 24 and lobbied vigorously to water down the regulations.

The Rodríguez Lara government made no attempt to mobilize popular support or create new organizations to support reform in the style of the Peruvian SINAMOS. It did, however, find a vocal ally in Ecuador's largest trade union, the communist Confederación de Trabajadores del Ecuador (CTE). On the whole, labor fared well under Rodríguez Lara. Union membership grew with the economic boom, and so did the minimum wage, which was raised three times by Rodríguez Lara. These hikes were combined with the creation of a new bonus system and cost of living adjustments.[33]

In Bolivia Of the three cases, policy struggles between business and government were the least visible in Bolivia. Business had no reason to be unhappy with the Banzer government's tough labor policy, nor was it burdened by new forms of regulation. The major dispute that surfaced involved tax policy, specifically the taxes levied on the "medium mining" sector. Although the state-run COMIBOL retained its status as the largest single producer of minerals, the private "medium mining" sector had developed into a significant economic force. It was dominated by several large modern firms owned by La Paz–based economic groups. By 1977, medium mining firms produced 34 percent of the total mineral production of Bolivia.[34]

Following the upturn in world market prices for minerals, the Banzer government enacted a new export tax system on mining. The new tax was layered onto the already existing system of royalty payments. The mining companies attacked the tax as confiscatory. The charge was supported by foreign experts who saw the tax as a serious threat to reinvestment and growth in the sector.[35]

Conflict over tax policy fed a more general resentment among mining capitalists that their sector was misunderstood by government policy makers and being milked, while other sectors (finance, commerce, agro-industry) enjoyed overly generous incentives. Resentment over the "looting" of the mining sector had regional undertones; the burdened mining industry was located in the altiplano whereas the government-induced boom was based in Santa Cruz in the eastern lowlands. The mining lobby failed in its repeated efforts to revoke the tax, and the conflict simmered throughout the Banzer government period.

Lurking under the surface of business-government relations in Bolivia was a growing unease about the long-term effects of the statist development model. Business leaders inside the Confederación de Empresarios Privados de Bolivia (CEPB) began expressing concerns about the proliferation of public enterprises and their possible preemption of private sector investment in lucrative activities. Particularly disturbing was the creation of the Corporación de las Fuerzas Armadas de Desarrollo Nacional (COFADENA), a diversified corporation managed by the armed forces whose activities ranged from leather goods manufacture to truck assembly.[36]

The business sector's resistance to select policies involved obvious objections to their immediate effects and more deep-seated fears about the future should certain precedents be allowed to stand. Peruvian and Ecuadorean capitalists clearly were worried that state interventions could lay the basis for even more of a power shift in favor of the "dangerous classes." In Bolivia, the controversy over tax policy rehearsed long-standing concerns about which region and which sector (and by extension, economic groups) would bear the burdens of financing the state and economic development. The struggle over discrete policies intertwined with the struggle over which ideas would inform the military rulers in the long run.

For businessmen to win the struggle over policies and ideas, they needed to secure reliable points of entry into the reigning circles of military and civilian technocrats. The search for access to the military regimes was a frustrating one—and one that helped invigorate businessmen's interest in democracy.

Other Anxieties: The Problems of Representation

Putting an end to "politics as usual" was an idea that animated the military governments under discussion here. All three military leaders justified their seizure of power on the grounds that the political arena required dramatic restructuring. But this restructuring of the political arena turned into one of the most problematic areas for military government. None of the juntas were able to reconcile societal demands for systematic representation with their own inclination to concentrate decision-making powers within an exclusive coterie of military and civilian policy makers.

In Peru, policy making was dominated by a cadre of top military officers organized as the Comité de Asesoramiento de la Presidencia (COAP), the cabinet ministries headed by active duty officers, and other consultants from within the armed forces. Civilian technocrats were drawn into the process as advisors but, typically, were not part of the inner circle around General Velasco.[37] In contrast, in Ecuador, civilians played a visible role, heading key ministries in the Rodríguez Lara administration. Similarly, in Bolivia, Banzer pressed civilians into service as cabinet officers. Despite the differences in the roles played by civilians, all three governments declined to institutionalize mechanisms to provide for civilian representation in the making of public policy. None ever contemplated the resurrection of a legislature, not even a controlled one in the style of the Brazilian Congress of the 1970s.

In Peru and Ecuador. The policy-making style that developed under these circumstances created an air of uncertainty and unpredictability in the policy environment. In the Peruvian case, Cynthia McClintock aptly described it as a "politics of stealth."[38] Policies were developed by the network of military groups with access to Velasco, with little in the way of public debate or even consultation with the affected groups. Once a consensus was reached inside the government, the policies were abruptly unveiled and imposed. A saying that circulated among businessmen captured the mood engendered by this style of policy making, "No sabemos con que ley amanecemos" (We don't know what law we'll wake up to).

The insular policy-making process in Peru went hand in hand with moves to strip officially recognized business interest groups of their corporate status. Administrative reforms in 1969 removed interest groups from their seats on governmental bodies.[39] In 1972, the Velasco government forced the traditional landowners' lobby, the Sociedad Nacional Agraria (SNA), to cease operating, confiscating their property to boot. The industrialists' lobby, the Sociedad Nacional de Industrias (SNI), lost its recognition as an official representative of the industrial sector in 1973.[40] While the SNI was not subject to takeover, it was forced to remove the term *national* from its title, to acknowledge its loss of status. New government-created organizations were mounted within the institutional framework of SINAMOS and charged with representing the "popular" interests of the sector. Peasant cooperatives were represented within the Confederación Nacional Agraria (CNA); the workers' industrial communities were represented by the Confederación Nacional de Comunidades Industriales (CONACI).

The mixed military-civilian government under Rodríguez Lara was marked by some of the same insularity in decision making. Traditional interest groups also found themselves stripped of their voting rights inside government entities such as the Monetary Board and the National Finance Corporation. The shutdown of Congress also deprived interest groups of the representation they had traditionally enjoyed through the private sector "functional senators."

As the discussion in the next chapter will show, the distancing between business interest groups and the military governments was not complete. Despite the absence of clear institutional channels, lobbying did not cease and informal channels of influence, working behind the scenes, were still used. Still, the reformist regimes of Velasco and Rodríguez Lara were the first to clearly challenge the entrenched powers of traditional business interest groups. Reformist discourse combined with this assault on the status of business interest groups induced a state of anxiety within the business community. It is impossible to assess the impact of these experiences on the psychology of business elites as a whole, but the testimonies of individual business leaders are revealing and suggest that military-led reformism was traumatic, especially in Peru. In our interviews with businessmen, bellicose language often surfaced in their descriptions of the period. The Velasco years were "war," a "frontal attack," on business. One of the most outspoken opponents of Velasco was Raymundo Duhuarte, who served as

SNI president and who was exiled as a result of his criticisms of Velasco. Duhuarte reminisced about contemplating arson, rather than have the SNI suffer the fate of the SNA:

> [Velasco] always wanted to take over the SNI. That was his dream. . . . He was against us and we were against him. The first time I spoke out against the government was in Chimbote and I called Velasco a communist. Everybody thought I would be shot . . . this provoked the conflict. At certain times, Velasco was getting ready to take over the buildings [of the SNI]. And I was thinking of burning the building myself to prevent him from taking it. I was thinking about buying some gasoline and putting it inside the building so I could do it so they couldn't do the same thing they did to the SNA. They took their furniture. They took everything . . . their antiques![41]

In Bolivia In Bolivia, the character of the regime engendered a different type of "representation" anxiety than in Ecuador and Peru, where businessmen feared that what they were experiencing was a prelude to even further political and economic marginalization. In Bolivia, there was nothing radical to fear in the Banzer administration. Nonetheless, there was still uncertainty in the policy making and problems in reference to representation, which were rooted in the neopatrimonial dynamics of the regime itself.

In the 1972–74 period, the Banzer government appeared to be moving toward the installation of "privatist corporatism"—that is, a system of representation that excluded labor but included a role for capitalists through appointments to the cabinet and through a formal incorporation of their interest group representatives in governmental agencies.[42] Along with this arrangement, the collaboration of center-right parties (the MNR and the FSB) also opened another channel for conservative business voices to be heard.

Dissent within the armed forces over the role of civilians in the regime ultimately forced Banzer to retreat from the corporatist blueprint. Through the autocoup of November 1974, Banzer altered the regime by subjugating the civilian component to the military. As part of the "New Bolivia Plan," an executive decree allowed the government to "draft" civilians into the civil service. The decree was used to bring individual businessmen and technocrats into Banzer's service. The appointments were made on the basis of technical qualifications; individuals were not pressed into service as members of parties or as representatives of interest groups. The business confederation, the CEPB, was stripped of its official corporate status. Thus, Banzer replaced the aborted corporatist experiment with a system of personalistic ties between himself and his appointees.

Patron-clientelism became the glue that kept the Banzer government in place until 1978.[43] It was the instrument that he used not only to create pockets of support for himself in the private sector but also among factions in the military and in the urban middle class. The proliferation of government bureaucracies and public employment was the fruit of the clientelist dynamics undergirding the Banzer administration.

Well-known businessmen served in high-profile positions during both phases of the Banzer government. Among the most notable names were Carlos Calvo, Mario Mercado, and Carlos Iturralde. All three were important shareholders in medium mining operations. Yet, none of these individuals was able to act as effective representatives of the mining sector. Incorporated into this patrimonial system as individuals, they saw themselves primarily as *banzeristas*—that is, Banzer supporters whose personal loyalties to him superseded those of class or sector. They, and their fellow businessmen, recognized that their personal participation in the government did not translate into a systematic representation of interests for the sector. One of the banzerista businessmen flatly acknowledged this lack of "fit": "Many individuals from the private sector had positions in the Banzer government. I have been criticized for my role in the Banzer government. As a sector, medium miners were not influential in the Banzer government. *I was*" (emphasis ours).[44] Another banzerista businessman pointed to the confiscatory tax as an example of the lack of influence by medium miners:

> The left has always said that the bourgeoisie controlled the Banzer government. This was not the case. While there were businessmen in the government, we did not realize our private interests. You had someone like Jaime Quiroga who was minister of finance and an associate [of a medium mining firm] and yet he was the one who put taxes on the sector.[45]

A longtime leader of the medium miners' lobbying group underscored the problems of access and inability to affect policy making:

> Persons from our sector, when they assume positions in government, act like Caesar's wife (that is, not only are they honest, but they have to demonstrate they are honest). Sometimes they assume an incommunicative attitude vis-à-vis the sector. There was a time when someone from our group was the minister of finance. And there was a matter that we were having problems with, but we could never talk to that minister. He would not talk with us. I have here a black book of actions taken against our sector when members of our sector participated in government. The famous additional tax that Banzer created came with the signature of Carlos Iturralde on it, a well-known miner. So we did not have influence under Banzer.[46]

With access structured through personal ties to Banzer, businessmen without those ties or those who sought to put forth sectoral- or class-wide concerns were left without any direct avenues for influencing policy making. As Raymundo Duhuarte learned in Peru, the authoritarian nature of the regime made public criticism of policies a risky tactic. One CEPB leader recalled a telephone conversation with Banzer after he had published criticisms in the press: Banzer said, " 'Look, next time you publish something like that I'm going to throw you out of the country.' In spite of our personal relationship, it went as far as that. He was ready to exile me because I was very outspoken—and I thought I had to be.''[47]

This atmosphere effectively muted business criticism of the regime. Even for those inside the policy-making loop, dissent was difficult. Because personalistic ties were the basis of incorporation into the loop, any rift with Banzer could bring an ejection from the loop. One banzerista businessman confessed that his personal friendship with Banzer made it very difficult to express his disagreements on policies.[48]

The individual incorporation of prominent members of the private sector did not translate into a reliable avenue of corporate representation for the domestic bourgeoisie; and business leaders clearly perceived this to be the case. ''Business'' influence during the Banzer years was accorded to individuals—and the access that they enjoyed was conditional and contingent. Moreover, after 1974, military factions became even more influential inside the policy process and they saw civilians as rivals in a competition for control over resources and patronage.

Conclusion: The Right to Rule and Make Money

While all three military governments claimed to support the development of a vigorous private sector, their policies came with price tags that businessmen found increasingly unacceptable. The Andean private sector found itself at best with only episodic and contingent access to the policy-making process. As a result, business elites faced a crisis of representation under military rule. They were expected to react positively to (that is, invest in) government initiatives over which they had little or no say. The policies made by technocrats often presumed to define what were the ''legitimate'' interests of domestic capital in conjunction with their notion of what constituted the general ''national'' interest. Neither military nor civilian technocrats made any effort to consult with business elites in any systematic way—and businessmen in turn balked at their behavioral prescriptions.

In all three countries, civil society seemed progressively overshadowed by a larger and more demanding state apparatus—one out of the direct control of the privileged classes. This lack of control heightened feelings of uncertainty among business elites. No set of policies enacted by the military, however beneficial, could erase the unease bred by the lack of steady access and influence. It was within this environment that the private sector came to the realization that the

question of how to recalibrate statecraft and governance, in the wake of the demise of the oligarchical system, was of fundamental importance to them. Having made the public sector a pivotal actor in the economy, the military forced domestic businessmen to rethink their role and their relationship to political power. The

conclusion reached by the Andean businessmen was that they needed more direct

involvement in governance in order to assure that their "right to make money" would not be eroded by policy makers outside their control.

Unintentionally, the military rulers of the 1970s motivated business elites to organize themselves in new and more effective ways to confront the expanding powers of public authorities. To accomplish this, businessmen had to convert their previously unprofessionalized interest associations into effective instruments of political combat; moreover, they had to begin to develop new strategies to challenge the models of political economy authored by the military regimes. As our later chapters will show, business organizations began to develop their ideological counterpunch first in the form of antistatism. Armed with an antistatist discourse, business interest group leaders sought to regain the capacity to define on their own terms the key issues of political economy.

Antistatism was not a new intellectual current in these or other Latin American republics. What was new was the way in which antistatism became coupled to calls for a transition to liberal democracy. For business, liberal democracy combined with a renewed emphasis on the market seemed an ideal formula for both resolving their problems of representation and also beating back an all-too-intrusive state.

CHAPTER 4

The Antistatist Revival and Regime Transition

BY THE MID-1970s, domestic capitalists of the Central Andes found themselves enmeshed in contradictory relationships with their respective military governments. On one hand, domestic businessmen were the primary beneficiaries of the modernizing and expansionary policies of the period. They were quick to take advantage of the subsidized credit, protectionism, tax breaks, and consumption booms fashioned by the military regimes. Yet, as lucrative as these policies were for individual investors, domestic capitalists soon discovered the political and ideological costs of statism and military authoritarianism.

In all three countries, military control over economic policy making engendered a high level of anxiety in the business community. The hierarchical and insular character of decision making inside these regimes made it extremely difficult for business interest groups to penetrate and influence the process with any degree of regularity. Without reliable channels of influence, business interest groups and individual capitalists were left with two political options. To use Albert Hirschman's categories, they could choose to engage in open "voice" against governmental policies, or they could opt for a more muted combination of "voice and loyalty."[1] The "voice" option entailed overt criticism of the military's policies by business organizations in public forums, launched with the hope that high-profile opposition would force a policy reversal or retraction. The second option was an "insiders' lobby," that is, business interest group leaders burrowed inside the executive branch, using personal contacts and private persuasion to influence policy makers.

Neither tactic substantially reduced the uncertainty in the policy-making environment, however. Public criticism of the regime always carried the threat of deportation, imprisonment, or other reprisals. The insiders' lobby, while often effective in the short run, was also problematic. Since access was contingent on the maintenance of contacts among individuals, the relationships could always be endangered by personnel changes (either inside the state bureaucracy or within the interest groups). This type of selective influence also created enormous differentials in the access of individuals and factions of domestic capital to the policy-making machinery. Thus, the cost of military authoritarianism for the domestic bourgeoisie came in the form of a crisis of representation.

Ideological anxiety fed the political frustrations of domestic capitalists. In all three countries (albeit with important variations), the developmental models adopted by the military governments were built around the premise of an activist and expansionary state. The progressive assertion of the government's role as a regulator, consumer, and investor in the economy raised important questions concerning the long-term relationship between the public and private sector. Which would dominate? Which would assume a subsidiary role? From the perspective of domestic business elites, every new extension of state power stood as a dangerous ideological precedent; every new government intervention established public control over a previously private sphere of action. In Ecuador and Peru, military reformers posed an even greater ideological and material threat as government interventions legitimated the redistributive claims of workers and peasants.

Domestic capitalists profited from the policies of the 1970s; but they were also confused, frustrated, and frightened by the continuation of military rule. It was within this context that business elites became protagonists in a process of regime transition and ideological change, mobilizing through corporate interest groups and conservative parties. The aim of the mobilization on the right was twofold. First, it sought to turn the ideological tide away from statist approaches to economic management. Second, it pushed for a rationalization of the political process—the creation of clear rules of the game and a structured participation in decision making for business groups. This desire for a rationalization of politics overlapped with growing demands from the rest of civil society to return to elections and civilian rule. Thus, the bourgeoisie's campaign to contain the state became intertwined with calls for political democratization.

In this chapter, we describe the conservative mobilization that began under military rule and continued through the transition to civilian rule. In the course of the conflict with military governments, the domestic bourgeoisie developed greater class consciousness and cohesion, which was reflected in a new organizational prowess in interest groups and parties. Together, these interest groups and parties struggled to project an alternative political-economic model, built around a classical liberal commitment to political and economic competition. Beneath the cries for freedom lay the hope of fashioning a more predictable political game and a more stable investment climate.

Interest Group Activism

Business interest group activity in Bolivia, Ecuador, and Peru has a long history that can be traced back to the late nineteenth and early twentieth centuries. In the three countries, the pattern of interest group formation mirrored the contours of the dependent capitalist development that took place during the oligarchic period. Commercial and agricultural interest associations preceded the creation of industrial associations.

In Ecuador, business interests crystallized into two powerful sets of regional associations organized by economic sectors. Coastal businessmen from the Guayas province organized into separate chambers of commerce, industry, and agriculture, as did businessmen from the interior province of Pichincha where the capital city of Quito is located. In Peru, with the major economic activities concentrated in the city of Lima, businessmen were organized into national sectoral chambers—the Sociedad Nacional de Minería (SNM), the Sociedad Nacional Agraria (SNA), and the Sociedad Nacional de Industrias (SNI). In Bolivia, where mining dominated the economy, the Asociación Industrial de Mineros de Bolivia (AIMB) became the most powerful business interest group; but chambers of commerce and industry were also on the scene by the 1930s. Early on, these business groups developed close formal linkages to governmental agencies. The groups were legally sanctioned by the governments; in Peru and Ecuador, governments actively encouraged the formation of these interest associations. Thus, from the beginning of their institutional lives, business interest groups were sanctioned by governments to act as the official interlocutors for their economic sectors by representing those interests inside governmental bodies. With few exceptions, this special status was not accorded to trade union or peasant associations.

These corporatist linkages between business interest groups and governments were present to varying degrees in all three countries. In Peru, for example, the SNI enjoyed representation in twenty-three governmental entities prior to the military coup of 1968. SNI representatives sat on the boards of the Banco Central, the Banco Industrial, and the National Minimum Wage Commission, among others. Such business representation also took place in Bolivia until 1952. Prior to the revolution, business interest groups held positions in the Central Bank, the Exchange Control Board, and the Social Security Board.[2] In Ecuador, the same type of functional representation occurred and was even extended into the national legislature; the constitution of 1929 created functional Senate seats assigned to the chambers of agriculture, commerce, and industry.[3]

But the access and influence that dominant economic elites enjoyed over policy making extended well beyond the formal interest group structure. Indeed, the public lobbying performed by interest groups was often secondary to the more informal lobbying that took place among businessmen and government officials in elite social clubs and through familial-clientele networks.[4]

The breakdown of oligarchic politics and the economic modernization that ensued created the context for changes in business interest group structure and activity. While the advancement of interest groups was not completely parallel across the three cases, business interest group activity was marked by three important developments in the period between 1960 and 1980. First, there was a proliferation in the number of groups representing private sector interests. More specialized producers' associations (for example, milk producers, pharmaceutical manufacturers, and so on) sprang up alongside the older sectoral associations. But even as this differentiation took place, there were new institutional efforts to increase solidarity across the business community by bringing executives together in umbrella groups.

Second, business groups actively sought to endow their organizations with a higher degree of technical expertise and sophistication in reference to economic policy. Consultants were hired and technical staffs were created or expanded inside the associations. In short, business groups tried to project themselves as technocratic bodies, consciously seeking to shed the image of oligarchic clubs. This technocratic projection became an important component in the business groups' lobbying of technocrats charged with making economic policy making inside both military and civilian governments.

Third, business interest groups took a more active role in educating and promoting professionalism among their own membership. These educational efforts were aimed at developing a more competent managerial elite inside the private sector and also fed into the drive to remake the public image of the business elite. By the 1980s, business associations were actively promoting a more positive image of business through public relations and philanthropic activities.

In Peru and Ecuador. This organizational effervescence in Peru and Ecuador was manifested in a number of developments in the period from 1960 to 1980. New types of producers' associations were created to represent the changing interests in the business community. Of particular importance was the creation of associations to represent business in nontraditional export industries. In Peru, the organization was the Asociación de Exportadores (ADEX) founded in 1973; its Ecuadorean counterpart was the Federación Ecuatoriana de Industrias Exportadores (FEDEXPOR) created in 1976. But there were also efforts in this period to bring groups together into broad confederations. In Ecuador, national-level federations of commerce and industry were founded in 1969 and 1972 respectively. The Unión de Empresarios Privados del Perú (UEPP), founded in Peru in 1977, brought together eight major business interest associations. Although internal disagreements led to the dissolution of the UEPP by 1978, it set the stage for another attempt at a nationwide business organization founded in 1984, Confederación Nacional de Instituciones Empresariales Privadas (CONFIEP). There were efforts to create broader forums for business elites from across the spectrum to meet and discuss public policy issues. The Conferencia Anual de Ejecutivos (CADE) was launched in Peru in 1961, and it developed into an important institutional mechanism for interbusiness dialogue as well as a channel for business-government exchanges.[5] A similar attempt at a business forum on public policy was sponsored in Ecuador by the Asociación Nacional de Empresarios (ANDE).

New efforts to educate and promote professionalism among business executives also surfaced in the 1960s and 1970s in Peru. The Instituto Peruano de Administración de Empresas (IPAE) was founded in 1959 to disseminate to business executives the principles of scientific management; IPAE became the sponsor of the CADE meetings. Other educational innovations followed. The Escuela Superior de Administración de Empresas (ESAN) was created in 1966 to provide advanced instruction in business. With the same goal in mind, business contributors backed the creation of two private universities in the 1960s (Universidad de Lima, Universidad del Pacífico) to provide training in economics and business administration. A similar drive to professionalize business managers emerged in the early 1970s in Ecuador. The major business chambers joined together to contribute to the Servicio Ecuatoriano Capacitación Profesional and the Centro de Formación Profesional; both programs provided technical courses to business managers.[6] In Guayaquil, business seminars were sponsored by the Centro de Ejecutivos.

In Bolivia. While business organizations in Peru and Ecuador expanded activity in the 1960s, Bolivian businessmen were reconstructing the interest group structure that had been shattered by the 1952 revolution. The revolution dramatically restructured the private sector by eliminating the traditional landholding class and the old mine-owning elite represented by the Asociación Industrial de Mineros. By the 1960s, however, new economic groups in the revamped private sector started to emerge and formed two important representative organizations. One was the Confederación de Empresarios Privados de Bolivia (CEPB). Founded in 1962, the CEPB acted as a peak association for all business interest groups. After experiencing a decline in importance in the 1950s, the Asociación Nacional de Mineros Medianos (ANMM), representing medium-sized mine owners, regained its position as an influential interest group in the 1960s.

Business associations reflecting the growth of agro and agro-industrial enterprises in Bolivia's eastern department of Santa Cruz were also emerging. Cotton, sugarcane, milk, and beef producers all formed associations in the 1960s; soybean and corn producers followed suit in the 1970s. These producers' groups formed the core of the Cámara Agropecuaria del Oriente (CAO), founded in

1966. The CAO quickly became a powerful regional interest group, standing alongside the older Cámara de Industria y Comercio de Santa Cruz. Both business groups played a prominent role in the civic association, the Comité Cívico Pro–Santa Cruz. Similarly, leading businessmen in the city of Cochabamba sought to strengthen their organizations. In 1969, they founded a regional peak association, Federación de Empresarios Privados de Cochabamba. The founding groups included the local chambers of commerce and industry and the regional affiliate of the banking association.[7]

Certainly, the history of business interest groups indicates that a process of institutional modernization and growth was already under way prior to the installation of military governments in the 1970s. But the rocky relationships that developed between the military and the business groups gave further impetus to the process. In the struggle to be heeded by military policy makers, business interest groups became highly politicized organizations as they thrust themselves into the debates on economic models and regime transition.

Voice and Loyalty: Business Strategies Under Military Regimes

The antagonisms that emerged between business interest groups and the successive military regimes of the 1970s revolved around policy, procedural, and ideological issues (see chapter 3). The relative salience of these issue areas and the actual degree of open conflict among actors varied across the countries and the specific governments in question.

Of the three countries, the most intense conflict took place in Peru during the Velasco administration: the conservative turn under the subsequent military government of General Francisco Morales Bermúdez eased the disputes over ideology and policy, although the lack of participation in decision making continued to be a source of dissatisfaction. In Ecuador, a similar sequence occurred: interest groups leveled criticisms at the Rodríguez Lara government on ideology and policy. These attacks dissipated under the ensuing administration of Admiral Alfredo Poveda Burbano, but frustrations remained in reference to the structuring of participation and the mechanics of the political transition. Due partially to the patrimonial practices of the administration, business dissatisfaction remained muted in Bolivia under Banzer but exploded under subsequent military governments.

Business interest groups mixed both "voice" and "loyalty" as political strategies in their dealings with the military governments. For the most part, these strategies were not contradictory or mutually exclusive. Rather, the use of both was part of the business sector's push to gain or retain by whatever means available some modicum of influence inside the terrain of policy making.

The dynamics of business-government relations followed somewhat similar paths in Peru and Ecuador during the reformist phase of military rule under

Velasco Alvarado and Rodríguez Lara. In both countries, the interventions that brought the military to power entailed the closure of formal channels of societal representation (that is, legislative bodies) and threw the party system into limbo. The reformist governments in Peru and Ecuador also stripped business interest groups of their privileged corporate status inside policy-making bodies.

The shutdown of formal representation and the concentration of decision-making powers inside a small circle within the executive branch created serious problems for business organizations. Given the increasingly restrictive conditions prevailing inside the government, Peruvian and Ecuadorean business groups frequently chose to go public with their lobbying—and in doing so became the most prominent organized opposition to these governments.

The Ecuadorean Chambers of Production (that is, the regionally based chambers of agriculture, industry, and commerce) battled the Rodríguez Lara administration on virtually every piece of its reform program. They strenuously opposed (1) the proposals for moderate agrarian reform, (2) controls over foreign investors through the application of Decision 24 of the Cartagena Agreement, and (3) increased regulation over domestic firms.

The press and public meetings became the key vehicles for the chambers' resistance to the proposed reforms. In fact, the policy battles that took place from 1973 to 1975 acquired a near ritual form. The administration launched its proposals, usually with little or no prior consultation with business groups. The policies were, in turn, met by denunciations from business interest group leaders. These denunciations took the form of public communiqués, published in the leading newspapers, or were voiced at interest group meetings or private sector conferences covered by the press. On numerous occasions, the chambers came together as a unified opposition, issuing joint communiqués condemning the reform proposals. The response of the Rodríguez Lara administration to this strident and cohesive opposition was either to retreat from a strenuous implementation of the policy or to reverse itself altogether.[8]

Thus, a great deal of the lobbying that had gone on behind closed doors in the old oligarchic system was thrust onto a public stage, and this lobbying on the public stage placed new demands on the institutional capacity and political savvy of interest groups. The Rodríguez Lara regime had cast economic reforms within the framework of a new development model—with techniques and ideological underpinnings provided by military and civilian technocrats. To counter the technocratic and ideological offensive, business groups had to frame their proposals within a more elaborate technical and ideological framework. A longtime consultant to the Cámara de Industriales de Pichincha described the logic behind the buildup of technical expertise inside the organization:

> the technical development of the Cámara began with the government of Rodríguez Lara in 1972. This was the government that first began making plans that were disquieting to

> the industrial sector. The government began to deal with certain themes that could change the national economic focus. With Rodríguez Lara, . . . we thought that certain pronouncements, certain alignments toward a distinctly new economy had appeared. Rodríguez Lara began to talk about the democratization of the capital of business. Petroleum policies changed dramatically at the same time. The state grew in size since it owned petroleum. State power grew incredibly. . . . We understood that we were up against a new phenomenon. So in light of the evident growth of the state, it was logical that the Cámaras would create at least a small economic team to analyze, with much more interest, this economic, political, and social phenomena . . . to do a more technical analysis, not just the opinion of businessmen or a consultant or two. They don't just examine the interests of the sector anymore, but examine the interests of the sector within the context of the national reality.[9]

This is not to say that the private lobbying of policy makers by business leaders was completely disrupted. On the contrary, sporadic business-government interchanges did take place. For example, Rodríguez Lara called a secret summit of interest group leaders as tensions mounted in January 1974. But the administration did not act to institutionalize the dialogue. And whereas civilians did control the economic ministries throughout the Rodríguez Lara administration, the appointments did not come from the ranks of business elites. The lack of strong social ties between economic policy makers and business elites made the old method of lobbying informally through friendship and family cliques more problematic.

Highly charged confrontations also became part of the fabric of business-government relations in the first phase of the Peruvian revolution (1968–75) led by Velasco Alvarado. Because the Peruvian reformers were committed to a more radical restructuring of the economy, the material and ideological stakes in these battles were even higher than those in Ecuador. As such, Peruvian policy makers went much further than their Ecuadorean counterparts in restraining the capacity of business interest groups to publicly protest the reforms.

The Velasco government's efforts to deny "voice" to business groups was waged through a whole range of measures. Administrative reforms in 1969 removed business interest groups from their positions within policy-making bodies. The government offensive against the old interest group structure continued with the disbanding of the SNA in 1972 after its resistance to the agrarian-reform program of 1970. The agrarian reform was a conscious strike against the remnants of the traditional agro-export oligarchy of the northern coast. The banning of the SNA deprived the affected owners of their organizational vehicle to oppose the reforms. Mounting criticisms of the reform policies, especially the Industrial Community Law, by the SNI eventually resulted in its "derecognition" by the government in 1973. The government decision to strip corporate status from the organization came in the wake of the SNI's refusal to incorporate representatives from the *CIs* onto its board of directors. The organization continued to function as the Sociedad de Industrias (SI).

These assaults on elite interest groups were accompanied by efforts to create contending popular organizations to defend the reforms. Velasco began with the recognition of the communist trade union confederation, the CGTP, in 1971. This was followed by the launching of an ambitious program to create popular organizations under the umbrella of SINAMOS. The defense of the agrarian reform was delegated to a new agrarian organization, the CNA, in 1972. Similarly, the industrial communities reforms were to be overseen by a new organization, CONACI.

The government's attempt to check businesses' capacity to oppose its program extended into the media and resulted in a takeover of the leading newspapers used by the business community in its public relations campaign against the reforms. The takeover began with the confiscation of the Lima dailies *El Expreso* and *Extra* in 1970. The clampdown on the press eventually extended to other Lima dailies and culminated in a series of reforms that "socialized" the press in 1974.[10]

The crackdown on conservative opposition included the repression of individual critics in business groups and parties, who were deported or barred from reentering Peru. For example, the SNI president Raymundo Duhuarte, who had emerged as one of the most strident voices against the Velasco administration, was not allowed to return to Peru after a business trip in 1973. Other critics, such as AP party leader Javier Alva Orlandini, were also deported.

Confrontation was not the only route taken by Peruvian businessmen during the Velasco period, however; business interest groups opted for various different strategies in this period. After 1970, for example, the SNI opted for the confrontational approach. They were occasionally joined in their protests by other business groups such as those representing the mining and fishing industries. As government attempts to stifle the SNI escalated, so did the SNI's aggressiveness and its organizational prowess. In order to buttress its claim as the legitimate representative of the industrial sector, the SNI undertook a concerted membership drive. The drive changed the complexion of the SNI by incorporating small- and medium-sized industrialists who had not traditionally played an important role inside the SNI. Membership swelled to around four thousand affiliates and gave the SNI an increased capacity to engage in mass mobilization. In 1972 and 1973, the SNI convoked mass meetings to discuss government policies that drew over a thousand members to its Lima headquarters.

In contrast, other segments of domestic capital opted for a more conciliatory posture. In 1973, the SNI Export Committee (a group composed of industries engaged in nontraditional exporting) split from the SNI to form its own organization, ADEX (dominated by the leading economic groups), which eschewed the belligerence of the SNI and strove to maintain cordial relations with government policy makers. The rewards of loyalty for ADEX came in the form of more fluid access to the economic team and pro-export measures.[11]

The installation of the conservative military juntas in Ecuador and Peru brought the policy goals more in line with the antireformist postures struck by the private sector in both countries. Both the Morales Bermúdez and Poveda Burbano governments undertook a more repressive policy toward organized labor; both placed a new emphasis on export promotion over the domestic market. The Morales Bermúdez administration began a gradual dismantling of the Velasco reforms, including the industrial communities.

This convergence between the conservative military juntas and the private sector was, however, just that: a coincidence of ideas in respect to some, but by no means all, policies. Important areas of disagreement still remained. As our later discussion of transition politics will show, the Ecuadorean business chambers were unable to cajole the Poveda Burbano government into a constituent assembly formula for regime transition. Neither were chambers able to dissuade the administration from pursuing Andean Pact commitments.

In Peru, the SNI continued to badger the Morales Bermúdez government even after the administration had disavowed socialism. Disagreements between business groups and the administration on the extent and pacing of the reversal of the Velasco reforms were recurrent throughout Morales Bermúdez's term in office. These tensions came to the surface in conflicts between two civilian cabinet appointees, Javier Silva Ruete and Gabriel Lanata. In 1978, the technocrat minister of finance, Silva Ruete, clashed openly with the minister of industry, Gabriel Lanata, a well-known industrialist and high-profile leader of the SNI. Lanata pressed for a rapid turnaround in government policy; he favored, among other things, a privatization of some of the firms nationalized by Velasco. In contrast, Silva Ruete was less prepared to rescind the reforms.[12] Lanata lost the bureaucratic battle with Silva Ruete and resigned his post after only a few months. Both SNI and ADEX decried the exit of Lanata whose presence in the cabinet had been characterized as a "guarantee to the private sector."[13]

In their interactions with the conservative military governments, business interest groups in Ecuador and Peru discovered there were absolutely no guarantees under military rule. Even when convergences on policy did occur (as they frequently did), the business sector's frustrations over access to and influence over policy makers did not decline. Complaints by business associations in Peru over their lack of influence in cabinet appointments were constant throughout the Morales Bermúdez period. If anything, conflicts with the conservative juntas only underscored the problems involved in establishing mutually satisfactory relationships within the constraints posed by military dictatorship.

In Bolivia, business organizations generally opted for collaboration as a strategy during the military government of General Hugo Banzer. While there was growing discomfort among business leaders regarding state-centric economic policy and the lack of participation in decision making, these fears were offset somewhat by the benefits that flowed from Banzer's policies. Occasional opposition to specific economic measures was voiced through the press; but, true to the personalist style of the administration, Banzer was able to apply pressure to individual critics and thereby stifle conservative criticism of his policies.

The CEPB shifted into a more critical and activist stance during the subsequent military and civilian governments from 1978 to 1982. At this point, CEPB behavior began to resemble more closely the mobilizing strategies practiced by the Ecuadorean chambers and the Peruvian SNI. Public pronouncements questioned the economic model and decried the political instability of the period. Criticisms of economic policy were frequently lodged in "technical" analysis commissioned by the CEPB.[14]

"Exit" and Opportunism: Other Strategies

So far, we have focused on how business elites related to military governments through the formal interest group structure. It is important to appreciate, however, that individual businessmen coped in a number of other ways with the investment climate generated by the military regimes. These coping behaviors were not overtly political—but they did carry important implications for policy and the policy-making environment.

One of the classic coping mechanisms that is available to capitalists in a market economy is economic "exit"—that is, they can withhold their investments from the domestic economy and direct their resources to more profitable investments, be it a Swiss bank account or Miami real estate. Capital flight or "investment strikes" are what Charles Lindblom refers to as the "automatic punishing recoil" that business elites wield in their relationship with governments.[15]

In the absence of attitudinal data on investors, it is impossible to disentangle exactly to what extent the investment decisions made by Andean capitalists in the 1970s were a reaction to the military governments, per se, versus broad macroeconomic variables (for example, overvaluation of the exchange rate, high interest rates abroad, and so on).[16] It seems reasonable, however, to assume that the political environment did exert some influence over those decisions.

Economic data measuring the levels of private investment and of capital flight indicate that some economic "exit" behavior did take place and was probably most notable in Peru. Richard Webb's study shows that private sector investment as a percentage of gross domestic product (GDP) took a significant downward turn in the 1970s; it plunged to an average of 8 percent for the decade, after registering an average of 17.7 percent for the 1950s and 12.3 percent for the 1960s. Other studies of the period concur with the conclusion that Peruvian capitalists retreated from investment in the 1970s. In Ecuador and Bolivia, private investment as a percentage of GDP showed some growth in the first half of the 1970s, registering at 14.3 percent and 7.8 percent respectively by 1975.[17] That growth leveled off and began to erode by the late 1970s, however, with sharper declines by the early 1980s. While comparable data on capital flight over time is not available for all three countries, data on Bolivia and Peru suggest that both countries experienced flight in the 1970s, particularly in the last half of the decade.[18]

To reiterate, one must be cautious in interpreting aggregate economic data as evidence of capitalists' attitudes toward any particular regime. But it does not seem far-fetched to suggest that the apparent decline in investor confidence in Peru was connected to the pursuit of radical programs of reform by the Velasco government. Virtually every critic of Velasco's policies pointed to their deleterious effects on investment.

''Exit'' is one form of market behavior that business elites may turn to in order to cope with problems of uncertainty. ''One-on-one deal-making'' constitutes yet another type of coping behavior. Domestic business elites in the Central Andes have a long track record of turning to government officials to extract firm-specific concessions (that is, contracts on government projects, special tariff exemptions, and so on). This type of direct personal contact and business dealings with decision makers continued unabated during the military period. In all three countries, individual capitalists worked at cultivating personal ties to military policy makers. Research by Luis Soberón, for example, indicates that Peruvian businessmen sought out military officers for their boards of directors; the purpose was to assure the firm some entrée with high-level decision makers within the government.[19]

This kind of individualized deal making engenders a number of problems, however, from the perspective of the domestic bourgeoisie as a whole. By definition, access and benefits are unevenly distributed; certain types of firms are more likely to benefit from these relationships than others. Deal making during the Banzer government, for example, was a boon to construction companies in the form of government contracts; but this feeding frenzy in the construction industry left other firms out of the game.[20] Such dynamics create tensions across and within factions of domestic capital as those factions compete for scarce resources in an environment where rationality in decision making gives way to personalism. In a speech to the annual conference of executives in 1979, a Peruvian businessman summarized the problems inherent in this type of deal making in the period:

> Illegality and absolute power are conducive to corruption, deceit, abuse, and this collective attitude has degraded more than one person. This includes businessmen themselves who develop defensive attitudes (in regard to their enterprises) in circumstances in which there are no regular channels of discussion, criticism, or debate in governments. It is an illusion to think that personal friendships between businessmen and officials of de facto governments are going to result in greater influence or benefits. . . . The last several years have been truly tragic for business. One has seen in more than one case a lack of personal valor,

> a collective accommodation to the day-to-day circumstances, a lack of solidarity in the face of dictatorship. This lack of solidarity is a consequence of a speculative mentality of a good part of Peruvian businessmen.[21]

Individual firms flourished on the basis of this type of deal making during the military government, but such linkages could not supply economic or political certainty either to individual capitalists or to the class at large.

Lessons Learned: Interpretations of Statism and Militarism

Business interest group leaders drew a variety of important lessons from their experiences with military rule in the 1970s. In the late 1970s and early 1980s, these lessons fueled subsequent efforts to restructure the policy-making environment. Before we look more closely at the role of business in the political transition, it is important to understand how domestic capitalists interpreted the effects of military rule on themselves and on society at large. In the following discussion, we have chosen to synthesize the common themes that emerged in numerous interviews we conducted with business interest group leaders and in the documents issued by their organizations.

Domestic capitalists came to view the growing state as a type of Frankenstein—a lumbering uncontrollable force whose expansion threatened the private sector on a number of levels. This demonizing of the state took hold in business rhetoric during the military governments and continued to permeate business thought even after the military exit. For business interest group leaders, the state became a permanent obsession.

In their pronouncements, business interest group leaders interpreted state growth as a hydra-headed threat. The growth of public enterprises, for example, was portrayed as usurping the private sector's place in the market. Public enterprises were seen as entities that competed unfairly with private enterprise or effectively preempted future private investment. A related criticism had to do with the perceived economic inefficiency of state enterprises and of the public sector at large. The public bureaucracy was frequently accused of wasting scarce economic resources by directing them to nonproductive uses.

Thus, the state became identified by business organizations as the primary cause of economic stagnation. In Bolivia, the CEPB declared the public sector to be the "principal cause of the economic crisis." In a similar vein, the Cámara de Industria y Comercio de Santa Cruz, affirmed the view that the state capitalist model of 1970–80 had failed. The Peruvian SI published an economic analysis in 1980 that dubbed the 1970s the lost decade; it blamed the military regimes for the mismanagement of macroeconomic policies and the bloated public sector.[22]

In Ecuador and Peru, the expansion of the state's regulatory powers during the reformist phase of the military governments was portrayed as part of a movement to supplant capitalism altogether. This was a recurring theme raised by SNI presidents Raymundo Duhuarte and Alfredo Ferrand in their critiques of public policy.[23] The specter of communism was played on similarly by interest group leaders in Ecuador.

Business discourse also linked the statism of the 1970s to the proclivity of technocratic policy makers to import foreign models or theories of economic management. The Ecuadorean chambers frequently accused the Rodríguez Lara government of attempting to implant a Peruvian or a Chilean model (of the Allende variety). Business resistance to the proposal that firms be obliged to sell stock to the public was based on the fear that this would open the door to Peruvian-style industrial community reforms. In another attack on technocrats, the Bolivian CEPB asserted that economic planning should not be based on "theoretical schemes," but should be crafted to fit the national reality.[24]

This trepidation in reference to theory and technocrats did not, however, halt the development of in-house technical staffs inside business organizations. On the contrary, interest group leaders concluded that mounting a contending cadre of technocrats was critical in order to counter the arguments and influence of the technocrats lodged inside the state apparatus. This was one of the motivating factors behind the creation of a think tank, the Instituto de Estudios Económicos y Sociales (IESS), inside the SNI. The force behind the creation of the IESS in 1980 was none other than Gabriel Lanata, president of the SNI. Lanata had intimate knowledge of the power of technocrats, acquired during his brief tenure as minister of industry when he tangled with the finance minister Silva Ruete.[25]

Interest group leaders frequently cast their criticisms of the state within the framework of classical liberalism. State growth was posed as synonymous with the erosion of individual liberties. The president of the Guayaquil Chamber of Industry, León Febres Cordero, strenuously asserted that the state's role should be subsidiary and complementary to the private sector. In 1979, the Bolivian CEPB issued a call for a "new economic policy" that flatly demanded limiting the role of the state to provision of infrastructure and "leaving all other activities to the private sector."[26]

There is little doubt that the private sector of the Central Andes was completely disillusioned with the direction of state development in the 1970s. But it was the Peruvians who eventually emerged with the most theoretically ambitious analysis of what had gone wrong with the state. The critique was mounted in the early 1980s by intellectuals and technocrats linked to business organizations. 
Among the most notable early advocates of the new critique were Hernando de Soto, Felipe Ortiz de Zevallos, and Mario Vargas Llosa. The critique drew extensively on free market ideology as well as the "public choice" theory, especially the works of James Buchanan and Mancur Olson.[27] The basic thrust of these critics' analysis revolved around the notion that there was a direct relationship

between state growth and the operation of interest group politics—that is, they saw state growth (and the hyperbureaucratization it entailed) as a function of "rent-seeking" behavior on the part of interest groups.

We shall return to a discussion of the relationship between Peruvian technocrats and businessmen later. For now, two points are worth noting. First, by the early 1980s in Peru one can clearly identify the emergence of a new stratum of "organic intellectuals" linked to domestic bourgeoisie, busily working to elaborate a new right ideology.[28] Second, the critique put forth by right intellectuals was not simply critical of the previous military rulers or policies; rather, the analysis recognized the complicity of capitalists in process of "irrational" state growth.

This brings us to another important theme in business discourse—how domestic capitalists perceived themselves in this period. Hostility toward the state was matched by feelings of political weakness and economic incompetence on the part of business elites; this view was particularly striking in our discussions with Peruvian and Bolivian capitalists. Business leaders saw the military period as a period of failure for the bourgeoisie as a class—a moment when they were unable to act as a unified and coherent class with a hegemonic vocation. In Peru, this point was made repeatedly by SNI leaders in their descriptions of their battles during the Velasco period. One former ADEX and SNA leader summarized the trauma and disappointment of the Velasco period:

> Velasco's revolution was a real revolution. It was no joke. . . . Things like the UEPP and CONFIEP are definitely a response to a fear of a repetition of something like Velasco. Because there was no union in the private sector during Velasco, and Velasco was very clever in a way. He took the private sector by slices. The first, of course, was the agricultural side . . . and Velasco said the object of the revolution was to "break the spine" of the oligarchy—and the spine of the oligarchy was the SNA. And the SNI published a communication saying fine—that agrarian reform was necessary. Of course, after that they also came along with the industrial communities. They thought they were not going to be touched. But of course, they were. . . . Agriculture, fishing, industry, mining were affected one by one. . . . And now we have learned the lesson that we have to be together on the big issues.[29]

In Bolivia, concern about the character of the bourgeoisie surfaces as an important theme in CEPB documents and in the reflections of CEPB leaders on the period. There are glimpses of self-criticism in their reflections on their own development. Business leaders readily acknowledge the dependence on the state that the private sector developed in the post-1952 era, often with a certain amount of disdain. They also recognize how divisions within the business community facilitated the maintenance of state capitalism, with certain factions benefiting enormously from their collusion with the state. One informant, for example, made the distinction between what he called a "fast buck" bourgeoisie (that is, financial speculators, contractors) versus the "productive" sector of the bourgeoisie (that is, investors such as the mine owners with capital in fixed assets).

Despite this concern about the internal composition and lack of unity inside the private sector, the CEPB actively defended the "productivity" of the private sector—juxtaposing its contribution to economic development to the inefficiency in public sector enterprises. The assertion of private sector productivity in the "technical" analysis of the economy commissioned by the CEPB took place in tandem with CEPB calls for a reduction of the role of the state in 1979.

In all three countries by the end of the 1970s, the domestic bourgeoisie of the Central Andes had come to see itself as a group on the defensive—threatened by a state taken over by unreliable military leaders and technocrats and frightened by a growing militancy among popular classes. As we have seen, business associations responded in a variety of ways. Starting in the 1970s, they stepped up rhetorical attacks on statism. The business counteroffensive escalated in the early 1980s with efforts to spread antistatist ideology within the business sector's own ranks and to a broader public. In Bolivia, the CEPB sponsored the establishment of the Fundación Boliviana in 1981. Along with philanthropic activities, the foundation was charged with the task of fostering the "philosophy of private initiative" and facilitating the discussion of national problems among businessmen through studies and public forums.[30]

The same self-conscious promotion of probusiness attitudes was taking place in Peru in the late 1970s led by the "organic intellectuals" mentioned earlier. Felipe Ortiz de Zevallos came on the scene in 1978 with the publication of a conservative monthly review called *Perú Económico.* In November 1979, a symposium on "Democracy and the Market Economy" was held in Lima's civic center. Among the organizers were Hernando de Soto and Miguel Alvear, a leading textile-company executive with close ties to ADEX and SNI. Invited participants to the symposium included free market theorist Friedrich Von Hayek and conservative writer Jean-François Revel.[31] Remaining funds from the symposium helped to give birth to a conservative think tank under the directorship of Hernando de Soto, the Instituto Libertad y Democracia (ILD). The declared purpose of the institute was to defend "liberty of thought and democracy" and to act as counter to the "monopoly of Marxist totalitarian" thought in Peruvian intellectual life. Joining de Soto as founders of the Institute were Mario Vargas Llosa and highly placed politicians from AP and APRA.[32]

By the late 1970s, the business sector's campaign to retake lost ideological ground was on track. What the antistatists needed, however, was a political opening—to retract the state, they needed to control it. The antistatist drive was part of the complicated prelude to democratization.

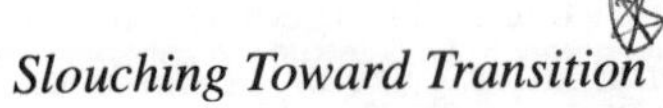

Slouching Toward Transition

The comparative history of business elites reveals a mixed picture of their role in the development of democratic regimes, in Europe and in North and Latin America. At some historical junctures, capitalist elites have been important actors inside the social coalitions that promoted political democratization; whereas on other occasions, businessmen joined with other groups in either slowing democratization or forsaking it completely by supporting authoritarianism. What stands out in this historical record are the shifts and deep-rooted ambivalences in the relationship between business and democracy. While democracy holds out the promise of access and influence for business, it also implies an openness to the demands of lower-class groups. It is simultaneously attractive and menacing.

It is not surprising then to find Andean capitalists cautiously supporting a transition to civilian rule as they grew disillusioned with military regimes. But their support for a transition was not an unqualified vote of confidence in democracy per se. Throughout the transition process, business organizations strove to limit the scope of democratization and to insure that checks on popular sovereignty were guaranteed. Some of these efforts were successful; others were not. As the transition unfolded in each country, business associations were sometimes eclipsed by other organizations in shaping the process. Political parties reemerged on the scene as important interlocutors and took a directive role in the constitutional and legal engineering that was part of the transition. In Bolivia, for example, the Catholic church took on a critical role as mediator. And, especially in Peru and Ecuador, the military retained a high level of control in setting the terms of its own retreat. Thus, business organizations must be seen as one of a number of protagonists in the transition process.

Domestic capitalists welcomed the military interventions that brought the Banzer, Velasco, and Rodríguez Lara administrations to power. These economic powerholders did not anticipate the problems over policy, ideology, and access that were to ensue. Business groups initially sought an accommodation with these de facto governments.

As accommodationist strategies failed to produce consistently satisfying results, the leaders of business organizations grew more insistent in their calls for participation in economic policy making. It is important to note that the initial calls for participation by business groups were just that—an insistence on the business sector's right to be consulted on major matters affecting the economy. The demand for participation was not, at least initially, framed as a broader claim for society at large. *Participation,* for business groups, was a code word that implied a renewal of corporatist linkages between these groups and the government.

Business discourse during the military period is strewn with references to business's right to be heard on economic matters. The Bolivian CEPB, for example, broached the issue in 1977. In a document on the role of the private sector, the CEPB underscored the need for private sector input in development planning, reminding the armed forces of their commitment to *participación concertada* (participation and consensus-building).[33] The Ecuadorean chambers of production registered the same dismay about a lack of consultation with the private sector in development planning. In a 1973 conference, León Febres Cordero, the president of the Guayaquil Chamber of Industry, voiced the concern in the following query:

> Is it possible that one could demand a genuine participation by private enterprise for the accomplishment of developmental goals while pretending that we should not have a role in the organs of planning, credit, or monetary policy? . . . We cannot accept the assignment of great responsibilities without participation.[34]

After 1970 in Peru, complaints over the lack of private sector participation in the formulation of such pivotal economic reforms as the Industrial Communities Law became a standard component of the SNI's attacks on the Velasco government. These calls for participation continued even after the removal of Velasco; and ADEX joined SNI in voicing such concerns.[35]

Business interest groups did not boldly leap from the idea of participation to calls for a transition to democracy. These groups played an important role in creating an atmosphere that was conducive to a transition—but, at least initially, the task of articulating an alternative political formula was in the hands of political parties. In Peru and Ecuador, parties of the center and the right played a pivotal process in the transition. Over all, organizations of the left (including trade unions and parties) were initially uninterested in pressing for a return to civilian rule; instead, they devoted their energies to pressing the reformist military governments to live up to their promises for structural transformation.

In Ecuador. While the Rodríguez Lara government in Ecuador barred partisan activity and initially jailed some party leaders in 1972, there was no systematic effort to eliminate parties. By 1974, centrist and rightist political activists were openly calling for a return to civilian rule. The demands by party leaders escalated in 1975 and led to the deportation of Conservative party leader and Catholic University administrator, Julio César Trujillo. The deportation of Trujillo sparked further protests by parties and student groups. And parties began to put forth contending views of exactly how the transition should take place. Suggestions ranged from the appointment of an interim civilian president to a constitutional referendum.[36]

This wave of partisan agitation coincided with another clash between the Rodríguez Lara government and the business chambers in the period from June to September 1975. In response to a balance-of-payments problem, the government decreed a series of import restrictions that provoked the ire of the Guayaquil and Pichincha Chambers of Commerce and Industry. Rather than agreeing to the austerity measures, the chambers blamed the crisis on the excessive public spending and the mismanagement of the petroleum sector by the government.

Against this backdrop of renewed business opposition, leaders of the Conservative, Socialist, Velasquista, Poncista, and National Revolutionary parties formed the Junta Cívica in August 1975. The junta's avowed purpose was to seek the "reestablishment of the constitutional order." Echoing the criticisms that had been voiced by business groups since 1973, the junta condemned the administration for its agrarian reform, collaboration with the Communist party, and "aggression against the private sector."[37]

The Junta Cívica subsequently endorsed the abortive coup attempt staged by General González Alvear on 31 August 1975. Rodríguez Lara rallied enough support within the armed forces to weather the attempt, but his administration was seriously weakened by the incident. The obvious lack of support for the government in business and party circles strengthened the position of the more conservative elements inside the military and paved the way for Rodríguez Lara's forced resignation in January 1976. The new military junta under the direction of Admiral Alfredo Poveda Burbano immediately announced its intention to initiate a *retorno constitucional* (return to the constitution).

In Peru. Parties in Peru similarly took the lead in pressing the military to return political power to civilians. This resurgence of parties came in conjunction with the political liberalization initiated by the Morales Bermúdez government in 1975; exiled party leaders like Fernando Belaúnde Terry were allowed to return. The liberalization was part of an effort to soothe relations with conservative critics and to turn away from the more radical postures struck during the Velasco period. The populist and right parties—AP, APRA, and Partido Popular Cristiano (PPC)—used the political opening to push for a military retreat and elections.

Partisan demands for democratization became more compelling as they converged with popular class mobilizations against Morales Bermúdez's economic stabilization programs in 1976 and 1977. We shall return to the contours of the economic crisis in Peru in chapter 5; for now, suffice it to say that Morales Bermúdez's reversal of the Velasco economic reforms and his economic stabilization measures put an end to whatever support the regime still enjoyed among popular class organizations.

Amid the economic crisis and growing public hostility in January 1977, the armed forces announced their program for a transition in their Plan Túpac Amaru. The plan outlined a transition that would proceed with elections for a constituent assembly, the drafting of a constitution by the assembly, and a subsequent scheduling of general elections. The announcement was followed by consultations between the government and political parties; but the government dragged its feet on announcing a schedule for the transition events.

In April, the SNI made public its position on the transition plan. The SNI endorsed the idea of a return to elections, the restoration of civil liberties, and the constituent assembly formula. Like parties, however, the SNI pressed for the fixing of a firm timetable for the transition. After the general strike of July, the government finally conceded to these demands and set June 1978 as the date for the Constituent Assembly elections.

In Bolivia. Once the military had set the transition in motion in Peru and Ecuador, the process remained on track; and political activity became focused on the tasks of constitutional engineering and electioneering. The transition in Bolivia, however, took a more torturous route, beginning with Banzer's failed machinations to stay in office and winding through three aborted elections, five military juntas, and two civilian-led interim governments in the period between 1978 and 1982. In contrast to the Peruvian and Ecuadorean experiences, the Bolivian transition was neither controlled nor predictable. Rather, it was a process that both revealed and exacerbated the deep fissures in every part of Bolivian society; it was marked by power struggles inside the armed forces, extreme discord within the civilian political elites, and both class and regional conflicts.

During the turbulence of 1978 through 1982, the CEPB officially supported a transition to what it called ''un estado democrático de derecho'' (a democratic state under rule of law). The concept itself reveals the CEPB's reticence to offer anything close to a blanket endorsement of democracy. The CEPB leadership feared that the left and the militant trade union movement would take over democratic institutions and launch the country toward socialism. Thus, the CEPB's discussion of democracy always included references to coupling democracy with ''stability'' and ''ideological pluralism.'' CEPB leaders seemed to recognize, however, that the prospects for achieving ''bourgeois democracy'' were slight in the absence of a national consensus on the economic and political rules of the game. With this in mind, the CEPB repeatedly floated the idea of forging a *gran acuerdo nacional*—a national agreement among contending class, party, and regional groups on the appropriate economic and political model for Bolivia. The CEPB called for such a move in 1978, 1979, 1980, and 1981.[38]

Despite the CEPB's proposal, no *gran acuerdo* ever materialized. Indeed the CEPB's own rivalry vis-à-vis the COB mitigated against any movement toward a social pact and contributed to the divisiveness that stalled the transition. The two interim civilian governments of Walter Guevara Arce and Lidia Gueiler offered the opportunity to take cabinet positions and participate in a government of ''national conciliation,'' but the CEPB resisted the offers. The CEPB—along with the rightist Acción Democrática Nacionalista (ADN) led by ex-dictator Hugo Banzer—was also conspicuously absent from the front that formed to defend the Gueiler government amid rumors of an impending coup.

The rhetoric of democracy and conciliation put forth by the CEPB in this period contrasted sharply with its virulent antilabor posture. The behavior of prominent individuals associated with the CEPB and the rightist ADN did not reflect an unsullied commitment to democracy. Along with party officials, business elites were embroiled in the chronic coup-baiting of the period. This shortsighted behavior went so far as to include collaboration in the corrupt dictatorship of General Luis García Meza. With the tacit approval of Banzer, high-ranking ADN leaders took positions in the Consejo Nacional Legislativo (CONAL), the entity charged by García Meza with reforming the constitution. Although CONAL collapsed eight months later, it stood as the primary pillar of civilian support for García Meza.

It must be underscored that this sort of coup-baiting and opportunism was not confined to businessmen or the ADN. Other party elites and COB leaders practiced a provocative style of politics that courted military intervention. Congressional leaders played a large part in destabilizing the interim civilian governments of Guevara and Gueiler.[39]

The definitive rejection of military rule by every element in civil society came only after the noxious government of García Meza reduced the state to a "military kleptocracy." Not only was the administration highly repressive, but many of its own officials were openly linked to drug trafficking. The international community boycotted García Meza—refusing diplomatic recognition and financial aid.[40]

As Bolivia faced near complete international isolation and the collapse of public authority, the CEPB began to agitate in earnest for a retreat from militarism. They were joined in their efforts by the COB and political parties. The overthrow of García Meza by General Celso Torrelio in August 1981 reopened the question of a transition, and negotiations ensued under the succeeding government of General Guido Vildoso. One CEPB leader described the anxieties that animated the organization's efforts to secure a "real" transition:

> The Confederación first met in a group of very important entrepreneurs, who saw that there were great problems with García Meza—problems of trying to do things in ways that were not suitable for members of the private sector, problems of human rights, economic problems. And we saw that little by little, these problems were putting the military in a very difficult position. You see, we always looked at the military as an important means of saving us from the extreme left in this country. And the less prestige they had, the less we could count on them. . . . And we knew that this meant that the longer [the military] stayed, the greater the chances that the extreme left would take over the country in a coup. And if that happened, we thought it would be hard to remove them. [The left] would take measures like those in Nicaragua, and it would be hard for us to get them out [of government]. We could not allow the prestige of the military to suffer, so we started a campaign to begin a true democratic process.[41]

As in Peru and Ecuador, the business sector's support for democracy in Bolivia reflected a loss of faith in the military as a guarantor of the capitalist order. Domestic capitalists decided to gamble on democracy, hoping that Lenin's prognosis was correct—that democracy could become the "best possible political shell for capitalism."[42]

Designing the Democratic Shell

In each country, the transition from military to civilian rule involved a struggle between parties, interest groups, and the military to define the contours of the new legal and constitutional order. (Summaries of the key events of the transition process in each country can be seen in tables 1, 2, and 3.) Business elites, acting through their corporate organizations and through parties, entered the fray of transition politics with a decidedly conservative agenda. Because Ecuadorean and Peruvian businessmen had chafed under military reformism, their focus was on lobbying for a constitutional structure that would limit the prospects for a repeat of such reformism. In Bolivia, however, business did not look to constitutional engineering as the hedge against reformism. Rather, the CEPB opted for a

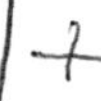

TABLE 1
CHRONOLOGY OF TRANSITION IN ECUADOR

September 1975	Abortive coup attempt by González Alvear.
January 1976	Resignation of Rodríguez Lara. Assumption of power by junta under Poveda Burbano. Junta announces it will oversee a transition to civilian government.
January–March 1976	"Dialogues" between government, parties, and interest groups over legal-constitutional engineering.
June 1976	Junta announces the transition plan with constitutional referendum as first step. Civilian commissions named to frame constitution and design party law.
January 1978	Referendum on constitution held. "New" reform constitution chosen by voters.
July 1978	First-round presidential elections held. Long recount process delays scheduling of second round. Jaime Roldós (CFP) and Sixto Durán Ballén (PSC) are elected as the second-round contenders.
April 1979	Second-round presidential elections and congressional races held. Victory of Jaime Roldós and the CFP by wide margin.
August 1979	Jaime Roldós and Osvaldo Hurtado are sworn in as president and vice-president.

TABLE 2
CHRONOLOGY OF TRANSITION IN PERU

January 1977	Morales Bermúdez government issues the Plan Túpac Amaru—pledging a transition via constituent assembly (CA).
March 1977	Acción Popular (AP) party announces its intention to abstain from CA election, calling for immediate direct presidential election. Other parties and interest groups pressure government to announce a specific timetable for the process.
July 1977	Official timetable announced. CA election scheduled for 1978 with transition to be completed by 1980.
August 1977	Government lifts state of emergency and restores constitutional rights.
July 1978	CA elections held. APRA and PPC win a majority of seats.
July 1979	Writing of constitution completed. Conflict between military and CA over certain provisions of the new charter. Direct elections delayed due to registration problems.
May 1980	Presidential and congressional elections held. Fernando Belaúnde (AP) elected. AP and PPC form a majority in Congress.
July 1980	Inauguration of Belaúnde.

Machiavellian high-risk strategy to discredit the leftist forces—by allowing them to come to power immediately after the military withdrawal in 1982.

In Ecuador. The jockeying among civilian groups to define the legal framework of the transition began even before the military exit was assured in Ecuador. In 1974, parties began to put forth proposals for how the changeover should take place. After the resignation of Rodríguez Lara in January 1976, the Poveda Burbano government opened up discussion of the transition to parties and interest groups through what it dubbed "dialogues"—public meetings, sponsored by the government, in which an array of groups and parties were invited to present their blueprints for a transition. The "dialogues" took place from January through March 1976.

The business chambers used the "dialogues" to reassert their ideological attacks on the statist development model. The presidents of the National Federation of Chambers of Industry, the National Federation of Chambers of Commerce, the Federation of Agriculture, and the Sierra Ranchers' Association issued a joint communiqué at their meeting, demanding a reduction of the state's role in the economy as part of the political restructuring.

In regard to the transition mechanics, the business chambers pointed to the plan put forth by four ex-presidents of the republic. The plan involved calling

TABLE 3
CHRONOLOGY OF TRANSITION IN BOLIVIA

December 1978	Banzer announces elections to be held.
July 1978	General Pereda wins presidential election marked by fraud.
November 1978	Pereda overthrown by General Padilla who calls for new elections.
July 1979	New elections held. Siles (UDP) wins plurality in presidential race. Election thrown into Congress for resolution. Stalemate in Congress results in election of Walter Guevara Arce as interim president for one year.
1–16 November 1979	Coup led by Colonel Alberto Natusch Busch deposes Guevara. Natusch sacked after Congress chooses Lidia Gueiler to serve as interim president.
July 1980	Gueiler overthrown in coup led by General Luis García Meza.
August 1981	García Meza forced out by General Celso Torrelio.
May 1982	Government lifts ban on parties and unions. Declares political amnesty for exiles. CEPB calls for the reinstallation of the Congress of 1980 to select civilian president.
July 1982	Removal of Torrelio. New government headed by General Vildoso. Vildoso calls for direct elections in April 1983.
September 1982	Popular mobilizations demand civilian rule. Broad consensus among parties and groups on the recall of the Congress of 80. Vildoso government accedes to the demand.
October 1982	Congress of 80 convened. Congress chooses Hernán Siles and Jaime Paz Zamora of the UDP coalition as president and vice-president.

elections for a constituent assembly, the indirect election of an interim president by that assembly, and a subsequent constitutional reform under the direction of the assembly. In short, the scheme envisioned a slow transition, one likely to be dominated by Ecuador's traditional parties. Center-left, populist, and left parties opposed the constituent assembly formula; they proposed a quicker move toward direct presidential elections.

The Poveda Burbano government disregarded the conservative formula. Instead General Richelieu Levoyer, the minister of government charged with managing the transition, opted for a sequence that undercut the right's ability to dominate the process. Levoyer created three civilian commissions and charged them with the duty of constitutional and legal restructuring. One commission was formed to rewrite the 1945 constitution while a second commission formulated an entirely new constitution. The public would then choose between the two in the first electoral exercise of the transition, a national referendum scheduled for

January 1978. This was to be followed by presidential and congressional elections. The third commission was charged with reforming the laws governing parties and elections.

Levoyer's transition scheme was an outright rejection of the right's bid to reinsert the old structures and dynamics of oligarchic politics. Not only did the Levoyer plan reject the right's institutional designs, but the composition of the civilian commissions mitigated against the takeover of the process by business groups or right-wing parties. Business chambers vociferously protested their assignment of a single seat on each commission. In fact, a new cohort of party leaders dominated the commissions. Jaime Roldós, a young lawyer from the populist Concentración de Fuerzas Populares (CFP), was appointed to direct the commission writing the new constitution; and Osvaldo Hurtado, a young sociologist, headed the commission on parties. Both were considered to be reformists and their positions gave them considerable influence over the design of the new regime. They later became the successful presidential and vice-presidential slate in the 1979 election.

The work of the commissions reflected a reformist bent. The commission drafting the new constitution proposed important departures from previous constitutional practices. The new constitution abolished ''functional'' representation in Congress, enfranchised illiterates, and mandated the development of a ''communal property'' sector of the economy along with the public and private sectors.

Forces on the right were divided in their reactions to the work of the commissions. Fearing that they would be punished by voters for opposing an extension of the franchise, rightist parties chose to endorse the new constitution (the only exception was the Conservative party). The business chambers reacted harshly to the work of the commissions. They complained again about a lack of representation; and the chambers eventually withdrew their single representative in protest. In Guayaquil, the Chamber of Industry denounced the referendum and led a campaign urging voters to cast ''null ballots.'' Notwithstanding this public relations blitz against the referendum and the new constitution, the new constitution emerged as the clear winner, taking 43 percent of the vote. Only 23 percent of the electorate cast null ballots.

Despite the defeat, the chambers continued to press their opposition to the reformist constitution. León Febres Cordero, president of the Guayaquil Chamber of Industry, belittled the results of the plebiscite and called its validity into question. The Chamber of Industry of Quito demanded a sober rethinking by the incoming civilian government of the application of the ''communal property'' provision of the constitution. It cautioned that any attempt at implementation would raise uncertainty and suspicion among businessmen.[43] The thrust of the chambers' pronouncements was to cast a pall on the new constitution, serving notice that the chambers would not tolerate attempts by any incoming civilian government to use the new legal framework for reformist ends.

In Peru The Peruvian Armed Forces, true to the highly centralized decision-making style that developed in this period, eschewed public consultations on transition mechanics. Instead, they imposed a constituent assembly formula in their Plan Túpac Amaru of January 1977; the plan called for elections to a constituent assembly, the writing of a constitution, and subsequent elections. Ex-president and AP leader Fernando Belaúnde rejected the plan and called for immediate direct elections. But most of the remaining parties from across the political spectrum acceded to the formula. After much foot-dragging by the government before specifying a timetable, the constituent assembly election was finally scheduled for January 1978. With AP refusing to participate, the major beneficiaries of this route were APRA and PPC. They struck an alliance that gave them a majority in the constituent assembly, allowing them to dominate the deliberations.

The constituent assembly became a focal point for business elites who sought to undo the ideological and legal assault on private property that had taken place through Velasco's industrial community and social property laws. The SNI sent a communiqué to the assembly demanding in no uncertain terms that guarantees for private property be included in the constitution.[44]

Closely linked by ideology and social ties to the private sector, PPC representatives pushed hard on the question of economic liberties in the assembly. The drive was successful. With APRA votes, PPC integrated three important principles into the new charter: the constitution assured *pluralismo empresarial* (pluralism in the economic realm), assured liberty in commerce and industry, and defined Peru as an *economia social de mercado* (a social market economy). In the social market theory, the state is assigned a subsidiary role in the economy—acting to set up the rules of the game for market actors, with only occasional interventions into the provision of goods and services (that is, social welfare or infrastructure).[45]

In Bolivia Business organizations in Peru and Ecuador actively sought to disengage the emerging civilian regime from the preceding experience of reformism and state growth. As we have seen, their energies were channeled in two directions. First, there was the day-to-day lobbying aimed at dismantling the reform policies and altering the policy-making environment even as the military still held power. Second, there were the efforts directed at influencing the constitutional engineering of the transition.

In Bolivia, on the other hand, the essential problem of the transition for business elites was not how to reverse reform—but how to stave off a complete collapse of public authority. As the García Meza government unraveled, business leaders in the CEPB looked to transition as a salvage operation, that is, public authority itself had to be resuscitated and restored before they could launch any concerted attempt to reshape it. These dire circumstances led the CEPB elites to advocate a transition route that (at least in the short run) entailed high risks for the private sector.

With the exhaustion of the military as a political option, CEPB leaders came to recognize that regime stability could only emerge with a popularly mandated civilian regime. The rightful heir of civilian government was the Unión Democrática Popular (UDP), the center and left electoral coalition headed by Hernán Siles Zuazo. The coalition included Siles's own Movimiento Nacionalista Revolucionario-Izquierda (a spinoff from the original MNR), the social democratic Movimiento de la Izquierda Revolucionaria (MIR), and the Bolivian Communist party (PCB). The UDP had, in fact, won a plurality in two of the three aborted elections of the post-Banzer period, but had been denied power on both occasions. In July 1979, the Congress deadlocked over approving Siles as president and appointed Walter Guevara Arce as interim president. The UDP earned another plurality in the elections of June 1980, but their accession was blocked by the García Meza coup of July.

It was with the UDP's electoral track record in mind that the CEPB made its proposal for the transition, following a meeting in April 1982. It advocated the installation of the unseated Congress of 1980; the Congress would, in turn, elect a civilian president for one term in office to be concluded with the convoking of a new round of presidential and legislative elections. The CEPB proposal was published in the newspapers as *¡Democracia ya!*[46]

This "Congress of 80" option was attractive to CEPB leaders for a number of reasons. First, it avoided the drawbacks of calling a new (and possibly destabilizing) round of elections; yet, it permitted a transfer that would enjoy legitimacy and popular acceptance. Second, the transition would obviously entail the installation of a UDP government, but it would be a weak UDP government: without a new round of elections, the UDP would be forced to take power without a unified majority in the legislature and would encounter enormous difficulties in governing. CEPB leaders believed that the left would discredit itself in power and pave the way for a subsequent electoral victory by conservative forces. Because of the somewhat improvised nature of the UDP's ascent to power, some CEPB leaders hoped that Siles could be forced into holding early elections if the situation deteriorated rapidly. A high-ranking leader of the CEPB described the Machiavellian reasoning behind the choice:

> Well, I don't want to be cynical about this, but I think we all realized that after the military government we were going to have a very difficult time. I was willing to see whether the

> left could do it [govern] . . . I wasn't surprised to see them fail. . . . Unless the left tried it, we would never have peace in this country. They had to try it. They were sure they had the majority; they had won democratically. Anything we would have done to change that and bring a government of the center or center-right would have been like snatching the government from their hands. We couldn't run that risk. We had to let them govern, although we knew they couldn't do it. . . . Now, our questions and frustrations were two: (1) How much of a mess were they going to make? (2) How long would they resist? But we knew that after this, we had to have a chance [to govern], which is exactly what happened.[47]

The CEPB's "Congress of 80" solution was supported by a group of seven parties. It included Banzer's ADN; the Christian Democratic party (PDC); Paz Estenssoro's Historic MNR; Lidia Gueiler's Frente Revolucionario de Izquierda (FRI); Walter Guevara's Partido Revolucionario Auténtico (PRA); Guillermo Bedregal's Unified MNR; and the Partido Socialista (PS). The social democratic MIR and the Socialist Party-1 (PS-1) subsequently endorsed the idea.

Opposition to the plan came from Hernán Siles Zuazo, the COB, and the PCB. All three favored a new round of elections, the option put forth by the military. They believed that new elections would strengthen the position of the UDP, giving it a broad popular mandate and perhaps control over both chambers of the legislature. This opposition dissipated, however, after the MIR sponsored an impressive mass rally in support of the plan. The COB followed suit by staging a hunger strike demanding the transition via the Congress of 80. The government of General Vildoso acquiesced in the face of the widespread consensus on the scheme; he announced on 17 September 1982 that the Congress would be convoked in October. It was, and as expected, Hernán Siles Zuazo and the UDP came to power.

Conclusion: Reconstituting the Right

Business interest groups were important protagonists in the transition from military authoritarianism to civilian rule in the Central Andes. Their presence in the process was by no means unusual. The decomposition of business support for military regimes has been part of the story of democratization in virtually every case of political transition. From the *antiestizacão* campaign of domestic industrialists in Brazil to the business sector's disengagement from the personalist authoritarianism in the Dominican Republic and Paraguay, economic elites have played a key role in determining the final denouement of dictatorships all over Latin America.

Notwithstanding their interest in shaping the transition process, business organizations in the Central Andes were unable to oversee a process completely to their liking. In Ecuador, business interest groups disapproved of parts of the new constitution and were wary of the new generation of party leaders that emerged in the transition process. In Peru, business interest groups groped through the transition process, disgruntled with what they regarded as the snail-paced dismantling of the Velasco reforms by Morales Bermúdez. After an extended period of aborted transition in Bolivia, the *realpolitik* of the situation paved the way for a major concession on the part of business elites—that they tolerate the accession of a center-left government to power. From the perspective of business organizations, the unfolding of the transition in each case was below the optimal, but nonetheless acceptable.

The politics of the transition period reinforced the lessons that business interest groups had already learned in the 1970s. To put it simply, they found that military governments (even when seeking alliances with the private sector) were unpredictable and prone to disregard pressures from civil society, even those from its most elite members. But business interest group leaders were neither disheartened nor defeated by their encounters with the military governments in the 1970s. On the contrary, they were invigorated by the experiences—and looked to the reinstallation of civilian rule as a way to build on the lessons learned. Business leaders actively revived antistatism as an ideological position and gave it a new currency in their own organizations. And this ideological revitalization of antistatist ideas spread through conservative and centrist parties, laying the basis for a sea change in the policy-making environment.

The conservative challenge to state-centered economic models gained even more momentum with the onset of economic decline and problems in the management of the foreign debt situation. Economic crisis, along with the organizational revival of the right, laid the groundwork for conservative electoral victories and the coming of neoliberal economic experiments.

CHAPTER 5

Crisis, Elections, and Neoliberal Coalitions

Starting with Peru in the mid-1970s, the Central Andes began to exhibit the first symptoms of what was to become a *continentwide* economic crisis in the 1980s. For the Central Andes and the rest of Latin America, the 1980s turned into the "lost decade"—a period of declining economic growth, the greatest single downturn for the region since the Great Depression in the 1930s. While the exact onset and precise configuration of macroeconomic problems differed among the countries, shared structural features were at the root of this regional crisis: troubled export performance; a continuing dependence on imports, and the high costs associated with import-substitution industrialization strategies; and the burdens of servicing the ballooning foreign debt.

The growing economic crisis fed the antistatist upsurge we described in chapter 4 in a number of ways. The crisis imparted a new sense of urgency and credibility to antistatist advocates who argued in favor of a fundamental reorientation of the developmental model. By the early 1980s, the promarket ideology espoused by domestic actors converged with directives from powerful external actors in the international financial community. Both the IMF and the World Bank imposed "conditionality" in their loan agreements that pushed for both short-term stabilization measures and economic restructuring to promote market rather than state-centric models.[1] The increasing emphasis placed on such structural reforms by these international institutions was, of course, no accident. It reflected the changes in the intellectual and political climate of the advanced capitalist economies. By the early 1980s, Ronald Reagan and Margaret Thatcher had already launched their own assaults on state intervention, and economists were proclaiming the death of Keynesianism and the welfare state. Antistatism acquired a new cachet and legitimacy in the political discourse of the 1980s; and the incipient neoliberal coalitions forming in the Central Andes found their point of view enthusiastically reinforced by international institutions, foreign creditors, and the Reagan administration.[2]

Even before the neoliberal projects were launched, the economic crisis and international pressures were pushing Andean governments away from their expansionary postures of the early 1970s. In each country, balance-of-payments problems forced the implementation of short-term stabilization measures by non-neoliberal governments (Morales Bermúdez in Peru, Hurtado in Ecuador, Gueiler and Siles in Bolivia). Ironically, the popular discontent generated by such austerity measures bolstered the presidential hopefuls of the center-right who were able to portray themselves as "opposition" candidates.

The challenge for antistatist forces was to seize upon the unique opportunities for change made available by the confluence of economic crisis, shifting international circumstances, and the political transition. In order to proceed with their plans for economic restructuring, the loose antistatist movements centered in the business communities of the three countries faced political and organizational tasks. First, they needed to fortify their links to the party system because parties were the primary vehicle for entrée into the new electoral game. Second, they needed to forge a technocratic cadre capable of formulating and undertaking the reforms, once political power was secured by the center right. Thus, business interest group leaders began to come together with conservative party leaders and technocrats in pre- and post-electoral alliances.

We have divided this chapter into two parts. The first part summarizes the special features of the economic crisis in each country and the stabilization efforts that took place prior to the installation of the neoliberal governments; as we show in this and the following chapter, the specific character of each crisis and the initial stabilization efforts undertaken in each country were important elements in influencing the development of subsequent neoliberal programs. The second part focuses on how neoliberal policy coalitions crystallized—composed of capitalists, technocrats, and politicians—and how they were able to capitalize on the crisis conjuncture. Since these processes did not unfold either simultaneously or uniformly across the three countries, we have chosen to treat each country separately and draw our comparisons at the conclusion of the chapter. The time periods under discussion are 1975–80 in Peru, 1978–85 in Bolivia, and 1979–84 in Ecuador.

Part 1: Crisis and Stabilization

Peru: The IMF's Vietnam

By the time of Velasco's ouster in August 1975, Peru's economic upturn was clearly at an end. Serious economic disequilibria were reflected in balance-of-payments problems, budget deficits, and inflation. The crisis that surfaced in

1975 was the product of long-standing structural difficulties in the Peruvian economy combined with the effects of Velasco's economic strategies.[3]

Despite the enormous changes wrought by the Velasco government, the reformist program did not effectively address one of Peru's most serious ongoing problems—the constraints on growth emanating from the stagnation of the export sector. By the mid-1960s, Peru had exhausted all the "easy" routes to export expansion. Agricultural and mineral exports had reached the physical limits to expansion. The limited supply of irrigated lands restricted the possibility of increasing agricultural exports such as cotton and sugar. In the mining sector, the most accessible deposits of high-grade ores were depleted; a turn toward new types of mineral exports demanded new technology and investment.[4]

The stagnation in the export sector created foreign exchange bottlenecks. And, with the pursuit of import-intensive industrialization in the post–World War II period, the scarcity of foreign exchange proved increasingly problematic. The balance-of-payments crises of 1957 and 1967 were evidence of the growing structural bind at work in the Peruvian economy. Certainly, this foreign exchange constraint was in place prior to 1968. It was, however, aggravated by Velasco's economic policy, which ignored export promotion while fueling industrial expansion for domestic consumption.[5]

In addition to reinforcing an anti-export bias in development policy, the Velasco administration exacerbated the decline in private investment with its pursuit of reformist policies. The Industrial Community Law (see chapter 3) antagonized a broad segment of the business community and was probably one of the main causes of capital flight during the Velasco government. The tough regulations over foreign capital enacted in the first years of the administration discouraged new investment by multinational corporations; for the most part, multinationals remained wary of sinking new capital into long-term investments in Peru despite the efforts of the government to entice some firms into new relationships.[6]

As Rosemary Thorp and others have argued, Velasco's economic model was based on a number of false assumptions regarding how the reforms would affect both public and private sectors.[7] Velasco's economic policy makers sought to capture a greater part of the economic surplus for the state and readjust the behavior of domestic and foreign capitalists. They gambled on the belief that capitalists would accommodate to the new rules and invest. They did not—and the central government was forced to compensate for the lack of private initiative. Whereas Velasco's planners had envisioned a leading role for the state through the development of public enterprises in strategic industries, public sector expansion exceeded the original conception. By 1974, the state accounted for more than half of the total investment in the Peruvian economy.

Favorable terms of trade for Peruvian exports helped the administration to pursue its heady spending and investment policies in the first part of the administration. But foreign financing proved critical to the administration's ability to pursue its ambitious investment projects. The Velasco government took advantage of the bonanza conditions in the international financial markets and contracted substantial foreign debts from private commercial banks. Peru's foreign debt increased substantially during the Velasco years, accelerating during the 1974–76 period.[8]

The fiscal limits to Velasco's model were in evidence by mid-1975. Foreign banks balked at the idea of continuing loans to the overextended Peruvian state. Declining investment and a shrinking tax base made it impossible to raise new revenues domestically. The economic indicators shown in table 4 tell the story of the distressed state of the Peruvian economy by mid-decade; deficit spending and inflation were coupled with rising unemployment.

The takeover of the presidency by General Francisco Morales Bermúdez initiated phase two of the revolution—that is, the end of the reformist experiment and the ascendance of more conservative elements within the armed forces. Morales Bermúdez was known to favor fiscal conservatism. In fact, while still serving as minister of finance in July 1975, he launched what became the first in a series of stabilization measures. His program included gasoline price increases and hikes on other price-controlled items.[9]

The march toward economic stabilization continued with Morales Bermúdez's appointment of the first civilian finance minister under the military, Doctor Luis Barua Castañeda. One of Barua's first measures after he took the post in September 1975 was a currency devaluation. This was followed by a fresh package of austerity measures in January 1976. The package included tax and price increases and budget cuts. Yet another package was enacted by Barua in June 1976; it included another devaluation and price increases.

The stabilization measures of 1976 were offered up to the international banking community as a sign of Peru's willingness to put its fiscal house in order. Nonetheless, while Morales Bermúdez sought a rapprochement with foreign banks, he wanted to avoid the implementation of a draconian austerity plan under IMF supervision. In an unorthodox move, the government opened up direct negotiations with private creditor banks in March 1976. Peru asked banks to roll over the debt without the usual IMF standby agreement. Hoping that such an agreement would shore up the Morales Bermúdez government and facilitate repayment, the banks agreed. In exchange for new loans, the government pledged itself to continued austerity and promised to reverse many of the Velasco reforms affecting domestic and foreign capital. The most unusual aspect of the agreement was the role to be played by the foreign banks in monitoring the agreement. A steering committee composed of Citibank, Bank of America, Chase Manhattan, Manufacturers Hanover, Morgan Guaranty, and Wells Fargo took responsibility for overseeing the arrangement.[10]

TABLE 4

PERU: SELECTED ECONOMIC INDICATORS, 1973–83

Short-Term Indicators (growth rates)	*1973*	*1974*	*1975*	*1976*	*1977*	*1978*	*1979*	*1980*	*1981*	*1982*	*1983*
GDP	6.2	6.9	3.3	2.0	−0.1	−0.5	4.1	3.8	3.9	0.4	−11.8
Per capita GDP	3.3	4.0	0.5	−0.6	−2.7	−3.1	1.4	1.1	1.2	−2.2	−14.[illegible]
Consumer prices (Dec. to Dec.)	13.8	19.2	24.0	44.7	32.4	73.7	66.7	60.8	72.7	72.9	125.[illegible]
Real Remunerations											
Salaries	—	0.1	−8.1	−8.9	−12.5	−14.6	−8.7	−7.4	1.7	8.3	−15.1
Wages	—	−2.1	−17.6	8.5	−15.6	−9.9	−3.2	9.9	−2.0	1.4	−16.9
Unemployment (nonagricultural)	7.1	6.7	8.1	8.4	9.4	10.4	11.2	10.9	10.4	10.6	13.[illegible]
Fiscal Deficit (as percentage of total central government expenditure)	35.9	30.5	33.1	30.2	33.9	24.4	6.0	12.2	21.4	18.1	38.0
Public Sector deficit (as percentage of GDP)	—	—	—	10.0	9.8	6.2	1.1	4.7	8.4	8.5	12.0
Debt	*1973*	*1974*	*1975*	*1976*	*1977*	*1978*	*1979*	*1980*	*1981*	*1982*	*1983*
Total external debt (in millions of dollars)	1,424	1,814	2,563	3,474	3,987	4,759	5,597	9,594	9,688	11,340	12,442
Service (as percentage of exports)	29.7	23.5	26.1	26.1	30.7	31.5	22.7	32.7	44.9	49.1	60.3

Sources: Figures are taken from United Nations Economic Commission for Latin America and the Caribbean, *Economic Survey of Latin America and the Caribbean* (Santiago: United Nations, 1980–87), as follows: for 1973–75, from *Economic Survey, 1978* (1980), 427; for 1976–83, from *Economic Survey, 1983* (1985), 558; debt figures for 1973–79, from *Economic Survey, 1980* (1982), 466; debt figures for 1980–83, from *Economic Survey, 1985* (1987), 565. Debt services ratios are taken from Junta del Acuerdo de Cartagena, Luis Abugattás "Crisis económica y programas de estabilización en los países andinos: Una visión comparativa," (paper delivered at the Seminario sobre el Grupo Andino: Nuevos Enfoques para el Desarrollo y la Integración Subregional, 17–19 September 1985. Junta del Acuerdo de Cartegena, Lima, Peru).

Despite another round of austerity measures in January 1977, the agreement with the banks unraveled as the government failed to meet any of the targets for spending cuts. Unhappy with their monitoring role, the banks retreated to their traditional position and demanded an agreement with the IMF as a condition for disbursing any further loans. As expected, the IMF mission that visited Lima in March 1977 proposed deep budget cuts that included slashes in defense spending and the selling of public enterprises.

The negotiations with the IMF caused serious conflicts within the Morales Bermúdez administration and keen resistance to the notion of defense cuts within the armed forces. Faced with internal opposition, Finance Minister Barua resigned. He was replaced by Walter Piazza, another civilian, who lasted only fifty-six days in office. Piazza enacted a fifth austerity package of price increases, which touched off a new wave of riots and demonstrations.

Popular rejection of the austerity program culminated in a nationwide general strike in July 1977. The strike was a watershed for the Morales Bermúdez government. It was the first general strike in Peru for twenty years and it underscored the extent of public disaffection with the regime. The strike forced the government to back down from its announced price increases. And to defuse the mobilization against the economic measures, Morales Bermúdez turned to political reforms. In August, he lifted the state-of-emergency decree that had been in effect since July 1976; he also finalized the timetable for the constituent assembly election and the promised transition to civilian rule.

Still in need of an IMF endorsement to calm the bankers, Morales Bermúdez continued negotiations, and a standby agreement was struck with the IMF in November 1977. The IMF laid down targets for the reduction of the fiscal deficit through tax hikes and price increases in goods supplied by public enterprises. Especially notable was the 20 percent increase in gasoline prices mandated by the agreement. The November accord was followed by the application of the austerity measures in December.

The inability of the Morales Bermúdez government to control the fiscal deficit, especially defense spending, triggered a new crisis in Peru's relations with the IMF in February 1978. The IMF mission of February 1978 declared Peru to be in massive violation of the conditions set down in the standby. With the credibility of the economic team at a new low, Finance Minister General Alcibiades Sáenz laid out another set of draconian measures as prelude to his resignation in May 1978. Riots broke out as the government announced hikes of from 50 to 60 percent in the cost of food and public transport. Sáenz was replaced by a civilian technocrat, Javier Silva Ruete. As part of the same shuffle, Manuel Moreyra took over as head of the Central Bank. The Silva Ruete–Moreyra team immediately sought to secure a new standby with the IMF, but with less stringent conditions.

The IMF compromised with Peruvian negotiators and a new agreement went into effect in August 1978.

The policies pursued by Silva Ruete to some extent presaged policy directions followed by President Belaúnde's neoliberal economic team of 1980. Silva Ruete concurred with the findings of a Dutch advisory mission—and followed some of the directions suggested in its 1978 report.[11] He began to lower tariffs in order to open up the economy. But Silva Ruete's turn toward conservatism stopped short of a wholesale attack on the directive role of the state in the economy. For example, he approved the extension of tax breaks to nontraditional exports—an incentive that would be stripped away by hard-line neoliberals in the Belaúnde team. Silva Ruete also resisted pressures to move rapidly on the privatization of public enterprises.

Javier Silva Ruete and Central Bank president Manuel Moreyra found themselves at the helm of economic policy in the most propitious of circumstances. The Peruvian economy rebounded in 1979–80, largely because of a boom in international prices for Peru's principal mineral exports. By 1979, there was a foreign exchange surplus and a substantial reduction in the public sector deficit, and conflicts with the IMF had ebbed. How this short-term boom was interpreted and acted on by the incoming economic team of President Belaúnde is treated in the next chapter. For now, suffice it to say that the configuration of problems underlying the 1975–78 crisis reappeared during Belaúnde's term, undoing the neoliberal experiment and discrediting the administration.

Economic management during the Morales Bermúdez period was notable for the new ethos that took hold in the policy-making process. Morales Bermúdez replaced Velasco's ECLA-influenced economic advisors with businessmen and more conservative-leaning technocrats as he sought to rebuild relationships with the private sector.[12] At the same time, the catastrophic financial conditions between 1975 and 1978 drastically altered the parameters within which economic decisions were made and the policy options as they were perceived by the Morales Bermúdez teams. The range of economic discourse shifted; the debates over allocation of resources and the design of reforms that had dominated discussions between 1968 and 1974 were replaced by questions of how to appease foreign creditors and allocate the costs of economic stabilization among social groups.

The "right turn" of the Morales Bermúdez administration paved a way for the more concerted neoliberal experimentation of the subsequent Belaúnde government. The successive stabilization programs of the 1976–78 period were an attack on the subsidy-providing functions of public enterprises. To attack this subsidy-providing function was, of course, to challenge the state's role in expanding popular consumption. The imposition of price increases through stabilization programs became one component of the Morales Bermúdez administration's broader effort to discipline labor and popular organizations, which had grown out of the Velasco reforms. Along with stabilization, the push to subordinate labor included a piecemeal dismantling of the industrial community reforms. Lower-class resistance in the form of demonstrations, riots, and strikes were met with repression.[13]

The Morales Bermúdez interregnum closed the book on the reformist policies of the Velasco era. The retrenchment of 1976–79 suggested a different vision of Peru's future—one based on a more modest role for the state, a toned-down working class, and an increased emphasis on the market. This view was welcomed by antistatists in the business world; and they looked to a new civilian government to enlarge on the legacy of the Morales Bermúdez years.

Bolivia: The Road to Hyperinflation

Starting in 1978, Bolivia began to wrestle with many of the same problems that already plagued the Peruvian economy. Troubles in the export sector, a burdensome foreign debt, uncontrolled government spending, and the retreat of domestic and international capital were all components of the Bolivian economic crisis from 1978 through 1985.

Efforts to deal with the crisis seemed only to aggravate it. A succession of military and civilian presidents put the Bolivian economy through a series of incomplete and unsuccessful stabilization programs. The crisis and the policy failures during the Siles presidency culminated in one of the most intense hyperinflations of the twentieth century. The catastrophic conditions of the 1982–85 period laid the groundwork for the subsequent neoliberal experiment under the presidency of Víctor Paz Estenssoro. The catastrophe was the catalyst for an organizational offensive by antistatists and prepared the public for the dramatic measures that were to be taken by the Paz government. Before examining the impact of the crisis on the domestic political scene, it is important to appreciate the depth and the jarring character of the difficulties at work inside the Bolivian economy in the first half of the 1980s.

Paralleling the experience of Peru in the 1970s, Bolivian economic growth during the Banzer administration of 1971–78 was based on two exogenous factors: (1) buoyant prices on the international market for Bolivian exports; and (2) the boom in international credit markets that allowed for extensive foreign financing of government expenditures.[14] The inflow of resources during the Banzer years was used to expand the state bureaucracy and funnel millions of dollars in subsidized credit to the private sector (see chapter 3).

For a variety of reasons, the financial boom did not result in an expansion in the productive capacity of the Bolivian economy; and in that sense, there was an artificial quality to the growth experienced in the period. The influx of foreign credit helped fuel a consumption splurge; imports, especially of consumer durables, skyrocketed. The real estate market in the capital city of La Paz and the construction industry surged along with government spending.[15]

The collapse of commodity prices and a halt in the flow of foreign capital set the economic crisis in motion by late 1978. The expected boom in petroleum export—much heralded by Banzer and awaited by foreign lenders—failed to materialize. Bankers balked at the idea of increasing their exposure in Bolivia, especially as the political instability of the post-Banzer period unfolded.

The first attempt at economic stabilization came in late 1979 under the government of interim civilian president, Lidia Gueiler. Gueiler's own political circumstances were not propitious for launching austerity measures; she had come to the presidency as a compromise candidate, selected by Congress after the Natusch Busch coup of November 1979 and charged with presiding over a transitional administration until a new election scheduled for June 1980. Nonetheless, she plunged ahead with stabilization as a prelude to negotiations with the IMF. The package included a devaluation, a reduction in mining taxes, and an increase in the price of agricultural products and goods produced by public sector enterprises. This "good behavior" was rewarded by the multilateral lending institutions; the IMF approved a standby loan in January 1980 and the World Bank agreed to a structural adjustment loan in June 1980. These agreements were seen as a vital first step toward the reopening of foreign credit to Bolivia.[16]

But any credibility that Gueiler's initiatives may have engendered in international circles was completely undone by the military coup staged by General Luis García Meza in July 1980. García Meza's unsavory character and the administration's links to drug trafficking brought commercial and multilateral lending to a halt in 1980–81. Despite the financial crunch, García Meza was able to cover his current account deficit with a medium-term loan from the Argentine government and short-term loans from various Latin American central banks. Pressures from private commercial lenders for repayments eventually led to a rescheduling agreement between the García Meza government and a coordinating committee representing 128 creditor banks. The agreement converted short-term to medium-term loans but laid out tough terms for the scheduling and pace of repayments. The agreement was not made contingent on an IMF accord. While some payments were made, Bolivia fell into arrears once more in September 1982.

With the overthrow of García Meza in September 1981, the new military government under General Celso Torrelio sought to reestablish relations with the IMF. His attempted rapprochement began with a monetary devaluation in February 1982; interest rate hikes and elimination of subsidies on sugar, rice, and milk followed in March. An IMF mission visited Bolivia in May; but Fund representatives remained unimpressed. They urged further price hikes in the goods produced by public enterprises to offset the growing fiscal deficit.[17] Protests against the austerity moves and demands for a political transition made the Torrelio government reticent to press on with stabilization and no agreement with the Fund was reached. The Torrelio government was replaced by the last military government under General Guido Vildoso. As the economy continued to deteriorate, Vildoso agreed to the transition plan convoking the Congress of 1980 and the subsequent election of Hernán Siles Zuazo as president.

Redressing the ills of the Bolivian economy would have been a herculean task for any incoming administration in October 1982. A World Bank study enumerated the extraordinary set of problems that faced the Siles administration including (1) a ballooning fiscal deficit; (2) a 300 percent annual inflation rate for 1982 and a real decline in the purchasing power of large segments of the population; (3) shortages of food, medicine, and imported spare parts and supplies for industrial production; (4) falling mineral prices; and (5) mounting arrears on the foreign debt.[18]

Political conditions, however, severely exacerbated the difficulties of managing this stressed economy. President Hernán Siles Zuazo took the transition to democracy seriously—that is, he sought to differentiate his government from previous de facto governments by its commitment to political freedom.[19] The price of this new political freedom was that it allowed a variety of social groups—trade unions in the COB, business groups of the CEPB, and regional civic committees—the opportunity to mobilize against Siles's attempts to deal with the crisis with a stabilization program. Moreover, internal conflicts within Siles's unwieldy center-left coalition produced constant changeovers in the economic team and undermined the government's capacity to sustain a coherent economic formula.

What ensued under the Siles government was a macroeconomic nightmare. An examination of the economic indicators set out in table 5 convey the depth of the problems during the Siles period. Six successive stabilization packages were enacted from November 1982 through February 1985. Not only did these policies fail, but each successive failure undermined the credibility of the next set of measures.

Immediately after taking office in October 1982, Siles launched the first stabilization package. The November 1982 plan was the most heterodox of the six packages insofar as it combined fiscal austerity with a new incomes policy.[20] It reintroduced prices controls over food staples. Wages were hiked and indexed. At the same time, the price of publicly produced goods and services (utilities, gas) were increased. On the monetary side, exchange controls were established, the peso was devalued, and the controversial "dedollarization" measures were put in place. The measures were supposed to dampen internal demand for the dollar by allowing residents to convert their locally contracted dollar debts into pesos at a fixed rate.[21]

The reforms brought disappointing results. Despite dedollarization, domestic

TABLE 5

BOLIVIA: SELECTED ECONOMIC INDICATORS, 1980–85

Short-Term Indicators (growth rates)	*1980*	*1981*	*1982*	*1983*	*1984*	*1985*
GDP	0.9	3.2	0.3	−2.8	−6.6	−0.9
Per capita GDP	−1.7	0.5	−2.3	−5.4	−9.0	−3.5
Unemployment	—	5.8	9.7	10.5	14.2	15.1
Consumer Prices						
Dec. to Dec.	23.9	25.1	296.5	328.5	2,176.8	8,170.5
Variation between annual averages	47.2	32.1	123.5	275.6	1,281.3	11,749.6
Money (M1)	41.1	20.5	230.9	209.4	1,782.1	5,940
Fiscal deficit/total expenditure of government	45.2	44.0	85.5	86.8	93.2	94.8
Fiscal deficit/GDP	7.6	7.1	28.9	23.0	42.1	76.4
Debt (in millions of dollars)						
Total disbursed external debt	2,340	2,622	2,502	3,156	3,156	3,842
Total disbursed external debt (as percentage of exports)	224.4	259.1	274.0	367.8	386.9	—
Public debt service (as percentage of exports)	26.9	27.6	26.9	30.5	37.2	34.4

Source: United Nations Economic Commission for Latin America and the Caribbean, *Economic Survey of Latin America and the Caribbean, 1985* (Santiago: United Nations, 1987), 100, 115.

demand for dollars grew. Informal markets appeared to service the demand, giving rise to a wide gap between the government-controlled official exchange rate and the unofficial exchange rate. Local merchants, in turn, adjusted prices to reflect the unofficial rates and workers demanded wage increases in line with the price increases.

The exchange rate and escalating wage demands fed the inflationary pressures already embedded in the Bolivian economy. The driving force behind Bolivia's inflation of the early 1980s was the government's use of seignorage financing (that is, the printing of money) to cover its expenditures in the absence of fresh foreign credit.[22] As international credit dried up, the military governments and the Siles administration resorted to currency creation to underwrite the chronic fiscal deficit. The decisions taken in 1982 and 1983 to renew interest payments on the foreign debt further drained government coffers even as inflation heated up and eroded tax receipts.

The failure of a heterodox approach led to five subsequent stabilization packages. These packages were designed along more orthodox lines by Siles's "independent" technocrats in the cabinet. The key features of the programs included

(1) substantial monetary devaluations; (2) the use of more flexible exchange controls; (3) significant price hikes in publicly produced and price-controlled goods; and (4) wage increases lagging behind price increments and the devaluations. Along with these measures, the government renewed the commitment to pay arrears on the foreign debt as a way to reestablish Bolivia's standing with international financial circles.

The Siles government was unable to sustain any of the orthodox packages. Leaders of the COB resisted the proposed budget cuts, price hikes, and wage restraints; and they mobilized the public in demonstrations and strikes. Unwilling to use force against the opposition and unable to withstand the demand to maintain consumption, Siles continued on the path of financing the fiscal deficit by expanding the money supply. By April 1984, Bolivia had become Latin America's first textbook case of hyperinflation in the 1980s as average monthly price increases exceeded the 50 percent range. With the economy spinning out of control, Siles bowed to widespread pressures to exit office a year early. The schedule for the next round of presidential elections was advanced to July 1985.

So far, we have simply outlined the character and progression of the Bolivian economic crisis of the early 1980s. As we shall see in the second part of this chapter, the economic catastrophe that unfolded during the Siles years was fertile ground for the developing neoliberal coalition in Bolivia. Businessmen and political elites came together in opposition to the Siles government, looking to turn the debacle into a victory for antistatism.

Ecuador: The Boom-Bust Saga of Oil Export

In 1982, a downturn in international oil prices and the financial fallout from Mexico's moratorium on its foreign debt sent shock waves through the Ecuadorean economy. As a major oil exporter through the 1970s, Ecuador sidestepped the severe economic disequilibria that had already pushed Peruvian and Bolivian policy makers down the road to stabilization. But with the oil boom gone flat and foreign creditors in retreat, the dilemmas facing the Ecuadorean economic team of President Osvaldo Hurtado in 1982 were reminiscent of those already experienced by Ecuador's Andean counterparts.

The petroleum exports initiated in 1972 brought unprecedented wealth to Ecuador (see chapter 3). With control over the oil industry, the central government directly reaped the benefits of the new windfalls from oil, and these revenues were directed in a variety of ways. They were used to expand the public payroll, to create new public enterprises, and to make massive investments in infrastructure. At the same time, a significant portion of the oil windfall was channeled to the private sector through subsidized credits and tax breaks. Business and urban consumers also benefited from subsidies that kept low prices on gasoline, electricity, and foodstuffs. Petroleum-induced consumption turned Ecuador into one of the fastest-growing markets in Latin America in the 1970s.

The economic bonanza produced by oil export, however, both masked and aggravated underlying structural problems in the Ecuadorean economy; and in this sense, the Ecuadorean experience parallels that of Peru and Bolivia in the first half of the 1970s. The frenzy of consumption increased the demands for imports, especially by the industrialists who relied on imported raw materials and capital goods. The demand for imports outpaced export growth, putting pressure on the balance-of-payments situation. By 1975, the central government turned increasingly to foreign loans in order to cover the current accounts deficit.[23] Ecuador's status as a major oil exporter made it especially attractive to international bankers in the 1970s. The military government of Admiral Poveda Burbano (1976–79) made *endeudamiento agresivo* (aggressive indebtedness) an official component of economic policy. From 1975 to 1980 Ecuador's foreign debt increased sevenfold, and its debt service ratio climbed from 4 to 19 percent.

The major flaw in this development strategy—developed under the two successive military governments of the 1970s—was that it built the economy around monoexport dependence; growth in every sphere, from public investment to private industry, was intimately tied to the price of Ecuadorean crude oil on the international market. Oil export also provided the entrée into international financial markets and led to a spiraling dependence on foreign loans.

The end of military rule in 1979 did not bring about a major transformation in the conduct of economic policy or a reformulation of the development model. The newly elected civilian president, Jaime Roldós, faced formidable political conflicts when he assumed office in August 1979. Like Hernán Siles Zuazo in Bolivia, Roldós's task as the first postdictatorial president was to launch a new democratic political system and to distinguish it from the previous de facto regimes. As such, Roldós was preoccupied with managing political conflict and responding to the new socioeconomic demands articulated by the newly enfranchised electorate. The establishment of social security for female workers and the enactment of the forty-hour work week were part of Roldós's reformist efforts in social policy. Most of the energy of the administration in the first year was consumed by the executive-legislative impasse caused by the split within Roldós's own CFP.

For the most part, politics overshadowed debates over the economy for the first year of the Roldós government. Some members of the administration did, however, express concerns over the foreign debt. Vice-President Osvaldo Hurtado, charged with overseeing the National Development Plan, warned the public of the austerity that lay ahead. Nonetheless, buoyant oil prices in 1979–80 did not encourage austerity in the Roldós government. Current and capital expenditures rose in 1980; and the government agreed to Congress's generous salary increases for public sector employees. Subsidies on the domestic consumption of oil and electricity contributed to the still-accelerating public deficit.[24]

Although Roldós authorized some unpopular price increases in 1980, the first warning of the oncoming economic crunch came in February 1981 when the president enacted his first economic package, or *paquetazo*. Roldós's turn to austerity measures came on the heels of Ecuador's costly border clash with Peru and reflected a downturn in world oil prices. The package included an increase in the domestic price of oil products and a hike in public transportation fares. The measures constituted a major departure in economic policy—it was the first hike in domestic oil prices since oil exports took off in 1972. Trade unions, grouped together in the Frente Unitario de Trabajadores (FUT), responded by calling the first nationwide general strike since the transition to civilian rule.

Roldós's untimely death in an airplane crash in May 1981 thrust economic policy into the hands of his successor, Vice-President Osvaldo Hurtado. Rising interest rates on the foreign debt made for increasing balance-of-payments difficulties by 1982. With interest payments soaring and the prospects of future loans receding, a Central Bank advisory team authored a study outlining the basic elements of a stabilization program.[25] Hurtado made his first move in that direction in the form of currency devaluations in March and May 1982. Like Roldós's gas hike, Hurtado's action broke the long-standing political taboo against devaluation; Ecuador's exchange rate of twenty-five sucres to the U.S. dollar had been frozen since 1970. The May measures devalued the sucre by 33 percent and combined with other measures to restrict imports. The economic indicators found in table 6 show the growing problems facing the Ecuadorean economy by 1982.

International banks shut down credit flows to Latin America in the wake of the Falkland Islands–Malvinas War and Mexico's debt moratorium in the summer of 1982. By September 1982, Hurtado and his economic team were convinced that there was no practical alternative but to continue with austerity. Hurtado saw this as an essential part of laying the groundwork for a successful renegotiation of the debt with the IMF and private creditors.[26]

With Congress in recess, Hurtado went forth with a wide-ranging set of measures to increase central government revenues. This included new taxes on beer, cigarettes, and cars. Gas prices were raised and the wheat subsidy was eliminated.

Although Hurtado pledged some compensation for the price increases through modest salary increases, widespread public protest greeted the October package. The FUT staged demonstrations and convoked a twenty-four-hour national strike. Hurtado responded to the escalating street politics by declaring a state of emergency; and talks between labor leaders and the government led to a softening of some measures and a peaceful denouement of a serious conflict.[27]

TABLE 6

ECUADOR: SELECTED ECONOMIC INDICATORS, 1979–84

Short-Term Indicators (growth rates)	*1979*	*1980*	*1981*	*1982*	*1983*	*1984*
GDP	5.3	4.2	3.8	1.1	−1.2	4.5
Per capita GDP	2.3	1.3	0.8	−1.8	−4.0	1.6
Real minimum wage	21.1	71.6	−13.8	−9.7	−8.3	−1.7
Consumer prices (Dec. to Dec.)	9.0	14.5	17.2	24.4	52.5	25.1
Fiscal deficit/total expenditure of government	18.1	20.9	33.8	28.8	18.7	6.4
Fiscal deficit/GDP	2.2	3.4	5.8	4.5	2.5	0.8
Debt (in millions of dollars)						
Total external debt	3,554	4,652	5,868	6,186	6,690	6,949
Total external debt (as percentage of exports of goods plus services	174.4	162.3	201.4	230.0	253.1	230.1
Service (as percentage of exports of goods plus services)	66.6	49.2	73.4	73.8	34.2	35.6

Source: Statistics are taken from United Nations Economic Commission for Latin America and the Caribbean, *Economic Survey of Latin America and the Caribbean, 1985* (Santiago: United Nations, 1987), 288, 303.

A third phase in the adjustment and stabilization program came in March 1983. The sucre was devalued by 27 percent and a new system of automatic "minidevaluations" was created to adjust the exchange rate on a daily basis. The effect of these devaluations on the private sector was mitigated by the "sucretization" of the privately held external debt. Through the sucretization program, the Central Bank assumed responsibility for private firms' external debt in exchange for their assumption of a sucre debt to the Central Bank.

With an austerity program firmly in place, Hurtado's economic team entered talks with its international creditors. A new standby agreement with the IMF was followed by a deal with private creditors to consolidate and reschedule debt obligations in September 1983.

Hurtado's tenure as president set a new tone in Ecuador's political economy. Through his public pronouncements and his stabilization measures, Hurtado sent a clear message to the public that the golden age of the oil boom was over. In his first television address to the nation after Roldós's death, Hurtado laid out a new message of austerity:

We have become used to spending beyond the proportions and possibilities of our national economy. It is necessary to return to the limits of our economy, it is necessary to return to the austerity of the 1960s, it is necessary to come to the conclusion that the petroleum is *finished* and as a consequence, we must forget the lavish spending that characterized the 1970s.[28]

For the first time in a decade, notions of fiscal restraint and austerity were introduced into the political lexicon of elites and the mass public. But it is also important to note that economic management under Hurtado focused on short-term stabilization measures; that is, its major concern was crisis management, not a dramatic restructuring of the economy. Neither Hurtado nor his economic team called into question the principle of state intervention; Hurtado's measures did not significantly reduce the state's regulatory capacities or its presence in the economy as a whole.[29] Moreover, in other policy spheres, Hurtado's commitment to an activist state was plainly in evidence. In his parting speech to Congress in 1984, Hurtado credited his administration with fomenting the development of over four thousand new unions and popular organizations in rural areas.[30]

Like Morales Bermúdez and Siles, the Hurtado administration acknowledged the fiscal constraints on state activism and attempted to curb the spending policies that were the legacy of the 1970s. But, just like his Andean counterparts, he did not make a complete policy or ideological break with that past. His administration was the target of deep animosity from antistatist advocates in business organizations and rightist parties. As in Peru under Morales Bermúdez and as in Bolivia under Siles, the economic crisis and the pain of stabilization in Ecuador laid the groundwork for a conservative electoral victory and the launching of an alternative economic model cast along neoliberal lines.

Part 2: Casting the Coalitions

So far, our analysis has focused on the conditions leading up to the formation of neoliberal coalitions in the Central Andes, taking into account both the long-term structural developments and the immediate conjuncture that preceded the launching of the neoliberal experiments. Before proceeding into the second half of our story, let us briefly summarize the central themes of our argument.

First, we pointed to the surge in antistatist ideology among business groups in the 1970s as the domestic bourgeoisie evolved and reacted to the respective military governments of the period. Second, the ensuing economic crisis of the late 1970s and early 1980s strengthened a growing consensus in business circles that it was time to challenge the state-centric model. This position was reinforced by international actors whose influence in the domestic policy-making environment was heightened as the debt crisis developed. Third, the political transition from authoritarianism to democracy (a process in which business interest group leaders played an important part) opened up opportunities for antistatists to vie with each other for policy-making positions, through the electoral process and through the jockeying for appointments that accompanied it.

So, we have established both motive (to lift a phrase from murder mysteries) and opportunity for some of the important protagonists of our story—domestic capitalists. But how did domestic capitalists come together with politicians and technocrats to form neoliberal coalitions? How did the antistatist sentiments held by business elites first turn into collective political action and eventually translate into concrete policies aimed at restructuring the politicoeconomic system?

Let us now turn our attention to the actual formation of the neoliberal coalition, that is, the concrete processes through which dominant social groups became linked with political power brokers.[31] Elections triggered the process of alliance building; the campaigns and the pact making that ensued became crucibles for the development of the neoliberal coalitions.

Peru: From Cordiality to Pact

As the presidential and congressional campaign unfolded in 1979, antistatists in the Peruvian business community could look to at least three political parties as possible electoral vehicles for their point of view—Partido Popular Cristiano (PPC), Acción Popular (AP), and Alianza Popular Revolucionaria Americana (APRA). Each party had its liabilities as a standard-bearer for antistatists; yet, each could count on loyal partisans in the business community, who were often attached to a party on the basis of personalistic or clientelistic ties. Close cooperation between PPC and AP—prior to and immediately after the election of Fernando Belaúnde Terry—was the foundation of the neoliberal coalition in Peru.

Of the three parties, PPC emerged as the most outspoken critic of the statist economic model to develop under Velasco's military government. Prior to 1968, PPC was still a minor party; it was formed in 1966 after a split within the Partido Demócrata Cristiano (PDC). During Velasco's tenure, PPC consistently attacked the growth of state power; it denounced virtually every initiative of the Velasco government, ranging from agrarian reform to the creation of the social property sector of the economy. It also made frequent calls for a return to the constitution and civilian rule. Cordial relations developed between PPC and AP. In the wake of the government takeover of the major newspapers, PPC joined with AP to push for a return of the confiscated papers to their owners.[32]

The AP decision not to participate in the constituent assembly of 1978–79 allowed PPC to assume the position of unequivocal representative of the center right throughout the deliberations. With the encouragement of business interest groups, the PPC delegation pushed the constitutional plank that defined Peru as a social market economy and enshrined business pluralism as a legal principle.

Luis Bedoya, one of the original founders of PPC and an aggressive antistatist rhetorician, became the party's presidential nominee for the 1980 contest. On the campaign trail Bedoya, in no uncertain terms, laid out his commitment to restructuring state-market relations. He started his television campaign with the following attack on the military's economic model:

> Where the revolution went wrong, more than any other sphere, was in economics. It drove the country through a process of *estatización* [''statization''] where the capital of the state substituted that of the private sector . . . driving away, creating disincentives, and punishing private sector initiatives. We will rectify this, defending the social market economy—and within that, private initiative.

Bedoya's antistatist rhetoric was laced with technomanagerial talk: ''To direct a country is to manage the most extraordinary of enterprises,'' or ''Government today is a technique and a science.'' Such discourse was designed not only to appeal to dominant-class groups but to members of the bureaucratic-technical strata of the middle and upper-middle classes.[33]

Bedoya's candidacy attracted business support, especially from important members of the SNI. During the Morales Bermúdez government, Bedoya had been highly critical of the lack of private sector representation in the cabinet. Bedoya strongly supported Gabriel Lanata, a businessman with close ties to the SNI, during his brief tenure as minister of industry in 1978. During the conflict that developed between Lanata and the finance minister Silva Ruete, Bedoya defended Lanata and referred to him as the administration's ''guarantee to the private sector.''[34]

The PPC platform drawn up for the 1980 election clearly situated the party on the right of the political spectrum. It reiterated the antistatist themes that had already been articulated by Bedoya. Here is a portion of the economic analysis put forth in the one-hundred-page document:

> The last decade has been characterized by a reduction of the sphere of the market (due to the recent direct intervention of the state in production and investment) and a severe deformation of its function (due to erroneous state intervention in the area of business's property rights, labor policy, and tariff policy). The consequence of this evolution is the deepening of a ''rent economy'' in which the market functions less and more imperfectly and in which political decisions supplant the market in the assignment and distribution of resources. This explains the lack of dynamism in the national economy, which contributes to poverty, and the decline of economic development over the last decade.[35]

The PPC program was written by a team of U.S.-trained professional economists who were ardent critics of the ''mercantilist'' state and the ''rent-seeking'' behavior among capitalists. Among the team members were Iván Rivera and Jorge González Izquierdo, who had both undertaken postgraduate work in economics at the University of Chicago. Joining them were Jorge Vega and Ruffino Cebrecos who were educated, respectively, at Boston University and Cornell. After the plan was completed, PPC party leaders also consulted with Richard Webb, the Harvard-trained economist who later became Belaúnde's director of the Central Bank.

Prior to working on the PPC program, Jorge González Izquierdo, with Daniel Schydlowsky and Roberto Abusada, coauthored a book that presaged some of the neoliberal program of the Belaúnde government. The work, commissioned by ADEX, strongly emphasized the need to develop exports; it suggested opening up the national market to imports as an anti-inflationary measure. The book also urged introducing more flexibility into labor laws and maintaining wage increases in line with productivity. In announcing the publication of the work, ADEX declared it to be a summary of its own policy recommendations.[36]

Even at this early stage of the making of the neoliberal coalition, the positions struck in the ADEX document penned by the three economists underscored contradictions that were taking shape in the neoliberal coalition. Domestic capitalists in all sectors wanted to see the state's penetration into the economy and its regulatory capacity scaled down; they also desired the reversal of what they saw as overly protective labor laws. But in other policy areas—on tariff structure, for example—there was considerable divergence of interest among business elites and technocrats. These divergences became more visible as Belaúnde's economic program unfolded and eventually undermined the coalition base of the Belaúnde program (see chapter 6).

As the party system developed during the 1979–80 campaign, PPC emerged as the major voice for business interests as well as the major magnet for capitalists seeking political office. Social and economic data on PPC congressional deputies confirm that they were drawn from the most privileged circles of Peruvian society and are closely tied to large enterprises. In a survey of congressmen elected in 1980, 100 percent of PPC deputies reported holding high managerial positions in industrial or mining firms. Despite PPC's strong probusiness position and the ties that developed between individual businessmen and the party, the business sector's corporate organizations (SNI, ADEX, and so on) refrained from throwing their institutional support to PPC. Instead, SNI and ADEX urged parties to come to a consensus on economic objectives and to promote *concertación* between the incoming government and the private sector.[37]

Fernando Belaúnde and his AP also enjoyed some ties to important groups inside the Peruvian business elite. The embryonic industrial bourgeoisie had been a major supporter of Belaúnde's modernization drive during his first presidency (1965–68); and a number of important AP leaders were important businessmen. The young technocrats who had served in the first Belaúnde administration had gone on to work in international business and banking circles. Manuel Ulloa, Belaúnde's last finance minister, spent his exile working with the First Bank of Boston. Belaúnde's Central Bank manager, Carlos Rodríguez Pastor, took a position with the Wells Fargo Bank of California. Pedro Pablo Kuczynski was an executive with Halco Mining in the United States and was a partner in the investment bank of Kuhn Loeb. Thus, important figures within AP did have important ties to segments of the domestic elite and international banking circles.

Still, the overall makeup of AP leadership remained more diverse than that of PPC with more middle-class activists. The presence of more middle-class members in the party can be traced to the populist origins of AP. When it was founded in 1956, Belaúnde had fashioned the party as an alternative to APRA. But clientelism was a key element in the building of AP, as it was in APRA, and as was the personality cult that developed around Belaúnde himself.

The third alternative for conservatives lay in APRA. After the death of APRA founder, Víctor Raúl Haya de la Torre, in 1979, the party split into two competing factions. On one side stood Armando Villanueva, a longtime party bureaucrat who identified with the early leftist thrust of the party. Contesting Villanueva's bid for power was Andrés Townsend. Townsend represented the right wing of APRA, taking a tough anticommunist and probusiness stand. Townsend's rightist credentials included his participation, along with Mario Vargas Llosa and other conservatives, in the founding of Hernando de Soto's Instituto Libertad y Democracia (ILD).

But Townsend did not capture the party's presidential nomination. Instead, to avoid an official split, a compromise was reached that placed Villanueva at the top of the ticket with Townsend in the vice-president's slot. The compromise proved disastrous, however, as Villanueva and Townsend sniped at each other throughout the campaign. Given this organizational and ideological disarray, APRA was perhaps the least appealing nonleftist option to businessmen and antistatist advocates seeking a political vehicle in 1980. Nonetheless, individual businessmen and the large economic groups cultivated their connections to APRA during the campaign in an effort to ensure some level of access to the government should APRA win. Such a win seemed likely, given that an important segment of the military (including General Morales Bermúdez) favored an APRA succession—seeing it as a way to contain the growth of the left.[38]

At the beginning of the electoral campaign in 1979, Luis Bedoya urged the formation of a PPC-AP-APRA alliance, and although a united electoral front never materialized, AP and PPC leaders were cordial throughout the campaign. In September 1979, Manuel Ulloa of AP proposed the formation of a "Pacto de Punto Fijo" among the mainstream parties to ensure democratic and economic stability after the transition was completed.[39] Ulloa's use of the name Punto Fijo was a direct reference to the 1958 agreement drawn up among Venezuela's three major parties; the agreement was struck at the conclusion of the Pérez Jiménez military dictatorship and pledged the parties' support for democracy and mutual power sharing. Thus, even before Belaúnde's victory, Ulloa was sending strong signals that AP was interested in close cooperation with other parties on the center right. After Belaúnde's win in May 1980, AP established a Punto Fijo commission that was charged with managing interparty relations. As part of the effort to forge a progovernment majority in Congress, the commission offered cabinet positions to PPC and held discussions with APRA.

With Bedoya and PPC clearly situated on the right of the spectrum, Belaúnde chose to play on the populist themes reminiscent of his early political career. Trained as an architect, Belaúnde had always been fascinated with public works; and now he promised massive new construction programs to voters. Belaúnde also played on the democratic image of AP, its resistance to the military governments and its refusal to collaborate in elongating the transition through the constituent assembly process. On the economic front, Belaúnde was studiously vague. Indeed, AP issued no detailed economic program during the campaign.

Belaúnde's victory in May 1980 surprised political analysts and the public. He took a commanding 46 percent of the vote. APRA's Villanueva pulled a disappointing 27 percent; and Bedoya trailed behind with only 10 percent. The overall vote for parties of the left also fell off from their previous performance in 1978, coming to just 17 percent of the vote. Given Belaúnde's commanding lead in the first round of the election, Villanueva decided to forgo a runoff and he conceded defeat.

The period between Belaúnde's election and his inauguration (May–July 1980) was the crucial "foundational moment" of the neoliberal coalition—that is, it was the period during which the loose antistatist movement (the individuals and groups scattered across civil society) came together through a concrete political pact engineered between AP and PPC. The neoliberal coalition combined party leaders, business constituents lodged in parties and interest groups, and orthodox economic technocrats. The pact was forged as a vehicle to provide political support as well as programmatic direction for the Belaúnde government.

For AP, the pact was a necessity. Despite Belaúnde's impressive personal victory, AP had not won a majority of congressional seats and it needed to establish an alliance to ensure that Congress would not emerge as a stumbling block to the new government. Belaúnde was particularly sensitive to the obstructionist role that an opposing legislature could assume; bitter executive-legislative conflicts were one of the many problems that had undermined his first presidency.[40] As Ulloa's earlier Punto Fijo overtures demonstrated, AP was anxious to seal a pact with PPC. PPC agreed and took two ministries in Belaúnde's first cabinet.

This political deal between AP and PPC had profound implications for the course of economic policy. The AP-PPC pact set the stage for a fusion of ideological positions and a transfer of technical expertise between the two parties. AP's lack of a concrete economic program allowed for a transfer of ideas from the shadow economic team of PPC, which had been assembled during the political campaign. Manuel Ulloa (Belaúnde's designated finance minister and prime minister) facilitated the transfer. Ulloa was already predisposed toward many of the recommendations floated by economists close to PPC. His own background in international banking and his desire to assure a flow of credit from organizations such as the World Bank made him interested in the favored orthodox formulas (opening up the economy to imports, for example, and the promotion of exports).

The outline of Belaúnde's experiment was hammered out in meetings behind closed doors and through an exchange of memoranda within a small circle of technocrats chosen by Ulloa. Among the players were Richard Webb, who had agreed to become the director of the Central Bank; Roberto Abusada, a Cornell-trained economist, who was brought in to serve as vice-minister of commerce; the two University of Chicago-trained economists Iván Rivera and Jorge González Izquierdo; and Brian Jensen, a former manager from Wells Fargo Bank. Consultations between Ulloa and World Bank personnel were an important part of this first phase of policy formulation. As Richard Webb later pointed out, the World Bank perspective was already well known and widely accepted within the team; both Webb and Abusada had worked in various capacities with the Bank.[41]

The Neoliberal Coalition. We discuss the neoliberal program itself in detail in chapter 6. For now, we want to draw attention to the similarities in the processes through which neoliberal coalitions were formed in Peru, Bolivia, and Ecuador. As we have just seen in the Peruvian case, cooperation among parties of the center right was a critical factor in launching the neoliberal experiment. This cooperation provided the executive with the political clout to undertake the program and bred an important cross-fertilization of ideas on the right. The pact succeeded in bringing neoliberals together in a concrete set of working relationships, that is, by virtue of their positions within the executive branch, technocrats and party leaders were empowered to use the policy instruments at their disposal to launch the restructuring of state-market relations. Another crucial point, one that will become more evident as we examine Bolivia and Ecuador, is the multiplicity of roles that technocrats play in the making of these coalitions. On one level, through their role as "experts," technocrats act as ligaments—attaching dominant-class groups, interest associations, and parties to governmental power. They distill the "interests" of these groups and carry them into the inner circles of policy making. At the same time, they are more than the simple conduits for interests. Technocrats also bring theoretical approaches and worldviews to the policy process, which inform how they conceptualize what is in the "national interest." Their theoretical predispositions, in turn, may bring them into conflicts with different interest groups over what policies indeed are in the "national interest."

As all three of our cases show, technocrats play a crucial "bridging" function in the process of coalition formation, weaving together ideas, interests, and organizations. In the Ecuadorean and Bolivian cases, individual businessmen also emerged in these bridging roles—using their vision and leadership to tie interest groups to parties, and ultimately to executive power.

Bolivia: Business Opposition and the Rightist Revival

No brief discussion can do justice to the complexity and drama of Bolivian politics from 1982 to 1985. In many ways, the tribulations of the Siles government were reminiscent of those faced by President Salvador Allende of Chile from 1970 to 1973.[42] In both countries, class conflict and social mobilization reached unprecedented levels. And like Allende, Siles was the man in the middle of this upheaval; Siles headed an unwieldy center-left coalition that cracked under the strains exerted by labor, business, and international creditors. Siles was ultimately able to avoid Allende's tragic fate, but he was forced into an early retirement from office. As in Chile, the economic crisis that unfolded in this period set the stage for the neoliberal experiment that was to follow. Chile and Bolivia stand together as cases of the most draconian economic restructuring in contemporary Latin America.[43]

We described the contours of the economic crisis and the policies pursued by Siles previously (see part 1 of this chapter). Here we would like to consider how the crisis accelerated the development of the neoliberal coalition in Bolivia. The anxieties and frustrations that were already building inside the domestic bourgeoisie reached an apogee during the Siles period. The crisis atmosphere that prevailed between 1982 and 1985 was in a number of ways crucial to the process of coalition building. First, the crisis united all sectors of the domestic bourgeoisie in a common project of opposition to the Siles government. As part of the project of opposition, the bourgeoisie (especially CEPB) intensified its organizational efforts and increased its capacity to engage in class mobilization. Second, the crisis was used by the opposition to discredit the left and labor as economic managers; the depth of the crisis called into question the entire state-centric development model. This eclipse of the left opened up new space for parties of the right to contest the 1985 election. In short, the crisis electrified the domestic bourgeoisie; fears about the future of private enterprise threw business groups and the political right into new efforts to gain political power and to recast the policy-making environment.

From the start, the CEPB was skeptical of the Siles administration (see chapter 4). The CEPB's acceptance of the Siles presidency was based on the notion that there was no alternative. CEPB leaders believed that a transition to civilian rule was imperative and that any attempt to deny the center left's claim on the presidency would jeopardize the transition altogether. But it did not take long for the CEPB's discomfort with Siles to turn into outright hostility. By February 1983, just three months after Siles's inauguration, the CEPB was complaining of government attacks on the private sector. The CEPB's opposition revolved around what its leaders saw as Siles's excessive attentiveness to the demands made by labor (the COB) and the extreme left of his UDP coalition, the PCB.

That Siles had ceded great influence to both COB and PCB was not an exaggeration; they had a profound effect on the conduct of economic policy. The COB exercised veto power over Siles's successive stabilization programs. James Malloy and Eduardo Gamarra describe the near ritual process that surrounded Siles's attempt to implement stabilization packages:

> Over the next three years [1982–1985] a drama with minor variations was played out repeatedly. A designated economic team within the government would devise an austerity package, usually guided mainly by how the package would sit with the IMF and other interested international actors. In pursuit of consensus Siles would submit the package to the cabinet, which usually transformed it into a much watered down version that was issued by decree. The COB immediately attacked the package as being antipopular and restated its own growing set of demands. The packages as well as the COB's reactions set off further negative reactions from other groups and segments, which immediately mounted their own defensive positions. The government, battered from all sides, usually gave concessions to the COB and other naysayers, which not only weakened the policy even more but also provoked reactions from yet other groups like the CEPB and regional *comités cívicos*.[44]

According to his economic advisers, Siles's willingness to accede to COB demands was based on his belief that the government had to secure a pact with the COB in order to govern. This was—in the words of one cabinet member, Flavio Machicado—the "reigning myth" of the Siles government. Siles's efforts to secure COB cooperation on economic policy went as far as offers of *co-gobierno,* that is, offers of cabinet positions to COB officials. The COB, however, refused the offer.[45]

From the CEPB perspective, Siles had extended a carte blanche to an increasingly unruly working class. The PCB's control over the ministry of labor was seen as a fundamental threat to the private sector. The CEPB denounced the ministry's failure to incorporate private sector representatives into the wage negotiations it oversaw and charged the ministry with a violation of the principles of tripartite bargaining. The CEPB blamed the ministry and the PCB for inciting workers to take over facilities during labor conflicts. CEPB leaders believed that the takeovers were part of a larger plan to nationalize enterprises. In repeated public pronouncements, the CEPB warned of the government's plan to *comibolizar* the country's productive apparatus (that is, turn companies into state enterprises, à la COMIBOL).[46]

The increasing incidence of labor conflict was perhaps the most worrisome development to domestic capitalists. There was a significant increase in the number of workplace disruptions during the UDP government. In 1981, Bolivia registered 31 industrial disputes; in 1982, there were 301. As hyperinflation took off in 1984, the number of industrial disputes totaled 500. Strike activities not only affected private enterprises but paralyzed important offices in the public sector, including Bolivia's Central Bank.[47] In addition, the COB called a total of nine general strikes under Siles.

Strikes were just one component of the intensive mass mobilization that took place during this time. Roberto Laserna reports that there were roughly 53 "collective action events" (such as strikes, marches, takeovers, blockades) per month during the Siles administration. In fact, 1,799 such events took place from 1982 to 1984 (see table 7). This means that 40 percent of all collective political action that took place in Bolivia in the period between 1970 and 1984 occurred during Siles's term in office. Regional-based events were an important subgroup of this increasing collective action. A total of 15 provincial and 16 department "civic strikes" were staged between October 1982 and December 1984; hunger strikes, marches, and road blockades brought the number of regional events sponsored by local civic committees to a total of 51 for that period.[48]

Siles balked at using repressive tactics to deal with the popular protests; he believed that such a response was antithetical to democratic principles and that the preservation of the constitutional order was his foremost responsibility. In explaining his position Siles remarked, "I don't care if I'm judged as indecisive or a bad administrator. What's important to me is having my hands clean of

TABLE 7

COLLECTIVE PROTESTS IN BOLIVIA, 1970–85

Government	*Months in office*	*Number of events*	*Monthly average*
Ovando/Torrés	19.6	705	35.8
Banzer	82.9	876	10.5
Pereda/Padilla	12.5	265	21.2
Guevara/Gueiler	11.4	346	30.4
García Meza/Vildoso	26.7	473	17.7
Siles Zuazo	33.9	1,799	53.1
Total	187.2	4,464	23.9

Note: The "events" measured in the table include regional and departmental civic strikes, road blocks, marches, demonstrations, and hunger strike.

Source: Figures are taken from Roberto Laserna, "La protesta territorial (La acción colectiva regional y urbana en una coyuntura de crisis democratica)," in *Crisis, democracia, y conflicto social: La acción collectiva en Bolivia: 1982–1985,* ed. Roberto Laserna (Cochambaba: CERES, 1985), 226.

repression and that history recognizes the extent of my commitment that Bolivia continue to be a land of free men.''[49]

From the perspective of the domestic bourgeoisie, the threat posed by this undisciplined left and labor movement was real. By 1984, the convulsive state of the society and economy placed Bolivia at the brink of what Guillermo O'Donnell terms ''a crisis of social domination, i.e., a situation in which disruptions in the capital accumulation process are accompanied by lower class behavior that undermines the social relations upon which the capitalist order is built.''[50] In short, the future of the capitalist order seemed to be at stake. The COB made its revolutionary intentions explicit in September 1984 when it issued its emergency plan; it called for the installation of socialism and a popular democracy. To the domestic bourgeoisie, these were not just slogans; they were the confirmation of the bourgeoisie's worst fears about the COB.

The domestic bourgeoisie responded to the lower-class mobilization with a mobilization of its own. The CEPB, under the leadership of Fernando Illanes, struck a combative stance and launched virulent attacks on the Siles government and the COB. The press and public forums were the principal instruments used by the CEPB in its effort to put pressure on the Siles government and undo the left. But other pressure tactics emerged in the course of the conflict. In February 1984, the CEPB called a forty-eight-hour business strike to protest the government's conduct of economic policy. Another day-long business halt was staged in September 1984 to protest the murder of a prominent businessman by a worker; the CEPB cast the homicide as a class attack on the private sector.

As these business strikes indicate, the CEPB placed a new emphasis on directly mobilizing its membership during this period. Like other groups in Bolivian society at this time, the CEPB became organizationally hyperactive. In 1983 and 1984, the CEPB called a series of ''extraordinary assemblies'' and conferences to discuss the economic situation and its policy recommendations. A newsletter, *El Empresario* (The Businessman), was launched in order to communicate regularly with CEPB members. The number of organizations affiliated with the CEPB also rose in this period.

As president of the CEPB, Fernando Illanes sought a new organizational sophistication for the CEPB. He created a professional staff, installed a computer in the office, and hired economists to act as consultants. He was concerned with the public image of the group; he contracted a public relations firm to correct the ''distorted image of the private sector'' and commissioned a Gallup poll to tap public opinion on issues close to the CEPB. A high-ranking member of the CEPB described the upsurge in activity during the Siles period:

> The fight was clearly identified. You had an enemy—socialism. And Mr. Siles represented something that we didn't want because he was out to get our heads and wipe us out. . . .

Everybody rallied around Fernando Illanes . . . and we put up money, we hired economists, we hired lawyers. And we created a staff for the CEPB, and a budget.[51]

In the minds of CEPB leaders, the struggle during the Siles years was a heroic moment—a time of frenzied activity done with the aim of saving Bolivia from complete social and economic disintegration.

The expertise provided by the economists allowed the CEPB to cast its policy positions in more technocratic terms. In 1983, the staff began work on macroeconomic modeling.[52] In 1984, Illanes presented a policy paper to President Siles that provided a detailed outline of the CEPB's program for economic recovery. The program contained forty-five specific proposals on monetary, fiscal, labor, and trade issues. What the document reveals is the extent to which a consensus on economic restructuring was being developed inside the CEPB. Indeed, many of the recommendations made by the CEPB presaged the neoliberal measures that were enacted under the subsequent government of Víctor Paz Estenssoro. In keeping with its strong antistatist stance, the document identified state expansion as the principal source of Bolivia's problems:

The state, overblown and inefficient, has taken away resources from productive activity and generated within itself an unhealthy situation of disguised unemployment. This deformation is reflected, on the economic side, by a deficit and substantial losses that are covered by inorganic emission, provoking the inflation that, in the final analysis, is the most unjust tax that the state collects from Bolivians.[53]

Along with a freeze on public sector growth and deficit reduction, the document recommended other stabilization measures and deregulatory policies. These included (1) the elimination of price controls, especially on agricultural products; (2) the elimination of consumption subsidies; (3) the introduction of more flexible labor laws. The document also urged a renegotiation of the external debt so as to reestablish the flow of international credit to Bolivia.

By the second quarter of 1984, the Bolivian economy had become a textbook case of hyperinflation. Between March 1984 and August 1985, the average monthly rate of inflation was 46 percent. The annual average for 1984 was 1,281.4 percent; in 1985, inflation reached a staggering 11,749.6 percent.[54]

By September 1984, forces on all sides of the political spectrum were clamoring for an end to the Siles government, although it was unclear how such a change could be engineered without endangering civilian rule. The COB and the left had failed in its attempt to push Siles into an auto-coup (an executive-led coup) through which he would shut down Congress and enact the COB's emergency plan by executive decree. The two major parties, Banzer's ADN and Paz Estenssoro's MNRH, had also been unsuccessful in their efforts to remove Siles through a *golpe constitucional* (an impeachment of Siles followed by a succession by Vice-President Jaime Paz Zamora).

The impasse was resolved through the intervention of the Catholic church. The National Conference of Bishops called a conference of parties and interest groups in November 1984 to "find a way out of the crisis and save the country."[55] Out of these meetings came an agreement on a proposal floated by ADN to schedule early elections in June 1985. Siles accepted the idea, which allowed him to maintain the principles of constitutionality while making possible an immediate political fix to end his wounded presidency. The COB and leftist parties opposed the deal, knowing that leftist parties would fare poorly because in the minds of voters they were associated with the UDP government.

The early election deal undoubtedly favored the two parties on the right, Banzer's ADN and Paz Estenssoro's MNRH. Both had virulently opposed the Siles government; and they could easily cast themselves as the only alternatives to save Bolivia from the disastrous policies enacted by the left. Both parties were perfectly positioned to play on popular disillusion and frustration with the conduct of the left.

ADN made no bones about classifying itself as a party of the right in 1985. The party was founded in 1978, as a political vehicle for the ex-dictator Hugo Banzer. At the leadership level, the party attracted a broad range of activists who were previously associated with the Banzer government. At least three sorts of individuals were found within the upper ranks of ADN: (1) professional politicians who had defected from other parties to serve during the Banzer administration; (2) notable businessmen who had served in Banzer cabinets; (3) young technocrats who had manned a variety of bureaucratic positions in the Banzer administration.

In the years immediately following its formation, such individuals gravitated toward ADN because of their personal ties and loyalties to Banzer himself. Many high-ranking party militants openly described themselves as *banzeristas*. But this personalism was coupled with a push by Banzer to develop the party as the principal voice for the Bolivian right. Like the Peruvian PPC, ADN adhered to the notion of *economia social del mercado*. The party also reinforced its sober image by signing an accord with the U.S. Republican party.

The other option for conservatives lay in Víctor Paz Estenssoro's MNRH, the product of Paz's decision to lead the populist MNR into an alliance with the Banzer dictatorship in 1971. That decision split the party; Siles led the dissident faction of MNR to form his MNR-I. Paz was left with his followers inside MNR, which transmuted into MNRH for the 1985 electoral contest. Paz's part of MNR was still built on a clientele network, which revolved around him. Patronage concerns, not ideology, was the glue that held Paz's MNRH together. The party's clientele was drawn largely from the dependent middle class and the peasantry, but high-profile businessmen were also found in MNR. The most notable *movimientista* from the business community was Gonzalo Sánchez de Lozada, Paz's campaign manager in 1985. A major stockholder in one of Bolivia's largest private mining companies, Compañía Minera del Sur S. A. (COMSUR), Gonzalo Sánchez de Lozada was already an MNRH deputy and his family loyalties to MNR dated from the 1950s. Sánchez de Lozada was a member of the *grupo consultivo* inside the CEPB and was an ardent supporter of Illanes's tough opposition of Siles, and (as we shall see further on) he later emerged as a central architect of Paz's neoliberal experiment. He was a pivotal character in the making of the neoliberal coalition—rallying business elites of the CEPB, technocrats, and the international financial community to support the experiment.

Paz and MNR were the original authors of Bolivia's state-centric model of development starting with the revolution of 1952 (see chapter 2). But by 1985, Paz was personally disenchanted with his legacy to Bolivia. According to one of his closest advisors, Paz was becoming increasingly interested in the idea of economic liberalization and was digesting much of the 1980s' intellectual attack on the welfare state.[56] But whereas Paz entered the 1985 presidential race in an antistatist mood, little of his new thinking was divulged during the campaign. He projected a thoroughly mixed message concerning the policies he would adopt if elected. He reiterated his support of the "nationalist revolutionary" model of a mixed economy based on a coexistence of state, private, and communal sectors. He advocated a "rationalization" of public enterprises while at the same time acknowledging the need to negotiate and work with the trade union movement in promoting economic change. He promised to end hyperinflation by cutting the fiscal deficit, but his promise was short on the specifics of how that would be accomplished.[57] The vagaries in MNR's economic platform fueled speculation during the campaign that an agreement between ADN and MNR was in the making. Following a CEPB-sponsored panel discussion in May 1985, Banzer was reported to have told Paz that he would not be alarmed if MNRH won, given the similarities to the ADN philosophy.[58]

Emerging as an early front-runner in the presidential race, Hugo Banzer sought to refine ADN's economic program and prepare a more detailed agenda for his prospective government. He had already assembled the core of an economic team by January 1985. The team included Ronald Maclean and David Blanco, both graduates from Harvard's Kennedy School and former functionaries in the Banzer administration. Mario Mercado, head of the Emusa mining firm, also joined the deliberations. Internal disagreements within the team led Ronald Maclean to suggest that Banzer and the team hammer out a final consensus through a seminar at the Kennedy School. Banzer agreed and the ADN economic team traveled to Boston. Joining in the seminar were invited political "independents," among them Juan Cariaga. Cariaga, a Bolivian economist and banker, had already been working on a macroeconomic model to cure Bolivian hyperinflation. Harvard participants at the seminar included the American economist

Jeffrey Sachs, who was to play a continuing role in Bolivian economic policy making. Sachs later traveled to Bolivia for further consultations with the ADN team in July. The seminar produced an outline of a neoliberal economic program for Bolivia. On their return home, the ADN team stopped in Washington for informal conversations with World Bank officials; their seminar work was greeted with enthusiasm.[59]

Despite Banzer's attention to economic policy during the campaign, ADN's public relations machine did not reveal the prospective neoliberal shock program to the public. Both Banzer and Paz chose to cast the election more as a retrospective judgment on the Siles government than as a preview of what was to come. Both candidates played on their past associations with economic good times. ADN's economic program was never made public.

After a campaign notable for its excessive spending (particularly on the part of ADN), the elections were held on 16 July 1985. As expected, Banzer edged out Paz by a slight margin, winning 28 percent of the vote to Paz's 26 percent. Parties on the left were punished severely by voters. Jaime Paz Zamora, the candidate of the social democratic MIR and Siles's former vice-president, polled just 8.8 percent of the vote. The candidate of Siles's MNR-I, Roberto Jordan Pando, turned in an embarrassing performance, winning just 4.8 percent of the vote. By constitutional law, Banzer's plurality win automatically threw the elections into Congress for a final decision.

After some intense politicking, Paz emerged as the winner in Congress based on a combination of votes from his own party and the MIR. While Banzer was unhappy with Paz's political horse-trading in Congress, he decided to accept the outcome. Banzer's decision to accept Paz as president laid the basis for a postinaugural political pact between the two parties in October 1985. This *pacto por la democracia* (pact for democracy) pledged legislative cooperation between the two parties and support for Paz's economic program.

Unlike Banzer, Paz had no detailed stabilization program prepared to enact, nor did he have a cohesive and technically competent economic team. A working group had been formed within MNR during the campaign under the direction of Guillermo Bedregal. Whereas Bedregal was an experienced MNR politician, he was not an experienced economist, nor was he especially inclined toward talk of orthodox economic stabilization.

Unhappy with the work of the Bedregal group, Paz moved to assemble an emergency task force to formulate an economic plan, just days after his August inauguration. He turned to Gonzalo Sánchez de Lozada, now an MNRH senator, to head the group. Among the team members were Juan Cariaga (the independent economist who had consulted earlier with ADN) and Fernando Romero (another independent, a businessman and member of the *grupo consultivo* of CEPB). Consulting with the team on the politics of the economic plan were Guillermo Bedregal and Roberto Gisbert, the ministers of planning and government.

The task force was consciously designed to be small, exclusive, and secretive. Paz's idea was to minimize any interference by parties or pressure groups in the formulation of the plan. Paz made it clear to the team that he expected to take harsh stabilization measures and that he was committed to dismantling the state-centric model. For seventeen days, the team worked furiously in the home of Sánchez de Lozada with intermittent visits from Paz. Sánchez de Lozada recalled the advice Paz offered on his visits to the team:

> Paz used to quote Machiavelli, ''Do bad things all at once and do good things little by little.'' So [Paz] kept saying, ''If we don't do this now, we'll never do it. Do it! Do it!'' He kept telling us that people were ready, that they were going to accept it. He'd come in and find us wishy-washy and he'd be hard-line. He kept saying, ''If you are going to do it, do it now. I can't operate twice.''[60]

The team emerged with the neoliberal shock program that President Paz issued as D.S. 21060 on 29 August 1985. (We examine its design and implementation at greater length in chapter 6.)

As in Peru, the making of the neoliberal coalition in Bolivia involved businessmen and technocrats who straddled party and interest group structures; they disseminated new ideas and they brought fellow businessmen, technocrats, and politicians together in new ways. Two individuals are especially notable in these bridging roles in Bolivia: Gonzalo Sánchez de Lozada and Juan Cariaga. Both brought considerable business savvy and technical expertise to the process. Both had close ties to important business and financial circles. Cariaga, a political independent, also had dealings with the ADN economic team and was well acquainted with their proposals for economic stabilization and liberalization. Sánchez de Lozada, MNR militant, was an important voice inside the CEPB. In other words, they occupied strategic positions inside the constituent parts of the neoliberal coalition. By assuming proactive roles, Sánchez de Lozada and Cariaga were able to give form and content to the antistatist consensus that had evolved among various groups in Bolivian society by 1985.

Ecuador: Febres Cordero and the National Reconstruction Front

As in Bolivia, the transition to civilian rule in Ecuador did not yield an immediate political victory for antistatists. Ecuadorean antistatists were forced to tangle with two successive presidents who sought to distance themselves from the right. As in Bolivia, the ensuing business-government conflicts galvanized groups with antistatist sentiments into a more cohesive neoliberal coalition, which brought León Febres Cordero to the presidency in 1984.

The neoliberal coalition emerged in Ecuador in the wake of the electorate's dramatic rejection of the right in the 1979 presidential runoff election. The race pitted Jaime Roldós, a young lawyer of the populist CFP against Sixto Durán Ballén, an ex-mayor of Quito and candidate of the rightist Social Christian party. The Roldós–Durán Ballén runoff finally took place in April 1979 after a long recount process of the July 1978 results; the recount was widely interpreted as the military's way of whittling down Roldós's winning margin and improving Durán Ballén's chances in the second round.

A lack of unity among parties of the right weakened Durán Ballén's electoral bid. Instead of supporting his candidacy in the first round, the Liberal party chose to field its own candidate, Raúl Clemente Huerta. After the unimpressive performance of the rightist candidates in the first round of congressional elections, the right split on its approach to the second round. Some leaders challenged the validity of the results in the electoral court, the Tribunal Supremo Electoral. Although the rightist parties officially endorsed Durán Ballén, support for him was lackadaisical, and his own lackluster personality contributed to the uninspired (and somewhat unorganized) style of the campaign.[61] León Febres Cordero, a Social Christian deputy elect, supplied the anticommunist flavor of the campaign; he frequently drew analogies between Roldós and the deceased Salvador Allende of Chile.

In contrast to the unimaginative campaign on the right, the Roldós campaign was built on multiple strengths. Roldós engineered an alliance with the Christian Democratic party, which placed its leader, Osvaldo Hurtado, on the ticket as vice-president. Like Roldós, Hurtado was a young professional who had served ably in the civilian-led commissions preparing the legal framework of the transition. Together, Roldós and Hurtado represented a generational change in the political class and conveyed the sense that a new politics was under way, a politics untainted by any association with older oligarchic parties. Their campaign slogan was one with a decidedly reformist ring—*fuerza del cambio* (the force of change).

Thus, Roldós's campaign appealed to many of the young first-time voters in the newly expanded electorate who had no previous partisan affiliations. At the same time, he drew on the clientele networks developed through his work with the populist CFP in Guayaquil.[62]

Roldós won a sweeping victory in the second-round race in April 1979. He took 68 percent of the national vote, winning in all but one province. Even on Durán Ballén's home turf of metropolitan Quito, Roldós managed to score 69.6 percent of the Pichincha vote. In Guayas, Roldós fared even better with a smashing 75.9 percent of the vote.[63] In addition to this broad personal mandate for Roldós, CFP won 29 congressional seats out of a total of 69 in the unicameral body. An additional 15 seats won by the social democratic Izquierda Democrática party (ID) appeared to assure that a progressive majority would control Congress. The six parties on the right won only 23 seats.

The seeming triumph of center-left populism was short-lived, however. Fissures inside CFP paved the way for a chronic executive-legislative battle throughout Roldós's first year in office. A political feud over the control of CFP broke out between President Roldós and Assad Bucaram, president of Congress and longtime CFP leader. This intraparty dispute rent CFP's congressional delegation in two rival factions; and the dissolution of the CFP bloc opened the doors for rightist parties to assert themselves. In his struggle to control Congress, Bucaram engineered an alliance with deputies from the Conservative and Liberal parties. With this hybrid alliance in hand, Bucaram forced the Roldós administration to play defense. Roldós had to veto congressional initiatives and devoted much of his energies to managing the political crisis. (Roldós finally broke the impasse by threatening to call a plebiscite on a constitutional reform that would allow him to dissolve Congress and call elections. With the specter of a new election hanging over their heads, the conservatives and liberals drifted out of the Bucaram camp.)[64]

At the same time, leaders on the right began brainstorming on future strategies. Sixto Durán Ballén, a longtime proponent of a unified right, reopened the discussion of pulling parties together into a single electoral front. And the alliance of right-wing deputies in Congress spawned an atmosphere of cooperation that facilitated such discussion.[65] But given the right's long tradition of fragmentation and competition, it was unclear as to which of its leaders as the presidential nominee could hold together an electoral front.

By 1983, León Febres Cordero had emerged as the most likely "agglutinating" personality on the right.[66] His political career was launched with his election in 1979 as a national deputy of the Social Christian party. Educated as an engineer at Stevens Institute in Hoboken, Febres Cordero rose to prominence as a manager of several enterprises in the powerful Noboa group conglomerate of Guayaquil. In the 1970s, Febres Cordero enjoyed public attention as an outspoken president of the Guayaquil Chamber of Industry and president of the National Chamber of Industry, striking a virulently antistatist pose. By 1980, Febres Cordero was clearly staking out an alternative neoliberal model for Ecuador. In an interview in that year, he stated his seven rules to promote Ecuadorean economic development: (1) balance the budget; (2) do not permit the expansion of the money supply to exceed the rate of growth; (3) open Ecuador to foreign capital; (4) eliminate government-owned enterprises; (5) halt politically inspired agrarian reform; (6) stop blaming entrepreneurs for the country's problems; (7) and love Ecuador more.[67]

Febres Cordero sought the advice of technocrats on how to turn his ideas into a more coherent government program. He began informal meetings in 1980 with three *guayaquileños* who were to become the intellectual architects and implementors of his 1984 neoliberal experiment: Carlos Julio Emanuel, Francisco Swett, and Alberto Dahik. All three were young professionals with close ties to the Guayaquil business community. Prior to his appointment as chief of the Guayaquil branch of the government's Banco Central, Emanuel had headed the Banco del Pacífico, a leading bank closely linked to the Noboa economic group. Swett and Dahik had worked as consultants to the Cámara de Comercio de Guayaquil. Like Febres Cordero, all three were educated abroad. Swett and Dahik did their postgraduate work in public policy and economics, respectively, at Princeton University; Emanuel had studied economics at the University of South Carolina. Out of these discussions with Febres Cordero sprang the outline of a program of neoliberal reforms that incorporated many of the policy positions of the Cámara de Comercio de Guayaquil. Swett put together the initial version of the government plan in Febres Cordero's platform for the 1984 presidential race.[68]

As he prepared the neoliberal agenda, Febres Cordero drew increasing media attention with his steady criticism of the government; the attacks accelerated after Roldós's death and Osvaldo Hurtado's succession to the presidency in May 1981. The deterioration of the economy and Hurtado's unpopular stabilization measures made the government an easy target, and Febres Cordero led the assault in Congress. Interpellations and obligatory appearances were used frequently to harass Hurtado's cabinet ministers. The attack by the right was facilitated by the ambiguous pose struck by parties of the left and center left, particularly the social democratic Izquierda Democrática. ID's veering in and out of the opposition at times made for strange bedfellows in Congress. For example, Febres Cordero joined with his arch rival, Rodrigo Borja of the ID, in launching four official investigations of government economic policy in 1981.[69]

The attacks on the government by rightist parties were accompanied by aggressive behavior on the part of business interest groups. During the first wave of the stabilization program in late 1982, the Federation of the Chambers of Industry called for the formation of a new interim government. This came on the heels of Febres Cordero's clearly extraconstitutional call for Hurtado's resignation and his replacement by the president of Congress.[70] In March 1983, the chambers of commerce of Quito and Guayaquil staged business shutdowns. While industrial firms did not join in the action, the chambers of industries endorsed the strike. The actions were taken to protest Hurtado's economic measures, which included a devaluation, tight money policies, and import restrictions.[71]

The assault on the Hurtado government had a clear political motivation; it was launched by rightist parties' leaders with an eye toward positioning themselves for the 1984 race—and perhaps even forcing an early retirement for Hurtado. According to Hurtado and many of his closest advisors, civilian elites made numerous attempts at coup-baiting the military in this period. Hurtado wryly observed in 1983 that "there isn't a cocktail party or a social event where there are members of the armed forces in which some civilians don't try to initiate a conspiracy to overthrow the constitutional regime."[72]

By identifying the economic crisis with parties of the center and left—that is, Hurtado's Democracia Popular (DP) and the parties that veered in and out of alliance with it—rightist leaders sought to capitalize on public discontent and portray the right as the only real opposition. But along with this instrumental political logic, the mobilization against the Roldós-Hurtado governments in this period was fueled by the bourgeoisie's deep anxiety over issues of ideology and influence. Both Roldós and Hurtado identified their governments as reformist. Their presidential rhetoric sent mixed signals to an already hypersensitive bourgeoisie; sometimes they railed against *la oligarquía* and sometimes they seemed to court private sector cooperation on economic matters. Moreover, while important businessmen occupied positions within both Roldós and Hurtado cabinets, they were not perceived as part of the "establishment." A major Quito financier who served as Roldós's minister of finance, Rodrigo Paz reported that, for joining the government, his fellow businessmen referred to him as an *oligarca equivocadó* (a mistaken oligarch).[73]

The enmity between business groups and government reached a zenith during 1982–83 under the Hurtado administration. Notwithstanding Hurtado's conservative moves to stabilize the economy and his enactment of important probusiness measures, business interest groups resented their lack of direct input in policy making and chafed at Hurtado's reproaches. One leader of the Chamber of Industry described the business sector's unease with the Hurtado administration:

> The Hurtado government was very negative toward the private sector in the sense of doubting what we do for the country. The propaganda that you found in most government speeches was a very negative attitude toward the private sector. For example—something that I must say because it bothers me a lot—President Hurtado coined a new term in our lexicon, "Miami Boys." That means you take your money out of the country and buy apartments in Miami and enjoy your money in Miami. So those things were very worrisome to the private sector (and disagreeable to me) because we were trying to present our views all the time on what to do to help the national economy. But with that attitude toward the private sector, the government would not listen to us under any circumstances.[74]

Hurtado made no effort to conceal his personal disdain for business interest groups. He later acknowledged that business attacks on him were fueled by the animosity he projected. According to Hurtado, businessmen "knew they couldn't pick up the phone and give me orders in a country where the government traditionally ruled in consultation with the chambers."[75]

A number of factors allowed the Hurtado government to survive this coup-mongering. First, American officials put out strong signals to the armed forces that the U.S. government would not look favorably upon any move against Hurtado. Second, business leaders were divided among themselves as to how far to pursue hostilities. Finally, professional politicians of all stripes feared that any interruption of the constitution could threaten the scheduling of the 1984 election. This lack of consensus on the right coupled with the military's desire to steer clear of the fray dissipated any potential pro-coup coalition.

With an election on the horizon, groups on the right refocused their energies on campaign strategy. Meetings among rightist party leaders began in early 1983 to discuss the formation of a coalition. Among the party negotiators were congressional deputies such as Blasco Peñaherrera (Partido Liberal Radical [PLR]), Carlos Julio Arosemena (Partido Nacionalista Revolucionario [PNR]), and Eduardo Carmigniani (Partido Social Cristiano [PSC]). Playing the role of the éminence grise was Sixto Durán Ballén. Febres Cordero used his close personal advisors to take an active role in negotiations on his candidacy.

The discussions culminated in the founding of the Frente de Reconstrucción Nacional (FRN) in August 1983. The FRN brought the Conservative, Nationalist Revolutionary, Liberal, Social Christian, and the Institutionalist Democratic parties together in support of Febres Cordero's presidential bid. Joining Febres Cordero on the ticket was Blasco Peñaherrera. FRN unity applied only to the top of the ticket: each party remained free to run its own congressional slate, although some local agreements were struck that gave multiparty support to individual congressional candidates.

According to Blasco Peñaherrera, the FRN was based on a shared attitude by its leaders that it was time to reverse the statist model of economic development in Ecuador. The business community wholeheartedly supported this consensus, and FRN coffers swelled with campaign contributions from business elites. Peñaherrera described the character of the consensus:

> The multiparty agreement had, implicitly and even explicitly, concrete purposes that went beyond personalities and the interests of candidates and its leaders. It was conceived, in short, as the suitable instrument to redesign the model of development that had been implanted in the country during the wave of the petroleum boom and with the support of all-embracing [government] powers (first, of the dictatorships, then of the ''million'' votes). . . . [The model] tried to ''transform'' or at least change Ecuador with inveterate measures used for this effect: pseudo-left populism; partial and frustrating agrarian and tax reforms; expansion of the powers and functions of the state, especially in the economic realm; a broadening of the benefits and rights of employed workers; restrictions on foreign investment in all forms; a more or less open and systematic strangling of entrepreneurial activity.[76]

While Febres Cordero's coalition on the elite level was built on the promise of a probusiness and socially conservative agenda, his rhetoric to the popular classes was built on populist appeals, a large dose of machismo, religious imagery, and regionalism. He charged the Hurtado government with creating "hunger, unemployment, poverty, immorality, and corruption" and mercilessly derided the characters of his opponents, especially Osvaldo Hurtado and Rodrigo Borja.[77]

The electoral prospects of the FRN were greatly enhanced by the lack of cooperation among parties of the center and left. Instead of uniting around a single presidential candidate in the first round, these parties launched seven different nominees. Rodrigo Borja, the front-runner of ID, was forced to run in a crowded field that included presidential candidates from Hurtado's DP, the populist CFP and Frente Radical Alfarista (FRA), and the leftist Movimiento Popular Democrático (MPD).

The first-round race held in January 1984 yielded a slim victory margin for Rodrigo Borja and a second-place finish for León Febres Cordero. Borja took 28.7 percent of the valid vote while Febres Cordero received 27.2 percent. Since no candidate had won a majority, the two top-ranking candidates were slated for a runoff in May 1984. In a deft political move, Febres Cordero reoriented his campaign for the second round. He made his populist appeal even more explicit with the campaign slogan "Pan, techo, empleo" (Bread, housing, employment). In addition, he abandoned the staging of high-profile media events such as demonstrations and opted for a more concerted door-to-door effort in the poor neighborhoods of Guayaquil.

Tensions and rivalries among center-left and left parties continued to undermine the prospects for unity on the second round. With his pollsters projecting an easy win, Borja steadfastly refused to negotiate with other parties on the allocation of posts in his administration. This contributed to a lack of support for Borja from two key parties of the coast, CFP and FRA. CFP officially abstained from supporting Borja in the second round; and after considerable internal disputes, the FRA pledged its support for the "center left" but declined to endorse Borja by name. As a result, CFP and FRA leaders in Guayaquil openly campaigned for Febres Cordero. On the left, PS and MPD also declined to support Borja. Seeking to distance himself from the Hurtado government (and its association with the economic crisis), Borja remained cool to offers of campaign assistance from Hurtado's DP and the allied Partido Demócrata (PD). Only the Frente Amplio de Izquierda (FADI), the left coalition led by the Communist party, actively campaigned on Borja's behalf. Borja's brewing defeat was sealed by the worst decision of his political career: he agreed to a televised debate with León Febres Cordero in the last weeks of the campaign. Febres Cordero used the opportunity to hurl personal slurs at Borja.

Buoyed by Borja's mistakes, Febres Cordero squeezed a narrow victory in the second-round contest in May 1984. He took 51.5 percent of the valid vote nationwide to Borja's 48.5 percent. His winning margin was provided by coastal voters responding to regionalist and populist appeals.

Febres Cordero's victory met with a wide range of reactions. The event so shocked parties of the center and left that they were able to overcome their mutual animosities to form a congressional majority bloc called the *bloque progresista.* The bloc brought congressmen from the ID, DP, FADI, MPD, and PD together in opposition to Febres Cordero's neoliberal project.[78]

In contrast to the congressional reaction, business interest groups were elated at the FRN's win and quickly lined up to endorse the Febres Cordero government. Pedro Kohn, president of the Cámara de Industriales de Pichincha, declared that Febres Cordero's economic program was similar to the "recipe" put forth by the Cámara. The presidents of the commercial and agricultural chambers expressed satisfaction that a man from the private sector would be at the helm of economic policy.[79] In the words of one business-group leader, businessmen regarded Febres Cordero as "one of their own," someone who would be responsive to the business community and assure a stable investment climate.

By 10 August 1984, the day of Febres Cordero's presidential inauguration, the raw materials for the neoliberal experiment were in place. The new administration enjoyed the strong backing of all the major business interest groups in Ecuador. Febres Cordero had prepared a bright economic team dedicated to reasserting the market, and he had extracted a general agreement from the parties of the FRN that gave the team carte blanche on the economy. As head of the executive branch, Febres Cordero had the instruments at his disposal to act on his commitment to the restructuring of the economy. In short, a solid domestic coalition of businessmen, politicians, and technocrats had finally come together and secured a hold over executive power.

Crystallizing Policy Coalitions

A web of anxieties and frustrations brought businessmen, politicians, and technocrats together around the idea of retracting the state from the economy. After the transition to civilian rule was secured, these antistatists threw themselves into electoral politics. Political campaigns became the crucibles in which elites began to hammer out more specific policy prescriptions and to solidify ties among themselves. In each of the three countries, technocrats played a central role in this process. They straddled business interest groups and political parties; they articulated business concerns, but they also injected their own professional views and values into the debates on how best to move from state-centric to market-oriented economics. In all three cases, we have also noted the emergence of "political businessmen" who became advocates for the new antistatism and major players in the making of neoliberal programs—for example, Ulloa, Sánchez de Lozada, and Febres Cordero. Like technocrats, these individuals linked different business interests and linked business groups to parties.

In all three countries, the exact contours of the neoliberal programs that were to come were never revealed to voters during the political campaigns. Candidates on the right pledged to undertake market-oriented policies, but the new promarket rhetoric was mixed with a large dose of populist language. Belaúnde, Paz, and Banzer came to their respective campaigns with the historical baggage of their previous presidencies in tow—the baggage of a populist and statist past. Febres Cordero was the only candidate openly identified with neoliberal thinking, but even his campaign was marked by traditional populist appeals ("Pan, techo, empleo") and plenty of diversionary discourse (personal attacks). These elections were not so much cast as straightforward plebiscites on future policies as they were defined by the antistatist opposition as referenda on outgoing administrations.

With presidential victories in hand, the right turned from rhetoric to the complicated task of enacting and sustaining policies aimed at restructuring the economy. As the track records of the neoliberal experiments show, the political management of the economic projects proved more problematic than that of electioneering. Even among its supporters, antistatism in theory was often more attractive than antistatism in practice.

CHAPTER 6

Theory Into Practice: From Antistatism to Neoliberal Experiments

THE NEOLIBERAL COALITIONS of the Central Andes were built through the concerted efforts of individual leaders from the business community and rightist parties. Emergency meetings, "extraordinary assemblies," protests, and intense public relations activity were all among the methods used by business interest groups to build and strengthen ties among conservative forces. Luncheons and conferences were important occasions for diffusing antistatist perspectives on policy problems, and they served a ritual function of building solidarity among leaders and the rank and file of business organizations.[1]

The problem with the coalitions, however, was that they were built on a vague negative consensus around antistatism; whereas businessmen, capitalists, and technocrats all favored market-oriented reforms, there was no clear agreement among them concerning the precise design of the reforms. Each of the groups came to the coalition with different understandings of what antistatism would actually look like in practice.

How antistatism was translated into a specific package of neoliberal measures varied significantly in the three countries. These variations reflected the peculiarities of each national economic situation, the structure of interests inside the coalitions, and the conflicting imperatives at play inside the executive branch. In Peru and Ecuador, the neoliberal projects eventually unraveled; in Bolivia, the neoliberal project was successfully sustained by the Paz Estenssoro government. In this chapter we examine the launching of the economic experiments and the dynamics of policy making in the initial stages of the programs. In the next chapter, we examine why the neoliberal project was viable in Bolivia when it faltered in Peru and Ecuador. Before analyzing the political management of these economic programs, we begin with a look at the key components in each of the programs and the concerns that shaped policy formulation.

Variations on a Theme: The Policy Axes

The initial programs pursued by Presidents Belaúnde, Febres Cordero, and Paz Estenssoro reflected important differences in the immediate economic and political conjunctures faced by the incoming governments. The initial neoliberal projects differed significantly in the design, breadth, and pacing of the measures. In each country, the axis of the neoliberal program was distinct: exchange rate policy was the cornerstone of the effort in Ecuador whereas trade liberalization dominated the Peruvian mode; the most draconian and speedy restructuring was launched in Bolivia, whereas Peruvian and Ecuadorean policy makers opted for a more gradual and piecemeal approach. (The key features of each program as it was implemented over the first two years of its administration are presented in table 8.)

In Peru. In the months immediately following Belaúnde's election in 1980, the task of assembling an economic team and drafting an economic program in Peru fell to Manuel Ulloa. Belaúnde's choice as finance minister and prime minister, Ulloa enjoyed a carte blanche in the process. True to his usual style, Fernando Belaúnde showed little interest in complicated economic issues; his primary concern was to assure a steady flow of foreign credit to Peru in order to finance development projects. Belaúnde believed that the appointment of Ulloa would facilitate good relations with private creditors and multilateral agencies. Belaúnde's interest in macroeconomics ran so low that there was no attempt to author a comprehensive economic plan for his government prior to his election.

The specifics of the Belaúnde economic program were worked out in private exchanges within Ulloa's technocratic team, most of whom held fairly orthodox views. The monetarist bent of the economic team was reinforced through consultations with World Bank staffers. Belaúnde's dependence on World Bank loans for infrastructure projects insured that the team would be prone to accept Bank and IMF policy advice.

A short-term boom in 1979 based on rising prices for Peru's exports was an influence on the team's overall approach. The dramatic surge in revenues generated by petroleum, copper, silver, and coffee exports remedied the immediate balance-of-payments problem and generated some recovery. Peru's net international reserves recuperated to over $5 billion in 1979; and after two years of negative rates, the GDP rebounded to register a 3.3 percent growth rate in 1979. According to Richard Webb, Belaúnde's appointed president of the Central Bank, the recovery in Peru's balance-of-payments position that resulted from the export boom allowed policy makers to ignore unresolved structural problems in the economy and reinforced the orthodox focus on monetary and fiscal policies.[2] The

TABLE 8

SUMMARY OF INITIAL ECONOMIC PROGRAMS

Policies	*Peru 1980–82*	*Ecuador 1984–86*	*Bolivia 1985–87*
Prices	Removal of controls. Reduction of consumption subsidies on food, gas.	Removal of controls on most items. (Sept. 1984) Reduction of consumption subsidies.	Removal of controls on agricultural products, petroleum, and gas.
Exchange rate	Periodic small devaluations.	Reforms in multiple system. (Sept. 1984) Creation of uniform free market system. (Sept. 1986)	Massive devaluation. Rate set through daily auction system at Central Bank.
Trade liberalization	Tariff reduction from 115 to 60 to 30%.	Tariff reduction to maximum protection of 90%.	Single uniform tariff at 20%.
Foreign capital	New foreign investment statute to modify Decision 24. Major effort to attract foreign capital in mining, oil, banking.	Modifications to Decision 24. Revision in petroleum law to encourage new investment. Agreement with OPIC.	Agreement with OPIC.
Wages	Wage increases kept below rate of inflation.	Wage increase kept below rate of inflation.	Wage freeze
Debt	Negotiations opened with IMF on rescheduling.	Negotiations opened with creditors.	Negotiations opened up with creditors. IMF Standby (June 1986)
Monetary	Increase credit to private sector.	Restrictive; increase interest rates.	Problems in disbursement of reactivation credit; high interest rates.
Taxes	Income tax reduced.	Increased tax.	Tax reform.
State enterprises	No significant privatization.	No significant privatization.	No significant privatization. Restructuring and dismissals at COMIBOL.

team did not anticipate the downturn in international commodities prices that came into play in 1982.

Against the backdrop of this transitory economic upswing, the team fixed its attention on the problem of inflation. Ulloa feared that a buildup of foreign exchange reserves would generate excess liquidity in the banking system and lead to renewed inflation. The concern with the foreign exchange reserves, coupled with a demand-pull perspective on inflation, became paramount in the formulation of economic policy in 1980–81.

Unleashing imports was the method Ulloa fixed on to cure the problem of excess reserves. Continuing with the tariff liberalization already undertaken by the outgoing economic team of Javier Silva Ruete and Manuel Moreyra, the Ulloa team opted for a further dismantling of tariff barriers. The expectation was that the foreign exchange reserves would be burned up in financing imports. But tariff liberalization was not considered solely a short-term anti-inflationary device; it was seen as a pivotal part of the long-term program to restructure the economy. Moreover, trade liberalization had become part of the conditions imposed by the IMF and the World Bank in exchange for loan assistance.[3]

Other measures aimed at deregulating and opening up the economy included relaxing the rules governing foreign investment, stripping away price controls and subsidies, and privatizing state enterprises. While a consensus on the need to take such measures had solidified inside the team, no single comprehensive plan or package was developed. Instead, the neoliberal project evolved through the exchange of ideas and memoranda among team members.

The public got its first taste of the program when Prime Minister Ulloa unveiled the government's initial measures in September 1980. The probusiness slant of the government was clearly in evidence in the increase of credit for the private sector, the income tax reductions, and an aggressive campaign to attract foreign investment through new incentives. The controversial Certificado de Reintegro Tributario a la Exportación (CERTEX), the tax rebate to exporters, was left untouched in the September package. The September measures were deliberately moderate; the slow start on the neoliberal project was probably connected to the municipal elections that were scheduled for November 1980. Rather than arouse controversy, Belaúnde held back on restructuring measures.

Once the municipal race was out of the way (with a strong showing by Belaúnde's AP), Ulloa and his "dynamo" team were free to unleash their more serious restructuring effort in 1981–82. In January 1981, the team enacted substantial hikes on fuel and basic foodstuffs. Even though the hikes had an inflationary effect, they were seen as a necessary component in the team's efforts to "get the prices right," that is, allow prices to find their appropriate levels by reducing government controls. At the same time, Vice-Minister of Commerce Roberto Abusada struck abruptly with a reduction in tariff rates. This was followed in February by reduction and restriction in the application of the CERTEX tax rebates to nontraditional exporters.

Finance Minister Ulloa and Mining Minister Pedro Pablo Kuczynski also moved in early 1981 to entice foreign investors to Peru. New tax incentives were granted to foreign oil companies; this led to the signing of new oil exploration contracts with multinational corporations in 1981–82. Deregulation of the banking system also permitted greater foreign participation in the financial sector.

In his first year in office, Prime Minister Ulloa aggressively sought to cement good relations between Peru and the international financial community. To demonstrate its credibility to lenders, the government repaid $377 million in refinancing credits. The show of good faith and Belaúnde's probusiness image worked, bringing in a flow of $1.7 billion in medium-term credits in 1981–82.[4]

Trade liberalization emerged as the centerpiece of Peru's neoliberal experiment. The economic team looked on tariff liberalization as the cure for a variety of ills: it would eliminate excessive government interference in commerce; it would discipline inefficient import-substituting industries; and it would act as an anti-inflationary measure. The opening of the economy to trade and investment was viewed as the way to guarantee fresh finance from international creditors. In its initial formulation, Peruvian neoliberalism was structured to favor the traditional export sector, finance, and foreign investors.

In Ecuador. The immediate economic circumstances that prevailed in Ecuador in 1984 did not closely parallel those of Peru in 1980. The incoming economic team of the Febres Cordero government was not favored by bonanza conditions in the export sector. On the positive side, the Ecuadorean economy was showing signs of recovery from the downslide of 1982–83. The GDP grew by 3 percent because of improved performance in the agricultural and petroleum sectors. The stabilization measures launched by President Osvaldo Hurtado had cut back the inflation rate by half, bringing it down to 25 percent in 1984. Nonetheless, despite a trade surplus, payments on the external debt were creating an imbalance in Ecuador's current account; the result was a balance-of-payment deficit and a loss of $6 billion in reserves in 1984.[5] Given this weak reserve position, trade liberalization did not emerge as the dominant strand in Ecuador's neoliberal program. Finance Minister Francisco Swett was in no hurry to burn up Ecuadorean reserves by facilitating imports. As our later discussion shows, industrialists were able to lobby effectively to keep tariff reforms moderate.

In Ecuador, exchange rate reforms emerged as the pivot of the neoliberal program. The long-standing manipulation of multiple exchange rates by the central government was viewed as a primary source of distortions in the economy; the dismantling of exchange rate controls was assigned the highest priority by the economic team. Almost immediately after assuming office, Febres Cordero issued the first move toward exchange rate deregulation. On 4 September 1984, multiple exchange rates were collapsed into an official and free-market-intervention system controlled by the Central Bank. At the same time, 70 percent of all private exports were designated "free market" transactions. The rationalization laid the basis for a complete flotation of the exchange rate and the transfer of transactions to the private banking system in August 1986. Interest rates were also freed as part of the August 1986 reform.

Other types of deregulation proceeded alongside the gradual exchange rate reform. In September 1984, price controls were lifted from a wide range of agricultural commodities. Price hikes on gasoline and electricity rates stripped away some consumption subsidies during the first year of the administration.

As in Peru, an essential part of the program by Febres Cordero and his team was conceived to be the attracting of direct foreign investment and fresh international credit. The government moved rapidly during its first year in office to send the right policy signals to U.S. and foreign investors. A new agreement was signed with the Overseas Private Investment Corporation (OPIC) in December 1984. The agreement came in conjunction with a series of measures taken to weaken Ecuador's adherence to Decision 24 of the Cartagena Agreement and facilitate increased foreign participation in petroleum and financial sectors. Negotiations on the rescheduling of the foreign debt yielded agreements with the IMF, the Paris Club, and the Management Committee of Creditor Banks in 1985.

Both the Peruvian and Ecuadorean programs combined immediate stabilization measures with restructuring measures. The measures, however, were not taken simultaneously in a single comprehensive policy package. Instead, the neoliberal program was disaggregated into a series of measures that were spread out over the first two years of the respective administrations. As we see in the next chapter, the two programs were also marked by serious deviations from orthodoxy. Neither Belaúnde nor Febres Cordero were able to control the fiscal deficit; nor did they make significant inroads in restructuring the public sector through cuts or the privatization of state enterprises.

In Bolivia. In contrast to Peru and Ecuador, the incoming government of President Víctor Paz Estenssoro in Bolivia faced catastrophic conditions upon assuming office in August 1985. Bolivia was in the throes of intense hyperinflation and bordered on economic collapse (see chapter 5). There was consensus among Paz and his economic advisors that the new government's response had to be swift and dramatic. The extremity of the situation seemed ripe for shock treatment.

Stopping hyperinflation was the immediate task of the emergency economic team led by Gonzalo Sánchez de Lozada. In the analysis developed by the team, deficit spending by the central government and public enterprises was pinpointed as the immediate cause of the inflation. This focus on the state's lack of fiscal control fit in with the broader view held by Paz and others that the Bolivian state itself was decomposing. In an address to the nation, Paz put it in stark terms. In his view, the country was dying and the economy was in a coma. Sharing that view, Gonzalo Sánchez de Lozada depicted the political and economic crises as closely intertwined:

One comes to the conclusion that the state is practically destroyed. The fundamental institutions of the state's productive apparatus have been feudalized, corruption has been generalized and is being institutionalized, and the mechanisms of oversight have stopped operating. In this context, the state is unarmed and lacks the capacity to execute and implement any economic policy that the government proposes to put into practice. Therefore, the first political goal consists of reestablishing the authority of the state over society.[6]

Acting on the conviction that the erosion of state capacity was at the root of Bolivia's ills, Paz's team formulated a plan of stabilization-cum-liberalization that was designed to restore the authority of the state by making it more efficient. In short, the radical neoliberal package in Bolivia was launched with the idea of creating a ''leaner and meaner'' (a smaller but more effective) state. The program was conceived and presented in a comprehensive package with all measures to be applied simultaneously. It was issued as an executive decree, D.S. 21060.

At the core of Bolivia's *Nueva política económica* (NPE) contained in D.S. 21060 was a series of fiscal correctives aimed at restraining public sector spending over thc short and long haul. Fuel prices were hiked, public enterprise rates were increased, and the government declared a year-long wage freeze. Tax reforms were envisioned as part of the fiscal correction along with tighter budgetary procedures for public enterprises. Along with these measures, D.S. 21060 committed the government to a fundamental restructuring of public sector enterprises. This eventually translated into a drive to cut public employees; especially hard hit was the state mining corporation, COMIBOL, which saw its workforce of nearly thirty thousand decreased by twenty-three thousand in the period 1986–89.

Fiscal discipline was just the beginning. The team also sought to withdraw the state from its regulatory functions in the economy. The rationale was that, in addition to stimulating private sector activity, deregulation would reduce opportunities for corruption and place responsibility for economic outcomes in the marketplace.

A uniform tariff was enacted as part of the NPE, lowering the rate to 20 percent. Price controls on privately produced goods were lifted. Liberalization also extended to financial systems where ceilings and floors on interest rates were eliminated. Exchange rate unification ensued. A managed float system was devised, which involved a daily auction of foreign currency supervised by the Central Bank. This system removed the central government from day-to-day decision making on the exchange rate. According to Juan Cariaga, one of NPE's intellectual architects and minister of finance from 1986 to 1988, the advantage of the new system was that it forced the exchange rate to a realistic level at the same time as it eliminated the politicization and corruption surrounding the setting of exchange rates.[7]

Notwithstanding the team's commitment to radical restructuring, the NPE deviated from orthodoxy in two areas. First, the program did not mandate an immediate resumption of payments of Bolivia's foreign debt. Instead, the team embarked on a two-year process of negotiations with creditors that was aimed at securing special treatment for Bolivia. Second, there was no push (not even rhetorical) to privatize public enterprises. Instead, the team emphasized asserting central government control over the financial conduct of state enterprises.

Differences in the policy instruments, sequencing, and pacing of neoliberal reforms reflected the variations in the immediate economic circumstances faced by each team and its particular diagnosis of those circumstances. In Bolivia, draconian fiscal corrections dominated the NPE, whereas trade liberalization and exchange rate reforms emerged as the pivots of the programs in Peru and Ecuador. It is important to note that in each case the government's proclivity toward orthodox formulas was reinforced by interactions (or anticipated interactions) with private and multilateral creditors. In Peru, for example, World Bank personnel played a role in the deliberations of the Belaúnde team over its program. In Ecuador, the World Bank also had discussions in July and September 1984 with government officials in which the Bank laid out its recommendations for liberalization. These talks were followed by a visit from a U.S. agricultural mission, the Wheeler mission, which urged a similar package of price decontrols, export incentives, and the unification of exchange rates. In Bolivia, the team believed that the NPE was the only way to reestablish the country's credibility with international lending agencies. USAID, the IMF, the World Bank, and the Inter-American Development Bank favored the NPE, although there was a great deal of initial skepticism about the prospects for its successful implementation.[8]

Policy Making by Decree

We now turn to a discussion of the politics of policy implementation during the first two years of these administrations. In each country, the adroit use of executive power and maneuvers to neutralize Congress as a potential source of opposition greatly facilitated the initial implementation of the neoliberal reforms.

The constitutions of Bolivia, Peru, and Ecuador assign great discretionary powers to the president, especially in regard to economic policy. The presidents of all three countries are empowered to enact economic measures by executive order should circumstances deem it necessary. Along with this power of decree, presidents are also permitted to exercise broad powers should they declare a state of emergency. These far-reaching legal powers allowed presidents and their economic teams to develop and enact policy without public debate or consultations with the legislative branch. In all three countries, the core components of the neoliberal programs were enacted through executive decree.

The Peruvian constitution of 1979 provided two mechanisms for executive dominance over economic policy. Decree powers were delineated in Article 211, which gave the president the right to issue executive orders when dictated by "national interest." In addition, Article 188 of the constitution also permitted Congress to delegate its legislative functions to the president for any period of time designated by it. Article 65 of the 1978 Ecuadorean constitution gives the president the power to sign into law any measure deemed urgent in the event of congressional inaction on a measure; the Congress subsequently has a right to alter or derogate "urgent" decrees. A Bolivian president also can emit economic measures by executive decree, using the powers ascribed in Article 96 of the constitution.

In all three countries, the neoliberal economic teams made extensive use of these powers. Of the 675 laws promulgated in Peru between 1980 and 1984, 463 were issued as decrees by the executive branch. The largest number of decrees were generated by the Ministry of Economy and Finance. The import liberalization, removal of the CERTEX, and new mining laws were all issued as executive decrees. The Febres Cordero government in Ecuador issued twenty-six "urgent" economic decrees encompassing the entire range of the neoliberal reforms from the exchange rate system to deregulating foreign investment in the petroleum sector.[9] In Bolivia, the Paz government issued all the key policies of the shock treatment in a single executive decree, D.S. 21060. Subsequent decrees followed that elaborated on the principles established in D.S. 21060.

These decree-making powers gave presidents great discretion in the launching of economic policies. Other "emergency" powers ascribed to presidents in their constitutions facilitated policy implementation. In all three countries, presidents were endowed with exceptional powers—the right to declare a state of emergency or a state of siege in order to maintain "internal order." Once such a state was declared, all constitutional guarantees were suspended, allowing for the arrest and detention of individuals deemed dangerous by officials. As we shall soon see, presidents used these emergency powers in dealing with social protests against neoliberal policies.

While presidents enjoyed extensive legal powers to enact and implement economic policy, their powers were not completely unfettered. According to all three constitutions, the legislatures retained a role in the budgetary process and could exercise oversight functions by using their powers to call on economic ministers for public reports on their policies. In addition, Congress in all three countries could censure cabinet ministers through a process known as interpellation.

To keep Congress at bay, all three presidents depended on political deals. In Peru, Belaúnde struck a postelection pact between his AP and the right-wing PPC. In exchange for their congressional votes, PPC received two cabinet posts. This pact gave Belaúnde control over both the Senate and the House; it brought together the votes he needed to be granted the discretionary powers laid out in Article 188.

In Bolivia, the issuing of D.S. 21060 in August 1985 set off a wave of protest, and the Paz government faced immediate congressional opposition in the form of an interpellation of the cabinet. To deal with the growing opposition to the economic program, President Paz opened up discussions with Hugo Banzer's ADN. The result was the historic Pact for Democracy on 16 October 1985, which brought together MNR and ADN. The understanding laid out in the pact was built around ADN's promise to support the government's economic efforts in exchange for MNR support on the reform of electoral laws. With the pact, Paz was given legislative endorsement for his declaration of a state of siege.

Like Paz and Belaúnde, Febres Cordero in Ecuador enjoyed support of his policies from a right-wing alliance, the FRN. But FRN did not constitute a legislative majority. Instead, Febres Cordero confronted a center-left opposition bloc, the *bloque progresista,* which controlled Ecuador's unicameral Congress. The bloque vowed to oppose any neoliberal experiment. In face of this opposition, the administration opted for a two-pronged attack on the congressional opposition. First, the administration turned to aggressive legal and procedural challenges to the legislative actions taken by the bloque progresista majority. Within days of the presidential inauguration in August 1984, a full-blown executive-legislative battle was under way over the issue of Supreme Court appointments. According to constitutional law, Congress has the right to make the appointments. But the president and his FRN supporters denounced the partisan appointments made by the bloque and challenged the constitutionality of their actions. Febres Cordero sent the police to bar the new Supreme Court justices from entering their offices.

The conflict paralyzed Congress until December 1984; business came to a standstill after fistfights and walkouts by legislators marred the sessions. The resolution of the dispute came when bloque leaders finally agreed to parcel out some of the appointments to FRN candidates. This initial battle set the tone for subsequent confrontations. In a struggle over a minimum wage increase in March 1985, Febres Cordero once again challenged the constitutionality of congressional action. The president also refused to publish the congressionally mandated wage increase in the official government publication, the *Registro Oficial.*

A second tactic used by the government—inducing desertions from the ranks of the bloque—eventually succeeded and obviated the need for strong-arm tactics. Along with putting pressure on individual deputies to leave their parties, the government was able to strike an alliance with two "independent" populist parties, CFP and FRA, that had lent support to the president's campaign. Desertions coupled with CFP-FRA votes sealed a government majority in August 1985. This effectively eliminated Congress as a threat to the neoliberal program in Ecuador during the legislative year 1985–86. With a congress that would not override his decrees, Febres Cordero issued a batch of "urgent" economic decrees in 1985–86. Finance Minister Francisco Swett described policy making during this period:

> It seemed that the president dominated Congress in every political skirmish, and the deficit of four votes was converted into a majority with six votes in 1985. Using every power resource available within the law, the executive not only controlled the important instruments of the economy (exchange and interest rates, tariffs, and public spending), but promoted legal reforms. A total of seventeen laws were reformed, including the Law of Hydrocarbons, which resulted in seven new exploration contracts, when none had been signed since 1973. Reforms to banking and monetary laws gave monetary authorities greater liberty to establish finance and credit policies; discrimination against foreign investment was dismantled. . . . The president vetoed every decision of the Congress that ran contrary to the reordering of the economy.[10]

In every case, executive dominance was central to the implementation of neoliberal reforms. Presidents enjoyed great latitude over economic policy, and this enabled the economic teams to launch reforms without any worry that a legislature might reverse them. But Congress was not the only site of potential opposition. The economic teams recognized the potential threats posed by societal opponents—and defusing that threat was another important dimension of policy implementation. Strategies to deal with popular opposition ran the gamut from the intermittent use of force to simply ignoring public outcries.

Opposition from Below

The trade union movement constituted the most visible and organized source of popular opposition to neoliberalism. In all three countries, previous attempts at stabilization had already taught workers much about the costs associated with orthodoxy. The neoliberal teams fully expected to see labor take to the streets to protest the changes, especially the price hikes in food and gasoline, and the governments resorted to force to derail popular protests. At the same time, internal fragmentation among the trade union movements and within the labor force at large reduced the capacity of lower-class groups to resist the reforms.

In all three countries, general strikes became the primary method for the trade union movement to contest the stabilization programs. In Peru, two mammoth strikes were called by the CGTP in response to Morales Bermúdez's stabilization packages in July 1977 and May 1978. The 1977 strike was called to protest price hikes that included a 30–50 percent jump in bus fares; approximately 272,000 workers participated in the strike. The 1978 strike was called to demand wage increases as compensation for the stabilization measures. An estimated one million workers joined in the event. Thus, Peruvian workers had already established a track record of resistance to such measures even prior to Belaúnde's program. On the governmental side, however, there was also a tradition of responding with force; the Morales Bermúdez government enacted restrictions on the right to strike and reverted to the use of "emergency powers" in dealing with the 1977 and 1978 strikes.

Two general strikes were called in response to Peruvian stabilization in 1981. The price hikes announced by Finance Minister Ulloa in January were met by a general strike involving 326,000 workers. It was followed in September by another general strike protesting the economic program.[11] The government responded by deriding the strikers.

In a similar vein, the Ecuadorean trade union movement had gathered experience in mobilizing against stabilization efforts under the government of Osvaldo Hurtado. The trade union confederation FUT launched three general strikes during Hurtado's stabilization program in 1982–83; Hurtado responded by declaring a "state of emergency." This trade union opposition to stabilization continued during the Febres Cordero administration. General strikes were called in January 1985 and March 1985 to protest the price increases and Febres Cordero's move to reduce congressionally mandated wage hikes. Both strikes ended in violence between police and protesters, demonstrating Febres Cordero's tougher law-and-order line.

By 1985 in Bolivia, resistance to stabilization measures had become the trademark of the COB. General strikes were part of a spiral of collective action that characterized Hernán Siles Zuazo's term in office. Nine general strikes, ranging from twenty-four hours to fifteen days in duration, were launched by the COB in the period from December 1983 through March 1985.[12]

Given Siles's experience, Paz and his cabinet fully expected the COB to mobilize and reject D.S. 21060. Less than a week after the decree, on 4 September 1984, the COB called a general strike to oppose the measures. The strike was originally called for twenty-four hours but it was extended, and COB leaders launched a hunger strike. The COB's call set off a wave of marches, roadblocks, and building occupations throughout the country. Troops surrounded COB headquarters in La Paz. As popular challenge to the plan mounted, Paz decided to move definitively against the COB. In the early hours of 19 September, Paz declared a "state of siege"; he ordered police and the armed forces to search out and arrest the hunger-striking COB leaders. Over two hundred leaders, among them the legendary Juan Lechín Oquendo, were arrested. Lechín, along with a hundred others, was sent to internment camps in the remote provinces of the Beni and Pando. They were detained without legal recourse until 5 October when the COB agreed to suspend the general strike and enter into dialogue with the government. Reflecting on their tactics, one member of Paz's cabinet later admitted, the government "behaved like authoritarian pigs." But the moves effectively defused the COB whose capacity for mobilization had already begun to wane by the end of the Siles administration. By December, the state of siege was lifted.[13] The Paz government did not shy away from reapplying repressive measures when deemed necessary: in August 1986, a massive protest march of miners, the *Marcha por la vida* (March for life), was physically barred by the army from entering La Paz.

But repression was not the only factor inhibiting the development of an effective trade union opposition to neoliberalism. In all three countries, the economic marginality of the traditional working class undercut the threat posed by trade unions and the force of their mobilizations. As recent research by Alejandro Portes and others demonstrate, the world of the Latin American working class is complicated by its position within both formal and informal sectors of the economy. The traditional terrain of trade unionism was the formal sector of the economy—that is, that segment of the economy dominated by large modern firms in which wages, working conditions, and benefits are established via contractual relations and government regulations.[14] But a significant portion of the ''laboring classes'' fall outside this organized world of the formal sector. Instead, many people find employment in the informal sector of the economy, where work is not governed by contracts or monitored by state. According to Portes, urban informal workers constitute 40 percent of the nonagricultural labor force in Peru, and 56 percent in Bolivia. In Ecuador, an estimated 52 percent of the urban population is located in the informal sector of the economy.

The heterogeneity of the labor force in the informal sector and the diversity of working conditions in the sector create enormous obstacles to organization. Orthodox Marxism was dominant in most trade union organizations during the 1960s and 1970s, which made those trade unions relatively uninterested in organizing outside the mainstream ''industrial proletariat.'' Rather than organizing around their work, popular classes have increasingly turned their energies toward other sorts of organizations, at the neighborhood level, ranging from self-help groups to church groups. Thus, fragmentation inside the workforce and popular organizations has contributed to the problems in mounting a concerted popular mobilization against neoliberalism.

The availability of opportunities in the informal sector and its attractiveness in terms of earning potential and flexible working conditions had important ramifications for working-class response to neoliberalism. Jorge Parodi's insightful work on Peru points to how industrial workers in Peru aspired to leave factory life for the informal sector. According to Parodi, this ''exit'' calculus affected the strategy of many trade unions during the Belaúnde period. Instead of resisting the wage ceilings set by the neoliberal team and protesting the layoffs caused by import liberalization, trade union members became more concerned with negotiating severance payments that would give each of them the capital to start up an informal business.[15]

Similarly in Bolivia, the severance payments made to miners affected by the closing of COMIBOL mines defused some of the resistance to the cutbacks. As in the earlier neoliberal experiments in Chile and Argentina, the deindustrialization that accompanied tariff liberalization shrank and dispersed the constituency for industrial trade unions. Neoliberalism itself effected an atomization of individuals by forcing people out of their traditional workplaces and communities in search of employment. This "organic weakening of society" that came with neoliberal reform itself facilitated a continued application of the neoliberal program.[16]

Recognizing the severe social costs of neoliberalism, the Paz government also sought to mitigate some of its effects on lower-class groups through the creation of the Fondo Social de Emergencia (FSE), which began functioning in 1987 and was designed to provide the unemployed with temporary work on public works projects. According to FSE estimates, over a hundred thousand such jobs were generated in its first year of projects in 1987.[17] Funding for the program came from a variety of sources including the World Bank, USAID, and the governments of Switzerland, Holland, Sweden, and Canada.

In all three countries, governments met popular resistance to neoliberalism with a patchwork of repression, co-optation, and nonchalance. It is important to underscore that in all three cases the neutralization of Congress (through pacts and other maneuvers) was a critical factor that allowed executives to ignore popular opposition. In the absence of a sympathetic and activist legislature, trade unions and other organizations were without interlocutors inside the institutional apparatus of the state. As such, they could only revert to "street and strike" politics; and they were hampered by the liabilities inherent in that form of politics—from the dulling effects of government repression to the limits on people's energies to engage in mass mobilization while struggling for day-to-day survival.[18]

Business and Its Discontents

The reactions of domestic capitalists to initial implementation of neoliberal programs were diverse and complicated. After years of pushing an antistatist agenda, business interest groups finally saw concrete measures inspired by that agenda enacted by conservative administrations. Yet, the reality of neoliberalism did not evoke the across-the-board enthusiasm in the business community that had been inspired by the earlier antistatist campaigns. Conflicts erupted between business groups and the conservative governments, which revealed the lack of clear agreement between the business community and the political right over the structuring and pacing of economic reform. On one side stood the authors of the measures, the technocrats inside the economic teams, driven by theory, who saw themselves as the founders of a leaner and meaner state and an untainted market system. On the other side stood the more pragmatic members of the business community, who agreed with the broad principles underlying the neoliberal projects but believed that a kinder and gentler version should prevail—one that would allow business to gradually accommodate to new rules. The lessons learned by business elites in the unfolding of neoliberalism were not just economic, but political. To businessmen of the Central Andes, neoliberalism in practice demonstrated that democracy per se would not secure the kind of representation they envisioned. In short, the conservative governments showed that just putting your men in office was not enough—it did not guarantee palatable economic policy or a privileged position within the inner sanctum of policy making.

In all three countries, the liberalization of trade emerged as the most controversial component of the neoliberal programs. From its initial implementation in Peru and Bolivia, business groups affected by the measures (largely industrialists producing for the internal market) lobbied heavily to reverse the policy, but without success. In Ecuador, in contrast, industrialists were effective in limiting tariff reforms; negotiations were drawn out over the first two years of the Febres Cordero administration, and the final result reflected the moderating effect of the chambers of industry. Why did Ecuadorean industrialists fare better than their Andean counterparts in their lobby of a conservative government?

In Peru. Industry-government relations in Peru soured just weeks into the Belaúnde administration. Although the president of SNI, Alfredo Ferrand, had offered "unconditional support" to the new government in July 1980, SNI made a rapid about-face in September.[19] The source of the shift was D.S. 21080, the executive decree enacted on 13 September 1980 that authorized tariff reductions to a maximum of 60 percent ad valorem. The technocrat that designed the measure, the Vice-Minister of Commerce Roberto Abusada, took the action without any consultation with industrialists.

SNI responded with immediate public criticism of the government's economic policy, through repeated pronouncements by its leaders and the use of communiqués published in the Lima dailies. SNI decried the measures' anti-industrial thrust and their preferential treatment of financial and mining sectors. Ferrand argued that industrial firms were still hamstrung in the market by industrial community laws and other reforms passed during the Velasco period.[20] He rebutted the team's claim that the measure was anti-inflationary. The SNI leader painted an apocalyptic scenario of the results, predicting the loss of thousands of jobs as industrial firms went bankrupt. The industries most immediately affected included textile, footwear, and metal-working plants.

Along with their gloomy forecasts, the SNI leadership criticized the economic team for what they saw as a slavish adherence to economic theory. Ferrand accused the team of conducting a laboratory experiment that was inappropriate to Peru's special circumstances. He characterized economic policy as an attempt to "chileanize" Peru and suggested that the tariff reduction smelled like the work of "Chicago boys." In his yearly message to SNI members, Ferrand clearly laid out his objections: "Peru will not find its destiny if it departs from the road of industrialization. We must create *our own economic theories because we are different. Peru is not Chicago, nor Germany*" (our emphasis).[21]

ADEX sympathized with SNI's position and called for a more gradual adjustment in tariff rates. ADEX shared SNI's perspective on the mentality of the economic team, suggesting that they lived in "the land of economic theory and Milton Friedman's ideas" but not in the reality of Peru. To resolve the controversies over economic policy, ADEX proposed a *gran acuerdo nacional*—a dialogue that would bring together government officials, businessmen, union leaders, and party representatives.[22]

ADEX's opposition intensified when the Ulloa team stripped exporters of their CERTEX subsidy. Once again, business's objections not only revolved around the effects of the measure but included the lack of consultation between the economic team and the affected sector. In a magazine interview ADEX president, Boris Romero, criticized the "unilateral" and "nearly abusive" decision-making style of the economic team.[23]

SNI and ADEX tried various directions in their attempts to reverse government policy. Their lobbying efforts included applying direct pressure on players within the executive branch along with attempts to enlist support from AP and PPC congressional deputies. PPC's close ties to the industrial sector were reflected in the roles played by a succession of three PPC ministers of industry—Roberto Rotondo, Roberto Persivale, and Gonzalo de la Puente—each of whom attempted to act as a conduit for industrial interests inside the economic team. But this lobbying by industrial ministers proved ineffective; and it opened the first serious fissure within the economic team, casting Minister of Industry Roberto Rotondo against Prime Minister Manuel Ulloa.[24] Ulloa's dominant position inside the team and the government allowed him to overrule Rotondo's objections to the economic reforms of 1980–81.

In addition to seeking help from the minister of industry, business groups also directly hounded President Belaúnde. These pressures did yield intermittent meetings both with Belaúnde and with Prime Minister Ulloa. Belaúnde even called an economic "summit" in August 1981 to bring the economic team together with top business leaders. Yet, these meetings produced little substantive change in the economic model laid out by the team.[25]

SNI and ADEX also looked to leading legislators in their attempts to put pressure on the executive branch. Two congressmen emerged as representatives in the battle: Javier Alva Orlandini, the president of Congress and AP leader, and Miguel Angel Mufarech, a PPC congressman. Alva, acting with the support of a significant segment of AP, attempted to outflank Ulloa by presenting Belaúnde with a detailed critique of economic policy. In this effort at technical lobbying, Alva contracted a group of independent economists to author the study. But the study, presented to Belaúnde in April 1981, aroused little interest and was completely ignored by the economic team.[26]

With the efforts at persuasion yielding no results, SNI turned its attention to limiting the powers of the economic team through the passage of a new industrial development law. SNI and ADEX collaborated with the Ministry of Industry in the formulation of the proposed legislation. One of the key components of the new law included the creation of commissions to ensure consultation between government representatives and private sector groups on such key issues as the tariffs. After drawn-out deliberations over the law, the final version was passed by Congress in May 1982, but by the time it passed, it had substantially watered down the provisions concerning business-government consultation.

Throughout the behind-the-scenes maneuverings of 1981–82, SNI and ADEX kept up their public relations blitz against the policies. Part of the campaign involved the staging of high-profile public conferences where the policies were criticized by "experts." One such event, sponsored by SNI in May 1981, featured the Peruvian economist and Boston University professor Daniel Schydlowsky, denouncing every aspect of the economic program. Neoliberal proponents countered with a subsequent conference featuring Milton Friedman.[27]

The intense activity of SNI and ADEX leaders produced no substantial modifications of macroeconomic policy in the period from 1980–83. Prime Minister Manuel Ulloa resigned at the end of 1982, but he was succeeded by a fellow neoliberal, Carlos Rodríguez Pastor. Trained as an international banker at Wells Fargo, Rodríguez was committed to the same program of liberalization. It was only as the severity of the economic recession became clear and elections approached that the Belaúnde government abandoned liberalization (see chapter 7).

What SNI and ADEX rudely discovered in these first years of the new democratic government was the extent to which their specific grievances could be ignored, even by a conservative executive committed to a probusiness posture. As one business informant put it, the affected business groups discovered the problem of "access without receptivity." Business leaders had expected the new democratic state to be more open and pliable to pressure politics—but reality was quite different. Rather, the expected receptivity of economic policy makers was reduced by their adherence to economic doctrine that permitted little room for bargaining. With orthodox technocrats ascendant inside the economic team, a

mental curtain descended around the executive branch that was impossible for business lobbyists to puncture. The "power of economic ideas" became eminently clear to frustrated business lobbyists. An officer of the mining lobby, the Sociedad Nacional de Minería (SNM), underscored the centrality of economic ideas in the lobbying process:

There's plenty of access to ministers. The dialogue exists. We always talk with the minister of the economy or energy. . . . The problem is not one of dialogue—the problem is one of conceptions. The real key is the economic model that is adopted. If the conception is that export is the key, then the help goes to the mining sector. If your idea is that demand has to be stimulated and purchasing power increased in order to stimulate industry, then you are going to favor industry. Everything depends on the focus that is adopted.[28]

In our interviews with business leaders and dissidents inside AP, there were frequent references to the arrogance of the economic team and their complete lack of responsiveness to business's concerns. Simply put, while SNI and ADEX leaders frequently met with Ulloa, they felt that they were never really being heard.[29] One ADEX leader reported that Prime Minister Ulloa sat with his feet up on his desk when receiving an ADEX delegation in his office. The ADEX leader interpreted this as visible evidence of Ulloa's total disregard for the group. Business leaders attributed this insensitivity to dogmatism and the fact that Ulloa (and other team members) had never worked in the affected industries.

The intransigence of Belaúnde's economic team was not simply a demonstration of their own mental toughness and conviction. We are not arguing that the behavior of the team reflected a high level of "relative autonomy" for the Peruvian state. Rather, their steadfastness was based on a web of relationships that developed inside the executive branch, which fed on considerable support from external allies and pockets of sympathetic businessmen in Peru. President Belaúnde's unqualified backing for Prime Ministers Ulloa and Rodríguez Pastor was the basis of their considerable power and their ability to resist lobbyists. Belaúnde's principal concern was to use macroeconomic policy to curry favor with international lending organizations; and Belaúnde's ministers knew that trade liberalization was one of those agencies' preferred policies. Thus, the neoliberal clique inside the executive found a powerful set of external allies in the IMF and the World Bank. Moreover, not all of Peruvian business lined up with SNI and ADEX in their initial conflict with the government. As Francisco Durand points out, business groups with interests spanning the financial, commercial, and mining sectors were not adversely affected by the measures and did not mobilize to oppose them. Only as the recessive effects of the policies became evident in 1983 did opposition spread throughout the private sector.[30]

In Bolivia. The enactment of the uniform tariff in Bolivia also met with opposition from segments of business that were hurt by the measure. The most vocal opposition came from industrialists grouped in the Cámara Nacional de Industrias (CNI) and the agro-entrepreneurs of Santa Cruz organized by the Cámara Agropecuaria del Oriente (CAO). Both groups portrayed as unfair and destructive the indiscriminate opening of the internal market to foreign food and manufacturing imports. They argued that the overvaluation of Bolivian money vis-à-vis the currency of neighboring countries, the high cost of internal transport, and the absence of production incentives ensured that imports from surrounding countries would enjoy an undue advantage over Bolivian products. Moreover, the elimination of differential tariffs actually increased the cost of the capital goods and inputs upon which these producers depended.

As in Peru, the leaders of this business opposition to liberalization focused their energies on lobbying the executive branch, and they used similar tactics and rhetoric. CAO leaders criticized the measure as an abandonment of the defense of the national market and as a perpetuation of the old mono-export model. The CNI contracted experts to make technical arguments against the measure and, to present those arguments, mounted meetings such as its 1988 seminar on industrial policy.

Despite their efforts, CAO and CNI leaders encountered the same stone wall in the executive as had their Peruvian counterparts. President Paz Estenssoro stood solidly behind the program and his ministers. Gonzalo Sánchez de Lozada, the minister of planning and chief architect of the neoliberal package, firmly held that the package had to be maintained in its entirety, not just for technical reasons but in order to reestablish the government's credibility domestically and among international creditors. He believed that negotiations with any group to adjust the measures would open a floodgate of societal demands and unravel the entire economic program. Sánchez de Lozada consistently projected this no compromise position; although, in contrast to Manuel Ulloa, he used his affable personality and avoided the image of arrogance even as the economic team remained resistant to the business lobby. Although there was frequent contact with the economic team, this remained a "dialogue of the deaf." A leader of the industrial lobby characterized the contacts in this way:

> Bolivia is a very small country where we all get together to talk. We're friends of ministers, for one reason or another reason, and of the undersecretaries. So it isn't difficult. Nevertheless, although it might not be difficult to talk, they [the economic team] tell us—very cordially and in a very friendly way—that this is the model. So you could have a meeting once a week, but once a week they will tell you the same thing: "The economic policy is this and we aren't going to change it!"[31]

The relatively weak market position of industrialists and agrarian capitalists only reinforced the economic team's strong proclivity to ignore their specific sectoral demands. The manufacturing sector in Bolivia remained marginal as an employer and income generator. By the mid-1980s, Bolivia was still one of the least industrialized countries in Latin America. Manufacturing constituted only 9 percent of the GDP and most of Bolivian industry remained concentrated in simple import-substitution activities such as food processing and textiles. Only 8.7 percent of the EAP was employed in manufacturing; of those employed in manufacturing enterprises in the private sector, 66 percent were found in small firms employing fourteen persons or less. While some of the large economic groups did have interests in industrial firms, manufacturing was not the leading activity of most economic groups. According to Eckstein and Hagopian, the predominant activities of most economic groups were mining, agriculture, finance, and commerce.[32]

Similarly, by the 1980s, the agro-entrepreneurs of Santa Cruz found themselves in an increasingly marginal economic position. Whereas these firms had enjoyed a boom in the 1970s, based on state credit and buoyant commodities prices, they were already in a slump before the neoliberal package was enacted. Some of the most productive agricultural enterprises of Santa Cruz were not even in the hands of CAO entrepreneurs but were owned by the local Mennonite and Japanese colonies. These groups eschewed politics and were not part of the CAO lobby.[33]

The business peak association, the CEPB, did echo the CAO and the CNI's criticisms of the abrupt trade liberalization in its public pronouncements. The CEPB noted that even mining firms were hurt by the increased cost of capital goods under the uniform tariff. But the CEPB did not turn this into its own particular cause célèbre. This had to do, in part, with the diversity of business interests represented by the CEPB and the differential impact of the NPE on various types of businesses. Importers, who dominated the Chamber of Industry and Commerce of Santa Cruz, obviously benefited from liberalization. Even within the industrial sector, the effects of the NPE were not uniform. Given its role as a peak association and its mission to represent business at large, the CEPB focused on articulating broader business demands rather than specific sectoral ones. The CEPB president, Carlos Iturralde, placed more emphasis on the need for economic "reactivation," that is, a rapid disbursement of credit to business and the lowering of interest rates to end the stabilization-induced recession, so that the private sector could assume its role as an "engine of growth." The demand for reactivation was generalized among all business groups notwithstanding their sectoral concentration. With reactivation defined as the central demand of the CEPB, its lobby in the 1985–89 period focused not on opposition to neoliberalism per se but on how best the model could be pushed rapidly to promote economic growth.

Although some entrepreneurs within the Bolivian business community clearly were unhappy with trade liberalization, no frontal opposition to the neoliberal model developed as a result. Discontent with specific components of the package were blunted to a great degree by at least three other considerations. First, while trade liberalization may have been a controversial component of the package, other measures contained in D.S. 21060 (for example, deregulation of stringent labor laws, termination of price controls, and so on) were popular among businessmen. Second, all business organizations supported the ideological underpinnings of the model; they applauded the new respect for market principles and the government's commitment to reduce the role of the state in the economy.[34] Third, business leaders were heartened to see a strong government and the reestablishment of order after years of political uncertainty and isolation from the international financial community. The procapitalist rhetoric of the administration was music to the ears of businessmen who had felt profoundly threatened by the radicalism of labor and political unrest of the preceding Siles government. The situation that prevailed under Siles (see chapter 5) came perilously close to what Guillermo O'Donnell termed a ''crisis of social domination,'' that is, a situation in which disruptions of the capital accumulation process are accompanied by lower-class mobilization that undermines the social relations upon which the capitalist economic system is built. With this kind of system-threatening crisis in the immediate past, capitalists (even those suffering under the new orthodoxy) were loath to attack a government dedicated to reestablishing order.[35]

In Ecuador. In contrast to Bolivia and Peru, the trade liberalization component of the neoliberal package in Ecuador was the subject of bargaining between industrialists and the Febres Cordero government. A number of factors converged in this case to produce a greater receptivity to the idea of a more gradual and negotiated trade liberalization scheme.

Of the three presidents under consideration here—Fernando Belaúnde, Víctor Paz Estenssoro, and León Febres Cordero—only Febres Cordero had firsthand experience as a business executive and industrialist. Throughout the 1970s, he served as general manager of the Noboa group enterprises in Guayaquil where he oversaw the operations of Industrial Molinera (a flour milling plant) and Industria Cartonera (a cardboard plant). In addition, his family was a major stockholder in Ecuatoriana de Sal, a desalination plant, owned in conjunction with Morton's Salt of the United States. He made his way into the public spotlight as president of the Guayaquil Chamber of Industry and as president of the National Federation of Chambers of Industry of Ecuador. Prior to the military coup of 1972, he had served as the ''functional'' senator representing industry in Congress in 1966, 1968, and 1970. Febres Cordero was intimately acquainted with both the day-to-day problems of individual industrial firms and with the corporate demands of the sector.

Febres Cordero was ideologically committed to neoliberalism, but he frequently stressed his own pragmatism and belief in a more gradual approach to economic restructuring. In the early 1980s, he came out in favor of tariff reductions but argued that they would have to be phased in slowly to give industry time to adjust.[36]

The idea of a gradualist route to economic restructuring was shared by Minister of Finance Swett and Central Bank director Carlos Julio Emanuel. They believed that Ecuador was not a country accustomed to radical discontinuities in economic policy and that a slower restructuring would be politically more palatable. Febres Cordero believed that political constraints (for example, an opposition majority in Congress in his first year in office) also ruled out a shock treatment approach.[37]

The bias toward gradualism and the fact that trade liberalization was not defined as the centerpiece of the program allowed the issue to be opened up to consultations between officials and the affected business groups. The minister of industry, Xavier Neira, was designated the chief negotiator in the process. Neira, who had worked as a functionary in the Guayaquil Chamber of Industry alongside Febres Cordero, was a sympathetic interlocutor. From the start, Neira underscored his own commitment to gradualism, emphasizing that the government was not seeking to destroy import-substituting industries but to make them more efficient and to promote an increased export capacity.[38]

The chambers of industry were quick to express their concern about the prospective reform and moved to open talks with Neira. The discussions dragged on for a year and a half. When the new tariff schedule was finally enacted in February 1986, it reflected the long process of horse-trading among the affected businesses and the Ministry of Industry. A total of 5,067 products were considered in the negotiations. Of those, the tariffs on 1,870 items were left unchanged while the remaining 3,197 were altered. Tariffs on 1,470 locally produced items increased; tariffs on 1,737 items decreased. These tariff reductions largely affected capital goods and industrial inputs. Tariffs on luxury items were reduced from 200 percent to a maximum of 80 percent. On nationally produced goods, the new tariff schedule varied from 20 to 90 percent. In short, although the process did bring a reduction in the overall level of protectionism, it did not subject industry to an immediate and drastic restructuring.[39]

Neoliberalism Unleashed

All three narratives on the launching of neoliberal programs point to common factors that worked in favor of their initial implementation. In every case, a strong executive was pivotal to the process. While extensive powers were ascribed to each president in the constitution, presidential power was not simply an artifact of the legal structure. In all three countries, presidents worked actively to enhance their power, especially to neutralize Congress as a potential site of opposition to their programs. In Peru and Bolivia, this was accomplished through political pacts whereas in Ecuador the task involved considerable maneuvering and confrontational tactics by Febres Cordero. This marginalization of Congress was essential to the capacity of the executives to undertake neoliberal programs. With Congress subordinated, presidents were able to protect their economic teams from interpellation and keep them intact. Furthermore, the marginalization of Congress deprived social groups of an institutional base from which to oppose the measures and gave the administrations a freer hand in dealing with dissidents.

Some opposition did surface. Lower-class opponents took to the streets, and some business elites took to intense lobbying efforts to alter specific components of the program. For the most part, such efforts had little effect. Antiliberalization lobbies within the private sector were weakened because of the differential effects of the measures on business; some businesses benefited while others did not.

The capacity of the economic team to resist domestic pressures to alter the program was not simply a function of the weakness of societal forces. In all three cases, the apex of the administration's economic team was occupied by "true believers," convinced neoliberals who approached their jobs with near missionary zeal. Only in Ecuador was the economic model somewhat tempered by a concomitant belief in gradualism. In all three cases, the economic teams firmly believed that liberalization was the appropriate method to send the correct signals to international creditors. They also shared a certain disdain for civil society and political parties, tending to see social groups and other politicians as disruptive rent-seekers. Thus, there was a predisposition not to take public criticism too seriously, even when presented in the form of technical critiques of the measures.

Individual motivations behind each president's decision to back a neoliberal program varied—but once made, continuing presidential support for the economic team was the glue that held the programs in place. Of the three presidents, Belaúnde had the most instrumental and least ideological commitment to neoliberalism; he backed the program in order to ensure a continued flow of international credits for his public construction projects. Disinterested in economics per se, Belaúnde wanted to be remembered as Peru's great builder. Paz Estenssoro looked to the neoliberal project as a way of gaining control over the hypertrophied state he had helped create in the wake of the 1952 revolution. He saw neoliberalism as a way to salvage the Bolivian state, so he might conclude his political career as the president who brought Bolivia back from the brink of disaster. For Febres Cordero, the neoliberal project was the culmination of his lifelong campaign to dismantle the statist developmentalist model and put in place the kind of policies he had advocated as a business leader.

In all three cases, the constitutional prohibition on continuing in office beyond one term gave the presidents both the urgency to get on with their agendas and the freedom to ignore public criticism, including those criticisms emanating from their own parties. None of the presidents would personally pay any direct electoral cost for their association with painful economic adjustments.[40] Neither Belaúnde nor Febres Cordero were great party builders, and Paz was known to be pessimistic about MNR's future.

Ultimately, presidential commitment to neoliberal reforms dissolved in Ecuador and Peru. Rapidly deteriorating economic circumstances pushed these presidents further away from their original programs. As each crisis mounted, each president made improvisational adjustments while the original neoliberal coalition itself unraveled. The last two years of the Febres Cordero and Belaúnde administrations were marked by a "muddling through" approach to economic policy. In chapter 7, we shall examine the conditions that eroded the neoliberal projects in Ecuador and Peru and conditions that account for Bolivia's being the exception during this period. Why was the neoliberal experiment sustained in Bolivia when neighboring attempts failed?

CHAPTER 7

Some Things Fall Apart, Some Don't: Exhaustion and Survival of Neoliberal Experiments

THE ABILITY OF Central Andean governments to sustain their own particular versions of neoliberalism varied significantly. On one side of the divide are the Peruvian and Ecuadorean experiments, which dissolved during the last two years of the Belaúnde and Febres Cordero presidencies. These failures stand in sharp contrast to the Bolivian experience. The Paz Estenssoro government was not only successful in holding its ground on economic policy but forged a consensus, among the major parties, on the desirability of continuing with the model beyond the conclusion of Paz's own term in office.

Our concern in this chapter is to examine the causes underlying these remarkably different outcomes in neoliberal experimentation. The exhaustion or the survival of any type of economic policy, orthodox or heterodox, is of course a complicated affair. Circumstances outside the control of the economic team—fluctuations in export revenues, or production losses due to natural disasters—have implications for the pursuit of economic policy. In Ecuador and Peru, such external and internal shocks played an important role in derailing the neoliberal reforms. The Ecuadorean economy was damaged unexpectedly by a plunge in world oil prices in 1986; that shock was followed in 1987 by an earthquake that disrupted oil exports for months. In Peru, the economy was affected by the halt in the flow of international credits following Mexico's 1982 moratorium and the Falkland Islands–Malvinas war. Widespread flooding and temperature changes in 1983 ruined crops and sent domestic prices soaring. In both countries, this combination of external troubles and internal shocks from natural disasters led to deteriorating economic conditions, which had not been foreseen by the neoliberal economic teams. Under the strains of coping with such unexpected events, both presidents began their drift away from structural adjustment policies.

This is not to argue, however, that neoliberal experiments simply dissipated in the face of uncontrollable events. Bad luck certainly affected presidential decisions, but it was not the only factor at play. Bolivia also experienced a dramatic drop in international prices for its mineral exports in the latter part of 1985, which could have undermined the neoliberal reforms, but Paz Estenssoro acted decisively to keep the program from running aground. Just as skillful political management was crucial to the launching of the experiments, it was critical for their survival. Belaúnde and Febres Cordero progressively lost their capacity to keep in place the building blocks of the neoliberal experiments: a strong economic team, a subordinated Congress, a muted civil society, and pliant coalitional partners inside the business community.

The following discussion is divided into two parts. The first half examines the dynamics that eroded the neoliberal projects in Peru and Ecuador. The second part analyzes the sources of Bolivia's "exceptionalism."

Part 1: The Slide From Orthodoxy

On Economic Shocks and Unintended Consequences

Neither Fernando Belaúnde in July 1980 nor Febres Cordero in August 1984 faced catastrophic economic conditions when he was inaugurated. A relative economic recovery was under way in both countries as these presidents took office. The Belaúnde government commenced during an export boom that brought Peru's foreign exchange reserves to a high of $1.3 billion (see chapter 6). GDP growth rates for 1979 and 1980 were 4.1 percent and 3.8 percent, rebounding from the negative rates registered in 1977 and 1978. By 1984, in Ecuador, economic indicators showed that the recession that had accompanied Hurtado's stabilization measures was abating. The GDP increased by 4.8 percent in 1984 after its downward dive to −1.2 percent the previous year. Inflation was down to 25 percent after hitting 50 percent in 1983.[1]

The economic upturn that served as the backdrop to the launching of neoliberal programs in Peru and Ecuador did not last, however. In both cases, events unforeseen by the economic teams changed the parameters within which decision making took place. As the deterioration of the economies became more pronounced, the Belaúnde and Febres Cordero governments fell into short-term crisis-containment approaches to economic policy while the larger goals of economic restructuring receded. As our discussion in the next section will show, the crisis atmosphere was exacerbated by deteriorating political conditions, which directed presidential attention to other concerns.

In Peru. It is important to appreciate the magnitude of the economic crisis that had unfolded in Peru by 1983. Peru suffered its worst single economic decline in modern history in 1983; the drop in Peru's GDP registered at −12 percent. This brought per capita GDP down to its 1962 level. Inflation, as measured by the consumer price index, increased to 125 percent. Open unemployment reached 13 percent; real wages registered a 17 percent decline, receding to two-thirds of their 1976 value.[2]

In the case of Peru, it is difficult to disentangle the effects of unexpected economic shocks from the problems being generated by specific components of the neoliberal program itself. No doubt the economic shocks seriously aggravated design flaws in Belaúnde's program. In retrospect, the most striking aspect of the Peruvian case is the economic team's inability to anticipate these problems and to react to changing economic circumstances. An inflated optimism about the program blinded Belaúnde and his team to the danger signs, which if heeded could have prompted corrections in the program.

As Richard Webb and others have argued, overheated commodities prices in 1979–80 were not interpreted as aberrant but were taken for granted by the economic team. By 1983, however, Peru's long-standing vulnerability to price fluctuations in the international market was once again in evidence. Mineral prices had declined from the 1979–80 highs; by 1983 prices were down and production had slumped. Natural disasters also played a role in Peru's declining export performance. The climactic disorders caused by changes in the El Niño current wreaked havoc on the fishing industry, and production declined by one-third in 1983.

Poor export performance alongside import liberalization sped up the process of "burning up" foreign exchange reserves. Yet, as Richard Webb points out, Peru's weakening exchange position was masked initially by an influx of foreign credit.[3] By the end of 1982, this foreign credit cushion was also disappearing, however. Panic in international banking circles over the Mexican debt moratorium dried up new lending across Latin America.

Domestic agricultural production was also affected by poor weather conditions, which ranged from floods in the north to drought in the southern departments. In 1983, Peruvian agriculture suffered its worst contraction on record. Crop-farming production fell to −17 percent. These dramatic production losses contributed to inflationary pressures. The consumer price index rose from 64 to 111 points in 1983; food prices in the index more than doubled from 53 to 126 percent.[4] Thus, even though the government had defined the control of inflation as one of its primary goals, inflation resurged dramatically in 1983. The policy of periodic exchange rate devaluations reinforced inflationary expectations.

While mining and agriculture were suffering natural disasters and pricing problems, domestic manufacturing was being pummeled by the effects of trade liberalization and tight money policies. Adhering to monetarist assumptions, the economic team prescribed restrictive monetary policies to control inflation. The money supply decreased in real terms by 21.5 percent in 1983, and credit to the private sector shrank by 11 percent. The credit squeeze created serious liquidity problems for industries that were already contending with the effects of the increased foreign competition triggered by the tariff reform. To add to these industries' problems, inflation depressed domestic demand for their products. Among the industrial branches most affected were textiles, footwear, machinery, and transport equipment.

Public sector finance also fell victim to the spiraling economic crisis. As domestic business floundered, tax receipts decreased. In 1983, overall tax revenues declined in real terms by 29 percent. Prime Minister Ulloa had been able to disguise the state's growing fiscal crisis by contracting short-term loans in 1982, and by early 1983 even that option was gone. His successor, Carlos Rodríguez Pastor, had to reopen talks with the IMF to solve the growing fiscal jam. The effect of the new agreement with the IMF in February 1983 was to reinforce the notion that Peru required more, not less, orthodoxy to deal with its crisis. The IMF focused on the public sector deficit as the source of inflationary pressures and demanded further cuts in government spending. This demand was made even though real government spending had already been slashed, because the cuts could still not match the losses in revenues.

There was a remarkable lack of flexibility in the approach to economic policy under the stewardships of Manuel Ulloa and Carlos Rodríguez Pastor. Even in the face of altered and ominous circumstances, they remained wedded to a set of strict monetarist measures. But as Richard Webb notes, the neoliberal package had been predicated on rather propitious circumstances:

> Retrospectively, government policy during 1982–83 looks remarkably blind. The economic programme was designed for a benign balance of payments context that first evaporated gradually during 1981–82, as the fall of commodity prices continued to outlive the world recession, and then shattered in 1983 when the international banking system panicked and withdrew. The programme was also designed for a domestic economy much closer to full capacity, and with more flexibility to adjust to new relative prices than was the case, particularly after mid-1982.[5]

In other words, the landscape on which the economic team originally had conceived its program was completely altered by 1983—in part due to exogenous events such as natural disasters, but also because some of the measures in the neoliberal program were generating unintended and less than salutary effects.

The unwillingness to adjust to changing circumstances reflected a certain intellectual rigidity on the part of Ulloa and Rodríguez Pastor, which business  leaders interpreted as arrogance. But the inflexibility was a product also of serious misconceptions and miscalculations concerning trends in the national and international economy. These mistakes were reinforced by the sanguine predictions of IMF and World Bank experts. Both the IMF and the World Bank assured the Peruvian team that external markets would rebound and allow for a recovery of export revenues. With the assumption of such a recovery, both organizations remained insistent that Peru stick to its radical tariff liberalization even as the interconnected balance of payments and fiscal problems became evident.

The monetarist approach to inflation was reiterated constantly in discussions between Rodríguez Pastor and the IMF. Already quite sympathetic to the interpretation, Rodríguez plunged ahead in 1983 with tougher measures, aimed at squeezing demand out of the economy even as the economy descended into deeper recession. It was Rodríguez Pastor's attempt to force down further monetarist medicine that led to a rebellion against orthodoxy inside the economic team. And it was this public split inside the economic team that began the retreat from the neoliberal experiment.

In Ecuador. As in Peru, Ecuador experienced an external shock and a natural disaster that created unforeseen problems for Febres Cordero's economic team. The economic deterioration that occurred in 1986–87 combined with serious political problems to undermine Febres Cordero's commitment to continuing neoliberal reform.

An unprecedented collapse in the international price for oil, Ecuador's major export, took the administration's team by surprise in 1986. Whereas the price per barrel of Ecuadorean crude oil averaged $26 in 1985, changes in OPEC policies triggered a decline that brought the price down to a low of $8.60 in July 1986. The effects of the price drop were staggering. The government budget and the economy as a whole were dependent on oil revenues: in 1985, for example, petroleum accounted for 60 percent of all exports and about the same percentage of government income. The loss of revenue caused by the price decrease was estimated between eight and nine hundred million dollars.

The economic team was flabbergasted by the sudden turnabout in the international petroleum market. According to Minister of Finance Francisco Swett, the team had calculated the effects of a price decrease—but using what they believed was the worst-case scenario of a drop to $18 per barrel. World Bank and IMF experts, along with petroleum analysts, concurred with the team's projection that the price would not sink below their worst-case projection.

The potentially catastrophic effects of the crash were cushioned by new foreign loans. Because Ecuador had been servicing its foreign debt and was clearly committed to liberalizing reforms, the American government and multilateral agencies were sympathetic to Ecuador's plight. The U.S. government lent $150 million while the World Bank offered another loan of $145 million. The IMF agreed to a standby credit of $75 million along with another $40 million to compensate for the petroleum revenue loss.

But even as oil prices began to recover in 1987, the petroleum industry suffered another major setback. On 6 March 1987, a severe earthquake ruptured Ecuador's trans-Amazonian pipeline, which connected the Lago Agrio fields in the east with the refinery on the Pacific coast. Oil exports were severely disrupted for five months. The pipeline break resulted in a 40 percent drop in petroleum production in 1987. The loss of revenue was estimated at $400 million. Coming on the heels of the 1986 price crash, the 1987 earthquake dealt another critical blow to the budget of the central government. According to Febres Cordero, the two events together deprived his government of the equivalent of one year's budget. "I governed for four years with the equivalent of a three-year budget," he later remarked.[6]

Unlike in Peru, the crisis in the external sector and the deterioration in public finances in Ecuador did not inspire a last-ditch effort to apply more monetarist prescriptions. Unlike Belaúnde, León Febres Cordero was an active participant in the design of macroeconomic policy. According to his advisers, Febres Cordero always demonstrated a keen sense both of the political repercussions of economic measures and of what was politically feasible under the conditions at hand. Unlike Belaúnde, he never ceded his authority to the more theoretically driven technocrats on his economic team. By mid-1987, Febres Cordero's pragmatism was the guiding force of economic policy, not economic theory. The crisis in the oil industry deeply affected Febres Cordero's thinking on economic matters and changed his orientation. In his view, he was managing, "an economy of crisis, an economy of war where market laws don't apply." He saw no alternative but to maintain public spending, arguing that the country could not tolerate a deeper recession. Febres Cordero's refusal to cut public spending in 1986–87 was the first indication of the slide away from strict orthodoxy.

The sense of emergency that gripped the Febres Cordero administration in 1987 was not simply the product of the economic downturn. Febres Cordero recognized that the political conditions that had allowed him to go forward with economic reforms were dissipating. By 1987, Febres Cordero was forced to put aside the grander goal of economic restructuring, and his attention turned to the more primal task of political survival—simply completing his term in office.

Political Meltdown

The initial success achieved in implementing neoliberal packages was contingent on a special set of political conditions (see chapter 6). Namely, neoliberal programs were products of policy-making environments that were highly exclusionary in character. By "exclusionary environment," we mean one that is characterized by (1) an extreme concentration of decision-making powers in the hands of the president and a small economic team; (2) a near complete marginalization of Congress from economic policy decisions; (3) a marked resistance within the economic team to any compromise with dissenting social groups or party elites; and (4) a willingness on the part of the executive to use repressive measures (albeit not illegal ones in most instances) to pursue the program.

Maintaining such an exclusionary policy-making environment was not an easy task. The authoritarian structure of the Southern Cone military governments of the 1970s automatically created an institutional framework that facilitated the implementation of neoliberal experiments. But the Andean presidents of the 1980s had to maneuver to seal off economic policy making from pluralist pressures while at least appearing to remain within the bounds of democratic constitutionalism. Presidents labored to create an ''authoritarian bubble'' inside the democratic system—a space in which economic policy could be hived off from normal politicking and be less subject to reversals. To maintain this bubble of space, presidents had to make optimal use of the political resources at their disposal. Their formal powers as prescribed by the constitution were stretched to the limit (or perhaps even beyond the limit, as many critics of Febres Cordero contended). At the same time, they used the informal presidential powers of persuasion and intimidation to keep their administrations on track and their opponents off balance. In short, neoliberal policies were an act of political construction as well as economic design. In the final analysis, Febres Cordero and Belaúnde were unable to maintain the political conditions necessary to keep their reforms afloat.

In Ecuador. Of the two presidents, Febres Cordero used the most aggressive tactics in his drive to establish the executive's monopolistic control over economic policy. During his first months in office, critics pointed with alarm to the authoritarian style of the new administration. Analysts referred to it as a ''muscled presidency,'' ''civilian dictatorship,'' and even a *rambocracia*.[7] Febres Cordero moved decisively during his first year in office to break any opposition, toward him and toward the neoliberal reforms. A critical component of this process was his attack on the antigovernment bloque progresista majority that controlled Congress. His approach to undoing the bloque was anything but subtle: it included enticing deputies to desert their parties, questionable legal maneuvers that tied up congressional legislation, and the use of physical force to intimidate Congress.

That Febres Cordero struck an aggressive posture in his dealings with the opposition was not particularly surprising. His belligerent personal style was something of a trademark throughout his public career. A deep bitterness and mistrust, reinforced by the 1984 electoral campaign, permeated the relation between Febres Cordero and opposition forces of the FRN. From the start of the administration, Febres Cordero and his advisors saw themselves as besieged by a communist opposition. The idea of seeking a pact with opposition forces, which would allow neoliberal reforms to go forth with multipartisan support, was never seriously contemplated. The bloque progresista was formed in July 1984 with the express purpose of opposing neoliberalism.

Acrimony ensued between the executive and legislative branches during the first year of the administration. But Febres Cordero's persistent assault on the bloque progresista eventually proved successful. By August 1985, the bloque majority had been wheedled away by defections and opportunistic alliances between the FRN and two populist parties. In place of the bloque, a progovernment majority crystallized in Congress, and Averroes Bucaram of the populist CFP was elected president of Congress. The newly compliant Congress allowed Febres Cordero to issue a number of the most important legal reforms of the neoliberal package as "urgent economic decrees."

In early 1986, Febres Cordero and the neoliberal project appeared unstoppable. Yet, the administration found its political fortunes rapidly reversed in the months from March through June 1986. What started as a bizarre protest by a senior air force officer dramatically changed the political landscape and opened the doors to a resurgence of civilian opposition to the administration.

On 7 March 1986, a coastal air force base in the province of Manta was seized by Air Force General Frank Vargas Pazzos. Joined by five hundred troops and support personnel, Vargas took over the base to protest what he characterized as examples of government corruption. Specifically, Vargas charged high-ranking administration officials with graft in the purchase of two Fokker airplanes from a Dutch firm. The takeover of the base was staged to draw attention to Vargas's charges, and he called for the resignation of Minister of Defense Luis Piñeiros and Commander General Manuel María Albuja. Vargas did not call for an overthrow of the Febres Cordero government, but his action did reflect dissatisfactions within the officer corps over Febres Cordero's interference with promotion procedures in the armed forces. Vargas's protest was the first public act of military insubordination to a civilian executive since the reinstallation of civilian rule in 1979.

As news of the event spread, civilian supporters flocked to the base to join Vargas. Initial negotiations between Vargas and a variety of government negotiators failed. In a televised address on 10 March, Febres Cordero announced his decision to use the army to recapture the base by force. On the following day, Vargas ended the showdown by declaring that a deal had been struck. Vargas agreed to surrender himself in return for the resignations of Piñeiros and Albuja. The legal charges against Vargas for the uprising were to be handled by a military tribunal. Upon his surrender, Vargas was taken to the Mariscal Sucre air force base in Quito, where the story took another bizarre turn. In the early evening of 13 March, Vargas took over the Quito air base where he was being held. Vargas maintained that the administration reneged on its Manta agreement, and he called for a mass mobilization against the government. Febres Cordero immediately declared a state of emergency, cordoned off the area around the air base, and ordered a news blackout. On the morning of 14 March, army troops retook the base by force, recaptured Vargas, and sent him to yet another base outside Quito.[8]

Vargas's outburst turned him into a cult figure and popular symbol of opposition to the government. The events themselves, along with Vargas's charges of corruption, were deeply embarrassing to the government—and highly advantageous to opposition parties who were preparing for midterm congressional elections in June 1986. Vargas's protest seemed to energize public opposition to the government by rupturing its image of invincibility.

In fear of losing control over Congress, Febres Cordero had floated a plan to postpone the midterm election in 1985. He abandoned that plan, however, in the face of strong opposition by the U.S. government to any plan to scuttle elections. After returning from a visit to Washington in January 1987, Febres Cordero announced his commitment to go ahead with the June races, but with the inclusion of a referendum. The referendum put forth by Febres Cordero proposed a change in the law of political parties, which would permit "independent" candidates to stand for election. The proposed change would have fundamentally altered the logic of the party law, which was designed originally to strengthen party organizations, professionalize the political class, and rid the system of "personalist" parties organized around individual leaders. Febres Cordero had always disagreed with the ban on independents. Moreover, a win on the referendum would be seen as a political repudiation of his arch rival and critic, Osvaldo Hurtado, who had led the commission that designed the law in 1978.

Osvaldo Hurtado responded to the administration's political challenge and led the opposition to frame the plebiscite as a popular referendum on the conduct of the government. In the initial salvo of the NO campaign, a fellow Christian Democratic party leader laid out the themes of the opposition's mobilization:

> We say NO to the violence; NO to the authoritarianism; No to despotism; NO to the high cost of living; NO to deceit and lies; NO to political perjury; NO to the oligarchy; NO to cheating; NO to persecution; NO to torture; NO to the violation of human rights; NO to crime and fraud; NO to Latin American disintegration; NO to incompetence; NO to maneuvers; NO to opportunism; NO to unchecked political ambition; NO to injustice; NO to dictatorship; NO, a million times NO to Febres Cordero.[9]

The election results were another setback for the Febres Cordero administration. The No vote in the referendum garnered 69.5 percent of the votes cast; the Yes option failed to win a majority in any province, including Febres Cordero's home turf of Guayas. In addition to this humiliating personal blow to Febres Cordero, the midterm congressional elections held concurrently with the referendum undid the government's majority in Congress, and picking up some new seats, the bloque progresista parties were able to regain control of Congress. In August

1986, Andrés Vallejo of the social democratic ID, was sworn in once again as president of Congress.

The return of the bloque progresista majority brought a renewal of executive-legislative tensions; and it indirectly fueled a further deterioration in civil-military relations. In September 1986, the bloque progresista voted an amnesty for General Frank Vargas. Although opposed by the military court, the amnesty was upheld by the Tribunal de Garantías Constitucionales (TGC). Despite the TGC ruling, however, Febres Cordero refused to comply with the amnesty, and Frank Vargas remained in jail.

With the president and Congress at odds over the amnesty issue, Vargas supporters among the elite paratroopers stationed at the Taura air force base decided to take matters into their own hands. On the morning of 16 January 1986, air force troops attacked President Febres Cordero and his entourage as they disembarked from their plane at Taura. Two presidential guards were killed in the assault. Febres Cordero, his minister of defense, and other high-ranking officials were taken hostage. The rebel troops threatened to kill Febres Cordero and his fellow hostages if Frank Vargas was not immediately freed. By early evening, the rebels secured their demands. A visibly shaken Febres Cordero was forced in front of television cameras to sign a deal to free Frank Vargas and guarantee no reprisals against the Taura rebels.

The entire Congress condemned the attack on the civilian president, but bloque progresista deputies wasted no time in seizing the moment to undermine the government. Opposition legislators characterized the Taura incident as a product of the climate of violence induced by the administration and directly linked to Febres Cordero's blatant disregard for the constitutional powers of Congress.

Four days after the kidnapping, Congress's President Andrés Vallejo opened a special legislative session to discuss a motion drafted by bloque legislators requesting the resignation of Febres Cordero. The motion condemned the president for misconduct ranging from human rights abuses to violations of the constitution. Two days of emotional debate ensued; opposition legislators used the sessions to slam everything from Febres Cordero's foreign policy to his governing style. The debate concluded with a vote of 38 deputies in favor of the motion, 29 opposed, and two abstentions.

The motion was not an impeachment, however. Because the bloque lacked the two-thirds majority required for impeachment, the motion did not legally bind Febres Cordero to resign. To no one's surprise, Febres Cordero refused to heed Congress's call and characterized the motion as irrelevant and antidemocratic. Coming on the heels of his kidnapping, this vote of no confidence by the Congress was seen by Febres Cordero as a cruel blow and as evidence of the bloque's commitment to force him out of office.

Febres Cordero survived the immediate fallout of the kidnapping, but the events had a profound effect on how he perceived his own presidency and his policy options. As he later put it in an interview, he felt as if he were governing "with a pistol to the throat." He believed from that point on that his presidency (and perhaps his own life) were at risk.[10]

To understand the unfolding of public policy in 1987–88, it is important to keep in mind that the political shock of the kidnapping was immediately followed by the devastating earthquake of March 1987. With renewed fiscal problems engendered by the natural disaster, Febres Cordero made the critical decision not to press for a drastic stabilization program to correct the government's budget deficit. Instead, Febres Cordero decided to push on with his spending for public works projects. Political considerations, rather than economic ones, influenced this choice.

Like Belaúnde, Febres Cordero was committed personally to public works spending. As an engineer, he strongly believed that infrastructure projects were crucial for economic development. As a *costeño,* he also had an abiding interest in ensuring that the coastal provinces received a generous share of public works expenditures. Moreover, his presidential campaign heavily emphasized his commitments to public works. Early in his administration, Febres Cordero set up a special office to oversee public works and community projects, known as *unidades ejecutoras*. Situated in the office of the president and headed by the president's closest personal advisors, the unidades were projects authorized directly by the president, which were not subject to the rules and regulations of the normal bureaucratic channels for such spending (for example, the Ministry of Public Works, municipal governments). As the government's popularity faded, the continuation of the obras policy became an obvious route to shore up some support for the government and allowed Febres Cordero to leave some tangible legacy from his term in office.[11]

In his weakened political position, Febres Cordero believed that his presidency would not be able to survive the congressional agitation and public protest that would accompany any renewed effort at austerity measures. With congressional opposition firmly in place, Febres Cordero saw no prospects for either moving ahead with deep structural reforms (for example, privatization of public firms, cutbacks in government bureaucracies) or instigating short-term stabilization. Moreover, he reasoned that any attempt to breach the constitutional order (for example, closing Congress) would bring sanctions from the United States and international isolation. Thus, an overtly authoritarian project capable of forcing neoliberal reforms was not a viable option. In the crisis conjuncture of 1987, Febres Cordero fixed on a new goal—finishing his prescribed term in office and handing power over to his elected successor.

In Peru. While civil-military conflict did not figure into the erosion of neoliberalism in Peru, the electoral cycle did. Although Belaúnde did not have to contend with midterm congressional races, municipal elections were scheduled for what was to be the worst year of the economic crisis, 1983. APRA and the leftist parties—united in the Izquierda Unida (IU) front—jumped on the opportunity to cast the November election as a referendum on Belaúnde's economic policies. Predictably, Belaúnde's AP was routed. APRA took 38 percent of the vote nationwide, while AP totaled only 10 percent. IU scored 23 percent nationwide, and IU candidate Alfonso Barrantes won the important mayoralty of Lima. This humiliating defeat for AP confirmed the fears among party leaders that they were heading for an even bigger electoral debacle in 1985 if economic policy was not redirected. From within his party, pressure intensified for Belaúnde to dump Rodríguez Pastor and to move away from his ultraliberal line. With his party in a state of frenzy, Belaúnde finally recognized the election results as a rejection of his policies and promised a change in the economic team.

It would have been difficult for Belaúnde to ignore popular frustrations, as they were being increasingly expressed on the street as well as in the ballot box. Two nationwide general strikes were staged in 1983. The first came in March in response to Rodríguez Pastor's call for more spending cuts; a second followed in September. Two more general strikes protesting economic policies were called in March and November 1984. Along with the resurgence of general strikes, workers also resorted to more aggressive tactics in their workplace conflicts, such as the seizure of plants. This tactic was even used by the Lima police, who went on strike in May 1983 and seized their headquarters. High-profile strikes by municipal workers and bus drivers added to the sense of public disorder. By December 1983, Belaúnde's approval rating as president stood at 19.7 percent (his 1981 approval rating had been 56 percent). Another poll showed that 48 percent of the public believed a coup was possible. In mid-1983, the coup fears were fed by near daily speculation in the press.[12]

The image of the government as under siege by Peruvian society was heightened by the growing presence of the guerrilla movement Sendero Luminoso. Founded in 1970, the Maoist Sendero had transformed itself from a tiny insurgent group located in Ayacucho to a disruptive guerrilla force.[13] By 1983, Sendero was rocking Lima with explosions and electricity blackouts. In May 1983, Belaúnde ordered the first state of emergency aimed specifically at dealing with Sendero. A massive military campaign against Sendero ensued, and the overall level of political violence climbed. Deaths in the guerrilla war in 1983 came to 1,979 in contrast to the 187 deaths registered in 1982. The 1984 death toll mounted to 3,588.[14] The escalating political violence only reinforced the public's sense that the government was ineffective and that Peru was drifting out of control.

As their terms entered the second half, Febres Cordero and Belaúnde both found themselves facing hostile actors they could no longer ignore, co-opt, or easily repress. Political conditions and the prestige of their governments had deteriorated to the point where steamrolling ahead with economic experimentation was no longer viable. Their decision to back away from neoliberalism was not just a product of the politician's aversion to unpopularity. At the base of the decision was also a suspicion that the political regime itself might be at stake. In the mind of Febres Cordero, the terms of the trade-off were clear. He believed that any further pursuit of neoliberalism within the context of the deteriorating political conditions could provoke a rupture in the constitutional order. As he later put it, "I thought it was preferable that the economy deteriorate a little in order to save democracy."[15] The capacity of the two presidents to maintain an authoritarian-style grip over economic policy was progressively eroded—by societal forces, the effects of economic crisis, and nagging fears that the regime could break down.

Technocrats in Retreat

As we have seen, neoliberal projects were launched by a coterie of technocrats who were ideologically committed to market-oriented reforms and who also believed strongly in their own technical expertise and sophistication. They resented attempted intrusions into the rarefied realm of economics by nonspecialists and "rent-seeking" interest groups.[16]

This combination of ideological passion and professional confidence (which many in the opposition frequently read as arrogance) created a mental shield that heightened the proclivity of these technocrats to resist societal demands to alter economic policy. But the resurgence of militant opposition and the ensuing attrition of presidential power, however, made it difficult for presidents to hold their neoliberal cadres in place. Key ministers were forced out of office, and each administration's commitment to neoliberalism waned in the absence of a strong economic team.

In Peru. In Peru, as the dimensions of the economic crisis became evident in 1983, the decomposition of the neoliberal team involved both the exit of key individuals and a breakdown of consensus within the team itself. In fact, there had never been complete harmony within Belaúnde's cabinet on the direction of economic policy. All three PPC ministers of industry, for example, lobbied alongside industry for a more gradual approach to liberalization. Belaúnde's first minister of labor, Alfonso Grados Bertorini, promoted *concertación* and advocated a more conciliatory stance toward unions. But during the first part of the administration these dissenting voices in the cabinet had been ignored and outmaneuvered by the predominant prime minister, Manuel Ulloa.

Ulloa's resignation from the government in December 1982 did not signal a significant reorientation of economic policy. Belaúnde's choice as his successor was Carlos Rodríguez Pastor, an experienced international banker and convinced monetarist. His concern on assuming office was to remedy Peru's balance-of-payments problem and to negotiate new international credit. To create a credible image for international lenders, Rodríguez Pastor knew that a fresh round of price increases, government budget cuts, and a reduction in the money supply would be necessary. In his initial pronouncements to the public, he warned that even greater austerity lay ahead.

With the economy already in a deep recession by early 1983, Richard Webb began what he termed a "common sense rebellion against orthodoxy" from inside the government. Webb was the Harvard-trained economist who had accepted Belaúnde's offer to head the Banco Central de Reserva (BCR). Webb, who had largely supported the orthodox line, broke ranks with Rodríguez Pastor and took antirecessionary measures from his post at the bank. In open defiance of the policies outlined by Rodríguez Pastor and the IMF, Webb refused to undertake a credit crunch by raising interest rates. In another move to fight the contraction of the business sector, Webb authorized an expansion of BCR lending. The BCR also supported the move by Congress to place a ceiling on the monthly increases of government-controlled prices, including the exchange rate.

Webb's actions effectively created a "dual power" situation within the economic team as Rodríguez Pastor lost control over key components of economic policy. Belaúnde had no legal way to control Webb. As president of the BCR, Webb enjoyed a fixed term in office and could only be removed by congressional impeachment.

The mutiny inside the economic team and AP's electoral defeat in November 1983 set the stage for the final dissolution of the neoliberal experiment. Immediately following the election, Belaúnde indicated that a change in economic policy would be forthcoming. Rodríguez Pastor was kept in place, however, until work on a new accord with the IMF was near completion in March 1984. The terms of the agreement were predictable: the Fund demanded massive cuts in government spending as the sine qua non for new lending. Rodríguez Pastor resigned just days before another general strike was called to protest austerity measures.

Despite the budget cuts set out in the agreement with the Fund, Belaúnde announced at the end of March that the government would embark on a new policy of "austerity without recession." What this meant was that Belaúnde was ready to spend \$600 million in soft-term loans to reactivate the economy with more public works spending. This public dissociation of Belaúnde from the orthodox line triggered the resignation of his prime minister and minister of foreign relations, Fernando Schwalb, who was an ardent supporter of Rodríguez Pastor and the fiscal austerity line. Schwalb's exit in April 1984 opened the doors to a complete cabinet reshuffle and a revamping of economic policy.

Belaúnde's new cabinet appointments were experienced politicians drawn from the ranks of his own party. Several had been active in the anti-neoliberal agitations inside AP. One was Sandro Mariátegui, an AP senator, designated as Belaúnde's prime minister and minister of foreign relations. Another critic of neoliberalism in the Chamber of Deputies, Valentín Paniagua, took the post of minister of education. José Benavides, who had served in the Belaúnde cabinet in the Ministries of Education and Energy, became minister of the economy. PPC officially withdrew from its cabinet positions, and an AP appointee, Alvaro Becerra Sotero, took over the Ministry of Industry.

The new ministers shared the belief that the economy needed reactivation, and they endorsed Belaúnde's public spending plans. They also moved to dismantle trade liberalization policies. The minister of industry imposed new import prohibitions to protect those domestic industries that were suffering under liberalization. Over a hundred items—including textiles, footwear, vehicles, and cigarettes—were banned from importation. Export incentives for industries were hiked through an increase in the CERTEX.

The turn away from neoliberalism did not, however, put an end to the feud between Belaúnde and Webb. Webb harshly criticized what he saw as the completely contradictory initiatives emanating from the government—that is, the promise to meet IMF targets and continue debt repayments while reactivating the economy through public spending. Fearing that increased liquidity would fuel capital flight, Webb pulled the Central Bank back to restrictive monetary policies in 1984. Just as he had used the BCR as a counterweight against recessionary government policies in 1983, Webb in 1984 used it to oppose the government's policy reversal.

By Webb's own account, there was a complete "balkanization" of economic policy by 1984–85; ministers proceeded with their own initiatives without direction or coordination. The abandonment of the neoliberal project and the exit of its technocrats left the government without a clear core of ideas (or personnel) around which to organize economic strategy. Belaúnde's only real priority was to complete his public works projects prior to the 1985 presidential election. In pursuit of this objective, he kept his economic ministers in rounds of negotiations to seek new funds even while Belaúnde's domestic policies were completely at odds with the conditions being stipulated by international lenders.

In Ecuador. Febres Cordero's fixation on controlling Congress stemmed in part from his desire to keep his economic triumvirate—Emanuel, Dahik, and Swett—intact and protected from partisan harassment. Ecuador's constitution allowed Congress to exercise oversight of cabinet ministers in two ways. First, ministers can be required by Congress to present reports *(informes)*. Second, congressional deputies also have the right to launch an interpellation of a minister, which could in turn lead to a vote of censure and his or her forced resignation. In the interpellation process, a minister is served with a specific list of questions or charges and is expected to answer them in person before a session of Congress. If Congress is dissatisfied with the minister's defense, it can subsequently vote a motion of censure.[17] Even if an interpellation does not result in censure, the process can be politically damaging for the government. Moreover, interpellation can be time consuming, diverting the minister's attention away from other business. So, like his predecessors, Febres Cordero wanted to limit his ministers' exposure to interpellations.

But warding off interpellation became impossible once the antigovernment majority was reconstituted after the midterm elections in August 1986. By that time, the economic team had already suffered its first turnover; Finance Minister Francisco Swett left his post in June and was replaced by Alberto Dahik, who had been heading the Monetary Board. The congressional attack commenced in September 1984 in the wake of the elimination of multiple fixed exchange rates in favor of a uniform rate to be determined by marked forces. Interest rates were also deregulated in the August measures. Congressional critics charged Finance Minister Dahik with constitutional violations in the enactment of the new monetary reforms and called for his interpellation.

Febres Cordero believed there were no legal grounds for censure proceedings since Dahik had not headed the Monetary Board at the time of the exchange rate reform; he held a vote as minister of finance, but the Monetary Board was a collegial body. Moreover, the head of the Monetary Board could not be interpellated by Congress. Febres Cordero likened the proceedings to the "crucifixion of an innocent man." Vice-President Blasco Peñaherrera portrayed it as a straightforward attack on the government's philosophy, "an inquisition-like impeachment of an ideology."[18]

Interpellation procedures began in early September. Ten legislators drafted nineteen questions for Dahik; most focused on the legal bases for the Monetary Board's actions. Dahik's responses to the questions turned into a kind of filibuster. He held the floor for nearly a month as the government proceeded to implement the flotation. Dahik's long rebuttals covered a wide range of topics from Ecuador's economic history to a review of the regulations governing economic policy making. In the course of his testimony, Dahik was hospitalized several days for exhaustion. He finally concluded his defense on a strange note. After having defended the legality of the Board's actions for weeks, he argued that he could not be held accountable for any actions by the Monetary Board since he had actually stepped out of the room just prior to the vote. He noted that BCR President Emanuel had actually led the meeting, not him.[19] Opposition legislators scoffed at Dahik's attempt to escape on a technicality. The proceedings concluded with 39 deputies voting in favor of censure, 21 voting against, and 7 abstentions.

Febres Cordero accepted Dahik's resignation but did not reverse the exchange rate reform. Congressmen subsequently took their claims regarding its unconstitutionality to the constitutional court, the Tribunal de Garantías Constitucionales (TGC). Like Francisco Swett, after his resignation, Dahik continued to act as informal economic advisor to the president and even maintained an office in the Central Bank. The administration dismissed the Dahik censure as a partisan affair. According to Emanuel, Febres Cordero never considered rescinding the exchange rate reform in response to congressional action.[20]

Whereas Dahik's censure did not immediately redirect economic policy, it did have repercussions for how the neoliberal project was to fare in the long run. The exits of Swett and Dahik, two of the original architects of the project, deprived Febres Cordero of important managers. Along with Emanuel, they had provided the technical expertise that gave life to Febres Cordero's aspirations for economic liberalization. They had worked together with Febres Cordero on these ideas since 1980. As Febres Cordero put it, they brought a common *bagaje de lucha* (shared history of struggle) to their jobs. This common understanding and the close working relations were lost with the breakup of the team. In July 1988, Emanuel left to prepare for a presidential bid in the 1989 race.

With the attrition in the economic team and the mounting problems he faced in 1987, Febres Cordero lost his moorings as an economic policy maker. His new cabinet appointments did not have the same missionary zeal as their predecessors. The dominant personality in the economic team in the last two years of the administration was Rodrigo Espinoza Bermeo, who served as head of the Monetary Board and minister of finance. Espinoza, who had headed the BCR during the Poveda Burbano military government, was not a hard-core neoliberal and professed a belief in the need for state intervention to redress income inequalities. He concurred with Febres Cordero that freezing public works expenditures in 1987 would only prolong the recession. Neither Espinoza nor the other new members of the economic team were inclined to press Febres Cordero for fiscal austerity.

The exit of neoliberal technocrats from the Febres Cordero and Belaúnde governments was an important dimension in the collapse of the coalitions that had launched neoliberalism. As the economic crisis deepened in both countries, business backers joined the exit too.

Business and the End of Neoliberalism

An explanation of the collapse of the two policy experiments would not be complete without consideration of the behavior of the business sector during the period. The Ecuadorean and the Peruvian experiences show how problematic business's relationships to such experiments can be. Business joined with rightist politicians and technocrats in the antistatist movement; but the solidarity among the three groups did not translate into a commonly held and enduring understanding of what neoliberalism would look like in practice. This was the weakness of the coalition: support for the executives and technocrats from the business sector, their coalitional partner in civil society, was always tenuous. Its tenuous character was exacerbated by the proclivity of executives and technocrats to keep their coalitional partner "out of the loop" of economic policy making. Support for neoliberalism within the private sector was always tempered by the immediate effects of the measures on specific sectors of the business community. Whereas businessmen supported the ideological foundations of the respective governments, they were not willing to put aside the defense of their immediate economic interests to stand by those governments in hard times. In both countries, the market behavior that businessmen engaged in to defend themselves during economic crises actually helped sabotage the reforms. Currency speculation and capital flight helped trigger the reversals of the reforms.

The flotation of exchange and interest rates decreed by the Febres Cordero government in August 1986 were frequently depicted by members of the administration as a "historic" achievement—that is, a sign of the definitive break with Ecuador's "statist" past.[21] Yet, on 13 March 1988, the free market in foreign exchange was abolished by Febres Cordero. In its place, a government-controlled system was reestablished that forced business transactions back into a market whose rates were determined by the Central Bank. Febres Cordero described himself as heartbroken over the reversion to regulation, characterizing the decision as "the hardest step I ever had to take in my life."[22]

Febres Cordero's reluctant decision to step back from his historic reform came in response to rampant currency speculation that pushed the value of the national currency to a record low. The speculation against the sucre was fueled by the uncertainty that pervaded political and economic spheres in 1987–88. The presidential kidnapping of January 1987 was followed by the earthquake in March and the start-up of the presidential election campaign for 1988. The deterioration of economic conditions and the unstable political atmosphere encouraged investors to protect themselves—and they did so by rushing to buy dollars.

Stability in the free foreign exchange market depended to a great extent on the steady sale of dollars, from hard-currency generators (or exporters) to other businessmen (or importers, industrialists). The transactions were handled by private commercial banks. From the start, however, there were fears that the agroexporters of Guayaquil could exploit their market position by withholding currency in order to force up the price. To guard against that possibility, the Central Bank sold surplus dollars on the free market to buoy up the sucre. One source estimates that the Central Bank injected at least $500 million into the free market system between August 1986 and the beginning of 1987.[23] But the loss of revenue from the halt of petroleum exports in 1987 made it impossible for the BCR to continue to prop up the sucre through this ''dirty float.''

As the demand for dollars increased, exporters used their oligopolistic position to push dollar prices ever higher. Febres Cordero began steps in May 1987 to relieve pressure on the sucre. He started by reducing liquidity in the banking system. Starting in May 1987, the reserve requirements for banks were hiked. A new round of increases followed in September and another in October. The government also imposed new prior deposits for imports.

Despite these moves, the value of the sucre steadily declined, however, helping to fuel inflationary pressures in the last quarter of 1987. An even wilder frenzy of speculation ensued in the wake of the first round of the presidential elections held in January 1988. Neither of the two candidates who emerged from the first round were particularly appealing to the business sector. The two contenders scheduled to face off in the May runoff were Rodrigo Borja and Abdalá Bucaram. Borja was the social democrat who had lost to Febres Cordero in 1984. Bucaram was the demagogic leader of the populist Partido Roldosista. The election results fueled investors' nervousness. By 1 March, the price of the dollar on the Quito market stood at 398 sucres. One year earlier, the exchange rate had stood at 153 sucres. In a country accustomed to stability in the exchange rate, the surge was a source of anxiety to the public at large as well as to business. Both the Chamber of Industry and the Chamber of Commerce urged the government to take steps to stop the increase, although neither body advocated the dismantling of the free market system.[24]

In an effort to save the system, Febres Cordero personally lobbied exporters in February, urging them not to constrict the dollar supply. His appeal fell on deaf ears. In total frustration, on 2 March 1988, Febres Cordero and his economic team mandated the renewal of Central Bank control over the foreign exchange market. In a new three-tiered system, exporters were obliged to see their exchange in a ''controlled-free'' market in which the rate was regulated by the Central Bank. An ''intervention'' market controlled by the BC determined the rates for public sector transactions. Finally, a nonregulated ''free'' market was allowed to function to supply the residual demand for dollars.

Even after re-regulation, guayaquileño exporters remained recalcitrant and continued to withhold exchange from the controlled-free market, while trafficking on the free market. By 24 March, the exchange rate on the free market stood at 475 sucres. In the controlled-free market, the rate was 275 sucres; but there were virtually no dollars available for purchase in that market. Outraged by the coastal exporters' ongoing defiance, Febres Cordero called a meeting with business leaders in Guayaquil on 23 March to pressure them to comply with the new system. On hand for the meeting were the top exporters, including Febres Cordero's ex-boss Luis Noboa Naranjo. Days after the meeting, Febres Cordero publicly castigated two top exporters, Hugo Albán and Miguel Marchán, by jailing them for violations of the exchange regulations.[25]

The pursuit of short-term profit-maximizing strategies by key individuals within the Ecuadorean private sector set the forces in motion that led to the demise of financial liberalization. In this denouement of the neoliberal project the irony was that these were the same business groups (the Guayaquil Chamber of Commerce, for example) that had long championed the idea of a free market in foreign exchange. In the context of the highly uncertain political and economic environment of 1987–88, the behavior of exporters was indeed rational, at least in the short run. In the long run, however, a concerted push by the bourgeoisie to maintain the system may have been more advantageous. Yet, such an effort did not materialize. Looking back on the event, Febres Cordero bitterly blamed the private sector for ruining the reforms:

> They [the businessmen] never understood the crisis—or they wanted to take advantage of it to rob the country. Nobody can question my business background. I was one of the top businessmen in the country. I was their leader for ten years. I didn't lose faith in the system, I lost faith in the men that didn't understand the system and defend it. . . . I never thought they would do what they did. If you want to call me naive, then call me naive. I never thought they would run over the interests of the country in favor of their own pockets. They demonstrated they were capable of this. . . . They are going to pay the price for twenty more years for their lack of vision. Because they destroyed the public image of the only system that works—but it was they who destroyed it.[26]

In Peru, business defended itself against the economic crisis through a combination of "voice" (public protest) and "exit" (capital flight). The business groups immediately and most adversely affected by Belaúnde's economic policies swung into action first (see chapter 6). These were the domestic industrialists represented in SNI and the nontraditional exporting industrialists of ADEX. The lobby was not initially effective, but it gained support from other strategic players in the private sector (some of the large economic groups) as the recession swept through every productive sector in 1983. All the major sectoral lobbies pressed for reactivation policies. The growing unity in the private sector finally culminated in the formation of the Confederation of Private Business Institutions (CONFIEP) in October 1984. CONFIEP brought together all the major business interest groups—spanning commerce, manufacturing, mining, construction, and fishing.[27]

Whereas business leaders voiced their disillusion with Belaúnde's economic policies publicly, individual investors registered theirs in market behavior. Defensive reactions by investors had the cumulative effect of deepening the recession. One of the primary strategies used by all types of firms was to try to increase (or at least maintain) their ratio of liquid assets, particularly in the form of holdings in foreign currency. In the quest to maintain liquidity, firms delayed payments on accounts, defaulted on debts, and withheld tax payments. The aim behind this strategy was to keep liquid assets intact while throwing the costs of adjustment onto other actors (the state, other firms, or banks, for example). Along with the turn toward currency speculation, there was also a marked surge in capital flight. Calculations estimating the magnitude of flight differ, but all the sources concur that a significant external transfer of capital occurred in the latter part of the Belaúnde administration.[28]

Thus, during the recession, business used strategies that only served to aggravate it. The tendency to hold assets as liquid instruments and move them out of the country contributed to the decline in production, investment, employment, and wages in this period. Private investment as a percentage of GDP fell to 13 percent in 1984 in contrast to 20 percent in 1981. Richard Webb noted in his study of the period, ''it can be said that the financial experience of the enterprises during the crisis period under consideration contained a paradox: although they withstood the crisis with surprising success, their survival mechanisms had a high social cost and probably helped to aggravate the global crisis.''[29]

In both countries, business elites opted for short-term profit maximization over any residual loyalties they may have had to the center-right governments. Certainly, it was a ''rational'' choice on their part. This rational behavior in the marketplace had destructive macroeconomic effects, however, and exacerbated the developing economic crisis. Not only did the economic crisis undermine the viability of market reforms, but it also undercut the notion that such reforms could be beneficial. As Febres Cordero noted, the predatory behavior of some capitalists called into question the credibility of deregulation policies. The actions of capitalists belied the argument that the private sector would behave reasonably if unfettered by the state.

Economics as Political Construction

Economic policies can fail for a wide variety of reasons. Unexpected events can radically alter the economic landscape for policy makers. Crops fail, natural disasters strike, international markets change—all of these events are outside the control of economic teams and can wreak havoc with the best-laid economic plans. Policy makers may find that *fortuna*, or just plain luck, can be an extremely important part of the stories of success or failure.[30]

But fortune is not the only factor at work in these stories. Presidents can ply their political skills in ways to facilitate the success of their economic policies. Both Belaúnde and Febres Cordero seized on propitious circumstances and helped create conditions to launch neoliberal programs. Both were able initially to concentrate decision-making powers in an economic team and to subordinate potential opponents. But neither president was able to maintain the conditions necessary to

sustain the policies through to the conclusions of their terms. The failure of Febres Cordero and Belaúnde as economic managers was not simply a matter of faulty technique (that is, bad policy design, unwise timing of measures, and so on). Certainly technical mistakes can be important in unraveling economic programs. But the real failure of Febres Cordero and Belaúnde was their inability to manage the economic projects politically. Neither president directed his attention to transforming the elite-centric neoliberal coalition that brought him to power into a durable political force capable of backing reforms over the long haul. In other words, there was no attempt on the part of Febres Cordero or of Belaúnde to build political organizations dedicated to generating mass support to sustain neoliberal reforms. This was evident in their attitudes toward their own parties.

The lack of concern with party-building on the right was evident throughout the Febres Cordero administration. Whereas he had won the presidency as a candidate of a united front of rightist parties, he gave no serious thought to developing FRN as a permanent organizational entity to unite the right around neoliberal reform. On the contrary, Febres Cordero marginalized FRN leaders from his government. Most of his key cabinet appointments went to independent technocrats and businessmen. Like many another political leader in Ecuador who conceptualized politics in personalist terms, Febres Cordero had a disdain for parties and saw no particular use for them other than electioneering. Febres Cordero's lack of interest in building support for his government by strengthening partisan organization on the right was connected to the notion that political organization was irrelevant to the fate of economic policy. Febres Cordero and his troika of technocrats believed that the neoliberal reforms would create a "natural" constituency for the right among those who benefited from the reforms. In their minds, the political support necessary to sustain the policies would be generated by the economic success of those policies alone. Cultivating support through the development of a strong society-penetrating party organization was never seen as vital to the fate of their economic reforms. When asked in 1987 why the administration did not pay more attention to organizing active political support to ensure the maintenance of their policies, Carlos Julio Emanuel explained:

> the measures that have been taken are going to be analyzed by the public on the basis of whether they help or hurt. You go to the coast in Ecuador and talk to agricultural producers and you'll see that their situation has improved. So how politically are you going to change that? If a government of a different tendency than ours decides to overrule the measures, that is going to come out in the electoral campaign. And we'll see how the electorate reacts, the coffee pickers, the shrimp-farm workers, etc. . . . So my feeling is that the electorate is not going to go for a candidate who is going to abolish [the reforms] because they are going to have problems electorally. So that's why there is not much preoccupation in the government to set up a strong Social Christian party that can win another election to maintain policies, because the policies are going to be there.[31]

Emanuel's comments neatly capture the technocrat's tendency to underestimate the importance of politics and to overestimate the effects of pure economics. The economic team believed in a simple equation in which the application of "technically correct" policies produced predictable (and beneficial results). These, in turn, would automatically translate into support for Febres Cordero. Also note the belief in the immutability of policies once in place. The assumption that neoliberal policies would inevitably succeed did not lead Febres Cordero or his advisors to contemplate organizing support to guarantee that success. One can imagine, for example, a different outcome on exchange rate liberalization had Febres Cordero been able to persuade exporters to behave differently. Such persuasion might have been feasible had Febres Cordero actively sought to strengthen political loyalties among those groups through party ties or through *concertación* with interest groups.

Like Febres Cordero, Belaúnde failed to use parties to build support for policies. His approach to his own AP and the allied PPC was largely instrumental; they were to be used for electioneering and to guarantee Belaúnde's dominance over Congress. As in Ecuador, party leaders were kept away from economic decision making. AP and PPC were cast in the roles of spectator and passive supporter, and their party leaders were excluded from the inner circle of the administration. Parties were not seen as potential vehicles to draw constituencies around the neoliberal reforms; rather, they were seen by the economic team as havens for those who would disarticulate the model. And, as the exclusionary character of the game became more evident, AP and PPC did become vehicles that businessmen sought out in order to lobby against certain policies.

Febres Cordero blamed Ecuadorean capitalists for their lack of vision, which he believed contributed to the ruin of his reforms. But Febres Cordero and Belaúnde themselves demonstrated a certain lack of vision—the inability to see that their economic programs demanded political innovation on their part. These administrations did not actively work to maintain the alliance of technocrats, capitalists, and politicians that had elected them, nor did they reach out to other groups for support. There was no attempt to cultivate support in the party system or in civil society. Once in power, the economic teams sought to maximize the distance between themselves and everyone else for fear that the economic projects would be diluted by politicking. The neoliberal technocrats expected parties and civil society to simply wait in the wings as they restructured their respective economies with the advice of international technocrats from the IMF and the World Bank.

The isolationist stance of these governments worked initially but then turned out to be counterproductive when the experiments fell on hard times. Rather than defend the reforms, many capitalists turned to defensive postures. There was no heroic effort by business interest groups to salvage the reforms. Febres Cordero and Belaúnde failed to realize that neoliberal projects demanded an aggressive political and ideological campaign aimed at keeping them in place; simply launching them was not enough. By ignoring parties and by refusing to reach out to the disgruntled business community, these presidents consigned their policies to failure.

These failures were recognized by the electorate; each president's party was soundly punished by voters in subsequent elections. Febres Cordero's successor to the PSC presidential nomination in 1988, Sixto Durán Ballén, received only 14.7 percent of the nationwide vote and failed to qualify for the second-round runoff election. In Peru, AP presidential candidate Javier Alva Orlandini polled an embarrassing 7 percent of the vote in the 1985 election. In both countries, voters awarded the presidency to social democrats—Rodrigo Borja of the ID in Ecuador and Alan García of APRA in Peru—in the wake of failed neoliberalism.

Part 2: Explaining Bolivia's Exceptionalism

The Dimensions of Success

Bolivia and Chile stand together as examples of the most radical neoliberal restructuring that has taken place to date in South America. Before explaining why Bolivia was able to stay the course on neoliberalism, we should specify in what sense Bolivian neoliberalism can be regarded a success. The NPE begun in 1985 was successful, insofar as the government was able to define, implement, and sustain it as a set of coherent policies turning the country away from its previous state capitalist model. Like Chile, Bolivia was able to combine a short-term stabilization program with a deeper restructuring process. Unlike Chile, Bolivia undertook this effort under an elected civilian government rather than a military dictatorship. What is astonishing about the experiments in both countries is that, albeit under very different political circumstances, a consensus crystallized among contending party elites on the need to sustain the reforms beyond the tenure of the government that had initiated them. In both countries, the economy, polity, and society were profoundly altered by the neoliberal experiment.

Bolivia's neoliberal program has been characterized as stabilization-cum-liberalization, that is, standard stabilization measures coupled with a rapid-fire deregulation and opening of the economy.[32] The government's immediate objective was to eradicate hyperinflation, which had reached catastrophic levels in 1985. In the weeks just before the enactment of D.S. 21060, weekly inflation rates ranged from 6 to 19 percent. The stabilization effort included the unification and flotation of the exchange rate and a rapid reduction of the government's fiscal deficit in order to stop seignorage financing.

Within ten days after the decree was issued on 29 August, the effects of the measures were visible and inflation came to a dead halt. The government was able to maintain inflation at acceptable levels throughout the remainder of its term. From 1986 through 1989, yearly inflation rates were 65.9, 10, 21.5, and 16.6 percent respectively. This was a dramatic break from the 2,177 percent and 8,170 percent annual inflation rates registered respectively in 1984 and 1985.[33]

The structural reform measures also produced significant changes. Perhaps the most innovative reform was the restructuring of the state-owned mining enterprise COMIBOL. The restructuring involved a massive downscaling of its operations. The reorganization plan closed mines and forced 23,000 out of 30,000 mine workers off the COMIBOL payroll. The shrinking of COMIBOL was a pivotal component of the NPE—not only because it was part of the effort to reduce state expenditures but also because of its political and psychological significance. COMIBOL was the bastion of the militant mine workers union, which had traditionally dominated the leadership of the COB. Moreover, COMIBOL stood as the most potent symbol of the state capitalist model that Bolivia had embarked on in 1952. Thus, the COMIBOL reform simultaneously signaled both the government's commitment to curbing union power and the dismantling of the public sector labyrinth. Other state entities were also affected by reorganization plans. Overall budget cuts combined with this rationalization of the public sector made a significant reduction of the government deficit possible. The deficit of the nonfinancial public sector dropped from 26 percent of GDP in 1984, to 10.7 percent in 1985, to 3.2 percent in 1986.[34]

For the most part, the NPE lived up to the expectations of its designers. The policies put an end to hyperinflation, established a new fiscal discipline in the public sector, and began retracting the state from the overarching role it had come to assume in the Bolivian economy. The policies sent positive signals to the international financial community that Bolivia was putting its house in order and merited special consideration. There were, of course, certain policy initiatives in the NPE that were not fully realized. The proposal to decentralize the administration of health and education went down to defeat in 1987. The program to reactivate the economy by extending fresh credit to the private sector lagged. No significant headway was made concerning the privatization of public enterprises in the 1985–89 period. Some short-term macroeconomic problems reappeared.

At this juncture, it is important to note that the NPE's relative success described here entailed a great deal of pain, especially among the low-income groups who were affected by job cuts and slashes in government expenditures. As in Chile, the social costs of neoliberalism were high. The socioeconomic indicators of the period reveal some of the dimensions of those costs. Open unemployment soared under structural adjustment. The unemployment rate by 1987 was estimated at between 18 and 25 percent. Estimates are that between 40,000 and 60,000 jobs in the formal economy disappeared because of the cuts in public employment and because of the dismissals in private sector jobs made possible by the new "flexible" labor regulations. Real per capita GDP shrank by 5.6 percent and .6 percent in 1986 and 1987. The real minimum wage fell from 3,800 pesos in 1985 to 2,654 pesos in 1986. There was some recovery in the minimum wage by 1988, but it still remained below its 1985 level and well below the minimum wage levels that had been attained earlier in the decade. The average monthly wage was the nominal equivalent of $25 in 1987.[35]

That President Paz Estenssoro was able to keep such painful policies in place and sustain civilian rule was an unusual political achievement in Latin America in the 1980s. The scope of that achievement was extended by the way in which the NPE was accepted by rival political elites. In the presidential campaign of 1989, all three leading contenders for the presidency (Gonzalo Sánchez de Lozada, Jaime Paz Zamora, and Hugo Banzer) pledged their support in varying degrees to continuing the policies in their prospective governments.

Paz Estenssoro emerged as an adroit political manager of the neoliberal project in Bolivia. He drew on political skills that he had honed in his long career in Bolivian politics, and he demonstrated a shrewd capacity to capitalize on the peculiar conjuncture that prevailed in Bolivia during the last half of the 1980s.

Passions, Skills, and Opportunity

What distinguishes effective chief executives from lesser ones is a hotly debated topic among historians and political scientists.[36] The effectiveness of presidential leadership was a decisive factor in Bolivia's exceptional policy performance. No account of the neoliberal project would be complete without an appreciation of the extraordinary political prowess of Víctor Paz Estenssoro. From 1985 through 1989, Paz put together his political skills with a fierce commitment to economic restructuring; and this combination of political intelligence and presidential passion was crucial to keeping the neoliberal project on course.

Paz's personal commitment to economic liberalization may seem, at first glance, as an ideological turnaround and a repudiation of his own past as founder of the populist MNR. But Paz's adherence to neoliberalism was not a departure as much as it was the logical conclusion of his own political trajectory.

There was much in Paz's political past that presaged his behavior in the 1985–89 period. While Paz had presided over the creation of Bolivia's public enterprises during his first presidency from 1952 to 1956, he had never been hostile to the idea of fomenting a modern private sector. Many of the early economic development policies focused on helping private enterprise, particularly in the eastern region of Santa Cruz. His interest in private enterprise was matched by hostility toward the labor movement. Paz was no stranger to the idea that Bolivian labor needed to be "disciplined," nor was he unfamiliar with the notion that COMIBOL should be restructured. During his second presidency, in 1963,

Paz ordered the closures of COMIBOL mines that led to a serious confrontation with the COB.[37]

In his years out of power, Paz became increasingly interested in the debates on market reforms and discussions on the demise of the welfare state. According to Gonzalo Sánchez de Lozada, he was drawn to reading on China and New Zealand and was fascinated by the idea of leftist governments turning to conservative economic formulas.[38]

Along with his interest in market economics, Paz had a personal agenda that fit tightly into the neoliberal project. As one of Bolivia's major political figures in the twentieth century, Paz harbored concerns about his place in history and how the legacy of the MNR-led revolution of 1952 would be regarded in the long run. With political and economic instability reaching catastrophic levels under the Siles Zuazo administration, Paz believed that drastic steps would have to be taken to save the Bolivian state from complete collapse. Rather than seeing the NPE as an indictment of the economic model he had helped set in place in 1952, Paz saw it as the only medicine that could save the modern state he had fathered. In Paz's view the NPE was a preservative, not a repudiation, of his past. Unlike Belaúnde and Febres Cordero, Paz was not concerned about the pursuit of public works projects. Nothing competed with the NPE as top priority for this administration.

Paz's efficacy in executing the NPE was greatly enhanced by the crisis conditions within which it was launched (see chapter 5). The severity of the crisis profoundly affected public opinion, and Paz capitalized on the changing public mood. The loss of routine in social and economic life that occurred in Bolivia from 1982 to 1985 was a disconcerting experience for everyone, and Paz correctly perceived that the public was willing to tolerate harsh measures to restore some semblance of normality.

As in Chile, the national trauma that preceded the neoliberal project prepared the public to accept a dramatic effort to rectify the situation. This made it possible for Paz to project neoliberalism as the only alternative to such dire circumstances. Moreover, heterodox prescriptions were already discredited by the crisis itself. Indeed, the participation of the social democratic MIR and the Communist party in the Siles government discredited the left as economic theorists and managers. The Siles government's disastrous economic management cleared the playing field for Paz, because it destroyed credibility in the alternative policies proposed by the left and the trade union movement.

Public tolerance for neoliberalism was reinforced by the immediate payoff of the stabilization effort. The swift end of hyperinflation just weeks after the enactment of D.S. 21060 legitimated the Paz government's approach. That the Paz government immediately delivered on its claims was crucial to maintaining public confidence in the program. Trade liberalization also produced visible effects in the marketplace, especially for middle-class consumers who could afford to take advantage of the flood of foreign imports.[39] Thus, the immediate effects of the program also helped to maintain support for the Paz government.

Political Deals and Institutional Adaptations

In contrast to Belaúnde and Febres Cordero, Paz recognized that the consolidation of the neoliberal reform required a complicated mix of macroeconomic performance and politics; that is, the desired economic results would have to be coupled with political arrangements in order to sustain the policies over time. By exerting considerable control over his own party and by sealing a pact with the rival ADN, Paz ensured congressional support for the NPE and developed an institutional grid to keep it locked in place.

Throughout Paz's term in office, dissent over economic policy was recurrent within the governing party. Traditional populists inside MNR were uncomfortable with neoliberal ideas and were anxious about the future electoral effects of austerity policies. Guillermo Bedregal never openly broke with Paz, but he frequently voiced the concerns of this populist wing of MNR. And Paz did not immediately appreciate the problems that the populist wing posed for the implementation of the NPE. To unite the party behind the government, Paz named Bedregal as his first minister of planning, and Roberto Gisbert as minister of finance joined Bedregal on the original economic team named in August 1985. Neither of the two intellectual architects of the NPE, Sánchez de Lozada and Cariaga, held a post in the first cabinet.

An external shock in late October 1985 exposed the weakness of Paz's original economic team and forced an important reorganization of the cabinet. Prices for Bolivia's tin exports unexpectedly fell by 60 percent. The export crisis reverberated throughout the economy and led to pressures on the government to reactivate spending. The economic team responded with increased government expenditures and an expansion in the money supply. Opposing this departure from the NPE, Sánchez de Lozada denounced the reappearance of inorganic emissions as a ''punishment from God.'' Suddenly, the Paz government seemed perilously close to repeating the policy errors of Siles.

It was at this juncture that Paz turned to advice from Harvard economist Jeffrey Sachs. Sachs, who had worked with Banzer's shadow economic team during the presidential campaign, had not been consulted directly during the formulation and initial implementation of D.S. 21060. But at the invitation of the CEPB, Sachs returned to La Paz in November and prepared a memorandum to submit to Paz on how to save the NPE. Sachs recommended the creation of a stabilization council composed of cabinet ministers and charged with the task of monitoring and authorizing government expenditures. He also argued for a change of personnel within the economic team, suggesting that Sánchez de Lozada should take the helm at the Planning Ministry because of his commitment to the pursuit of the reforms.[40]

With Sachs's recommendations in mind, Paz reorganized his cabinet on 21 January 1986; and this move proved critical to the survival of the NPE. The reorganization moved Bedregal from Planning to the Ministry of Foreign Relations and Gisbert from Finance to Industry. In their place, Paz appointed Gonzalo Sánchez de Lozada and Juan Cariaga to head Planning and Finance respectively. The reorganization removed economic policy from the purview of the traditional *movimientistas* and placed responsibility for its implementation directly in the hands of its neoliberal designers.

Two important institutional arrangements reinforced the logic of the cabinet reorganization. First, the cabinet was divided into separate ''political'' and ''economic'' wings. The political cabinet, the Consejo Nacional Político (CONAPOL), was made up of several ministries including Foreign Relations and the Interior. It was headed by Bedregal. The economic cabinet, the Consejo de Economía Planeamiento (CONEPLAN), was led by Sánchez de Lozada and included the ministries of Planning, Finance, Industry, Urban Affairs, Housing, Energy, Information, and Agriculture. This division of the cabinet helped to insulate the economic team somewhat; it distanced the remainder of the cabinet from involvement in economic policy and placed the burden of defending economic policy squarely in the lap of the economic technocrats. CONEPLAN, for example, met frequently with regional civic committees in response to their complaints over cuts and the administrative reorganization of the budget.[41]

In addition to formalizing the split between the technocratic and the political wings of the cabinet, a special Commission on Stabilization was struck in January 1986. Sánchez de Lozada had demanded the body as a quid pro quo for entering the cabinet.[42] The idea was to create an institutional check on expenditures inside the executive branch, including those of the Central Bank and the Office of the President. No government disbursements could take place without prior approval by the commission. In effect, by agreeing to create the commission, Paz agreed on a check of his own powers to spend by decree. The general secretary was Sánchez de Lozada. Other members included the ministers of finance, labor, and the Central Bank.

Paz was the titular president of the Commission on Stabilization and astutely appointed Bedregal as its vice-president. Paz's appointment of Bedregal to this post was a good example of his wiliness in dealing with the traditional party *apparatchiks* of MNR. The appointment was a desirable one because it provided Bedregal with some entrée to economic matters and gave him another source of patronage jobs for the faithful movimientistas. But at the same time, Bedregal's minority position on the commission made it impossible for him to use the post to disarticulate the NPE. Bedregal himself acknowledged the political liabilities associated with being on the commission: "The most important commission is unfortunately this [Commission on Stabilization]. I suffer on it. . . . This body has a lot of power. As such, it puts a lot of the weight of the crisis on us. When there are tough decisions, Paz can say, 'I didn't do it! It's the Consejo.' "[43]

The cabinet reorganization did not completely resolve the tensions within MNR over economic policy, but there was no formal split of the party. Instead, the conflict crystallized as a power struggle between Bedregal and Sánchez de Lozada over the future leadership of the party. MNR's extremely poor showing in the 1987 municipal elections gave Bedregal the occasion to renew criticisms of the economic team. MNR won only 11.7 percent of the vote nationally, trailing behind ADN with 24.9 percent of the vote and MIR with 22.8 percent. This was a substantial drop from the 26.4 percent of the vote that MNR won in the 1985 presidential race.[44]

On the heels of MNR's worst electoral performance in its history, Bedregal began calling for cabinet changes and a reevaluation of economic policy. In contrast, Sánchez de Lozada was unwavering in his defense of the NPE. Just days before the election, Sánchez de Lozada announced that the 1988 budget would be the "toughest and most austere of recent years." He refused to interpret the election results as a rejection of the NPE and characterized them simply as a predictable slip in popularity, which comes with governing.[45] Paz, in turn, commissioned a postelection poll to determine the reasons for MNR's poor performance. The poll reportedly pointed to lackluster candidates and campaigning as the source of the defeat, not the NPE. Armed with the poll results, Paz ignored Bedregal's call for a cabinet reshuffle and kept the economic team intact.[46]

Paz's ability to keep MNR together despite the serious internal fissures reflected his unique status in the party as well as the pragmatism of fellow party elites. As an old leader of MNR, Paz could play on their deference and personal loyalties to keep the faithful from open revolt. Moreover, dissidents in the party recognized that a formal split would likely quash MNR's electoral prospects for 1989—and perhaps beyond.

Paz's personal hold over MNR paralleled that of Banzer's over ADN. The personal control that both exercised over their respective parties was crucial to the maintenance of the Pacto por la Democracia. Signed in October 1985, the pact was an official agreement between MNR and ADN pledging their support for the NPE. While the pact did not bring the ADN officially into the cabinet, it laid the basis for legislative cooperation and gave ADN a number of appointments in key state enterprises. Broad policy matters were negotiated directly by Paz and Banzer; the day-to-day operation of the pact was managed by a bipartisan committee of party leaders.

Banzer led ADN into the pact for a number of reasons. There was certainly some ideological affinity at work. First, the NPE was similar to the economic program devised by Banzer and ADN technocrats in their Harvard seminar with Jeffrey Sachs during the 1985 campaign. Second, Banzer's decision to cooperate with the new government as it faced a crisis situation helped in the effort to recast his public persona as a committed democrat and statesman. Since the transition to democracy, Banzer had worked hard at shedding his image of dictator. Third, Banzer was able to extract concessions from MNR as the quid pro quo for participating in the pact. Of particular importance was MNR's agreement to cooperate on electoral reforms. Fourth, the pact seemed to open the door to a permanent alliance between the two parties, which raised the prospect of perhaps alternating the two parties in power in the style of Colombia or Venezuela. In 1988, the two parties signed an addendum to the original agreement, promising to cast their congressional votes for whichever presidential candidate won a plurality of the popular vote. At the time, this implied MNR support for a Banzer presidency.[47] For both Banzer and Paz, the pact was a historic achievement—one that held out hope of achieving unprecedented political stability and an enduring elite consensus on economic policy.

The pact was critical for ensuring that Congress did not emerge as an institutional obstacle to the NPE, and it protected the economic cabinet from interpellations. On only one occasion did the pact fail as legislative insurance and an interpellation ensued. The civic committees of the gas- and petroleum-producing departments of Santa Cruz, Chuquisaca, and Tarija turned up their demands for financial reimbursements from the central government. The issue of departmental reimbursements for such production was a contentious budgetary issue; Planning Minister Sánchez de Lozada was reluctant to assent to the departments' ''rights'' to claim such payments.

After months of inconclusive meetings between Sánchez de Lozada and the civic committees, the committees lobbied their congressional representatives to censure the cabinet, as a protest. In the face of intense pressures from their constituents, ADN deputies voted in favor of the censure, as did four ''deserting'' MNR deputies. With only 67 deputies present for the vote, the censure passed by a vote of 66 to 1.

Rather than remove Sánchez de Lozada, Paz looked for a way out. Paz argued that the constitution did not legally oblige him to remove ministers in the event of a censure. While such a position could have provoked a full-fledged constitutional conflict, MNR and ADN deputies chose to ignore the issue. A face-to-face meeting between Paz and Banzer laid the basis for a negotiated settlement. A commission was formed to study the compensation issue; Congress subsequently passed a law that mandated a one-time-only payment to the departments of the amounts pledged by the previous Siles government, and the censured cabinet remained in place.[48] Of the four MNR deputies who had voted for the census, one was expelled from the party and the remaining three were suspended for breaking with party discipline.

The MNR-ADN stranglehold on executive and legislative power deprived leftist parties of any institutional levers to block the NPE. The left in Congress was further weakened by the transformation of MIR into a centrist social democratic party under the leadership of Paz Estenssoro's nephew, Jaime Paz Zamora. Originally founded by radical university students in the 1970s, MIR had shifted to a considerably more conservative stance by the late 1980s. The shift became visible during the Siles government in which MIR participated as coalition partner. In addition to MIR appointments to the cabinet, Jaime Paz Zamora served as Siles's vice-president. Recognizing the tremendous failure of the Siles government and worried about the possible electoral repercussions, Paz Zamora withdrew MIR support from Siles and began distancing the party from the more radical left. Disgruntled leftists subsequently split from MIR to form a new party, the Movimiento Bolivia Libre (MBL) under the leadership of Antonio Araníbar. This exit by the left gave Paz Zamora a free hand in refashioning the image of MIR as a young, progressive, but nonetheless sober party. With the remaking of their party underway, MIR leaders in Congress were not interested in heading the opposition to the NPE. On the contrary, Paz Zamora endorsed the basic design of the NPE in his 1989 presidential campaign. In a candidates forum sponsored by the CEPB in March 1989, the press noted how similar the economic positions of the three major candidates—Paz Zamora, Banzer, and Sánchez de Lozada—were.[49]

The perspicacity and political skills of Paz Estenssoro, Banzer, and Paz Zamora were vital elements in the development of a consensus on economic policy within the party system; that consensus, in turn, put an end to hostile intergovernmental relations that could have endangered the NPE. All three leaders used their personal control over their respective parties to tranquilize the party system and ensure that it would not emerge as an obstacle to maintaining the NPE.

Taming Civil Society: Repression and Dialogue

In his launching of the NPE, Paz employed the full range of repressive powers constitutionally prescribed to the president (see chapter 6). His declaration of a state of siege in September 1985 allowed the government to suspend civil liberties and to imprison COB leaders. The move was crucial in undermining labor's attempted mobilization against the economic program.

This initial use of state-of-siege powers by Paz set the tone of his administration. Unlike Siles, who had been preoccupied with establishing a democratic atmosphere after years of dictatorship, Paz Estenssoro did not hesitate to use force to defend his economic policies. Organized labor and university students were prime targets of much of the repression. Throughout 1986, the press was full of reports of arrests, injuries, and deaths that occurred in conjunction with strikes and protests against the NPE.[50]

Paz invoked state-of-siege powers for the second time in his administration on 28 August 1986, in response to the *Marcha por la vida* (March for life) organized by the COB. Led by five thousand miners in Oruro, the march was to protest the government's plan for restructuring COMIBOL. By the time the marchers reached the outskirts of La Paz, they had been joined by university students, leftist leaders, peasants, and representatives of the Catholic church. Cabinet ministers responded by denouncing the march as an attempt to overthrow the government. Fearing that the protesters would take over the city of La Paz, Paz ordered the army to encircle the protesters. Meanwhile, journalists and leftists in La Paz were arrested. Cut off from food supplies and facing possible military action, the marchers began their forced retreat on 29 August.[51]

Petroleum workers in the YPFB were also exposed to the government's strong-arm tactics. After government-union salary negotiations stalled in July 1987, Paz ordered the army to occupy YPFB offices and installations in anticipation of a strike. He also ''militarized'' YPFB workers, thereby making them subject to military command and indictments in military courts. Four days after the militarization of the conflict, the strike was concluded with a negotiated wage hike. The same scenario was repeated in a subsequent strike by YPFB workers in March 1988.[52] On the whole, petroleum workers generally fared better than other groups in such wage conflicts because of their strategic positioning in the Bolivian economy. (YPFB workers controlled petroleum and gas production, so strikes by these workers not only disrupted domestic gasoline supply but also disrupted Bolivia's natural gas exports.) The government played on the relatively privileged status of petroleum workers to keep them from joining forces with the COB.

In their public pronouncements, Paz's cabinet ministers routinely took a tough tone. Paz's two interior ministers, Fernando Barthelemy and Juan Carlos Durán, were outspoken in their defense of the use of force by the government. Government representatives always sought to delegitimize the opposition by characterizing groups as subversive and antidemocratic. This line of argument was used to discredit the COB's peaceful protest in 1986, the *Consulta popular* (Popular poll). After the government refused COB's request for a referendum, the COB sponsored its own mock referendum in July 1986. The government's proposed tax reform and the issue of foreign debt repayment was the specific matter at stake in the referendum; the broader aim was to frame the vote as a rejection of the NPE. Supported by leftist parties and regional civic committees, over a million citizens participated in the event and over half of them voted against the government's economic policy. Interior Minister Fernando Barthelemy charged that the *Consulta* was subversive, and he warned that any popular mobilizations in conjunction with it would be met with another state of siege. He accused COB and civic leaders of trying to destabilize the government and ominously declared, ''it is time to get rid of anarchy, we must act without contemplation.'' The minister of defense backed up Barthelemy's warnings.[53]

The intermittent use of force and verbal threats worked to create an atmosphere of intimidation, making the COB's efforts to organize against the NPE all the more difficult. There were occasional efforts by the government to derail popular protest through dialogues. Protesting the COMIBOL cutbacks in March 1987, Oruro miners staged a hunger strike that brought the economic cabinet to the negotiating table. Catholic church officials acted as intermediaries between the two sides. The talks and the strike came to an end, however, when the government threatened to impose a state of siege. In January 1988, COB and government leaders undertook a series of meetings to discuss the COB's alternative economic proposals, the *Pliego nacional* (National document). The *Pliego* included demands for a substantial wage boost and for increased spending on education, health, and housing.[54] The discussions dragged on for forty days but broke down after the COB rejected the government's offer of a 16 percent wage hike.

As these events illustrate, Paz made it a point not to completely eschew dialogue with opponents of the NPE. Catholic church officials played an important role in pressuring the government to the negotiating table. Once at the table, however, Sánchez de Lozada and the team were not inclined toward major concessions. Rather, they focused on negotiating at the margins of the NPE. The thrust of the NPE itself was not up for discussion or amendment. The projection of toughness by the team was not only a key component of domestic policy but also a critical part of the team's strategy to reestablish Bolivia's credibility in international financial circles.

Relief and International Allies

From the outset of the experiment, Sánchez de Lozada and the economic team were acutely conscious of the ''signaling'' function of their program. They knew that the program could be used to reshape the image of Bolivia among international financiers and to lay the basis for a more favorable position toward Bolivia on debt-related issues.

Payments on the Bolivian debt had been suspended in 1984, the last year of the Siles government. This suspension came after two years during which Siles had made interest payments amounting to 6 percent of Bolivia's GNP. By 1985, Bolivia's total medium- and long-term debt stood at nearly three and a half billion dollars. This translated into a debt-GNP ratio of 107 percent. A substantial portion of the debt, which had grown considerably during the latter 1970s, was comprised of loans from foreign commercial banks. Private commercial creditors accounted for 37.3 percent of Bolivia's debt in 1985. Thus, rectifying the debt problem required the cooperation of both multilateral and private lenders.

Straying from orthodoxy, President Paz did not pledge repayment of the debt as part of the NPE. Paz believed that public toleration of the NPE would completely break down if the NPE became a vehicle of debt repayment. Instead, Paz and his economic team sought to use the stabilization program as a vehicle to create support for debt relief. Jeffrey Sachs played an important role in lobbying international institutions on behalf of Bolivia's debt-relief strategy. Sachs had signed on as an official advisor to the Paz government in January 1986. The presence of Sachs on the Bolivian economic team helped to reinforce the image of sobriety and technical competence that the economic team was projecting toward the international community. Moreover, Sachs concurred with debt-relief strategy and was able to put forth compelling technical arguments concerning the benefits that could accrue to both creditors and debtors through comprehensive debt reduction.[55]

The comprehensive character of D.S. 21060 and the political zeal with which it was implemented were successful in attracting attention from multilateral institutions and the U.S. government. After some initial resistance in the spring of 1986, the IMF was convinced of the need to support the NPE without further modifications. Sachs served as a primary advocate for Bolivia in these discussions with the Fund. The IMF signaled its change in perspective by dropping its demand for further currency devaluation as a condition for new loans. In 1986, the IMF disbursed standby credits of SDR 51.9 million to Bolivia and, in 1988, agreed to a loan from its Enhanced Structural Adjustment facility for SDR 136.05 million.

The U.S. government agreed with the IMF that Bolivia could not be forced into debt repayments without seriously endangering the success of the NPE. The American policy reversal regarding the Bolivian debt coincided with U.S. efforts to gain Bolivian cooperation on the ''militarization'' of the war on drug trafficking. In July 1986, the Paz government went along with Operation Blast Furnace, a joint U.S.-Bolivian military operation to root out drug operations in the Bolivian jungles.

Bolivia's new relationship with the IMF and the U.S. government opened the doors for the economic team to seek concessions from its private commercial creditors. Successful negotiations with the Paris Club concluded in 1987 and provided for a debt-rescheduling scheme. In addition, arrangements were made for Bolivia's repurchase of one-half of its commercial debt at eleven cents on the dollar. The money for the repurchase plan came from the United States and several other friendly governments.

The cooperative stance of international actors, especially the IMF, stands in stark contrast with what occurred in Belaúnde's earlier neoliberal experiment in

Bolivia; need need for new loans for public works so could decree stabilization policies at own pace + gained upper hand w/ IMF

Peru. In that case, in 1983, the IMF was unyielding in its insistence on further budget cutting and devaluation, even as Peru plunged deeper into recession. As leaders of the economic team, neither Manuel Ulloa nor Carlos Rodríguez Pastor resisted the prescription for further orthodoxy. Given Belaúnde's obsession with public works financing and the track record of failed IMF agreements under the Morales Bermúdez government, the economic ministers saw total adhesion to orthodoxy as the only way to assure a continued flow of credits.

The economic team in Bolivia by 1986, however, was working within a different framework on debt matters. Bolivia was already cut off from credit, so there were no immediate sanctions associated with the attempt to stake out a new position in the negotiations. And by the latter 1980s, it was apparent to many international actors that new arrangements on the debt had to be sought out. In addition, Bolivia's relatively small debt (in comparison with other Latin American debtors) could be used as a bargaining chip to convince creditors to settle for less, rather than to continue to press for payments that could not be made and that could endanger the viability of the Paz Estenssoro government. At the same time, the U.S. government was disinclined to pressure Bolivia on the repayment issue while it was seeking Paz's cooperation on the drug war. Thus, peculiarities in the international conjuncture gave the Bolivian economic team some leverage in their negotiations on debt relief. Changes in the international environment allowed the economic team more leeway in their negotiations, and international allies acted in ways that were supportive of the overall thrust of the program.

Support for the Bolivian experiment also came in the form of bilateral aid, which was especially useful in the development of a temporary employment program administered by the Fondo Social de Emergencia. The idea of the FSE was championed by Sánchez de Lozada. As in Chile, the neoliberal team sought to mitigate the recessionary effects of the NPE through public works employment projects. Founded in late 1986, the FSE distributed grants to local communities for construction projects running the gamut from sewer systems to health clinics. Finance for the FSE came from the United States (specifically USAID), Sweden, Switzerland, Canada, Holland, and the World Bank. According to the FSE, a hundred thousand temporary jobs were generated by the projects in 1987–88.[56] Thus, while the IMF offered no long-term solutions to the unemployment generated by the NPE, it did help ease the effects on some of the worst-hit communities. Foreign aid allowed the Paz government to engage in some skeletal welfarism to offset the social costs of stabilization and restructuring.

Informality and the Drug Economy

Paz's pursuit of the NPE was built around an elaborate carrot-and-stick strategy. The government sometimes used force to quell opposition, but then it reverted to conciliatory gestures; draconian cuts in public expenditures and employment came alongside an effort at compensatory social spending through the FSE. This picture of the pursuit of the NPE would not be complete, however, without an appreciation of how two interconnected features of the Bolivian economy—the existence of a large informal sector and Bolivia's involvement in the illegal drug trade—worked to cushion the effects of the NPE across all social classes.

The size of the informal sector of the Bolivian economy is substantial. Although statistics vary, estimates are that somewhere between 50 and 60 percent of the economically active population by the mid-1980s were located in the informal sector. Within the informal sector, activities related to the production of coca and cocaine processing significantly expanded after the mid-1970s. By the 1980s, Bolivia was supplying between 30 and 40 percent of the world demand for cocaine. Approximately 120,000 people are directly involved in the cultivation of the coca leaf, and an additional 30,000 people are involved in other activities related to the processing of cocaine (approximately 7 percent of the EAP). Other types of indirect employment connected with the drug trade bring the total number of people employed in the coca-cocaine business to over 350,000.[57]

Bolivia's participation in the narcotics trade has a significant impact on the domestic economy, although it is difficult to specify its effects with exactitude given the lack of reliable statistics. Estimates placed the value of Bolivian exports of cocaine at around $2 billion per year in the second half of the 1980s. In 1987, the value of cocaine exports was estimated at 196 percent of legal exports; a decline in the international prices of cocaine brought the figure down to 90 percent of legal exports in 1989.[58] Whereas much of the revenue generated by cocaine exits Bolivia in capital flight, most analysts agree that the business helps

buoy the economy, injecting approximately $600 million a year into the local economy; it boosts rural incomes, generates new employment, and increases consumer demand both for imports and for domestically produced goods.

The economic team was loath to publicly acknowledge the cushioning effect that the drug trade exerted during the stabilization program, especially given the intense pressures by the U.S. government to engage Bolivia in its campaign against drug trafficking. But there is little doubt that the drug trade (like the international aid that Paz received) helped soften the blows of stabilization. In addition to generating income, the injection of "coca-dollars" into the banking system is believed to have helped stabilize the currency during the second half of the decade.[59]

Business and the NPE

In all three countries under consideration, the relationships of the business sectors to concrete neoliberal packages enacted by the conservative governments varied. In Peru and Ecuador, the adverse market behaviors of some capitalists helped unravel the neoliberal projects of Belaúnde and Febres Cordero. Such a scenario did not develop in Bolivia, because of the structural position of Bolivian capitalists and the trauma they had experienced under the preceding government of Siles Zuazo. After years of political instability and poor macroeconomic management, business groups welcomed the order imposed by Paz Estenssoro. In the minds of businessmen, any disadvantages attached to the neoliberal program were outweighed by the benefits. In short, the position of business in Bolivia paralleled the stance of the bourgeoisie in Chile in the aftermath of the Allende years. As Alfred Stepan noted in that case, the fear that pervaded the bourgeoisie as a result of the Allende experiment overrode concerns about any costs that would accompany Pinochet's neoliberal program.[60]

To a great extent, Bolivian businessmen had already disengaged themselves from productive investment prior to the enactment of D.S. 21060. As Oscar Ugarteche and other analysts point out, capital flight accelerated during the latter half of the 1970s as investors redirected their government-subsidized loans to bank accounts outside Bolivia; and the process continued under the subsequent governments of García Meza and Siles Zuazo in the 1980s. Estimates are that capital flight in the period 1976–81 amounted to \$216.9 million; in 1982–83, capital flight was estimated at \$106.2 million.[61]

By the time the neoliberal team took over in 1985, a significant decapitalization of the Bolivian economy had already taken place. Business elites were experienced practitioners of a variety of defensive behaviors. These behaviors included currency speculation, recourse to capital flight, and proclivity toward liquid assets–holding. Many of the large economic groups profited handsomely from the economic disarray of the Siles government. The poorly designed policy to "dedollarize" the economy enacted by Finance Minister Ernesto Araníbar allowed heavily indebted businesses to pay off loans at a fraction of their worth. At the same time, volatility in the currency market allowed businesses to reap huge windfalls through speculation.

From the perspective of the business community, the Siles government gave new meaning to the phrase "it was the best of times, it was the worst of times." Many businessmen that we interviewed readily acknowledged that they made huge financial gains during the economic chaos of the Siles years; several even sarcastically suggested that businessmen erect a monument to the Siles government for its contributions to the private sector. Yet, they also pointed to the anxiety associated with making money during that period. Profiteering under conditions of extreme uncertainty entailed significant stress for the business executives who were managing firms. The hyperinflation disrupted virtually all normal practices of firms and instilled a crisis-management atmosphere. Even as executives adjusted to doing business under abnormal conditions, they faced a never-ending stream of crises. Industrialists, for example, found themselves immersed in near daily wage negotiations with workers. At the same time, the hoarding and consequent unavailability of raw materials created supply bottlenecks and constantly threatened to shut down production. Thus, while the Siles government unintentionally created unprecedented opportunities for profiteering, it was a fatiguing experience for all economic actors, even those who gained. By 1985, business executives were willing to exchange the windfalls associated with economic instability for a more routine and predictable environment.

This desire for normality on the part of the business elites explains their subsequent attitude toward the NPE, including the willingness of many to accept measures they were not in complete agreement with. As one industrialist in food processing described it, business had already been so disrupted by labor conflict and supply problems that the uniform tariff seemed like a small price to pay for a coherent and pro–private sector economic program. Moreover, while new competition was worrisome to some industries, it was less threatening to others because of the high costs of transportation inside Bolivia. The elimination of differential tariffs was also seen as having a cost-cutting effect because it eliminated the time spent in bureaucratic paperwork and in bribing public officials to expedite transactions.[62]

On the whole, business interest groups focused their demands around the idea of economic reactivation and did not engage in any war of attrition toward the NPE or the Paz government. Neither the competence of the economic team nor the basic direction of policy was questioned by business interest group leaders. The debate that unfolded between business and government through 1985–89 did not revolve around the essential ''correctness'' of the NPE but was confined to discussions of how to pull Bolivia out of the recession that accompanied stabilization. Business groups' main demands were for a lowering of interest rates and the provision of new credits to the private sector. The neoliberal team eventually responded in the form of D.S. 21660, which was issued in July 1987. The decree created a reactivation fund aimed at channeling $500 million annually to the private sector over a three-year period.[63] Despite the decree, business groups continued to hammer the government for not paying adequate attention to the question of economic recovery. In public pronouncements, CEPB leaders constantly reminded the public that the primary responsibility for revitalizing the economy lay with the government, not the private sector.

For the most part, business elites adopted a wait-and-see position with respect to the NPE. Considerable praise and ideological support for the NPE and the economic team was expressed by business interest group leaders. There was no concerted attempt to derail the NPE, either in the political arena or through economic sabotage. Yet, support for the NPE by the business community was passive, not active. Some capital was repatriated after 1985, lured by the high local interest rates. But the lion's share of this repatriated capital was placed in short-

term dollar and dollar-linked deposits in the banking system. An estimated 90 percent of banking deposits (as measured in June 1989) were located in such accounts. Of the 323 million dollars in such accounts, 175 million were in thirty-day accounts. The "hot money" character of these accounts became especially evident in 1989 when the outcome of the presidential election triggered a run on deposits.[64]

In fact, it was precisely this concentration of financial resources in short-term accounts that contributed to the overall credit crunch and business's demands for reactivation credits. Even after stabilization was secured, there was no rush to reinvest in Bolivia: levels of private sector investment remained unchanged. Private investment as a percentage of GDP remained stagnant in the period 1987–90, registering a high of 3.9 percent in 1988 and a low of 3.1 percent in 1989.[65] Bolivian businessmen emerged as cautious allies of the government, waiting to see if the experiment could be sustained over the long haul.

Reinventing Bolivia

The initiation and subsequent implementation of neoliberal policies in Bolivia were built on a convergence of special circumstances and effective political leadership. As in Chile, the national trauma that initiated neoliberalism created an unprecedented opportunity for policy change. Saddled with the blame for economic chaos, forces on the left were discredited—and society looked to the newly elected Paz Estenssoro for immediate relief. Drawing on his years of experience in politics, Paz quickly seized on the possibilities presented by the economic catastrophe and moved decisively in his first months in office to realize his new vision of what Bolivia should become.

Paz and his economic team recognized that their aspirations for structural reforms hinged on the success of the stabilization effort. Stopping hyperinflation was of critical importance in establishing the credibility of the government, both domestically and internationally. The stabilization measures produced quick results: within ten days of D.S. 21060, inflation came to a dead halt. Yet, Paz did not let up in his efforts to demonstrate the continuing commitment of the government to economic restructuring. Paz moved against the COB to stop its mobilization against the measures, and the government used intermittent shows of force to keep popular resistance under control.

The political will that Paz demonstrated vis-à-vis civil society was evident in his management of relations within the government. When Planning Minister Bedregal faltered in his management of the program in late 1985, Paz shuffled the cabinet and placed one of the intellectual architects of the NPE, Gonzalo Sánchez de Lozada, at the helm of economic policy. When troubles with Congress over regional issues threatened the removal of the neoliberal team, Paz intervened to keep the team intact. In every internal conflict that emerged inside the government, Paz used considerable political skill to ensure that the neoliberal team would remain in place and enjoy the upper hand.

Keeping the economic team together was important for the coherence of the program. Inside the economic team, a strong consensus on policies prevailed. This helped to keep the economic program on track and sent clear signals of the government's commitment to the program to the domestic and international audience. As head of the economic team, Planning Minister Sánchez de Lozada staked out something of a new political style in Bolivia. By combining humor and frankness with intellect, Sánchez de Lozada won a grudging respect for himself and the government even among ardent opponents. Both at home and abroad, the economic team projected an image of competence and commitment to stabilization—a very different image from the one projected by the constantly changing economic teams of the Siles government. Jeffrey Sachs's presence as an advisor added considerable cachet to the team, enhancing its credibility to international institutions.

In contrast to Febres Cordero and Belaúnde, Paz did not disregard the party system but looked to restructure relations within it in order to ensure support for the NPE. By striking the Pacto por la Democracia with the ADN and keeping it in place until the presidential elections of 1989, Paz laid the basis for an enduring elite consensus for neoliberalism, while guaranteeing that Congress would not emerge as an institutional obstacle to the policies.

What was common to the neoliberal experiments in both Bolivia and Chile was the recognition on the part of the respective executives and their economic advisors that economic transformation would have to be combined with political transformation. The political transformation forced on Chile by the Pinochet dictatorship was certainly more radical and repressive than in Bolivia. In Chile, Pinochet ordered a suspension of politics and the physical extermination of labor and left opponents before allowing a very limited political arena to eventually re-emerge along the lines provided in the 1980 constitution. In Bolivia, Paz's political agenda was less draconian, but his strategy was also rooted in the idea that neoliberal reform could not be successful without a fundamental recasting of politics—the party system would have to be harnessed, the labor movement weakened, and the ideological atmosphere shifted to the right. Bolivia, as it had functioned since 1952, would have to be undone.

In the final analysis, Paz's vision—his understanding of the intimate connection between political change and economic change—was what differentiated his administration from those of Febres Cordero and Belaúnde. Paz's accomplishments as an economic policy maker lay in his recognition that neoliberalism required reinventing Bolivia politically as well as economically.[66]

CHAPTER 8

Conclusion: Tocqueville's Fears

> Thus I think the type of oppression which threatens democracies is different from anything there has ever been in the world before. Our contemporaries will find no prototype of it in their memories. I have myself vainly searched for a word which will exactly express the whole of the conception I have formed. Such old words as "despotism" and "tyranny" do not fit. The thing is new, and as I cannot find a word for it, I must try to define it.
>
> ALEXIS DE TOCQUEVILLE

THE WEDDING of neoliberal economics and civilian government was common throughout Latin America by the end of the 1980s. Following the Central Andean lead, military rule gave way in Argentina, Uruguay, Brazil, Paraguay, and Chile, as well as in Central America. A string of elected presidents—from Carlos Menem in Argentina and Carlos Salinas in Mexico to Carlos Andrés Pérez in Venezuela—committed their governments to orthodox stabilization packages and programs of economic restructuring. Even in Peru and Ecuador, where initial neoliberal policies dissolved, the experiments were resurrected under subsequent governments of Alberto Fujimori and Sixto Durán Ballén.

Coinciding with the fall of communism in Eastern Europe and the Soviet Union, Latin America's turnaround seemed to confirm a new hegemony of free market capitalism and democracy across the globe. At least that is how a number of academics, journalists, and analysts sought to portray the changes of the 1980s. Perhaps the most extravagant statement in this vein came from Francis Fukuyama who glibly proclaimed the twin triumphs of capitalism and democracy as the "end of history." Journalists joined in the hyped-up pronouncements on the "new and improved South America," a region that "has surmounted despotism of the right and left and embraced free enterprise.'' In less overheated prose, economists applauded neoliberal programs as evidence of a ''new realism'' in Latin American policy circles and wrote damning critiques of populism.[1]

Even as the new era of capitalism and democracy was being hailed, unsettling events continued to raise questions about the supposed irreversibility of the region's politicoeconomic changes. For the first time in decades, a faction of the Venezuelan military stirred in abortive coups against President Carlos Andrés Pérez in February and November 1992; the attempt came amid widespread public discontent with his neoliberal program. Peru and Colombia continued to be racked by guerrilla movements and the presence of widespread drug trafficking. In April 1992, the first definitive rupture in Latin America's new constitutional order came in the form of the *Fuji-golpe,* the disbanding of an elected Congress by Peruvian president Alberto Fujimori. These outward signs of trouble in Latin American polities were coupled with other evidence of *desencanto* (disenchantment). The poor policy performance of many governments in the 1980s, the dismal leadership displayed by some presidents, and the resurgence of political corruption helped erode public confidence in the newly minted democracies.[2]

Looking out on this horizon in the early 1990s, political scientists have been hesitant to declare free market economics and democracy as a done deal for Latin America. Instead, scholars have preferred to characterize Latin American democracies as ''incomplete,'' focusing on the problems of consolidating democracy. As insightful as many of these discussions of consolidation are, one of their drawbacks is that they conjure up the image of Latin America as being somewhere on the road, either heading toward evolution to a familiar (that is, American- or European-style) democracy or backsliding into some previously identified form of authoritarianism.

But, as we believe our case studies suggest, the reality is far more complex—and, at least so far, has outstripped our ability to adequately characterize it. As Theodore Lowi recently observed, one of the great failings of contemporary political science has been its inability to recognize ongoing regime change. Too often, as Lowi notes in reference to American politics, the ''tendency was to render each change consistent with our own existing model of the political system.''[3] Our understanding of the current evolution of regimes in Latin America may similarly be clouded by an outmoded metaphor that conceives of democracy and authoritarianism as lying at opposite endpoints on a continuum of regime types.

The current challenge for scholars is not unlike the task that Alexis de Tocqueville wrestled with at the end of the second volume of *Democracy in America.* In his concluding chapters, Tocqueville sought to identify how tendencies within modern democracy might gradually transmute it into a wholly new regime type. Of particular concern to Tocqueville was the growing centralization of power in

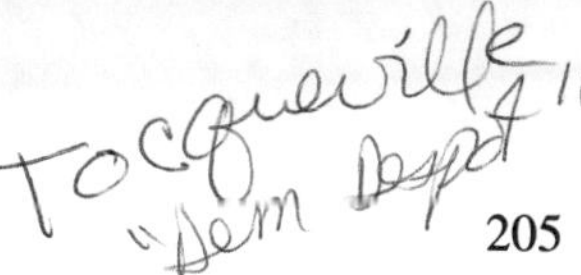

the state and how that might eventually lead to a progressive loss of participation and a surrender of citizens to a "guardianship" by the state. According to Tocqueville, periodic elections would turn into plebiscites legitimizing this type of rule by bureaucrats. Tocqueville settled on the notion of "democratic despotism" as a way to describe this type of regime.[4]

In the spirit of Tocqueville's effort to describe the mix of tendencies at work in modern regimes, we step back momentarily to summarize the findings of our case studies in order to highlight how the new Andean regimes were configured—how they combined contradictory principles of legitimacy, blended formal rules with informal political practices, and were shaped by new elite coalitions. As these regimes were taking shape, the economic crisis dwarfed virtually all other issues. It was the defining issue for governments and the core concern shaping the nature of the new regimes. Neoliberal economics became the preferred prescription of dominant coalitions of capitalists, conservative politicians, and technocrats and were implemented via practices that further defined the character of the regimes.

Unsolved Problems: Representation, Legitimacy, Class Compromise

By the end of the 1920s, signs of the breakdown of the old oligarchic order were in evidence in Ecuador, Peru, and Bolivia. Populist parties, leftist parties, and trade unions were the most visible manifestations of the change underway. The commodity export booms brought socioeconomic changes that wore away at the old order. New urban actors—labor and middle-class groups—began to organize around demands for political participation and social recognition.

The gradual disintegration of the oligarchic system opened the doors to what was to become a chronic crisis of representation in these political systems. Simply put, there was never any definitive resolution of how the interests of key groups—labor, the peasantry, business elites, middle classes—would be represented in government decision making. Neither military nor civilian regimes were able to construct viable systems that linked government to the central interests in Andean civil society on any stable basis. Indeed, the frequent recurrence to military rule was itself a manifestation of the problem: the legitimacy of civilian governments was often called into question by accusations that they functioned as instruments of elite domination or that they catered to the "dangerous classes." In the same vein, military governments fell prey to being depicted as *perros de la oligarquía* (watchdogs of the oligarchy) or as arbitrary rulers detached from civil society. Governments had little success in projecting themselves as an expression of the whole society, an embodiment of the national interest.

Lying at the base of the problem of representation was the highly inegalitarian socioeconomic structure of these countries. While upper classes were forced to make some concessions to lower-class groups, they maneuvered to stave off the full extension of citizenship rights to labor and to the peasantry. The circumscription of *las clases populares* was achieved by erecting legal and political obstacles to participation (restrictions on franchise, restrictions on participation of parties as in the case of APRA) and was facilitated by an atmosphere of social and racial discrimination.

A variety of civilian governments claiming to be democracies came and went in the twentieth century—but these governments were quite distinct from the kind of democratic civilian rule that evolved in Western Europe and the United States. Missing from the political development of the Central Andes was anything akin to the historic "class compromise" that was forged in the advanced industrial nations where Keynesian economic policies became the basis for a substantive consensus among workers and capitalists and laid the groundwork for stable democracy.[5] In the Central Andes, the upper classes were not prepared to compromise on either procedural or substantive issues.

The military governments headed by Velasco Alvarado, Rodríguez Lara, and Banzer were yet another installment in the ongoing crises of representation in Peru, Ecuador, and Bolivia. Each of the administrations came to power partly because of the previous government's inability to channel and process popular-class pressures through institutions and the party system. The Peruvian military's overthrow of Belaúnde in 1968 came after peasant movements revealed the explosiveness of the rural masses, and after the executive-legislative stalemate showed the inability of the party system to respond to growing pressures for change. In Ecuador, military intervention in 1972 followed two years after an *autogolpe* staged by President Velasco Ibarra shut down Congress. In Bolivia, Banzer's 1971 coup was staged to terminate the influence of left and labor groups.

None of the three military governments were able to resolve the basic issue of how contending social classes and interest groups were to be connected to the governing process. Certainly, the most creative—but nonetheless unsuccessful—effort by the military to create new avenues for representation and participation for lower-class groups came in Peru. Through SINAMOS and industrial communities, the Peruvian military sought to construct an institutional framework to facilitate popular participation at the local level (at the level of firms, cooperatives, neighborhood associations) and to tie those organizations into national-level organizations that would be accorded a place in policy-making bodies. At the same time, the Peruvian military lashed out at the traditional interest group structure and parties, hoping to force old constituencies into new structures. Of the three regimes, the Peruvian military came closest to forging institutions to facilitate some kind of class compromise. This proposed restructuring in class relations was never fully realized, with Morales Bermúdez beginning the retreat from Velasco's reforms in 1976. In Ecuador, the government of Rodríguez Lara was mute on the subject of representation and participation. In Bolivia, Banzer's project was an exclusionary one aimed at silencing labor and the peasantry.

Whereas business interest groups initially welcomed military interventions, an uneasiness settled on the business community as the contradictions became evident in its relationships with military governments. In the cases of Peru and Ecuador, the tensions evoked outright expressions of business opposition to the military governments. In Bolivia, the problems between business and the Banzer government remained more muffled, obscured by the general economic boom. Under the subsequent military governments of the post-1978 period, Bolivian businessmen joined their Andean counterparts in their challenge to military rule.

In all three countries, business benefited greatly from some of the economic policies authored by the military governments; protectionism, overvalued exchange rates, and subsidized credit were part of the policy packages of all three governments that provided lucrative ''rents'' to capitalists. But the provisions of rents by the military government did not satisfy business; multidimensional conflicts affected the tenor of business-government relations during the period. These conflicts prompted a revival of interest in democracy and economic liberalism within the business community.

In Peru and Ecuador, substantive conflicts over policies emerged as the military governments laid out reformist agendas. Of particular concern to business were the reforms that proposed to alter property rights and that affected managerial prerogatives in individual firms. In Bolivia, reformism was clearly not part of Banzer's agenda, yet questions over taxes and sectoral favoritism surfaced. However, objectionable policies were just the tip of the iceberg of what was bothering business during this period. Embedded within these discrete policy battles were businessmen's anxieties about their lack of representation, the arbitrary decision-making style of military governments, the aggrandizement of the size and regulatory functions of the state, and the role that the private sector would be assigned to play vis-à-vis the public sector.

Business saw the expansion of the state apparatus that took place under military rule as a potential threat to the private sector. Not only was business apprehensive about the ability of state enterprises to preempt private investment, there was also concern about how that expanding public sector would satisfy its financial needs. Business began to envision a voracious public sector that would require an ever greater share of the economic surplus. Hence, business interest groups began to voice worries about the long-term effects of the military's development model, which revolved around an activist state. Business interest groups became the standard-bearers of a revived antistatist discourse. Antistatism became an attractive ideological common ground upon which a new coalition of capitalists, technocrats, and politicians was constructed.

Antistatism was one of the products of the business sectors' encounters with the military governments of the 1970s. Another important effect of the encounters was a new interest in democracy within the business community. If anything, the military governments had added a new wrinkle to the chronic problem of representation in these systems by refusing to incorporate business interest groups into the policy-making process. Like the rest of civil society, business elites now found themselves without any institutional channels for representing their interests to government policy makers. Economic policy making in the military governments was dominated by a coterie of military and civilian technocrats, not unlike the situation that Guillermo O'Donnell described in the bureaucratic-authoritarian regimes of the Southern Cone. Whereas some individual capitalists and economic groups were able to gain informal access to some of the policy makers, domestic capitalists—as a set with organized interests—were shut out of decision making, and business lobbies were relegated to a reactive role.

In short, business elites found themselves caught in a crisis of representation under military rule. To use a theatrical metaphor, they found themselves being offered a part (that of the subordinate and complementary private sector) in a script (state-centric capitalism) that had been written and directed by technocrats and the military. Their absence of input into the policy-making process gave them no creative control whatsoever in the drama they were supposed to perform in.

Business—along with the rest of civil society—was subjected to at least two kinds of uncertainty under these military regimes. First, there was uncertainty as to outcomes. That is, the lack of representation heightened uncertainty as to what kinds of policies would be generated by governments. Second, another uncertainty concerned the arbitrary ways in which power was exercised by these governments. The military's suspension of the constitution and disbanding of oversight entities (Congress, for example) meant that these governments were essentially not bound by rules. The rules and procedures surrounding policy making were not explicitly defined, nor were they fixed; they could be altered at any time by executive fiat. In this fluid situation, policy making frequently devolved into a struggle for proximity and access to the junta leader; this was especially evident in the patrimonial style of Banzer's government in Bolivia.

One can contrast the type of uncertainty described here with the type of uncertainty that prevails in a liberal democracy. Adam Przeworski has characterized democracy as a system that "institutionalizes uncertainty," but this uncertainty is the uncertainty of outcomes.[6] In modern democratic systems, multiple political actors compete and employ a variety of strategies to affect policy outcomes—it is never clear, a priori, who the winners and losers in the system will be. In military regimes, an uncertainty as to outcomes also prevails, but it is

compounded by an uncertainty as to the procedures, rules, and personnel that

govern decision making. It is difficult for actors to know how to approach these governments and how to act effectively in order to influence the process, since power can shift in unpredictable ways inside the government. Moreover, the dictatorial character of the regime makes actors uncertain as to what types of public expression and behavior will be tolerated.

Business interest groups and individual businessmen in our three case studies used a variety of tactics (see chapter 4) in their attempts to exert influence over the military governments, and in some instances they were successful in altering policies. But business leaders soon began to realize the costs (in time, personal aggravation, and anxiety) involved in maneuvering in regimes where politics was akin to reading tea leaves—looking for nuances, straining for information about events within the insular institution of the armed forces.

The desire for transparency in decision making was one part of the bundle of concerns that brought business interest groups to support a transition to elected civilian governments. Rather than fearing democracy, business leaders believed that their interests would be better served in a system in which they could seek to shape policy through a variety of channels (through parties and elections, lobbying the executive and legislative branches, and so on). Given their control over economic resources in these highly inegalitarian societies, domestic capitalists were confident that their economic privilege would translate into political power—significant influence over parties, the outcomes of elections, and the behavior of elected officials once in office. Thus, democracy seemed like the obvious antidote to the business sector's own crisis of representation.

As the armed forces withdrew to their barracks in the 1980s, the Central Andes seemed poised for a new phase of political development. In Peru and Ecuador, literacy requirements for suffrage were removed, and this created a mass electorate for the first time. The reestablishment of elections and the reformation of the electorate did not, however, resolve the still-pressing question of how organized groups of interests within that electorate would be taken into account in policy making. As the economic crisis descended, and as neoliberal coalitions ascended to power, exclusion rather than inclusion became the order of the day.

Patterns in Governance: The Neoliberal Record

The transition from military to civilian rule did not produce daring attempts at political or institutional innovation in any of the three countries. In all three countries, the transition brought a refurbishing of presidentialism and a revival of preexisting multiparty systems. With the return of conventional politics, all the old problems that had plagued these political systems prior to the military interregnum reasserted themselves—the crisis of representation, the absence of a social compromise, the ill-defined relationships among governmental institutions, the chronic legitimacy deficit of public institutions. This time, however, the old problems would be further complicated by the most profound economic crisis that these countries had experienced since the 1930s. In fact, the act of managing the economic crisis came to be defined by leaders within the victorious neoliberal coalitions as completely at odds with any positive resolution of the old problems.

In Bolivia, the transition occurred without any constitutional reform; the transition arrangement involved only the seating of the 1980 Congress and the presidential selection by the Congress that had been interrupted by the García Meza coup. The 1967 constitution, promulgated during the military government of General René Barrientos, remained in place. Peru and Ecuador did undergo some constitutional alterations by virtue of a constituent assembly (in Peru) and a referendum (in Ecuador). Nonetheless, there was substantial continuity with previous constitutional arrangements. In all three countries, powers were highly concentrated in the executive. The decision to stick with presidentialism, rather than parliamentarism, was not particularly surprising. None of the countries had any prior experience with parliamentary government. The extreme concentration of power in the presidency was part of a centralist political tradition that dated from the nineteenth century. In Peru, the APRA-PPC majority in the constituent assembly pushed for an even greater fortification of the powers of the presidency.

In all three countries, presidents were provided with legal avenues to legislate without congressional approval, especially in emergency situations. And presidents made frequent use of these powers (as we have seen in the body of this study) to promulgate economic measures without legislative debate. Presidents also had the power to declare a state of emergency or state of siege, which allowed them to suspend the constitution and take whatever actions they deemed necessary to restore order. In every country, presidents invoked this power to quell popular disturbances in the wake of unpopular economic policies.

Although power was weighted heavily in favor of presidents, the constitutions ascribed enough powers to the national legislatures to allow for some oversight of the executive branch, especially through the practice of interpellation. This allows opposition deputies to call government ministers to account for policies and allows Congress to censure ministers. As we noted in our case studies, presidents usually maneuvered to avoid interpellations so as to keep their economic teams intact.

The alienated character of relations between the executive and legislative branches emerged as one of the most serious institutional strains in these polities, and it had profound repercussions on the way in which presidents approached the problem of governance. Elections almost always produced a divided government—that is, one in which a president lacked a legislative majority. Even in those cases where presidents did come to office with a congressional majority (or built one via coalition after the election), the absence of strong party discipline made those majorities seem tentative and suspect, at least from the president's perspective. So, as much as possible, presidents in these relatively weak legislatures sought to govern by bypassing even their own majorities.[7]

Presidents justified their actions, especially their proclivity to using executive decree to promulgate economic laws, by arguing the urgency of the situation and by calling into question competence of Congress to deal with such matters. This, of course, frustrated Congress—and left the institution struggling to define a role for itself and to establish its legitimacy in the public mind. With their legislative functions dwarfed by the decree-making presidents, congressmen often turned to their powers of investigation and interpellation. Congress increasingly appeared as a negative force, one that presidents liked to portray as inept, hounding, and obstructionist.

This problem of divided government was partially the product of electoral laws and the nature of the party system itself. In Peru and Ecuador, legislative elections were held concurrently with the first round of presidential elections, not the ensuing two person runoff. Given that elections were taking place within the framework of extreme multiparty systems, this electoral arrangement made it very likely that Ecuadorean and Peruvian presidents would come to power without a legislative majority. In Bolivia, the electoral system was even more problematical. Presidential and congressional elections are concurrent, but extreme multipartism and the absence of a presidential runoff complicate the outcomes. If no presidential candidate receives a majority, the contest is thrown to Congress for a decision. The successful presidential candidate must construct a coalition in Congress to vote him into office, but that coalition does not necessarily stay intact and ensure the president a working majority for his term. Thus, elections do not necessarily produce governments with the raw materials to govern.

But ill-designed election rules and multipartism per se were not the only sources of the divided government, ersatz congressional coalitions, and the hypertrophy of presidential power. The character and behavior of political parties facilitated presidential power-grabbing in a number of ways. For presidents, parties were a nuisance (or at best were irrelevant) in the organizing of an effective mode of governance. None of the Andean presidents of the 1980s gave their parties a decisive voice in economic policy making, nor did they evince much interest in developing their own parties to take on such a role in the future. Parties served primarily as campaign vehicles, and both presidents and technocrats, once in power, sought to subordinate and distance themselves from them. Apart from their role in elections, parties were bereft of the other functions democratic systems associate with them. They were not capable of turning the votes garnered in elections into stable broad-based coalitions to support or oppose policies. Nor did they perform a programmatic function, to generate policy blueprints for governments to put into practice after elections.[8]

Why have parties seemingly failed as interest aggregators, as accountable representatives, and as providers of choice in public policy? A complete answer to the question would have to begin with a deeper historical analysis of conditions under which party systems developed—and that would take us far beyond the scope of this concluding essay. For our purposes here, a few observations about the nature of political parties are germane to an understanding of their secondary standing in these polities and their disconnection from the important sphere of economic decision making.

First, political parties developed under an extremely averse set of structural conditions in the twentieth century. Elite attempts to forestall a full incorporation of the "masses" into political life—via restrictions on the franchise, repression, co-optation, and military dictatorships—hamstrung the development of mass-based parties. For the most part, parties were not able to forge enduring linkages to important segments of society—labor, peasantry, indigenous communities, and so on. Peru's APRA and Bolivia's MNR were partial exceptions in this regard. In the case of MNR, the populist alliance of labor, peasants, and middle-class groups was dashed, however, as MNR took a conservative turn under the presidencies of Siles Zuazo (1956–60) and Paz Estenssoro (1960–64). Bolivian labor never returned to the ranks of MNR, but looked to the left and divided its votes among a variety of leftist parties. In Peru, APRA developed strong ties to the early labor movement, but with its move to the right in the 1950s and 1960s, APRA relinquished its role as leader of "reformism" to a variety of new parties and lost any potential appeal it might have had to the new voting blocs, especially the peasantry.[9] Thus, parties have been at the historical center of the unsolved problem of representation in all three countries. The military interregnum temporarily suspended the party system, but its reinstatement occurred without any resolution of the disconnections between parties and civil society.

Rather than serving as the nexus for each group in civil society and the state, most parties developed as loose and ideologically ill-defined clientele networks, organized for the purpose of winning office and distributing *cargos y puestos* (positions and posts) to loyalists. Whereas all modern party systems to a certain degree are held together by clientelism, many of the Andean parties became examples in extremis of this logic. That clientelism became the central organizing component of party life is not particularly surprising, given the limited opportunities for white-collar employment in these economies. Job aspirants gravitated to parties as means to secure public sector posts. The instrumental character of attachment to parties was not just confined to lower- and middle-ranking militants but extended through the top rung of parties too. As dictated by career considerations, leaders routinely abandoned party organizations, joined up with other parties, or formed new parties. The amoebic proliferation of parties and the circulation of elites among parties were testimony to the intensity of the rivalries inside the clientelist parties for control of leadership positions and the inability of parties to contain the conflicts within the confines of the organization.[10]

Since their respective transitions, the primary focus of parties has been on electioneering and job-mongering. The result is that parties did not become venues for serious debates on policy or sites for generating alternative policy options. More often than not, parties were deemed to be incapable of serious formulations in regard to economic questions because of the absence of well-developed strata of economists within the parties' ranks. Many economists preferred to steer clear of any outright affiliation with a party. Whereas they sometimes surfaced inside political parties during election campaigns, many opted to maintain their status as independent consultants to individual politicians rather than become card-carrying partisans. The available data on congressional deputies in Peru and Ecuador in the 1980s show a continued domination of parties by lawyers. Economists accounted for only 2.6 percent of all deputies in 1978–88 in Ecuador, and 2.4 percent of all deputies in 1980–88 in Peru; in contrast, a little over half of the Ecuadorean deputies and a third of the Peruvian deputies were lawyers.[11]

The deficit of economic expertise in political parties and their inclination to oppose any policies that would have electoral costs helped presidents to rationalize their disregard for parties and legislatures in the formulation of policy. Instead, presidents looked to their "boys"—their economic teams. A team was a small circle of advisors, usually from three to five individuals, including the top economic ministers. Typically, the teams included professional economists and individuals with past work experience in the private sector, especially in the fields of banking and finance. Frequently, economic team members also had previously established contacts with international financial institutions.

As our case studies show, the economic teams practiced a very insular style of policy making, and the presidents' powers of decree allowed the executives to impose a broad range of policies without public debate. Economic technocrats believed that making policy was a technical exercise and that their technical prescriptions should not be subjected to second-guessing by nonexperts (politicians, legislators, representatives of interest groups, and so on). It is, of course, not unusual to have certain spheres of economic policy, particularly monetary policy, placed out of the grasp of politicians and the workings of interest group politics. Central banks were created for the purposes of overseeing such technical matters as exchange rate policy.

What is remarkable about these cases, however, is the extent to which virtually all matters of economic policy were defined as off-limits. In the three neoliberal governments we have analyzed, presidents and their economic teams sought to cut off debate on a whole range of fundamental issues, from the role of the public sector to the treatment of foreign capital. In many ways, the policy-making style that evolved in the new civilian regime closely resembled the "stealthy" style of the previous military regimes.[12] Policies were dictated by a small coterie in the executive, without much in the way of consultation except for exchanges with international institutions, the IMF and the World Bank.

The mentality that prevailed inside economic teams worked to reinforce the presidents' sense that it was both necessary and legitimate to place economic policy squarely outside the purview of interest groups, the public, and legislators. The economic teams viewed their task as the application of a science. Like all professionals, they were dismissive of all opinions rendered by nonexperts. This way of thinking was especially pronounced in the neoliberal economic technocrats; they were ideologically disposed to see almost everyone (politicians, interest groups, the masses) as voracious rent-seekers who, if given the opportunity, would unravel any coherent plan to reform the state and implement free market policies. As such, policy making had to be structured to prevent rent-seekers from influencing decisions.

The lame-duck status of Andean presidents also played a part in freeing presidents from feeling the need to be responsive to public opinion on matters of economic policy. In Bolivia and Peru, presidents were proscribed from seeking a second successive term in office, although they could seek reelection after sitting out a term. In Ecuador, the 1979 constitution contained a lifetime ban on reelection. The bans allowed presidents to act without having to consider the personal political costs of their behavior; they would not have to be subject to the humiliation of an electoral defeat. For a variety of reasons, presidents were not particularly concerned about the immediate electoral costs of their behavior for their respective parties.

What is especially notable about how these regimes evolved in the 1980s was the growing disconnection between elections and the policies that governments produced. Elections increasingly took on a plebiscitary quality—presidents were charged with "doing something" about the economic crisis, but exactly what they were being elected to do was never made clear. For the most part, it was in the interest of candidates and political parties to remain vague in their policy prescriptions for the economic crisis, and to frame an election more as a retrospective vote on the outgoing administration. In none of the neoliberal experiments we have discussed were presidents elected on an unqualified neoliberal platform. Instead, Paz Estenssoro and Belaúnde preferred to conjure up images of their previous presidencies and the populist associations those images provoked. While Febres Cordero was more open in his neoliberal leanings, his grassroots campaign played on populist themes, personality, and even religion. Thus, it is difficult to argue that any of these presidents took office with a clear public mandate to proceed with the neoliberal experiment, especially given the mixed results of the congressional races.

In the absence of clearly understood mass-based support for neoliberal policies, presidents proceeded in a variety of ways to create a political environment conducive to the neoliberal experiment. Formal arrangements were blended with informal practices. The subordination of Congress was crucial for allowing unobstructed decision making by the executive's economic team. In all three countries, presidents took actions to ensure that Congress would not emerge as a site of opposition to neoliberalism. Popular opposition was dealt with in a variety of ways, including selective repression. In Ecuador and Bolivia, strikes and protests against neoliberal policies were met with force.

In Ecuador and Bolivia, the use of force went hand in hand with government efforts to create a chilly atmosphere for the opposition. Febres Cordero's bellicose and unpredictable manner gave dissenters good reason to be fearful of retributions; rumors of government ties to paramilitary groups and street gangs were especially unsettling to the opposition. The aggressive behavior of Febres Cordero's FRN deputies in Congress contributed to an ambience of political violence. In Bolivia, Paz Estenssoro's deployment of force in the first weeks of the economic program set the tone of his administration; he left it to government ministers Fernando Barthelemy and Juan Carlos Durán to reiterate the government's intolerance of active opposition. While there was less in the way of physical intimidation of the Peruvian opposition, the tone of the Belaúnde administration was one of complete nonchalance vis-à-vis civil society. The stories told of Prime Minister Ulloa's receiving business leaders with his feet up on his desk are emblematic of the arrogant style of governing in the first half of the Belaúnde government. Criticism, no matter what the source, was simply dismissed.

As all three of our case studies indicate, presidents were the linchpin of this highly insular style of governance. Both presidential will and presidential skill were required to keep it in place. In Ecuador and Peru, Febres Cordero and Belaúnde eventually lost their capacity to deal, to force, to dismiss, to dictate. Events (natural disasters, military situations) overtook those presidents' capacity to maintain the political parameters necessary for the neoliberal experiments to continue. In contrast, Paz Estenssoro not only was able to launch his program but retained his ability to reproduce the political conditions that were crucial to sustaining it.

If effective governance is defined as the capacity of a government both to formulate policies to solve problems and to implement and sustain those policies over time, then democratic governance should be defined with an eye to at least the following three criteria: (1) Governments are constituted by political elites who have won public support for their policies through elections; (2) the implementation of policies does not undermine the functioning of democratic institutions themselves; (3) governments are able to sustain policies over time by having them deemed effective by the public and endorsed in subsequent elections.[13]

Using these criteria, it is clear that the principles of democratic governance were compromised to varying degrees in the elaboration of neoliberal economic programs in each of these cases. Neoliberal programs were embarked upon without any clear public mandate via the electoral process. Opposition groups in civil society were either ignored or repressed. The implementation of the neoliberal programs hinged on delegitimizing virtually every real or potential source of opposition and the engineering of a carte blanche for the executive. This is not to say that neoliberal economic programs singlehandedly account for the severe problems of democratic governance in the Central Andes. An unhealthy tradition of executive-centric constitutions, enfeebled legislatures, and weak political parties was already present in the Andes prior to the enactment of neoliberal policies.

What we suggest is that the mode in which neoliberal policies were pursued contributed to an accumulating set of political practices in these polities that contradict the principles of democratic governance. Neoliberal presidents set precedents that their successors took as cues for their own behavior. The denigration of the legislature, the privileging of the economic team as the sole legitimate source of opinion on economic matters, the derision of interest groups, the recourse to exceptional powers—all became conventional practices in the emerging imperial presidencies of the Central Andes.

Neoliberal Coalitions: Capitalists, Technocrats, and Politicians

It would be a gross oversimplification to view the neoliberal experiments of the Central Andes as policy packages that were unilaterally imposed by external agents such as the IMF and the World Bank. These entities did indeed play a critical role in shaping economic policy, both by providing technical assistance to local economic teams and by exercising their powers to grant or deny aid to these debt-ridden countries. Yet, they were not the sole authors of neoliberalism. In all three countries, business interest groups laid the groundwork for the development of domestic neoliberal coalitions with their antistatism campaigns that began during military rule. Young technocrats were enlisted into the campaign by business interest groups; they translated the antistatist mood into more systematic technical critiques of public policies. Many of the same business leaders and technocrats, in turn, gave voice to their concerns inside political parties, either as leaders or as independent advisors of the parties. Election campaigns became important crucibles for turning these loose antistatist movements into more concrete neoliberal coalitions as capitalists, technocrats, and politicians came together, usually behind closed doors, to hammer out agendas for incoming governments.

The revitalization of coalitions on the right was not a phenomenon confined to the Central Andes. In fact, the role played by business interest groups in the Central Andes bears a striking resemblance to that played by business in the resurgence of the right in the United States. By the mid-1970s, U.S. corporate elites were increasingly concerned about what they perceived as interconnected problems: their waning political influence, the rise of consumer advocacy groups, and the growth of an activist and regulatory state. Corporations as well as their interest groups went on the political offensive. Through campaign contributions, business helped strengthen the Republican party. At the same time, business sought to create its own strata of intellectuals and technocrats in conservative think tanks. Much like business leaders in the Central Andes, U.S. business elites were an active force in creating the conditions for "right turn" in the political and policy environment.[14]

Along other dimensions, however, the Andean neoliberal coalitions diverged sharply from the alliance around which Reaganism was built. The Andean coalitions were never more than a compact among political and economic elites. The coalition was not constructed as a cross-class alignment; it remained strictly an elite affair.

The narrow character of the Andean coalitions differs dramatically from the broad-based alignment that crystallized during the 1980s under the leadership of Ronald Reagan. In the United States, the Republican party became the home of a durable presidential majority—a majority that united corporate conservatives from the business community with white middle- and working-class voters who were concerned about racial, social, and tax issues. As a number of analysts have pointed out, racial polarization in the United States helped to swing white voters away from New Deal thinking and toward free market formulas. White discontent over welfare, affirmative action, and "racial quotas" in hiring was easily folded into a Republican discourse about the perils of state interference in the market that also appealed to the interests of the business community.[15]

Why were Andean leaders unable to construct such an alignment of elites and masses in support of neoliberal projects? Why wasn't Febres Cordero a Ronald Reagan? Part of the answer is obvious. It was evident to neoliberals that austerity and restructuring would be hard to sell to the popular classes, who would bear the brunt of the reforms (cutbacks in public services, loss of jobs in certain sectors, and so on). In these Andean economies, even the middle classes are highly dependent on the state as a source of white-collar employment. Thus, the reforms (particularly the shock stabilization measures in the form of wage freezes and price increases) in and of themselves had little immediate popular appeal; candidates recognized this and did not emphasize them in their campaigns. Moreover, there were no adjunct issues as in the United States—race, abortion, crime, family values, defense and foreign policy—that could be used to rally voters in support of these administrations.

Not expecting neoliberalism to elicit support in the short run and unable to tie it to other issues, the neoliberal elite coalition did not devote much energy to questioning how to organize support for their policies once in power. Instead, neoliberal policy makers looked for ways to either suppress or ignore the static coming from civil society. Even in Bolivia, Paz Estenssoro's Machiavellian political engineering stopped at the party pact; he did not use the presidency as a bullypulpit to lobby Bolivian society in favor of the reforms. Planning minister Gonzalo Sánchez de Lozada later admitted that one of the administration's biggest mistakes was its single-minded devotion to the technocratic application of the model and the absence of any attempt to sell the model to the public. ''We forgot to develop a constituency,'' he noted.[16]

This disconnection between policy makers and the public was a conspicuous feature of all three neoliberal experiments, and it explains a good deal of the frailty of the neoliberal coalitions themselves. In the absence of any developed and widespread public consensus and commitment to the reforms, politicians were prone to desert the experiments in the face of short-term crisis situations. In Ecuador, for example, the neoliberal experiment unraveled along with Febres Cordero's capacity to govern. The economic fallout from the earthquake, the deterioration of civil-military relations, and the resurgence of congressional opposition convinced Febres Cordero that he could not continue with the model. After the kidnapping incident, his major preoccupation simply was to complete his term in office.

Politicians were not the only sources of instability within the elite coalitions. In all three countries, serious fissures developed within the coalitions as actors differed on issues surrounding the design and implementation of policies. Whereas capitalists, technocrats, and politicians had all rallied around an antistatist discourse, they did not necessarily agree on the specifics and pacing of neoliberalism in practice. The business community itself was divided by diverging sectoral interests, and neoliberal policies had a differential impact on sectors. In all three countries, import-substituting manufacturers were the strongest opponents of a brusque dismantling of protectionist measures for industry.

For the most part, neoliberal economic teams tried to resist making adjustments in their programs in response to business criticisms. Neoliberal technocrats were animated by their ideological agenda and professional convictions; they were obsessed with the idea of unleashing market forces. Their concern was with aggregate economic performance, not the fate of particular capitalists or firms. Indeed, they hoped that market competition would eliminate the rent-seeking elements within the business community. In short, technocrats sought to impose on the economy an idealized and theory-derived model of capitalism. But some business groups balked at the idea of being subjected to what they considered radical experiments inspired by foreign academic theories. Instead, business leaders frequently argued for a fine-tuning of promarket policies to suit the ''national reality.'' In all three countries, neoliberal coalitions were marked by this conflict between the theorists of capitalism and its real-life practitioners.

Strains inside the tripartite coalitions of capitalists, politicians, and technocrats played an important role in determining how the policy experiments unfolded in reality and whether or not they were sustained over time. Tensions were most pronounced in Peru where industrialists mounted an all-out campaign against Belaúnde's economic policies. In Ecuador, the industrial lobby managed to water down tariff reforms in extended negotiations with the government. Later on, speculative behavior by exporters in the foreign exchange market led Febres Cordero to rescind currency flotation, the measure he had considered the historic achievement of his administration.

In contrast to Febres Cordero and Belaúnde, Paz Estenssoro in Bolivia proved more adept in managing the strains within the coalition and in keeping his experiment on track. The Bolivian business community was more manageable for a variety of reasons. Business elites, traumatized by their experience with the Siles Zuazo administration, were loath to attack a government that had restored order to the marketplace. And the policy reforms had different impacts both across and within economic sectors. As in Ecuador and Peru, industry was the sector most adversely affected by neoliberalism; but it was also the least important activity of the Bolivian private sector. Within the industrial sector, there were enormous differences in the extent to which the neoliberal reforms helped or hurt firms. Some manufacturers were felled by the competition that came with tariff liberalization, while other manufacturers benefited from the reduced costs of imported inputs and capital goods. For most of the business community, the positive effects of D.S. 21060 seemed to outweigh the costs. Other than the demands for government help with economic reactivation, business dissidence remained relatively muted throughout the course of the Paz Estenssoro administration. Paz never had to contend with a concerted antigovernment campaign by business, nor was he forced to deal with outright economic sabotage (capital flight, speculation) of his program—all this had already occurred during the previous Siles government.

The neoliberal coalitions of the Central Andes were founded on the adhesion of elites to antistatist ideology, which they believed could be played out to serve their immediate political and economic interests. The coalitions began forming in conjunction with the campaign to reestablish civilian rule and became more defined through subsequent electoral competition. But the coalitions never moved beyond the initial formative stage; they did not evolve into a more durable and institutionalized set of relations among actors, even in the case of Bolivia where neoliberalism remained intact. Looking at the coalitions in comparative perspective, we find no attempt to transform the coalitions into explicit networks linking economic decision makers with capitalists. As much recent work on political economy has shown, such networks have been critical in assuring close business-government cooperation on economic policy (including stabilization measures) in a number of countries, ranging from Taiwan to Switzerland.[17] Rather than seeking out ways to strengthen their relationships with business, neoliberal politicians and technocrats sought maximum autonomy and minimum business input. The neoliberal experiments brought no new institutional innovation to resolve the problems of inadequate representation that business was suffering from.

Democracy in the Americas: Parting Thoughts

One of Tocqueville's great insights in *Democracy in America* was to recognize that modern democracy is a composite phenomenon—a system of government built around checks on institutional power, animated by a robust civil society, and grounded in widely shared "habits of the heart" within the citizenry. Aware of the complexities of the mix that sustained democracy, Tocqueville was fearful of democracy's potential to slide into despotism. Tocqueville believed that the growth of the modern state would be characterized by an ever increasing centralization of power—and that the accumulation of such power in the state would open up endless possibilities for its abuse, either by individual leaders or by bureaucracies at large. In democratic systems, elections would be used to legitimize these practices by allowing citizens to periodically "choose their masters." Tocqueville described how democratic impulses mix with a perceived need for strong government:

> Our contemporaries are ever prey to two conflicting passions: they feel the need of guidance, and they long to stay free. Unable to wipe out these two contradictory instincts, they try to satisfy them both together. Their imagination conceives a government which is unitary, protective, and all-powerful, but elected by the people. Centralization is combined with the sovereignty of the people. That gives them a chance to relax. They console themselves for being under schoolmasters by thinking that they have chosen them themselves. Each individual lets them put the collar on, for he sees that it is not a person, or a class of persons, but society itself which holds the end of the chain.[18]

Our case studies focus attention on some of the disturbing tendencies at work in three Latin American countries that have made recent transitions from military authoritarianism to elected civilian rule. Unfortunately, our findings would give Tocqueville much to be dismayed about. The marginalization of the legislature; the arrogance and autonomy of the executive branch; the growing disjunction between electoral choice and public policy; the weakness of political parties; the devaluation of "politics" and the entrenchment of economics as the framing discipline of public policy; the forced contraction, through neoliberal policies, of the public sphere (and by extension, the contraction of what may be defined as rights)—all these phenomena constitute important features of these regimes. To focus solely on elections as the defining feature of these regimes misses much of how they operate. Elections are not a problem; the problem with Latin American democracy is what happens after elections. The real deficit within these democracies has to do with the absence of governmental responsiveness and accountability to the public.

The problematical tendencies we have outlined in these regimes should sound familiar to students of comparative politics. We do not believe that what we have just described is simply a regional pathology. Across the globe, long-standing democracies as well as those of more recent vintage are riddled with many of the same problems of governance we have described in this book. Rather than viewing the Central Andes as colorful but remote political exotica, it may be more instructive to regard the Andes as presenting bolder versions of some of the same problems at play in a variety of contemporary democracies. Might not the Andes tell us something about the dilemmas of postmodern political development—namely, the ways in which conventional democratic practices (that is, elections) are being forced into cohabitation with technocratic styles of governing?

Nowhere has the intellectual anxiety about many of the same problems of postmodern democracy been more acute than in the United States. A wave of recent writing by scholars and journalists has focused explicitly on the multiple sources of malaise in American democracy—the lack of meaning in elections, the decay of political parties, the autonomy of executive and bureaucratic power. It is an inventory of problems distressingly similar to those we have touched on in this study.[19]

The accretion and abuse of executive power is a persistent concern among analysts of American politics. The executive-led escalation of the Vietnam war in the 1960s and the Watergate scandal fueled the critique of the "imperial presidency."[20] The Iran-Contra affair during the Reagan administration was seen by many as yet another ominous sign of the executive's contempt for Congress and its proclivity to place itself above the law. The forces that have driven the growth of presidential power in the United States are not unlike those at play in the Central Andes. Presidents seek means both formal and informal to avoid the policy stalemates that almost inevitably arise in the context of divided government. Presidents, in turn, justify their end-runs around the legislature by invoking the notion of a "crisis" (either in national security or in economic terms).

The accumulation of power in the executive has gone hand in hand with the prevalence of weak party systems. On both sides of the equator, parties have performed poorly, both in linking the public to officials and in ensuring the policy responsiveness of those officials to the public. In the absence of strong parties, legislatures are further enfeebled and politics becomes unmediated by institutions. Presidential elections turn into personalized plebiscites on individual leaders, rather than the expression of an informed consensus on policy.[21]

The ascendance of technocrats and their growing domination over certain spheres of policy making, particularly economic policy, represents another serious problem in the organization of democratic governance, a problem that reaches far beyond Lima or Quito. Like the discourse of many professions, the discourse of economics is designed to restrict participation in debates to a field of designated experts. This necessarily narrows the range of debate on policy options and marginalizes the ability of nonexperts to participate in any meaningful way in deliberations on policy. In the case of the United States, Theodore Lowi argues that the rise of economics as the ''language of the state'' parallels the decline in the importance of Congress in policy making.[22]

The parallels between Latin America and the United States are not confined to the problems associated with presidentialism, divided government, and weak party systems. The substance of public policy itself is affecting the character of regimes and will have long-term implications for the future of democracy in the Americas. As in Latin America, the substance of public policy in the United States has been greatly affected by two developments in the 1980s: (1) the ideological and political surge of the New Right; and (2) the appearance of the interconnected problems of public debt, stalled economic growth, and the state's fiscal crisis. The right's attack on the welfare state coupled with the reality of diminishing economic resources induced a shift in public philosophy that even extended into the Democratic party. The result was a new emphasis on ''shrinking the state,'' that is, transferring functions previously performed by the central government to the local level or directly reassigning the functions to the market. By enlarging the scope of services that are to be provided by localities or by the market, the thrust of ''state shrinking'' is to reduce the range of claims that people can make on the state as part of the rights of citizenship. The wealthy, of course, can always compensate for the shrinking public goods with private goods—private schools, gyms, clubs, security guards replace public schools, pools, parks, and police. Lower-income groups are left to make do with downgraded public services or none at all. This combination of increasing privatization and decline in the availability and quality of public goods has led some analysts to talk about the ''Brazilianization'' of life in the United States.[23]

In both the United States and Latin America, the new austerity in public policy reinforces class divisions and fragments the citizenry into groups that are not joined in anything resembling a ''mutuality of experience.''[24] Like Latin America, the United States seems to have moved away from a broadly conceived notion of citizenship that incorporates social rights (welfare) with traditional political rights (freedom of speech, voting, and so on). With the demise of the New Deal coalition, substantive class compromise has given way and left the political system to operate on ''thin political consensus, limited largely to procedural matters.''[25] The combined effects of these shared institutional and policy developments have been to reduce the meaning of democracy to that of the holding of periodic plebiscitary-style elections. In between those elections, decision making is the province of unelected technocrats and unaccountable politicians.

In Tocqueville's estimation, the most effective checks on the development of despotism come from a combative civil society, one that jealously guards its powers to deliberate and participate by doing just that. More optimistic analysts of the U.S. regime would argue that American civil society is sufficiently robust and well equipped to combat the growth of technomanagerial government. As evidenced in the Watergate and the Iran-Contra scandals, the press acts as an important watchdog over the behavior of the executive branch. In addition to an aggressive press, a dense grid of interest groups and grassroots organizations are an entrenched part of American politics, compensating in part for the decline of parties.[26]

Yet, there are equally compelling signs that American society and its political institutions may be growing less capable of resisting the "de-democratizing" impulses of technocrats and executives. For the most part, American sociologists paint a rather unflattering picture of the state of American society. In the landmark study by Robert Bellah and associates, American society is a bleak landscape—a world organized around anomic individualism, obsessed with consumer capitalism, and increasingly devoid of "civic virtue."[27]

Moreover, as we have already noted, structural changes in the American economy are exacerbating the divisions among social classes. Analysts point to increasing class tensions among three distinctive strata: (1) an upper and upper-middle class who were the beneficiaries of the income-concentrating economic policies of Reaganism; (2) a middle and working class under increasing economic stress, induced in part by the loss of white- and blue-collar jobs; (3) a racially identified underclass composed of African American and other minorities—the unemployed, the underemployed, the workforce of a growing informal sector in the American economy.[28] In short, it is a class structure marked, like Latin America in the 1980s, by growing inequalities and polarization.

As class relations fray, the political system seems to be increasingly disconnected from the concerns of average (middle- and lower-class) citizens; the institutions that traditionally channeled the economic concerns of these groups (parties and unions) have lost their clout. In their place stands a dense grid of interest groups in Washington, but the grid is dominated by corporate interest groups and narrowly defined "issue constituencies." In conjunction with the operation of this interest group politics, the debates on policy become ever more subjected to the discourse of experts, and policy design takes place within the framework of reigning disciplines—economics, psychology, administrative sciences, criminology.[29]

In the Andes, civil society operates at a distinct disadvantage vis-à-vis the powers that have accrued inside the state apparatus, particularly the executive branch. Historically, the development of organizations in civil society, particularly those representing lower-class groups, has been hamstrung by the enormous inequalities in the distribution of income. The recent transition to civilian rule did not substantially alter the terrain on which society-state relations take place. By promoting a deproletarianization of the labor force and an expansion of the informal sector, neoliberal economic policies further aggravate the difficulties of organization and advance what Manuel Antonio Garretón called "an organic weakening of society"—the atomization of individuals and the disarticulation of traditional communal and workplace organizations that occur with the restructuring of the labor market.[30]

Could the United States and Latin America be moving toward civil societies and economic realities that are more alike than we might ever have imagined? The commonalities now seem as astonishing as our differences once were. On the economic side, we confront fiscal crisis, slowed economic growth, an expansion of informal sector employment and underemployment, and the presence of a seemingly permanent underclass. On the political side, we encounter the decay of trade unionism, the decline of traditional parties, plebiscitary presidential elections, and a variety of expressions of political alienation. Finally, given the penetration of neoliberal doctrine, we are joined in witnessing a dominant cultural milieu that exalts individualism and consumerism. Viewed within the context of the Americas, the divisions that once appeared to clearly separate the problems

of "late capitalism" from those of the "developing" countries now appear to be less definitive. How these problems (and the crises associated with these problems) are processed by the political systems may differ, but they will certainly impinge on the evolution of regime types.[31]

As we approach the end of the twentieth century, Tocqueville's warnings about the potential of democracy to devolve into new insidious forms of domination deserve our full attention. Reconciling effective governance with a meaningful practice of democracy is a conundrum for both North and South. Questions about the quality of democracy in our hemisphere are as pertinent in Los Angeles as they are in La Paz. For the United States and Latin America, democracy's future depends on a vigorous civil society, one capable of defending itself against arrogant technocrats and power-hungry executives. There are signs that such a civil society could be in the making for Latin America—in squatter settlements, in the environmental and indigenous movements, in women's groups, in human rights organizations.[32] But these signs of life in civil society cannot be taken for granted. Both in Latin America and the United States, democrats must make and

remake civil society to prevent the realization of Tocqueville's worst fears.

EPILOGUE

Unfinished Stories

As we prepare the final draft of this book in the fall of 1993, the denouement of the latest installments of democracy and neoliberalism in the Central Andes seems anything but clear. No definitive resolution of the economic and political dilemmas described in this book has yet been struck. Bolivia, Ecuador, and Peru have once again converged on neoliberal economic policies; but they all continue to struggle with the problem of how to achieve sustained economic growth in the wake of recessions induced by anti-inflation stabilization programs. At the same time, the political tendencies described in this book are still at play. In all three countries, presidents are driving toward an ever increasing concentration of power in the executive branch while relegating Congress and parties to minor roles in policy making.

It is not suprising that many of the individual players in the economic experiments described in this book remain on the scene as influential technocrats and politicians. After a failed attempt in 1989, Gonzalo Sánchez de Lozada won the Bolivian presidential election of 1993 and brought many veterans of the Paz Estenssoro government back on board his economic team. In Ecuador, Sixto Durán Ballén realized his dream of winning the presidency in 1992. His vice-presidential running mate was none other than Alberto Dahik, the zealous neoliberal technocrat of the previous Febres Cordero administration. León Febres Cordero remained politically active and won the mayoralty of Guayaquil in 1992. In Peru, many of the business leaders, technocrats, and conservative politicians (including Fernando Belaúnde and Luis Bedoya) who played roles in the initial neoliberal experiment regrouped around the presidential campaign of Mario Vargas Llosa in 1990. After the defeat of Vargas Llosa by Alberto Fujimori, neoliberal technocrats swooped in to influence the policies of the president-elect.

Among those technocrats who influenced the direction of policy were Hernando de Soto, Carlos Rodríguez Pastor, and later Roberto Abusada.

In Peru. The most dramatic drive to secure unquestioned executive dominance and neoliberalism came in Peru on 5 April 1992. As tanks rolled through the streets that evening, President Alberto Fujimori announced his decision to close Peru's Congress, dismiss the judiciary, and temporarily suspend the 1979 constitution. In his televised speech to the nation, Fujimori justified his autocoup as the only way to deal with Peru's extreme governability crisis. He blamed Congress and the traditional parties for obstructing his neoliberal economic program and his war on internal subversion.

Fujimori's autocoup aimed at putting an end to partisan opposition and clearing away any last institutional obstructions to executive rule. The coup came on the heels of a prolonged political and economic crisis. The collapse of Belaúnde's neoliberal experiment was followed by a complete policy turnaround under the leadership of President Alan García, the first APRA militant to hold executive power. Inspired by Argentina's turn to heterodoxy in the Plan Austral, García embarked on an economic program that aimed to reactivate the economy by boosting demand and industrial production. The costs of the plan were to be underwritten by savings garnered through García's policy to limit repayments on international debt to a ceiling of 10 percent. But García's experiment went awry: international financial flows to Peru were interrupted; reheating the economy brought hyperinflation; the economy deteriorated, and so did the social fabric. By the end of the 1980s, Peru was in the throes of a ferocious internal war with the revolutionary movement, Sendero Luminoso. Between 1980 and 1988, 12,870 Peruvians were killed in political violence; the toll had climbed to 26,000 by 1993.

As with Belaúnde, García's errors in policy making involved both style and substance. Decision making under García was marked by much of the same arrogance and arbitrary style that had permeated the Belaúnde government; but in contrast to Belaúnde, García personally took an active role in his own economic team. The most extreme example of the abrupt and nonconsultative style that emerged during the García presidency was the July 1987 decision to nationalize domestic banks. The decision signaled the end of any attempt to strike a proinvestment alliance between the government and the large economic groups. The ill-fated decision horrified middle- and upper-class Peruvians and galvanized an opposition movement that gave birth to the 1990 presidential candidacy of novelist Mario Vargas Llosa.

Yet, the seemingly powerful neoliberal coalition that rearticulated itself around the Vargas Llosa candidacy was repudiated by Peruvian voters. Vargas Llosa's unabashed commitment to the pursuit of "shock therapy" economic policies was unpopular with Peruvians who were already reeling from years of economic experiments. Unwilling to take a dose of the economic medicine promised by Vargas Llosa, Peruvians opted to elect the politically unknown Alberto Fujimori from a newly minted political party, Cambio-90. During the campaign, Fujimori denounced Vargas Llosa's economic plan but remained studiously vague as to how he would treat Peru's economic ills if elected. His appeal was based on his lack of association with what Peruvians perceived as a bankrupt party system and the resonance of racial-class appeal; he promised Peruvians "un presidente como tu" (a president like you).

The electoral rejection of neoliberalism did not undo the campaign to put Peru back on the road to economic orthodoxy. Technocrats of all persuasions jockeyed for Fujimori's attention in the weeks following his election. The heterodox pretenders, however, were unceremoniously unloaded by Fujimori after a pre-inauguration trip to the United States and meetings with World Bank and IMF officials. Sheparding Fujimori through this trip were Hernando de Soto and Carlos Rodríguez Pastor.

As Fujimori's July 1990 inauguration approached, it became evident that some sort of shock treatment lay ahead. Peru's annual inflation rate for 1990 stood at 7,500 percent, there were no foreign reserves, and public finances were in a state of complete collapse. The subsequent "Fuji-shock" included price hikes in gasoline and public utilities, emergency tax increases, and some trade liberalization. But conflicts over the pacing and the extent of the economic reforms surfaced quickly inside Fujimori's first cabinet. The exits of the minister of finance, Juan Carlos Hurtado Miller, and the minister of industry, Guido Pennano, in February 1991 cleared the way for more comprehensive orthodoxy. This time Fujimori chose a convinced neoliberal for the job of minister of economy, Carlos Boloña. Boloña, an Oxford-trained economist and former aide to Rodríguez Pastor, launched a broad plan of simultaneous structural reforms including financial deregulation, trade liberalization, and the privatization of public enterprises.

Like his predecessors, Fujimori made extensive use of his decree powers. Whereas his own party, Cambio-90, did not constitute a majority in Congress, deputies from the right voted to cede Fujimori further powers through the provision laid out in Article 188 of the 1979 constitution. Notwithstanding the existence of a largely sympathetic majority in Congress, Fujimori engaged in unrelenting attacks on the legislature and political parties, depicting them as obstacles to his plan of economic modernization. Executive-legislative conflicts over the 1992 budget and new antisubversion legislation were part of the poisoned political atmosphere that preceded the coup of 5 April 1992.

In retrospect, Fujimori's autocoup seems less of a departure from normal politics than a culmination of the unsettling styles of statecraft already set in motion by previous presidents. The autocoup on 5 April was the first installment in Fujimori's project to completely rewire Peru's political structures and subordinate them to the presidency. Under international pressures, the government allowed the resumption of elections but maintained tight controls over the subsequent timetables and the contours of the competition. In a plebiscite on 31 October 1993, voters narrowly approved the constitution written by the Fujimori-controlled majority in the constituent assembly. The new constitution further aggrandized the discretionary powers of the executive and allowed for presidential reelection; Fujimori is expected to take advantage of the provision and stand as a candidate in the election scheduled for 1995.

In Ecuador. As of this writing, Ecuador and Bolivia have not suffered a formal constitutional breach in the style of Peru's Fuji-golpe. Yet, the persistence of serious executive-legislative conflicts in Ecuador and continuing social resistance in Bolivia continue to complicate the implementation of neoliberal reforms. This chronic institutional, partisan, and societal "static" carries the potential either to disarticulate the neoliberal programs or to tempt executives to seek solutions that put future democratic political development at risk.

In Ecuador, Sixto Durán Ballén began his presidential term in 1992 with a round of shock therapy measures to combat inflation and a promise to set Ecuador firmly on a course of structural reforms. The attempted revival of neoliberalism by President Durán Ballén and Vice-President Dahik followed on the heels of a social democratic administration led by Rodrigo Borja. Elected in 1988 in the aftermath of Febres Cordero's failed policies, Borja shelved the neoliberal agenda while managing to avoid the excesses of García-style heterodoxy. His "gradualist" stabilization program consisted of periodic adjustments of exchange rates and fuel prices. Although inflation was contained in the 1988–90 period, it resurged during Borja's last two years in office with relaxations on government spending.

Promising to solve the economic disaster left by the outgoing administration, Sixto Durán Ballén initiated his economic program with fuel price hikes, devaluation, decrees that slashed government spending, and the elimination of public sector jobs. Yet, apart from the initial stabilization measures, the neoliberal revival stalled throughout the administration's first year in office. Many of the legal reforms proposed by the administration to facilitate measures like privatization either were rejected or simply languished in Congress, despite the presence of an ostensibly progovernment majority.

One of Durán Ballén's problems in moving ahead with neoliberal reform lay in the fragmentation of parties on the right. Durán Ballén's own party, the Partido Unidad Republicana (PUR), was the product of his split from the PSC during the fight over the 1992 presidential nomination. Founded as a personal electoral vehicle for Durán Ballén, PUR attracted into its ranks an ideologically heterogeneous collection of office seekers. The ensuing competition among parties of the right yielded a rightist congressional majority that spread across PUR, PSC, and the Partido Conservador Ecuatoriano (PCE), which had been revived as an electoral vehicle for Alberto Dahik. The result was an undisciplined and fractious conservative majority over which the government struggled to exert influence during the first year. Indeed, PUR deputies frequently voted against government-sponsored legislation. At the same time, electoral calculations made the PSC wary of appearing to be completely compliant to the government agenda.

Infighting inside the economic team also fed the disarray in policy making during 1992–93. Like Belaúnde, Durán Ballén is a professional architect who evinces little interest in the details of macroeconomic management. The absence of hands-on presidential leadership left the cabinet open to rivalries over who would control economic policy; by mid-1993, a series of resignations cleared the way for Vice-President Dahik to dominate decision making. Dahik's impact on economic policy in particular and the tenor of politics in general remains to be seen. Dahik's reputation as a "maximalist" on neoliberal reform was underscored in the 1992 campaign when his former boss, Febres Cordero, referred to Dahik as an "economic terrorist." Bitter exchanges between Dahik and the congressional opposition occurred in 1993; some opposition leaders accused the executive branch of exacerbating the executive-legislature conflict as a prelude to a Fujimori-style autocoup.

In Bolivia. In contrast to Ecuador, Bolivia's Congress has posed fewer problems for the executive in the elaboration of the neoliberal program, largely because of party pacts. The MNR-ADN Pacto por la Democracia engineered by Paz Estenssoro and Banzer in 1985 was followed by ADN-MIR's Acuerdo Patriótico in 1989. The ADN-MIR coalition denied the presidency to Gonzalo Sánchez de Lozada—the MNR candidate who won a plurality of popular votes in the election—by refusing congressional ratification of the popular result. Instead, ADN agreed to cede the presidency to MIR's Jaime Paz Zamora, who agreed to continue with the neoliberal economic program.

During his term in office from 1989 to 1993, Paz Zamora did nothing to alter the basic design of the neoliberal program laid out by the previous administration. But Paz Zamora's tenure in office did make clear the extent to which the maintenance of party pacts can eat away at the logic of neoliberal reform, especially regarding the downsizing of the public sector. Both in the Paz Estenssoro and Paz Zamora governments, party pacts were the key factors that allowed the presidents to go forth with economic reforms meeting virtually no institutional resistance. But patronage is the foundation of the pacts; and patronage politics became even more pronounced during the Paz Zamora administration, stoking charges of widespread corruption. Notwithstanding the neoliberal commitment to "state shrinking," Paz Zamora created three new ministeries and sixteen new vice-ministerial posts, and an estimated twenty thousand new employees were added to the public payroll.

The new government of President Gonzalo Sánchez de Lozada will not escape the pressures of *empleomania* (partisan job-seeking), which are part and parcel of maintaining pacts and keeping congressional opposition at bay. The president's congressional majority is diverse, composed of MNR, the populist Unión Cívica Solidaridad (UCS), and the once-leftist Movimiento Bolivia Libre (MBL). The most intense job pressures come from MNR itself, which was completely cut out of the patronage game during the Paz Zamora government. Sánchez de Lozada assumed office in August 1993 with a pledge to root out "hypercorruption" through an aggressive program of administrative streamlining; but serious doubts about the integrity of the program were raised in the first months of the administration when mass dismissals of employees were followed by a wave of rehirings of personnel from MNR. Meanwhile the Bolivian trade union movement has committed itself to mobilizing against further job reductions. By mid-November 1993, the popularity rating of the new government was declining.

After more than a decade of civilian rule, there is considerable public disenchantment with political life in the Central Andes. Public opinion polls in all three countries reveal low levels of public confidence in parties, the judiciary, and the legislature and show profound doubts as to the efficacy of democracy as a form of government. Much of this disapproval has to do with the public's continuing disappointment with economic performance. While economic stabilization programs have put an end to hyperinflation, the basic problems of unemployment, underemployment, and mass poverty remain. This discontent concerning economic issues is not confined to the lower classes but reaches well into the ranks of the middle classes who have been "pauperized" by job cutbacks and wage reductions in both public and private sector.

The underlying assumption of the neoliberal programs is that, once the investment climate is perceived to be stable, domestic and international capitalists will author a process of sustained economic growth. But whether capitalists will respond with long-term investments that provide some relief from the long-standing structural problems in these economies is still an unanswered question. GDP growth has recovered in the 1990s, but the benefits from neoliberal reform may not be evident to broad segments of the electorate for a long time, if ever. It takes no stretch of the imagination to understand how populist movements and demands for redistributive policies could reemerge under these circumstances.

We are not presumptious or foolish enough to conclude with a grand prediction as to the future of political development in countries as complicated as Bolivia, Peru, and Ecuador. As we have argued in this book, much of that future will depend on the choices made by their capitalists, technocrats, and politicians. But recent events in Peru cast a long shadow on the prospects for democracy, suggesting that civilian-led authoritarianism has not been ruled out as a political option by that triad of elites.

APPENDIX
NOTES
BIBLIOGRAPHY
INDEX

APPENDIX

Field Research and Methods

The book draws extensively on elite interviews and archival research conducted by the authors in Bolivia, Peru, and Ecuador in a number of trips that took place between 1986 and 1991. The bulk of the interviews were held between 1986 and 1989. Materials from interviews done by the authors in conjunction with other research projects on political parties and business groups were also utilized.

A total of 122 formal interviews were conducted specifically for this project: 35 in Ecuador, 33 in Peru, and 54 in Bolivia. The informants targeted for interviews were members of the elite class who were directly involved in some dimension of the economic-policy-making process, either as top decision makers or interest group leaders. For the most part, the informants were identified on the basis of their institutional positions. Interviews were conducted with former presidents, economic ministers and advisors, and congressional leaders of government and opposition parties. The leaders of major business interest groups in each country were also interviewed. All of the interviews were conducted by the principal researchers on the project. Some of the initial interviews in Lima in 1986 were conducted jointly by Luis Abugattás and Catherine Conaghan. Further interviewing in Lima was conducted by Conaghan. Interviews in 1986 in La Paz were conducted jointly by James Malloy and Catherine Conaghan. All subsequent interviews in Santa Cruz, Cochabamba, Guayaquil, and Quito were carried out by Conaghan.

The interview portion of the project was designed as qualitative research, that is, in-depth interviewing within a select group of informants rather than survey research. The subject matter of the study lent itself to this approach, given the small number of individuals involved in the policy-making circles in each country. In addition to providing the basis for the narrative as to "what happened" in the policy-making process, the interviews were structured to tap the informants' perceptions of the policy-making process and their sense of the historical peculiarities affecting the behavior of actors in the process. The interviews were based on a simple skeleton of open-ended questions; this opened up the discussion with the informants, which then led to more individualized questioning about their own particular experiences and behavior. Informants were asked to respond to the following introductory questions: (1) identify the persons or institutions most important in the formulation of economic policy; (2) compare the process of economic policy making with that which occurred under previous administrations; (3) discuss the role of business organizations in influencing economic policy; (4) evaluate the role of Congress and political parties in affecting policy formulation and implementation; and (5) assess the influence of international institutions.

Most of the interviews were conducted in Spanish. In most cases, they were tape recorded. The interviews cited in the text, along with the printed Spanish language sources, were translated by the authors. Because of the sensitive topics touched on by some of the informants, the anonymity of the informants has been maintained in the notes by referring only to the date and location of the interview. Individual informants are identified in the text in the cases where an event or the opinion of the individual was already a matter of public record.

In addition to the interviews, newspaper and periodical publications were an important source of information in constructing the narratives. In Lima, the bibliographic data bank at DESCO was utilized to do a subject search of newspapers for the Belaúnde period. Walter Spurrier, editor of the *Analisis Semanal,* generously allowed the use of his private newspaper files in Guayaquil. In Bolivia, subject searches of newspapers were done in the collection of the Centro de Documentación y Información in La Paz.

NOTES

Acronyms Used in the Notes and Bibliography

ADEX	Asociación de Exportadores
APRA	Alianza Popular Revolucionaria Americana
BAB	Banco Agrícola de Bolivia
CADE	Conferencia Anual de Ejecutivos
CEBRAP	Centro Brasileiro de Análise e Planejamento
CEDATOS	Centro de Estudios y Datos
CEDES	Centro de Estudios de Estado y Sociedad
CEDIS	Centro de Estudios y Difusión Social
CEDLA	Centro de Estudios para el Desarrollo Laboral y Agrario
CEDOIN	Centro de Documentación e Información
CEDYS	Centro de Estudios de Democracia y Sociedad
CEPAL	Comisión Económica para América Latina (in English: ECLA, Economic Commission for Latin America)
CEPB	Confederación de Empresarios Privados de Bolivia
CERES	Centro de Estudios de la Realidad Económica y Social
CFP	Concentración de Fuerzas Populares
CLACSO	Congreso Latinoamericano de Ciencias Sociales
CNI	Cámara Nacional de Industrias
COB	Central Obrera Boliviana
COFADENA	Corporación de las Fuerzas Armadas de Desarrollo Nacional
CORDES	Corporación de Estudios para el Desarrollo
DESCO	Centro de Estudios y Promoción del Desarrollo
FESO	Fundación Ecuatoriana de Estudios Sociales
FLACSO	Facultad Latinoamericana de Ciencias Sociales
FRN	Frente de Reconstrucción Nacional
FSE	Fondo Social de Emergencia
FUT	Frente Unitario de Trabajadores
IESS	Instituto de Estudios Económicos y Sociales

ILD	Instituto Libertad y Democracia
ILDIS	Instituto Latinoamericano de Investigaciones Sociales
IPAE	Instituto Peruano de Administración de Empresas
JUNAPLA	Junta Nacional de Planificación y Coordinación Económica
MNR	Movimiento Nacionalista Revolucionario
PPC	Partido Popular Cristiano
PREALC	Programa Regional del Empleo para América Latina y el Caribe
SENDIP	Secretaría Nacional de Información Pública
SI	Sociedad de Industrias
SINAMOS	Sistema Nacional de Apoyo a la Movilización Social
SNI	Sociedad Nacional de Industrias

1. Introduction

1. O'Donnell's influential argument was first elaborated in his *Modernization and Bureaucratic Authoritarianism: Studies in South American Politics* (Berkeley: Institute of International Studies, University of California Press, 1973). Also see his "Reflections on the Patterns of Change in the Bureaucratic-Authoritarian State," *Latin American Research Review* 12, no. 1 (Winter 1979): 3–38. For critiques of the O'Donnell argument, see David Collier, ed., *The New Authoritarianism in Latin America* (Princeton, N.J.: Princeton University Press, 1979). For O'Donnell's more detailed empirical study of the BA regime in Argentina, see Guillermo O'Donnell, *Bureaucratic Authoritarianism: Argentina 1966–76 in Comparative Perspective* (Berkeley: University of California Press, 1988).

2. For an argument in this vein, see Samuel Huntington's essay "The United States," in Michel Crozier, Samuel Huntington, and Joji Watanaki, *The Crisis of Democracy: Report on the Governability of Democracies to the Trilateral Commission* (New York: New York University Press, 1975), 59–113. For another argument on the "overload" of democratic systems, see Richard Rose and B. Guy Peters, *Can Government Go Bankrupt?* (New York: Basic Books, 1978).

3. See, for example, James O'Connor, *The Fiscal Crisis of the State* (New York: St. Martin's Press, 1973). Also see Jürgen Habermas, *Legitimation Crisis,* trans. Thomas McCarthy (Boston: Beacon Press, 1975). For a contrast of "overload" versus "legitimation" theorists, see David Held, *Models of Democracy* (Cambridge: Polity Press, 1987), 229–42.

4. Charles Lindblom, *Politics and Markets: The World's Political-Economic Systems* (New York: Basic Books, 1977).

5. This definition and the notion of these policies as experiments is taken from Alejandro Foxley, *Latin American Experiments in Neoconservative Economics* (Berkeley: University of California Press, 1983). Foxley preferred to use the term *neoconservative* for English-speaking readers, but we have chosen to use *neoliberal,* the word commonly used in Spanish to describe such policies.

6. For a discussion of most similar case approaches to comparative analysis, see Adam Przeworski and Henry Teune, *The Logic of Comparative Social Inquiry* (New York: Wiley, 1969), 31–43.

7. Poulantzas's position was laid out in *Political Power and Social Classes,* trans. Timothy O'Hagan (London: New Left Books, 1973).

8. Ralph Miliband's empirical approach to the study is found in *The State in Capitalist Society* (London: Weidenfeld and Nicolson, 1969). For Miliband's critique of Poulantzas, see "Reply to Nicos Poulantzas," *New Left Review* 59 (January–February 1970): 53–60; "Poulantzas and the Capitalist State," *New Left Review* 82 (November–December 1973): 83–92. For the reply, see Nicos Poulantzas, "The Capitalist State: A Reply to Miliband and Laclau," *New Left Review* 95 (January–February 1976): 63–83. For a summary of these issues, see Martin Carnoy, *The State in Political Theory* (Princeton, N.J.: Princeton University Press, 1984), 104–7.

9. Theda Skocpol, "Political Responses to Capitalist Crisis: Neo-Marxist Theories of the State and the Case of the New Deal," *Politics and Society* 10, no. 2 (1980): 157–201. Also see her "Bringing the State Back In: Current Research," in *Bringing the State Back In,* ed. Peter Evans et al. (Cambridge: Cambridge University Press, 1985), 3–43.

10. Although we have chosen to categorize these authors as part of a historical political economy school, they have also been referred to as practitioners of a "historical-institutionalist" or a state-centric approach. This stands in contrast to a "choice-theoretic" or rational-choice approach. For a look at the choice-theoretic literature on political economy, see William R. Keech, Robert H. Bates, and Peter Lange, "Political Economy Within Nations," in *Political Science: Looking to the Future,* ed. William Crotty (Evanston, Il.: Northwestern University Press, 1991), 219–64. The key works by the authors under discussion are Peter Gourevitch, *Politics in Hard Times: Comparative Responses to International Economic Crises* (Ithaca, N.Y.: Cornell University Press, 1986); Peter Hall, *Governing the Economy* (Cambridge, Mass.: Harvard University Press, 1986); Peter Katzenstein, *Corporatism and Change: Austria, Switzerland, and the Politics of Industry* (Ithaca, N.Y.: Cornell University Press, 1984); Peter Katzenstein, *Small States in World Markets: Industrial Policy in Europe* (Ithaca, N.Y.: Cornell University Press, 1985); David Vogel, *National Styles of Regulation: Environmental Policy in Great Britain and the United States* (Ithaca, N.Y.: Cornell University Press, 1986); John Zysman, *Governments, Markets, and Growth: Financial Systems and the Politics of Industrial Change* (Ithaca, N.Y.: Cornell University Press, 1983). Also see Kenneth Finegold and Theda Skocpol, "State, Party, and Industry: From Business Recovery to the Wagner Act in America's New Deal," in *Statemaking and Social Movements,* ed. Charles Bright and Susan Harding (Ann Arbor: University of Michigan Press, 1984), 159–72; Margaret Weir and Theda Skocpol, "State Structures and the Possibilities for Keynesian Responses to the Great Depression in Sweden, Britain, and the U.S.," in Evans et al., *Bringing the State Back In,* 107–68. For a review of how different explanatory variables are used in the analysis of Keynesianism, see Peter Hall's introduction to *The Political Power of Economic Ideas: Keynesianism Across Nations,* ed. Peter Hall (Princeton, N.J.: Princeton University Press, 1989), 3–26. In her most recent work, Theda Skocpol has characterized her approach to explaining social policies as a "structured polity" approach. See her discussion in *Protecting Soldiers and Mothers: The Political Origins of Social Policy in the United States* (Cambridge, Mass.: Harvard University Press, 1992), 41.

11. See the discussion in Gourevitch, *Politics in Hard Times,* especially chapters 1 and 6. Also see his essay "Keynesian Politics: The Political Sources of Economic Policy Choices" in Hall, *The Political Power of Economic Ideas,* 87–106.

12. See Peter Katzenstein, "Conclusion: Domestic Structures and Strategies of Foreign Economic Policy," in *Between Power and Plenty: Foreign Economic Policies of*

Advanced Industrial States, ed. Peter J. Katzenstein (Madison: University of Wisconsin Press, 1978), 306–23.

13. Katzenstein, *Corporatism and Change,* 19–33.

14. Adam Przeworski, *Capitalism and Social Democracy* (Cambridge: Cambridge University Press, 1985), 205–11.

15. Finegold and Skocpol, "State, Party, and Industry."

16. Hall, *Governing the Economy,* 61–62; Weir and Skocpol, "State Structures," 125–32.

17. Zysman, *Governments, Markets, and Growth,* 285–87.

18. In a similar vein, David Cameron consistently stresses the importance of a country's position in the global political economy when it comes to explaining domestic policy choices and economic performance. See, for example, his critique of Mancur Olson's singular fixation on domestic coalitions, "Distributional Coalitions and Other Sources of Economic Stagnation: On Olson's *Rise and Decline of Nations,*" *International Organization* 42, no. 4 (Autumn 1988): 561–604.

19. David Vogel, "Why Businessmen Distrust Their State: The Political Consciousness of American Corporate Executives," *British Journal of Political Science* 8, no. 1 (January 1978): 169–73. Also by Vogel, "The Political Power of Business in America: A Reappraisal," *British Journal of Political Science* 13 (1983): 19–43. His argument about the weaknesses in the American business class are made at length in *Fluctuating Fortunes: The Power of Business in America* (New York: Basic Books, 1989).

20. Zysman, *Governments, Markets, and Growth,* 307.

21. For a chilling description of the problems in the research environment, see Guillermo O'Donnell, "On the Fruitful Convergences of Hirschman's Exit, Voice, and Loyalty and Shifting Involvements: Reflections from the Recent Argentine Experience," in *Development, Democracy, and the Art of Trespassing: Essays in Honor of Albert O. Hirschman,* ed. Alejandro Foxley, Michael MacPherson, and Guillermo O'Donnell (Notre Dame: University of Notre Dame Press, 1986), 249–68.

22. It is also important to note that a third current in the recent literature is focused on the broader question of why particular countries chose certain developmental models, namely, those works concerned with explaining why Latin American countries embarked on and maintained import-substitution industrialization strategies. Among the interesting contributions on this question are Carlos Waisman, *Reversal of Development in Argentina: Postwar Counterrevolutionary Policies and Their Structural Consequences* (Princeton, N.J.: Princeton University Press, 1987); Stephan Haggard, *Pathways from the Periphery: The Politics of Growth in Newly Industrializing Countries* (Ithaca, N.Y.: Cornell University Press, 1990), 161–90; Kathryn Sikkink, *Ideas and Institutions: Developmentalism in Brazil and Argentina* (Ithaca, N.Y.: Cornell University Press, 1991). Also see the essays in Gary Gereffi and Donald Wyman, eds., *Manufacturing Miracles: Paths of Industrialization in Latin America and East Asia* (Princeton, N.J.: Princeton University Press, 1990).

23. Jonathan Hartlyn and Samuel A. Morley, "Bureaucratic-Authoritarian Regimes in Comparative Perspective," in *Latin American Political Economy: Financial Crisis and Political Change,* ed. Jonathan Hartlyn and Samuel A. Morley (Boulder, Colo.: Westview, 1986), 38–53. John Sheahan, "Market-Oriented Economic Policies and Political Repression in Latin America," *Economic Development and Cultural Change* 28 (January 1980): 267–91. Karen

L. Remmer, "The Politics of Economic Stabilization: IMF Standby Programs in Latin America, 1954–1984," *Comparative Politics* 19, no. 1 (October 1986): 1–24.

24. For further discussion of the impact of regime type, see Edward C. Epstein, "What Difference Does Regime Type Make? Economic Austerity Programs in Argentina," in *Paying the Costs of Austerity in Latin America,* ed. Howard Handelman and Werner Baer (Boulder, Colo.: Westview, 1989), 64–80. Economists, while less explicitly concerned with the political dimension, have evaluated the neoliberal economic programs of Southern Cone military regimes at great length. For example, see Foxley, *Latin American Experiments;* Sebastian Edwards and Alejandra Cox Edwards, *Monetarism and Liberalization: The Chilean Experiment* (Cambridge, Mass.: Ballinger, 1987); Joseph Ramos, *Neoconservative Economics in the Southern Cone of Latin America* (Baltimore, Md.: Johns Hopkins University Press, 1986). Also see the special issue, "Liberalization with Stabilization in the Southern Cone," *World Development* 13, no. 8 (August 1985).

25. Robert Kaufman, "Democratic and Authoritarian Responses to the Debt Issue: Argentina, Brazil, Mexico," in *The Politics of International Debt,* ed. Miles Kahler (Ithaca, N.Y.: Cornell University Press, 1986), 187–218. Also see his "Economic Orthodoxy and Political Change in Mexico: The Stabilization and Adjustment Policies of the de la Madrid Administration," in *Debt and Democracy in Latin America,* ed. Robert Kaufman and Barbara Stallings (Boulder, Colo.: Westview, 1989), 109–26.

26. Jeffry A. Frieden, "Classes, Sectors, and the Foreign Debt in Latin America," *Comparative Politics* 21, no. 1 (October 1988): 1–20. Also see his *Debt, Development, and Democracy: Modern Political Economy and Latin America* (Princeton, N.J.: Princeton University Press, 1991).

27. Stephan Haggard, "The Politics of Adjustment: Lessons from the IMF's Extended Fund Facility," in *The Politics of International Debt,* ed. Miles Kahler (Ithaca, N.Y.: Cornell University Press), 157–86.

28. For work that focuses on the impact of electoral cycles on policy making, see Barry Ames, *Political Survival: Politicians and Public Policy in Latin America* (Berkeley: University of California Press, 1987). For a summary of arguments made about the role of technocrats and administrative structures, see the introduction and the conclusions by Joan Nelson in *Economic Crisis and Policy Choice: The Politics of Adjustment in the Third World,* ed. Joan Nelson (Princeton, N.J.: Princeton University Press, 1990), 3–32, 321–61.

29. For an analysis of the effects of different modes of transition, see Terry L. Karl, "Dilemmas of Democratization in Latin America," *Comparative Politics* 23, no. 1 (October 1990): 1–21. For a critique suggesting that factors other than "mode" are crucial to understanding regime development, see Marcelo Cavarozzi, "Beyond Transitions to Democracy in Latin America," *Journal of Latin American Studies* 24, no. 3 (October 1992): 665–84.

30. Lourdes de Sola, "The Political Constraints to Heterodox Shocks in Brazil: Técnicos, Politicians, Democracy," *Journal of Latin American Studies* 23, no. 1 (February 1991): 163–95. William C. Smith, "Democracy, Distributional Conflicts, and Macroeconomic Policymaking in Argentina, 1983–1989," *Journal of Inter-American Studies and World Affairs* 32, no. 2 (Summer 1990): 1–42. Juan Carlos Torre, "El gobierno de la emergencia en la transición democrática: De Alfonsín a Menem" (unpublished paper, Instituto Torcuato di Tella, Buenos Aires, 1990). O'Donnell has been working on a com-

prehensive conceptualization of regime type in Latin America, focusing on the notion of "delegative democracy." For his reflections on the Argentine case, see Guillermo O'Donnell, "Argentina: De Novo," *Novos Estudos CEBRAP* 24 (July 1989). For a more recent discussion, see his "On the State, Democratization, and Some Conceptual Problems: A Latin American View with Some Glances at Some Postcommunist Countries," *World Development* 21, no. 8 (August 1993): 1355–69. Further work by Haggard and Kaufman discusses the connections between regime type and economic policy making: see Stephan Haggard and Robert Kaufman, "Economic Adjustment and the Prospects for Democracy," in *The Politics of Economic Adjustment: International Constraints, Distributive Conflicts, and the State,* ed. Stephan Haggard and Robert R. Kaufman (Princeton, N.J.: Princeton University Press, 1992), 319–50.

31. Similar trends have been visible in other cases: see Catherine Conaghan and Rosario Espinal, "Unlikely Transitions to Uncertain Regimes? Democracy Without Compromise in the Dominican Republic and Ecuador," *Journal of Latin American Studies* 22 (October 1990): 553–74.

32. For a reflection on these transitions in Latin America and Eastern Europe, see Adam Przeworski, *Democracy and the Market: Political and Economic Reforms in Eastern Europe and Latin America* (Cambridge: Cambridge University Press, 1991). See also Nancy Bermeo, ed., *Liberalization and Democratization: Change in the Soviet Union and Eastern Europe* (Baltimore, Md.: Johns Hopkins University Press, 1992).

33. This definition is taken from Alejandro Portes, "Latin American Class Structures: Their Composition and Change During the Last Decade," *Latin American Research Review* 20, no. 3 (1985): 7–39.

34. For a discussion of the notion of economic groups, see Nathaniel Leff, "Industrial Organization and Entrepreneurship in Developing Countries: The Economic Groups," *Economic Development and Cultural Change* 26, no. 4 (July 1978): 661–75.

35. Our use of the gender-specific term *businessmen* reflects the continuing domination of this sphere by men in Latin America. None of the top policy makers or interest group leaders we interviewed were women. Also, our use of the term *community* does not connote a complete convergence of interests or political consensus among business elites.

36. The population figures are for 1989 and were reported in the World Bank, *World Development Report 1991* (Washington, D.C.: Oxford University Press, published for the World Bank, 1991). The per capita GDP figures are for 1988 and were cited by Paul Kennedy, "Preparing for the Twenty-First Century: Winners and Losers," *New York Review of Books* 40, no. 4 (11 February 1993): 36. Hereafter, all references to dollars are to U.S. dollars.

37. For an overview of the history of the region, see Magnus Morner, *The Andean Past: Land, Societies, and Conflict* (New York: Columbia University Press, 1985).

38. Alexander Gerschenkron, *Economic Backwardness in Historical Perspective* (Cambridge, Mass.: Harvard University Press, 1962).

2. *Losing Control*

1. For a discussion of the notion of the privileged position that business occupies in capitalist democracies, see Lindblom, *Politics and Markets,* 170–213.

2. For a discussion of the different policy coalitions that formed around the issue of free trade in Europe, see Gourevitch, *Politics in Hard Times,* 71–123. For a comparative analysis that stresses the importance of different elite alliances in the development of democratic regimes, see Dietrich Rueschemeyer, Evelyne Huber Stephens, and John D. Stephens, *Capitalist Development and Democracy* (Chicago: University of Chicago Press, 1992).

3. For a collection of essays on the emergence of liberalism in nineteenth-century Latin America, see Joseph L. Love and Nils Jacobsen, eds., *Guiding the Invisible Hand: Economic Liberalism and the State in Latin American History* (New York: Praeger, 1988).

4. This fusion of economic elites from different sectors was not confined to our Andean cases. A number of historical studies have pointed to the phenomenon. See, for example, the discussion in Florestan Fernandes, *Reflections on the Brazilian Counter-Revolution: Essays by Florestan Fernandes,* ed. Warren Dean, trans. Michel Vale and Patrick M. Hughes (Armonk, N.Y.: M. E. Sharpe, 1981). Unfortunately, all three countries still lack a definitive treatment on upper-class culture in the nineteenth century. For an excellent discussion of how Euro-centric cultural style wove together Brazilian elites in this period, see Jeffrey Needell, *A Tropical Belle Epoque: Elite Culture in Turn-of-the-Century Rio de Janeiro* (Cambridge: Cambridge University Press, 1987).

5. The term *collusive quasi-rents* is taken from a discussion of the Argentine case by Guido di Tella. See his ''Rents, Quasi-Rents, Normal Profits, and Growth: Argentina and the Areas of Recent Settlement,'' in *Argentina, Australia, and Canada: Studies in Comparative Development 1870–1965,* ed. D. C. M. Platt and Guido di Tella (London: Macmillan, 1985), 37–51. For further discussion of business-government relations in this period, see Heraclio Bonilla, ''Peru and Bolivia from Independence to the War of the Pacific,'' in *The Cambridge History of Latin America* 3, ed. Leslie Bethell (Cambridge: Cambridge University Press, 1985), 539–82.

6. Our characterization of this period in Bolivian history is based on Herbert Klein, *Parties and Political Change in Bolivia 1880–1952* (Cambridge: Cambridge University Press, 1969), 1–88. See also Herbert Klein, ''Bolivia from the War of the Pacific to the Chaco War, 1880–1932,'' in *The Cambridge History of Latin America* 5, ed. Leslie Bethell (Cambridge: Cambridge University Press, 1986), 553–86.

7. For an excellent discussion of the conflicts that preceded the advent of liberalism in the 1850s in Peru, see Paul Gootenberg, ''Beleaguered Liberals: The Failed First Generation of Free Traders in Bolivia,'' in Love and Jacobsen, *Guiding the Invisible Hand,* 63–98. Also see Paul Gootenberg, *Between Silver and Guano: Commercial Policy and the State in Postindependence Peru* (Princeton, N.J.: Princeton University Press, 1989).

8. Our summary is based on Peter Klaren, ''The Origins of Modern Peru, 1880–1930,'' in Bethell, *Cambridge History of Latin America* 5:587–640; Steve Stein, *Populism in Peru: The Emergence of the Masses and the Politics of Social Control* (Madison: University of Wisconsin Press, 1980), 18–48. For further discussion of politics during the Aristocratic Republic, see Michael J. Gonzales, ''Planters and Politics in Peru, 1895–1919,'' *Journal of Latin American Studies* 23, no. 3 (October 1991): 515–41. Also see Dennis Gilbert, *The Oligarchy and the Old Regime in Peru* (Ithaca, N.Y.: Latin American Program Dissertation Series, Cornell University, 1977).

9. Key sources on this period are Linda Alexander Rodríguez, *The Search for Public Policy: Regional Politics and Government Finances in Ecuador, 1830–1940* (Berkeley:

University of California Press, 1985); Lois Weinman, "Ecuador and Cacao: Domestic Responses to the Boom-Collapse Monoexport Cycle" (Ph.D. diss., University of California, Los Angeles, 1970); Andrés Guerrero, *Los oligarcas del cacao* (Quito: Editorial El Conejo, 1980); Luis Alberto Carbo, *Historia monetaria y cambiaria del Ecuador* (Quito: Banco Central del Ecuador, 1978).

10. For a discussion of state weakness, as defined by an inability to control groups in civil society, see Joel Migdal, *Strong Societies, Weak States: State Capacity in the Third World* (Princeton, N.J.: Princeton University Press, 1988), 10–41.

11. Marcelo Cavarozzi notes the instability in the oligarchic state surrounding the question of elite rotation: see his "Elementos para una caracterización del capitalismo oligárquico" (documento CEDES/G.E. CLACSO no. 12, CEDES). For a further overview of the oligarchic state, see Marcello Carmagnani, *Estado y sociedad en América Latina, 1850–1930* (Barcelona: Editorial Crítica, 1984).

12. For a discussion of the limitations on hegemony in peasant societies, see James C. Scott, *Weapons of the Weak: Everyday Forms of Peasant Resistance* (New Haven, Conn.: Yale University Press, 1985), 304–50. There is a growing collection of historical work that documents the resistance of the Indian peasantry in the Andes. See, for example, Erik D. Langer, *Economic Change and Rural Resistance in Southern Bolivia, 1880–1930* (Stanford: Stanford University Press, 1989); Silvia Rivera, *'Oprimidos pero no vencidos': Lucha del campesinado aymara y quechua, 1900–1980* (La Paz: Hisbol, 1986); Florencia Mallon, *The Defense of the Community in Peru's Central Highlands: Peasant Struggle and Capitalist Transition, 1860–1940* (Princeton, N.J.: Princeton University Press, 1983). For an overview, see Florencia Mallon, "Indian Communities, Political Cultures, and the State in Latin America, 1780–1990," *Journal of Latin American Studies* 24 (Quincentenary supplement, 1992): 35–54.

13. For a discussion of the decline of business influence in the United States, see Finegold and Skocpol, "State, Party, and Industry," 159–72.

14. For further discussion of the Keynesian class compromise, see Przeworski, *Capitalism and Social Democracy,* 205–11. Also see John Goldethorpe, "Problems of Political Economy After the Postwar Period," in *Changing Boundaries of the Political: Essays on the Evolving Balance Between the State and Society, Public and Private in Europe,* ed. Charles Maier (Cambridge: Cambridge University Press, 1987), 363–408.

15. For an account of this crucial moment in the development of Ecuador's labor movement, see Ronn F. Pineo, "Reinterpreting Labor Militancy: The Collapse of the Cacao Economy and the General Strike of 1922 in Guayaquil, Ecuador," *Hispanic American Historical Review* 68, no. 4 (November 1988): 707–36.

16. The discussion of the Kemmererian coalitions and the reforms emanating from the Kemmerer missions draws extensively on the comprehensive work by Paul Drake, *The Money Doctor in the Andes: The Kemmerer Missions, 1923–33* (Durham, N.C.: Duke University Press, 1989).

17. Ibid, 268–70.

18. Stein, *Populism in Peru,* 57.

19. On the Compactación, see Agustín Cueva, *El proceso de dominación política en el Ecuador* (Quito: Ediciones Solitierra, n.d.), 28. Also Rafael Quintero, *El mito del populismo en el Ecuador: Analisis de los fundamentos socio-económicos del surgimiento del Velasquismo, 1895–1934* (Quito: FLACSO, 1980), 253–67.

20. Quintero, *El mito del populismo,* 236.

21. For a work that explores the relationships between the upper class and the state at greater length in the Bolivian case, see Carmenza Gallo, *Taxes and State Power: Political Instability in Bolivia, 1900–1950* (Philadelphia, Pa.: Temple University Press, 1991).

22. For further discussion of this period, see Leslie Bethell and Ian Roxborough, "Latin America Between the Second World War and the Cold War: Some Reflections on the 1945–48 Conjuncture," *Journal of Latin American Studies* 20, no. 1 (May 1988): 167–89.

23. Rosemary Thorp and Geoffrey Bertram, *Peru 1890–1977: Growth and Policy in an Open Economy* (New York: Columbia University Press, 1978); Gonzalo Portocarrero Maisch, *De Bustamante a Odría: El fracaso del Frente Democrático Nacional, 1945–50* (Lima: Mosca Azul Editores, 1983).

24. For a discussion of the development of the banana trade in this period, see Carlos Larrea, ed., *El banano en el Ecuador: Transnacionales, modernización, y subdesarrollo* (Quito: Corporación Editora Nacional, 1987).

25. The notion of "democratic parenthesis" in Ecuador is taken from Cueva, *El proceso de dominación política.* For a further discussion of contemporary Ecuadorean politics, see Osvaldo Hurtado, *Political Power in Ecuador,* trans. Nick D. Mills (Albuquerque: University of New Mexico Press, 1980). Also see John D. Martz, *Ecuador: Conflicting Political Culture and the Quest for Progress* (Boston: Allyn and Bacon, 1972).

26. For an overview of the alliance, see Tony Smith, "The Alliance for Progress: The 1960s," in *Exporting Democracy: The U.S. and Latin America,* ed. Abraham F. Lowenthal (Baltimore, Md.: Johns Hopkins University Press, 1991), 71–89. The most comprehensive critical appraisal is by Juan De Onis and Jerome Levinson, *The Alliance That Lost Its Way* (Chicago: Quadrangle Books, 1970).

27. Thorp and Bertram, *Peru 1890–1977,* 231–32.

28. Peasant mobilization in Peru and the La Convención movement is discussed in Jeffrey Paige, *Agrarian Revolution: Social Movements and Export Agriculture in the Underdeveloped World* (New York: Free Press, 1975), 124–210.

29. For a discussion of ideological development inside the Peruvian military, see Alfred Stepan, *The State and Society: Peru in Comparative Perspective* (Princeton, N.J.: Princeton University Press, 1978).

30. For further discussion of the period, see Julio Cotler, "A Structural-Historical Approach to the Breakdown of Democratic Institutions: Peru," in *The Breakdown of Democratic Regimes: Latin America,* ed. Juan J. Linz and Alfred Stepan (Baltimore, Md.: Johns Hopkins University Press, 1978), 178–206. Also see Pedro Pablo Kuczynski, *Peruvian Democracy Under Economic Stress: An Account of the Belaúnde Administration, 1963–1968* (Princeton, N.J.: Princeton University Press, 1977).

31. On the early development of the CFP, see John D. Martz, "Populist Leadership and the CFP," *Studies in Comparative International Development* 3 (Fall 1983): 22–50.

32. JUNAPLA, *Bases y directivas para programar el desarrollo económico del Ecuador* (Quito: JUNAPLA, 1958), 29.

33. R. J. Bromley, *Development Planning in Ecuador* (Sussex: Latin American Publications Fund, 1977).

34. John S. Fitch, *The Military Coup d'Etat as a Political Process: Ecuador, 1948–1966* (Baltimore, Md.: Johns Hopkins University Press, 1977), 136.

35. For a discussion of the modernization of agriculture and the agrarian reform in this period, see Osvaldo Barksy, *La reforma agraria ecuatoriana* (Quito: Corporación Editora Nacional/FLACSO, 1984).

36. For a detailed discussion, see James M. Malloy, *Bolivia: The Uncompleted Revolution* (Pittsburgh, Pa.: University of Pittsburgh Press, 1970), 179–82.

37. Richard Thorn, "The Economic Transformation," in *Beyond the Revolution: Bolivia Since 1952,* ed. James M. Malloy and Richard S. Thorn (Pittsburgh, Pa.: University of Pittsburgh Press, 1971), 157–215; Herbert Klein, *Parties and Political Change in Bolivia, 1880–1952* (Cambridge: Cambridge University Press, 1969), 396.

38. James M. Malloy, "Revolutionary Politics," in Malloy and Thorn, *Beyond the Revolution,* 111–56; James W. Wilkie, *The Bolivian Revolution and U.S. Aid Since 1952: Financial Background and Context of Political Decision* (Los Angeles: Latin American Center, University of California, 1969), 12–13.

39. The Bohan Mission is discussed in Mario Arrieta et al., *Agricultura en Santa Cruz: De la encomienda colonial a la empresa modernizada (1559–1985)* (La Paz: ILDIS, 1990), 74–80. For further discussion of the role of foreign advisors in this period, see Robert J. Alexander, *The Bolivian National Revolution* (New Brunswick, N.J.: Rutgers University Press, 1958).

40. For their report, see U.S. Operations Mission to Bolivia, *Problems in the Economic Development of Bolivia* (La Paz: U.S. Operations Mission to Bolivia, 1956). For a colorful and remarkably detailed discussion of the formulation and implementation of the 1956 stabilization program, see George Jackson Eder, *Inflation and Development in Latin America: A Case History of Inflation and Stabilization in Bolivia* (Ann Arbor: Bureau of Business Research, University of Michigan, 1968).

41. Arrieta et al., *Agricultura en Santa Cruz,* 271.

42. For an examination of how income inequality was re-created in the wake of the revolution, see Jonathan Kelley and Herbert S. Klein, *Revolution and the Rebirth of Inequality: A Theory Applied to the National Revolution in Bolivia* (Berkeley: University of California Press, 1981).

43. The figures quoted here and in the following paragraph are from Portes, "Latin American Class Structures," 7–39.

44. For a discussion of income distribution in Latin America, see David Felix, "Income Distribution and the Quality of Life in Latin America: Patterns, Trends, and Policy Implications," *Latin American Research Review* 18, no. 2 (1983): 3–33. Also see Alfredo Figueroa and Richard Weisskoff, "Viewing Social Pyramids: Income Distribution in Latin America," in *Consumption and Income Distribution in Latin America,* ed. Robert Ferber (Washington, D.C.: Organization of American States, 1980), 257–94.

45. The Peru figure is based on 1962 data. When income distribution in Peru was calculated for disposable income accruing to households, the top decile in Peru received 49.2 percent in 1972. These figures are taken from James Wilkie, ed., *Statistical Abstract of Latin America,* vol. 28 (Los Angeles: UCLA Latin American Center Publications, University of California Press, 1990), 392. For the most comprehensive discussion of income distribution in Peru, see Richard Webb, *Government Policy and the Distribution of Income in Peru, 1963–1973* (Cambridge: Harvard University Press, 1977). Other calculations of income distribution confirm this more extreme concentration in Latin America than in

other middle-income countries. For example, from estimates based on surveys from the late 1960s and early 1970s, Jeffrey Sachs estimates that, in Ecuador, the top quintile of households accounted for 72 percent of all income; in Peru, the top quintile accounted for 61 percent. See Jeffrey D. Sachs, *Social Conflict and Populist Policies in Latin America* (San Francisco: International Center for Economic Growth, Occasional Papers Series, no. 9, 1990), 7.

46. For a general discussion of the notion of economic groups, see Leff, ''Industrial Organization and Entrepreneurship,'' 661–75. For discussions of the development of Peruvian economic groups, see Eduardo Anaya, *Los grupos de poder económico: Un análisis de la oligarquía financiera* (Lima: Editorial Horizonte, 1990); Carlos Malpica, *El poder económico en el Perú* (Lima: Mosca Azul Editores, 1989); Germán Reaño and Enrique Vásquez, *El Grupo Romero: Del algodón a la banca* (Lima: Centro de Investigación, Universidad del Pacífico, 1988). For one of the first investigations of the topic in Ecuador, see Guillermo Navarro, *La concentración de capitales en el Ecuador* (Quito: Ediciones Solitierra, 1976). For a more recent treatment, see Luis Fierro Carrión, *Los grupos financieros en el Ecuador* (Quito: Centro de Educación Popular, 1991). On economic groups in Bolivia, see Susan Eckstein and Frances Hagopian, ''The Limits of Industrialization in the Less Developed World: Bolivia,'' *Economic Development and Cultural Change* 32, no. 1 (October 1983): 81–82. Also see Miguel Fernández Moscoso, ''La empresa privada y la reactivación: Apuntes para el debate,'' in *El rol de la empresa privada en el desarrollo,* ed. Taller de Investigaciones Socio-económicos (La Paz: Instituto de Investigaciones Sociales, n.d.), 27–75.

47. For further discussion of the Noboa saga, see Larrea, *El banano en el Ecuador,* 90–103.

48. Instituto de Investigaciones Económicas y Políticas, *El capitalismo ecuatoriano: Su funcionamiento* (Guayaquil: Facultad de Ciencias Económicas, n.d.), 140.

49. Data in these paragraphs are from E. V. K. Fitzgerald, *The Political Economy of Peru 1956–78: Economic Development and the Restructuring of Capital* (Cambridge: Cambridge University Press, 1979), 119.

50. For a discussion of the development of medium mining, see Manuel E. Contreras and Mario Napoleon Pacheco, *Medio siglo de minería mediana en Bolivia, 1939–1989* (La Paz: Biblioteca Minera Boliviana, 1989).

51. Grupo de Estudios Andrés Ibáñez, *Tierra, estructura productiva, y poder en Santa Cruz* (La Paz: Universidad Boliviana, 1983).

52. Eckstein and Hagopian, ''The Limits of Industrialization,'' 81–82.

3. Statism and Military Rule

1. Alfred Stepan, *The Military in Politics: Changing Patterns in Brazil* (Princeton, N.J.: Princeton University Press, 1971). O'Donnell's initial formulation of his argument came in *Modernization and Bureaucratic Authoritarianism.* Contending perspectives on his argument can be found in Collier, *The New Authoritarianism.*

2. For a work that traces the emergence of developmentalism during the government of Juscelino Kubitscek, see Sikkink, *Ideas and Institutions.*

3. The secretariat was originally created in 1953 and named the Comisión Nacional de Coordinación y Planeamiento. For an overview of the history of planning in Bolivia, see Gontrán Carranza Fernández, *El proceso histórico de la planificación* (La Paz: Editorial de la Universidad Mayor de San Andrés, n.d.).

4. Kuczynski, *Peruvian Democracy Under Economic Stress,* 47. The figures are from Felipe Portocarrero, Arlette Beltrán, and Alex Zimmerman, *Inversiones públicas en el Perú (1900–1968): Una aproximación cuantitativa* (Lima: Centro de Investigación, Universidad del Pacífico, 1988), 46, 52.

5. For Velasco's plan, see Instituto Nacional de Planificación, *Plan nacional de desarrollo 1971–75: Plan global* (Lima: Instituto Nacional de Planificación, 1971). For the Ecuadorean plan, see JUNAPLA, *Plan integral de transformación y desarrollo 1973–77: Resumen general* (Quito: JUNAPLA, n.d.). For Banzer's plan, see República de Bolivia, *Plan de desarrollo económico y social, 1976–80* (La Paz, 1976).

6. Carlos Parodi, "State Growth in Bolivia, Ecuador, and Peru, 1970–78" (unpublished paper, University of Pittsburgh, 1989).

7. For a list of the new entities created, see *Libro blanco de las realizaciones del gobierno de las fuerzas armadas: Bolivia, 1971–78* (La Paz, 1978), 16. Employment figures are from James M. Malloy and Silvia Borzutsky, "The Praetorianization of the Revolution," in *Modern-Day Bolivia: Legacy of the Revolution and Prospects for the Future,* ed. Jerry Ladman (Tempe: Center for Latin American Studies, Arizona State University, 1982), 54; and Richard A. Musgrave, *Fiscal Reform in Bolivia: Final Report of the Bolivian Mission on Tax Reform* (Cambridge, Mass.: International Tax Program, Harvard Law School, Harvard University, 1981), 108.

8. Fitzgerald, *Political Economy of Peru,* 194, 184.

9. The World Bank, *Ecuador: Development Problems and Prospects* (Washington, D.C.: World Bank, 1979), 642.

10. From the statement, "Filosofía y plan de acción del gobierno revolucionario nacionalista del Ecuador." Cited in Fitch, *The Military Coup d'Etat,* 145.

11. Aníbal Quijano, *Nationalism and Capitalism in Peru: A Study in Neo-Imperialism,* trans. Helen R. Lane (New York: Monthly Review Press, 1971), 85–90. See also Cueva, *El proceso de dominación política;* Augusto Varas and Fernando Bustamante, *Fuerzas armadas y política en Ecuador* (Quito: Ediciones Latinoamerica, 1978); Patricio Moncayo, *Ecuador: Grietas en la dominación* (Quito: Escuela de Ciencias de la Información de la Universidad Central del Ecuador, 1977).

12. For an in-depth treatment of politics and oil policy in Ecuador, see John D. Martz, *Politics and Petroleum in Ecuador* (New Brunswick, N.J.: Transaction Books, 1987).

13. Figures are taken from Rob Vos, "Structural Change and Macro Balances in a Small Open Economy," in *Theory and Policy Design for Basic Needs: A Case Study of Ecuador,* ed. Rudolf Teekens (Aldershot: Gower Publishing, 1988), 257.

14. Ibid, 241.

15. The rise of the cocoa processing industry is discussed at greater length in Catherine M. Conaghan, *Restructuring Domination: Industrialists and the State in Ecuador* (Pittsburgh, Pa.: University of Pittsburgh Press, 1988), 53–56.

16. Jorge Marshall-Silva, "Ecuador: Windfalls of a New Exporter," in *Oil Windfalls:*

Blessing or Curse? ed. Alan Gelb and Associates (New York: Oxford University Press, published for the World Bank, 1988), 183, 182.

17. Figures are from García-Rodríguez, "Structural Change and Development Policy in Bolivia," 181, and Jerry R. Ladman, "The Political Economy of the 'Economic Miracle' of the Banzer Regime," 322, both in Ladman, *Modern-Day Bolivia.*

18. The financial drainage of public sector enterprises by the central government is discussed in Michael Mortimore, "The State and Transnational Banks: Lessons from the Bolivian Crisis of External Public Indebtedness," *CEPAL Review* 14 (August 1981): 143–48. George Irvin, *Planning Investment in Bolivia: The Changing Role of the Public Sector* (The Hague: Institute of Social Studies, Research Report Series no. 6, 1979), 86.

19. Ladman, "Political Economy," 331. Figures on BAB credit are taken from Arrieta et al., *Agricultura en Santa Cruz,* 265–72.

20. See the analysis by Juan Antonio Morales and Jeffrey Sachs, "Bolivia's Economic Crisis," in *Developing Country Debt and Economic Performance,* vol. 2, ed. Jeffrey D. Sachs (Chicago: University of Chicago Press, 1990), 157–268; Horst Grebe López, "Innovaciones de las políticas económico-sociales en la Bolivia postdictatorial" (Documento de trabajo no. 17, Programa FLACSO–Bolivia, La Paz, January 1988).

21. For a discussion of business support for Banzer, see Christopher Mitchell, *The Legacy of Populism in Bolivia: From the MNR to Military Rule* (New York: Praeger Publishers, 1977), 122–24.

22. Anaya, *Los grupos de poder económico,* 60.

23. Stepan, *The State and Society,* 136–44.

24. Fitzgerald, *Political Economy of Peru,* 284–85.

25. Ibid, 158–59.

26. Figures are taken from Barbara Stallings, "International Capitalism and the Peruvian Military Government," in *The Peruvian Experiment Reconsidered,* ed. Cynthia McClintock and Abraham F. Lowenthal (Princeton, N.J.: Princeton University Press, 1983), 180.

27. Fitzgerald, *Political Economy of Peru,* 159.

28. For a fascinating case study of this group, see Reaño and Vásquez, *El Grupo Romero.*

29. For a discussion of agrarian policy in this period, see Peter S. Cleaves and Martin J. Scurrah, *Agriculture, Bureaucracy, and Military Government in Peru* (Ithaca, N.Y.: Cornell University Press, 1980); Cynthia McClintock, *Peasant Cooperatives and Political Change in Peru* (Princeton, N.J.: Princeton University Press, 1981).

30. For further description of the CI arrangement, see Peter T. Knight, "New Forms of Economic Organization in Peru: Toward Workers' Self-Management," in McClintock and Lowenthal, *Peruvian Experiment,* 250–401. The CIs are also discussed at length in Evelyne Huber Stephens, *The Politics of Workers' Participation: The Peruvian Approach in Comparative Perspective* (New York: Academic Press, 1980).

31. On SINAMOS, see Sandra L. Woy-Hazelton, "SINAMOS, Infrastructure of Participation," in *Political Participation in Latin America,* ed. John Booth and Mitchell Seligson (New York: Holmes and Meier, 1978); Cynthia McClintock, "Velasco, Officers, and Citizens: The Politics of Stealth," in McClintock and Lowenthal, *Peruvian Experiment,* 302–6.

32. Raymundo Duhuarte, president of the Sociedad Nacional de Industrias (SNI), did publicly accuse Velasco of being a communist. He was forced into exile shortly thereafter.

33. Nick D. Mills, *Crisis, conflicto, y consenso: Ecuador 1979–1984* (Quito: Corporación Editora Nacional, 1984), 130–31.

34. National Association of Medium Miners, *Annual Report July 1977–June 1978* (La Paz: ANMM, 1978), 24.

35. See Malcolm Gillis, "The Structure of Bolivian Mining Taxes," in *Taxation and Mining: Nonfuel Minerals in Bolivia and Other Countries,* ed. Malcolm Gillis (Cambridge, Mass.: Ballinger, 1978), 183–213.

36. Interview, La Paz, 11 February 1987 (see the Appendix for a description of our interview procedures). For a review of COFADENA's activities, see *Libro blanco.*

37. Peter S. Cleaves and Henry Pease García, "State Autonomy and Military Policymaking," in McClintock and Lowenthal, *Peruvian Experiment,* 222–23.

38. McClintock, "Velasco, Officers, and Citizens," 275–308.

39. David G. Becker, *The New Bourgeoisie and the Limits of Dependency: Mining, Class, and Power in "Revolutionary" Peru* (Princeton, N.J.: Princeton University Press, 1983), 257.

40. The word *nacional* was later restored to the Sociedad's title during the Belaúnde administration. To avoid confusion in our discussion of the organization, we refer to it as the SNI throughout the text.

41. Interviews, Lima, 4 and 6 February 1986; Duhuarte, interview, Lima, 22 January 1986.

42. The notion of privatist corporatism was developed by Guillermo O'Donnell. See O'Donnell, "Corporatism and the Question of the State," in *Authoritarianism and Corporatism in Latin America,* ed. James Malloy (Pittsburgh, Pa.: University of Pittsburgh Press, 1977), 74–77.

43. This argument was first developed and elaborated at greater length in James M. Malloy and Eduardo Gamarra, *Revolution and Reaction: Bolivia 1964–1985* (New Brunswick, N.J.: Transaction, 1988), 71–115.

44. Interview, La Paz, 20 February 1986.

45. Interview, La Paz, 21 February 1986. Jaime Quiroga served as minister of finance in the Banzer government from November 1973 to August 1974.

46. Interview, Asociación Nacional de Mineros Medianos (ANMM), La Paz, 19 February 1986.

47. Interview, La Paz, 11 February 1986.

48. Interview, La Paz, 21 February 1986.

4. The Antistatist Revival and Regime Transition

1. The reference is taken from Albert O. Hirschman, *Exit, Voice, and Loyalty: Responses to Decline in Firms, Organizations, and States* (Cambridge, Mass.: Harvard University Press, 1970).

2. Gonzalo Portocarrero Maisch, "Empresarios, Sociedad Nacional de Industrias, y proceso político, 1950–1968," Informe preliminar, Departamento de Ciencias Sociales,

Pontífica Universidad Católica del Perú, Lima, January 1978. William L. Lofstram, "Attitudes of an Industrial Pressure Group in Latin America: The Asociación de Industriales Mineros de Bolivia, 1925–1935" (M.A. thesis, Cornell University, 1968), 32–33.

3. Labor also had two functional representatives. In addition, there were four functional senators representing public education, private education, cultural associations, and the armed forces. For a description, see George I. Blanksten, *Ecuador: Constitutions and Caudillos* (New York: Russell and Russell, 1964), 105–9.

4. For a discussion of informal lobbying and the role that elite social clubs played in Peru, see Carlos Astiz, *Pressure Groups and Power Elites in Peruvian Politics* (Ithaca, N.Y.: Cornell University Press, 1969), 191–204.

5. For a discussion of the role of CADE, see J. Francisco Durand, "The National Bourgeoisie and the Peruvian State: Coalition and Conflict in the 1980s" (Ph.D. diss., University of California, Berkeley), 134–37.

6. Cámara de Industriales de Pichincha, *Cincuenta años de la Cámara de Pichincha, 1932–86* (Quito: Cámara de Industriales de Pichincha, 1986).

7. For a study of the development of this federation, see Alejandra Ramírez Soruco, "Empresarialismo regional, 1985–89," (tesis de licenciatura, Sociología, Facultad de Ciencias Económicas y Sociología, Universidad Mayor de San Simón, Cochabamba, 1992).

8. The dynamics of the policy process during this period are discussed at greater length in Conaghan, *Restructuring Domination,* 76–101.

9. Interview, Cámara de Industriales de Pichincha, Quito, 30 January 1987.

10. For a discussion of the press reforms, see Helan Jaworski, "Democracia y socialización en los medios de comunicación," in *El Perú de Velasco,* ed. Carlos Franco (Lima: Centro de Estudios para el Desarrollo y la Participación, 1983), 3:767–808.

11. The origins and approach of the early ADEX is discussed by one of its founders, Alejandro Tabini, in "¿Cómo y por qué nació ADEX?" *Perú Exporta* 99 (June–July 1983): 4–7.

12. In his inaugural remarks as finance minister, Silva Ruete declared his identification with the revolutionary process, including its "assets and debits." For his reflections on his term in office, see Javier Silva Ruete, *"Yo asumí el activo y el pasivo de la Revolución"* (Lima: Centro de Documentación e Información Andina, 1981).

13. In discussing the conflict betweeen Silva Ruete and Lanata, Luis Bedoya (leader of the right-wing party PPC) referred to Silva Ruete as "un gordito simpáticon" (a nice fat guy), but he characterized Lanata's presence in the cabinet as "a guarantee to the private sector." Bedoya's remarks are quoted in DESCO, *Cronología política, 1978,* 3199. The SNI published a protest after Lanata's resignation, accusing Silva Ruete of *continuismo* and of failing to restructure the economy along market lines (see ibid., 3220). For ADEX's dismay over the Lanata resignation, see ibid., 3225.

14. The technical studies are published in CEPB, *Pensamiento de la empresa privada* (La Paz: CEPB, 1981), 93–141.

15. Charles Lindblom, "The Market as Prison," in *The Political Economy: Readings in the Politics and Economics of American Public Policy,* ed. Thomas Ferguson and Joel Rogers (Armonk, N.Y.: M. E. Sharpe, 1984), 4.

16. For an excellent collection of essays that review contending explanations and

measures of capital flight, see Donald R. Lessard and John Williamson, eds., *Capital Flight and Third World Debt* (Washington, D.C.: Institute for International Economics, 1987).

17. Figures for Peru are from Richard Webb, "Internal Debt and Financial Adjustment in Peru," *CEPAL Review* 32 (August 1987), 57; and Thorp and Bertram, *Peru 1890–1977,* 309. The Ecuador figures are cited in Vos, "Structural Change and Macro Balances," 248. The Bolivian figure is taken from the World Bank, *Bolivia: Structural Constraints and Development Prospects* (Washington, D.C.: World Bank, 1983), 6.

18. For discussions of various calculations of capital flight for Peru in this period, see the chapter on capital flight in Anaya, *Los grupos de poder económico,* 141–62. For estimates on capital flight in Bolivia, see Morales and Sachs, "Bolivia's Economic Crisis," 213.

19. Luis Soberón shared his unpublished findings with us in an interview, Lima, 23 January 1986.

20. Interview, La Paz, 17 February 1986.

21. See the speech by Alfredo Novoa Peña, "Acción empresarial," in IPAE, *CADE 79: Anales de la XVIII Conferencia Anual de Ejecutivos, 1979* (Lima: IPAE, 1979), 123–24.

22. CEPB, *Pensamiento de la empresa privada,* 82; Cámara de Industria y Comercio de Santa Cruz–Bolivia, *El estado empresarial 1970–1980: Fracaso de un modelo* (Santa Cruz: Cámara de Industria y Comercio de Santa Cruz–Bolivia, July 1982); Alfredo Ferrand Inurritegui and Arturo Salazar Larraín, *La década perdida* (Lima: SI, 1980).

23. Alfredo Ferrand Inurritegui and Arturo Salazar Larraín, *La década perdida.* Raymundo Duhuarte, interview, Lima, 22 January 1986.

24. See the CEPB, "Memoria anual, 1981–82," *Pensamiento de la empresa privada,* 82.

25. For a discussion of the foundation of IESS, see "El IESS: Un lustro al servicio de la empresa privada," *Industria Peruana* 610 (August 1981): 18–23.

26. Cordero's speech cited in *Ficha de información socio-política,* 12 October 1974. CEPB, "Hacia una nueva política económica," *Pensamiento de la empresa privada,* 142.

27. For a full-blown elaboration of these ideas, see Federico Salazar Bustamante, "Mecanismos del estado." This was published as a chapter in *Proyecto Perú: Hacia un proyecto nacional de desarrollo a mediano y largo plazo* (Lima: IESS, 1986). This work makes extensive use of Buchanan's works. For a review of the political content of Buchanan's work, see David Reisman, *The Political Economy of James Buchanan* (London: Macmillan, 1990). Also influential was the work by Mancur Olson, *The Rise and Decline of Nations* (New Haven, Conn.: Yale University Press, 1982). Hernando de Soto, *The Other Path: The Invisible Revolution in the Third World,* trans. June Abbott (New York: Harper & Row, 1989), produced an international bestseller that focused heavily on "rent-seeking" behavior by economic agents and depicted Peru as a mercantilist state.

28. This point is made by J. Francisco Durand. See his "Mario Vargas Llosa o la nueva derecha peruana" (paper presented to the Fifteenth Congress of the Latin American Studies Association, 4–6 December 1989, Miami, Florida).

29. Interview, Lima, 4 February 1986.

30. CEPB, "Memoria anual, 1981–82," 81.

31. The symposium was reported in *Quehacer* 2 (November–December 1979). A transcript of the proceedings was published by the Instituto Libertad y Democracia (ILD), *Democracia y economía de mercado: Ponencias y debates de un simposio* (Lima: ILD, n.d.).

32. The institute was founded in December 1979. See DESCO, *Cronología política, 1979,* 3716. For a further declaration of principles, see DESCO, *Cronología política, 1980,* 3973.

33. CEPB, "La empresa privada y su papel en el desarrollo nacional," in *Pensamiento de la empresa privada,* 95.

34. See the speech by León Febres Cordero in *Guayaquil frente al futuro,* comp. Banco de Guayaquil (Guayaquil: Banco de Guayaquil, 1973), 129.

35. See the discussion by Giorgio Alberti, "Estado, clase empresarial, y comunidad industrial," in *Estado y clase: La comunidad industrial en el Perú,* ed. Giorgio Alberti et al. (Lima: Instituto de Estudios Peruanos, 1977), 31–104. The SI pressed for participation in a communiqué on 1 February 1977. See DESCO, *Cronología política, 1977,* 2428. ADEX's September statement is found in DESCO, *Cronología política, 1978,* 3225.

36. *Ficha de información socio-política,* 20 June 1975.

37. Ibid., 22 August 1975.

38. See CEPB, *Pensamiento de la empresa privada,* 17, 19, 69, 81.

39. The turbulent politics of this period is discussed at great length in Eduardo Gamarra, "Political Stability, Democratization, and the Bolivian National Congress" (Ph.D. diss., University of Pittsburgh, 1987).

40. For further discussion of this period, see Malloy and Gamarra, *Revolution and Reaction,* 117–55.

41. Interview, CEPB, La Paz, 20 February 1986.

42. Bob Jessop takes up Lenin's point in "Capitalism and Democracy: The Best Possible Political Shell?" in *States and Societies,* ed. David Held et al. (New York: New York University Press, 1983), 272–89.

43. See "Informe anual presentado por el Presidente de la Cámara de Industrias de Guayaquil," *Revista de la Cámara de Industrias de Guayaquil* 9, no. 38 (1978). See "Reflexión política," *Carta Industrial* 34 (September 1978, Cámara de Industriales de Pichincha).

44. For the communiqué, see DESCO, *Cronología política, 1978,* 3418.

45. See *Constitución política del Perú* (Lima: Editorial S.A., 1980), pp. 57–58. For a brief analysis of the politics surrounding the constituent assembly, see the introduction by Henry Pease García in *Perú: Constitución y sociedad política,* ed. Marcial Rubio and Enrique Bernales (Lima: DESCO, 1981); also Enrique Bernales, *Crisis política: ¿Solución electoral? Analisis de los resultados de las elecciones para la Asamblea Constituyente de 1978* (Lima: DESCO, 1980). For a discussion of the social market concept, see Fernando Sánchez Albavera, "La economía social de mercado: ¿Un modelo para rearmar el capitalismo?" *Quehacer* 2 (November–December 1979): 26–32.

46. The document is published in CEPB, *Pensamiento y acción de la empresa privada, 1982–1985* (La Paz: CEPB, 1985), 80–82.

47. Interview, CEPB, La Paz, 11 February 1987.

5. Crisis, Elections, and Neoliberal Coalitions

1. There is a large literature on conditionality in IMF agreements. See, for example, the essays in John Williamson, ed., *IMF Conditionality* (Washington, D.C.: Institute for International Economics, 1983). For a discussion of the evolution of conditionality in the World Bank, see Joan Nelson, "The Diplomacy of Policy-Based Lending," *Between Two Worlds: The World Bank's Next Decade,* ed. Richard E. Feinberg and Valeriana Kalb (Washington, D.C.: Overseas Development Council, 1986), 67–82.

2. For a discussion of the evolution of an international consensus on the desirability of market-oriented economic reforms in the Third World, see the discussion by Miles Kahler, "Orthodoxy and Its Alternatives: Explaining Approaches to Stabilization and Adjustment," in *Economic Crisis and Policy Choice: The Politics of Adjustment in the Third World,* ed. Joan Nelson (Princeton, N.J.: Princeton University Press, 1990), 33–61.

3. This discussion draws heavily on Rosemary Thorp, "The Stabilisation Crisis in Peru, 1975–78," in *Inflation and Stabilisation in Latin America,* ed. Rosemary Thorp and Laurence Whitehead (New York: Holmes and Meier, 1979), 110–43. Thorp cites the reference to Peru as the "IMF's Vietnam" from *Le Monde*.

4. The argument about the physical limitations on export growth is developed at length in Thorp and Bertram, *Peru 1890–1977,* 208–56.

5. This point is emphasized by Daniel M. Schydlowsky and Juan Wicht, "The Anatomy of Economic Failure," in McClintock and Lowenthal, *Peruvian Experiment,* 94–143.

6. Laura Gautsi, "The Peruvian Military Government and International Corporations," in McClintock and Lowenthal, *Peruvian Experiment,* 181–205.

7. Thorp, "Stabilisation Crisis," 115–16.

8. For a discussion of the growth of the Peruvian foreign debt, see Robert Devlin, *Debt and Crisis in Latin America: The Supply Side of the Story* (Princeton, N.J.: Princeton University Press, 1989), 139–78.

9. For further discussions of the stabilization policies under Morales Bermúdez, see Thomas Scheetz, *Peru and the International Monetary Fund* (Pittsburgh, Pa.: University of Pittsburgh Press, 1986); Adolfo Diz, "Economic Performance Under Three Stand-By Arrangements: Peru, 1977–80," in Williamson, *IMF Conditionality,* 263–73; Luis Abugattás, "Una década de estabilización: Perú 1975–1985" (paper given at the Séminario sobre el Grupo Andino: Nuevos Enfoques para el Desarrollo y la Integración Subregional, 17–19 September 1985, Junta del Acuerdo de Cartagena, Lima, Peru).

10. Barbara Stallings, *Banker to the Third World: U.S. Portfolio Investment in Latin America, 1900–1986* (Berkeley: University of California Press, 1987), 279–85.

11. Rosemary Thorp, "Peruvian Adjustment Policies, 1978–85: The Effects of Prolonged Crisis," in *Latin American Debt and the Adjustment Crisis,* ed. Rosemary Thorp and Laurence Whitehead (London: Macmillan, 1987), 212. Silva Ruete's reflections on his term in office can be found in *"Yo asumí."*

12. Daniel M. Schydlowsky, "The Tragedy of Lost Opportunity in Peru," in *Latin American Political Economy: Financial Crisis and Political Change,* ed. Jonathan Hartlyn and Samuel A. Morley (Boulder, Colo.: Westview Press, 1986), 217–42.

13. Pion-Berlin estimates that repressive measures directed against workers and their trade unions increased by 300 percent in the period between 1975 and 1978. See David

Pion-Berlin, *The Ideology of State Terror: Economic Doctrine and Political Repression in Argentina and Peru* (Boulder, Colo.: Lynne Rienner Publishers, 1989), 146–47.

14. The Bolivian debt is discussed by Devlin, *Debt and Crisis,* 139–80. Also see Mortimore, "The State and Transnational Banks," 143–48.

15. Grebe López, "Innovaciones de las políticas económico-sociales."

16. The World Bank, *Bolivia: Structural Constraints,* 4–7.

17. Ibid., 8.

18. Ibid., 11.

19. Arturo Núñez del Prado, "Bolivia: Inflación y democracia," *Pensamiento Iberoamericano* 9 (2d semestre, 1986): 249–76.

20. Juan Antonio Morales, "Las políticas de estabilización en Bolivia, 1982–89" (paper presented to the Fifteenth Congress of the Latin American Studies Association, 4–6 December 1989, Miami, Florida).

21. For a discussion of the dedollarization measures, see Kenneth Jameson, "Dollarization and Dedollarization in Bolivia" (photocopy of an unpublished paper, Department of Economics, University of Notre Dame, Indiana, 1986).

22. Morales and Sachs, "Bolivia's Economic Crisis," 226–27.

23. The World Bank, *Ecuador: An Agenda for Recovery and Sustained Growth* (Washington, D.C.: World Bank, 1984), 20–21.

24. Marshall-Silva, "Ecuador," 170–96. For further discussion of the continuities in the spending patterns of the military and the Roldós government, see David W. Schodt, "The Ecuadorian Public Sector During the Petroleum Period: 1972–83" (Technical Papers Series no. 52, Office for Public Sector Studies, Institute of Latin American Studies, University of Texas, Austin, 1986).

25. Abelardo Pachano, "Políticas económicas comparadas: Ecuador 1981–1987," *Neoliberalismo y políticas económicas alternativas,* ed. CORDES (Quito: CORDES, 1987), 205–42.

26. Osvaldo Hurtado, interview, Quito, 19 March 1986. For further discussion of the stabilization program, see Germánico Salgado, "Ecuador: Crisis and Adjustment Policies," *CEPAL Review* 33 (December 1987): 129–43. Also see Adrián Carrasco Veintimilla, "Los límites del reformismo: La política económica de Roldós-Hurtado y Hurtado-Roldós," in *El estado y la economía: Políticas económicas y clases sociales en el Ecuador y América Latina,* ed. Luis Pacheco (Quito: Instituto de Investigaciones Económicas, Pontificia Universidad Católica del Ecuador, 1983), 179–220.

27. For further discussion of the labor movement in this period, see Jorge León and Juan Pablo Pérez, "Crisis y movimiento sindical en Ecuador: Las huelgas nacionales del FUT (1981–1983)," in *Movimientos sociales en el Ecuador,* ed. Manuel Chiriboga et al. (Quito: CLACSO, 1986); Mills, *Crisis, conflicto, y consenso;* Juan Pablo Pérez Sáinz, *Clase obrera y democracia en el Ecuador* (Quito: Editorial El Conejo, 1985).

28. The speech is reproduced in Osvaldo Hurtado, *Política democrática II: Testimonios: 1964–1989* (Quito: FESO, Corporación Editora Nacional, 1990), 278.

29. Hurtado emphasized this point in our interview, Quito, 19 March 1986.

30. Hurtado, *Política democrática,* 354.

31. The idea of dominant groups and political power brokers coming together to form a ruling coalition is from Katzenstein, "Domestic Structures," 306.

32. Alvaro Rojas Samanez, *Partidos políticos en el Perú: Desde 1872 a nuestros días* (Lima: Ediciones F & A, 1985), 223–27.

33. Bedoya is quoted from DESCO, *Cronología política, 1980,* 3870, 3889. In his study of Latin American class structure, Alejandro Portes defines the bureaucratic-technical stratum as "middle-level managerial and technical personnel in foreign, domestic private, and state enterprises; career functionaries of state bureaucracies including the armed forces; and independent professionals employed by contract by the state or private sector" ("Latin American Class Structures," 11).

34. DESCO, *Cronología política, 1978,* 3199.

35. This is taken from PPC, *Programa de gobierno* (photocopy, Lima, May 1980).

36. At the time, Daniel Schydlowsky was an economist at Boston University. He was a tough critic of the economic policy under the military; and he went on to be just as severe in his judgment of Belaúnde. The work was entitled *Propuestas para el desarrollo peruano como aporte al país y al nuevo gobierno*. Its publication is described in DESCO, *Cronología política, 1980,* 3997.

37. Fernando Tuesta Soldevilla, *El parlamento en el Perú: Un perfil social y político de sus representantes* (photocopy of an unpublished manuscript, Lima, 1986). Francisco Durand, *Los industriales, el liberalismo, y la democracia* (Lima: Fundación Friedrich Ebert, DESCO, 1984), 21.

38. Cynthia Sanborn, "El APRA en un contexto de cambio, 1968–1988," in *El APRA: De la ideología a la praxis,* ed. Heraclio Bonilla and Paul Drake (Lima: Editorial y Productora Gráfica "Nuevo Mundo" EIRL, 1989), 105–06. Julio Cotler, "Military Interventions and the 'Transfer of Power to Civilians' in Peru," in *Transitions from Authoritarian Rule: Latin America,* ed. Guillermo O'Donnell, Philippe Schmitter, and Laurence Whitehead (Baltimore, Md.: Johns Hopkins University Press, 1986), 148–72.

39. DESCO, *Cronología política, 1979,* 3622. For further discussion of party relations in Venezuela, see Daniel H. Levine, "Venezuela Since 1958: The Consolidation of Democratic Politics," in *The Breakdown of Democratic Regimes: Latin America,* ed. Juan J. Linz and Alfred Stepan (Baltimore: Johns Hopkins University Press, 1978), 82–109; Terry Lynn Karl, "Petroleum and Political Pacts: The Transition to Democracy in Venezuela," in O'Donnell, Schmitter, and Whitehead, *Transitions from Authoritarian Rule,* 196–219.

40. For a discussion of executive-legislative conflict during the first Belaúnde administration, see Cotler, "A Structural-Historical Approach," 178–206.

41. Jürgen Schuldt and Luis Abugattás cite Rivera, González, and Jensen as participants in the formulation of policies, see "Neoliberalismo y democracia en el Perú, 1980–1985," in *Neoliberalismo y políticas económicas alternativas,* ed. CORDES (Quito: CORDES, 1987), 80–81. Webb's observations are from an interview, Lima, 16 July 1990.

42. A detailed history of the Siles Zuazo government has yet to be written. For our discussion, we draw on analyses found in Malloy and Gamarra, *Revolution and Reaction,* and in Roberto Laserna, ed., *Crisis, democracia, y conflicto social: La acción colectiva en Bolivia: 1982–85* (Cochabamba: CERES, 1985). For a succinct account of the politics of the Allende period, see Arturo Valenzuela, *The Breakdown of Democratic Regimes: Chile* (Baltimore, Md.: Johns Hopkins University Press, 1978).

43. Chile's economic reforms under the Pinochet dictatorship have been the subject

of extensive analysis. For a look at the debate on the reforms in Chile and the Southern Cone, see Foxley, *Latin American Experiments;* Ramos, *Neoconservative Economics;* Edwards and Cox Edwards, *Monetarism and Liberalization;* Vittorio Corbo and Jaime de Melo, ''Lessons from the Southern Cone and Policy Reforms,'' *World Bank Research Observer* 2, no. 2 (July 1987): 111–42.

44. Malloy and Gamarra, *Revolution,* 164–65.

45. Flavio Machicado, interview, La Paz, February 1987. The COB had previously participated in a cogoverning arrangement immediately following the 1952 revolution in the first government of the MNR. The COB had been given control over the ministries of mines, peasant affairs, labor, and transport, but it was eventually ousted from these positions in 1957 during the first presidency of Hernán Siles Zuazo. Siles's attack on the COB in the 1950s was part of his stabilization program. This earlier hostility between Siles and the COB contributed to his difficulties in dealing with the COB in the 1980s (the antagonism between Siles and COB leader Juan Lechín was legendary). For a discussion of the COB's experience in the 1950s, see Bert Useem, ''The Workers' Movement and the Bolivian Revolution,'' *Politics and Society* 9, no. 4 (1980): 447–69. For a discussion of the COB's experience with the principle of co-gobierno, see Jorge Lazarte, *Movimiento obrero y procesos políticos en Bolivia: Historia de la COB (1952–1987)* (La Paz: ILDIS, 1988), 121–33. Also see Ricardo Calla Ortega, ''La encrucijada de la COB: Temas del movimiento obrero boliviano en lay coyuntura democrática,'' in *Crisis, democracia, y conflicto social,* ed. Roberto Laserna (La Paz: CERES, 1985), 65–128.

46. See, for example, ''Sin libertad económica no hay democracia política,'' and ''El rescate de la democracia,'' in CEPB, *Pensamiento y acción,* 84–87, 89–90.

47. Figures are taken from *Business Latin America,* 25 July 1988 and 3 April 1989. For a discussion of the work actions at the Central Bank, see María Isabel Arauco, ''Los trabajadores del estado y del Banco Central de Bolivia (1982–85),'' in *Crisis del sindicalismo en Bolivia,* ed. FLACSO–ILDIS (La Paz: FLACSO–ILDIS, 1987), 175–200.

48. Roberto Laserna, ''La protesta territorial (La acción colectiva regional y urbana en una coyuntura de crisis democrática),'' in Laserna, *Crisis, democracia, y conflicto social,* 203–52.

49. Quoted by Núñez del Prado, ''Bolivia,'' 274.

50. O'Donnell, *Bureaucratic Authoritarianism,* 24–30.

51. CEPB official, interview, La Paz, 18 February 1986.

52. CEPB, *Pensamiento y acción,* 266.

53. ''Lineamientos y proposiciones de la empresa privada para un programa de recuperación económica,'' in CEPB, *Pensamiento y acción,* 301–13 (304).

54. Juan Antonio Morales, ''Inflation Stabilization in Bolivia,'' in *Inflation Stabilization: The Experience of Israel, Argentina, Brazil, Bolivia, and Mexico,* ed. Michael Bruno et al. (Cambridge, Mass.: MIT Press, 1988), 307–46.

55. The documents from this conference are in Müller y Machicado Asociados, ed., *El diálogo para la democracia* (La Paz: Müller y Machicado, 1986).

56. Interview, La Paz, 22 February 1986.

57. See the interview with Paz Estenssoro in Ronald Grebe López et al., *¿Qué ofrecen los candidatos? Elecciones 1985* (La Paz: Educación Radiofónica de Bolivia, 1985), 120–27.

58. This information on the 1985 campaign is taken from Eduardo Gamarra, ''Between Constitutional and Traditional Coups: The Bolivian Elections of 1985'' (photocopy, Florida International University, 1985).

59. Interview, La Paz, 17 February 1986.

60. Gonzalo Sánchez de Lozada, interview, La Paz, 22 February 1986.

61. For a discussion of the Durán Ballén campaign, see Howard Handelman, ''A New Political Direction?'' in *Military Government and the Movement Toward Democracy in South America,* ed. Howard Handelman and Thomas Sanders (Bloomington: Indiana University Press, 1981), 26–66.

62. For a discussion of Roldós's clientele networks in Guayaquil, see Amparo Menéndez-Carrión, *La conquista del voto: De Velasco a Roldós* (Quito: Corporación Editora Nacional, 1986), 396–407.

63. The results of the election are discussed in FLACSO, ed., *Elecciones en el Ecuador, 1979–1980* (Quito: Editorial Oveja Negra, n.d.).

64. For a retrospective on the Roldós government, see Jaime Roldós Aguilera et al., *''¡Viva la Patria!''* (Quito: Editorial El Conejo, 1981). The dynamics of party behavior in this period are also discussed in Catherine Conaghan, ''Party Politics and Democratization in Ecuador,'' in *Authoritarians and Democrats: Regime Transition in Latin America,* ed. James M. Malloy and Mitchell Seligson (Pittsburgh, Pa.: University of Pittsburgh Press, 1986), 145–63.

65. Sixto Durán Ballén, interview, Quito, 2 September 1983. Blasco Peñaherrera Padilla, interview, Pittsburgh, July 1987.

66. Blasco Peñaherrera Padilla, a Liberal party leader and vice-president in the Febres Cordero government, refers to him as the ''factor aglutinante'' in the formation of the FRN. His stinging criticisms of Febres Cordero were published as *El viernes negro: Antes y después de Taura* (Quito: Editorial El Conejo, 1988), 217.

67. León Febres Cordero, interview, Salinas, 27 April 1980. Febres Cordero's declarations against statist models of economic development are cited in Conaghan, *Restructuring Domination,* 88.

68. Francisco Swett, interview with author, Guayaquil, 5 February 1987. ''Sinopsis de los lineamientos y principios del plan de gobierno de Ing. León Febres Cordero'' (photocopy, Guayaquil, 1984).

69. Borja joined Febres Cordero in requesting ministerial *informes*. See Mills, *Crisis, conflicto, y consenso,* 76–77.

70. *El Comercio,* 15 November 1982; *Hoy,* 23 October 1982.

71. This was the first organized business lockout in Ecuador since 1966 when the chambers protested the economic policy of the military junta led by General Ramón Castro Jijón. The protest is described in Fitch, *Military Coup d'Etat,* 69.

72. See Hurtado's interview with Benjamin Ortiz in CORDES, *Democracia y crisis: Diálogos del Presidente Osvaldo Hurtado con la prensa, 1981–1984,* vol. B (Quito: CORDES, 1984), 240.

73. Rodrigo Paz, interview, Quito, 21 January 1987.

74. Interview, Quito, 20 January 1987.

75. Osvaldo Hurtado, interview, Quito, 10 December 1984.

76. Peñaherrera, *El viernes negro,* 216.

77. For a collection of Febres Cordero's colorful epithets, see Ramiro Rivera, *El pensamiento de León Febres Cordero* (Quito: Ediciones Culturales, 1986).

78. For the *bloque*'s formal declaration of purpose, see *El Comercio,* 17 and 20 July 1984.

79. For these declarations, see *Hoy,* 8 May 1984. Romulo López, president of the Federation of the Chambers of Industry, made similar statements in *Hoy,* 22 May 1984. Nahím Isaías, president of Guayaquil's Filanbanco Bank, declared that Febres Cordero would guarantee a strong and stable investment climate (*El Expreso,* 11 May 1984). Ironically, Isaías became a casualty of the Febres Cordero administration. Isaías was killed in a shoot-out in 1985 between government troops and the Eloy Alfaro guerrillas who had kidnapped him. Much to the dismay of the Isaías family, Febres Cordero himself issued the order for the troops to storm the hideout.

6. Theory Into Practice

1. For a discussion of how rituals can be used to build solidarity within groups, see David I. Kertzer, *Ritual, Politics, and Power* (New Haven, Conn.: Yale University Press, 1988), 57–101.

2. See UN Economic Commission for Latin America and the Caribbean, *Economic Survey of Latin America and the Caribbean, 1979* (Santiago, 1981), 438–61; Richard Webb, *Stabilisation and Adjustment Policies and Programmes,* Country Study no. 8, Peru (Helsinki: World Institute for Development Economics, Research of the UN University, 1987), 15.

3. For a discussion of the broadening of conditions on the part of the IMF and the World Bank by the early 1980s, see Kahler, ''Orthodoxy and Its Alternatives,'' 40–44.

4. Carol Wise, ''Peru in the 1980s: Political Responses to the Debt Crisis'' (Papers on Latin America no. 2, Institute of Latin American and Iberian Studies, Columbia University, 1988).

5. UN Economic Commission for Latin America and the Caribbean, *Economic Survey of Latin America and the Caribbean, 1984* (Santiago: United Nations, 1986), 283–310.

6. Gonzalo Sánchez de Lozada, ''La nueva política económica,'' *Foro Económico* 5 (September 1985): 6.

7. Juan Cariaga, ''Bolivia,'' in *Latin American Adjustment: How Much Has Happened?* ed. John Williamson (Washington, D.C.: Institute for International Economics, 1990), 7.

8. Cariaga makes this point in ibid., 42. A World Bank mission visited Ecuador in October 1983; its report and recommendations to the Ecuadorean government can be found in the World Bank, *Ecuador: An Agenda.* The recommendations of the Wheeler mission are discussed in Manuel Chiriboga, ''Política agropecuaria: La búsqueda del imperio del mercado,'' in *Los placeres del poder: El segundo año del gobierno de León Febres Cordero, 1985–86,* ed. María Arboleda et al. (Quito: Editorial El Conejo, 1986), 166–80.

9. Figures for Peru are from Enrique Bernales, *El parlamento por dentro* (Lima: DESCO, 1984), 81, 85. The legality of Febres Cordero's use of ''urgent'' decrees in

Ecuador was widely questioned by the opposition. For an analysis of the legal questions, see León Roldós Aguilera, *El abuso del poder: Los decretos-leyes económicos urgentes aprobados por el gobierno del Ing. León Febres Cordero* (Quito: Editorial El Conejo, 1986).

10. Francisco Swett, ''Vuelta a medias: Los vaivenes del liberalismo económico en el Ecuador, 1984–1988'' (unpublished ms., Guayaquil, 1989).

11. Information on the general strikes is taken from Jorge Parodi, ''Los sindicatos en la democracia vacía,'' in *Democracia, sociedad, y gobierno en el Perú,* ed. Luis Pásara and Jorge Parodi (Lima: CEDYS, 1988), 81–124.

12. For data on strikes and collective action during the period, see Roberto Laserna, ''La insurrección de la democracia,'' in *La acción colectiva en Bolivia: 1982–1985,* ed. Roberto Laserna (Cochabamba: CERES, 1985), 12.

13. Interview with member of Paz's cabinet, La Paz, 29 May 1988. For further discussion of the weakening position of the COB, see the collection of essays in FLACSO–ILDIS, *Crisis del sindicalismo en Bolivia* (La Paz: FLACSO–ILDIS, 1987); also see Lazarte, *Movimiento obrero y procesos políticos.* For a review of government actions in this period, see CEDOIN's monthly publication, *Informe ''R,''* for September, October, November, and December 1985.

14. The definitions are taken from the discussion by Portes, ''Latin American Class Structures,'' 8–16.

15. See Jorge Parodi, ''La desmovilización del sindicalismo industrial peruano en el segundo Belaundismo,'' in *Movimientos sociales y crisis: El caso peruano,* ed. Eduardo Ballón (Lima: DESCO, 1986). For an insightful and sensitive treatment of the world of the working class in Lima, see Jorge Parodi, *Ser obrero es algo relativo* (Lima: DESCO, 1986).

16. The notion of the organic weakening of society is taken from Manuel Antonio Garretón, ''Chile: In Search of Lost Democracy,'' in *Latin American Political Economy: Financial Crisis and Political Change,* ed. Jonathan Hartlyn and Samuel A. Morley (Boulder, Colo.: Westview, 1986), 197–216.

17. FSE, ''Estadísticas básicas'' (photocopy, La Paz, 18 April 1988). For a description of the objectives of the program, see Luis Fernando Campero et al., ''Costo social de la crisis y el ajuste,'' in *Costo social de la crisis y del ajuste* 6, ed. Taller de Investigaciones Socio-económicas (La Paz: ILDIS, n.d.). A temporary employment program, the Programa de Empleo Mínimo, was also launched under Pinochet during the neoliberal experiment in Chile.

18. Clearly in the case of Bolivia, the COB membership was exhausted by its hyperactivity during the Siles Zuazo administration. Albert Hirschman has argued that there are limits on the extent to which people can remain committed to intense political activity over time, see his *Shifting Involvements: Private Interests and Public Action* (Princeton, N.J.: Princeton University Press, 1979).

19. Ferrand's statement of support was reported in *El Comercio,* 17 July 1980.

20. *La Prensa,* 5 April 1981; and *El Comercio,* 16 September 1980.

21. *El Diario,* 27 September 1980. Ferrand's yearly message is quoted in *La Prensa,* 5 April 1981.

22. Quotation is from *El Diario,* 19 November 1980. Proposals are from *La Prensa,* 18 September 1980; *Opinion Libre,* 11 December 1980.

23. Business's objections are in *Opinion Libre,* 19 February 1981; *Oiga,* 23 February 1981. Romero's interview is in *Oiga,* 20 April 1981.

24. Interviews, Lima, 18 and 28 January 1986.

25. *El Comercio,* 22 November 1981.

26. *El Diario,* 26 March 1981. Interview, Lima, 4 February 1986.

27. For the SNI event, see *Correo,* 16 May 1981. For the neoliberal event, see Durand, *Los industriales,* 34.

28. Interview, Lima, 6 February 1986.

29. Interview, Lima, 4 February 1986.

30. Durand, ''The National Bourgeoisie and the Peruvian State,'' 154–62.

31. Interview with CNI official, La Paz, 12 February 1987.

32. GDP figures are from Víctor Chuquimia and Emilio Tórrez, ''Productividad y competividad de la pequeña y mediana industria,'' in *La industria: Problemas y perspectivas* (La Paz: ILDIS, 1990), 99. EAP figures are from Luis F. Baudoín, ''Capacidad de generación de empleo de la industria manufacturera,'' in *La industria: Problemas y perspectivas* (La Paz: ILDIS, 1990), 44. Eckstein and Hagopian, ''The Limits of Industrialization,'' 81–82.

33. Alan Bojanic, ''Evaluación de la estructura agraria en el area integrada de Santa Cruz,'' *Tenencia y uso de la tierra en Santa Cruz,* ed. Talleres CEDLA (La Paz: CEDLA, 1988), 9–67.

34. For an expression of the business sector's ideological agreement with the model see, for example, ''Exposición del presidente de la CEPB Licenciado Carlos Iturralde con motivo del XVII aniversario de la Federación de Empresarios Privados de Cochabamba,'' 29 August 1986 (photocopy, CEPB, 1986).

35. O'Donnell, *Bureaucratic Authoritarianism,* 24–30. Alfred Stepan also points to how the bourgeoisie's traumatic experience during the Allende period in Chile blunted business opposition to some of the components of the ensuing neoliberal model under Pinochet. See ''State Power and the Strength of Civil Society,'' in Evans et al., *Bringing the State Back In,* 321.

36. He projected a five-year phase-in of the program in the interview ''Apuntando al '84,'' *Vistazo,* 6 August 1982. He reiterated his commitment to gradual neoliberal reforms in another interview, ''Febres Cordero: La gente dice que mi imagen ha crecido,'' *Impacto* 44 (1983).

37. León Febres Cordero, interview, Guayaquil, 28 July 1989. The third member of the neoliberal troika—Alberto Dahik, who headed the monetary board—later characterized the gradualist approach as a major mistake. He claims he advocated a more radical shock treatment approach but this suggestion was vetoed by Emanuel (interview with Alberto Dahik, Quito, 18 July 1989).

38. For Neira's early declarations, see *Hoy,* 14 September and 18 October 1984.

39. Figures on the tariff schedule are taken from CEDIS, *La política económica del gobierno de Febres Cordero* (Quito: CEDIS, 1986), 39–41.

40. In Ecuador, the 1978 constitution limits a president to only one term in office in

his or her lifetime. Under the constitutions extant in Bolivia and Peru in the 1980s, presidents could not hold consecutive terms but could be reelected. In the case of Paz Estenssoro and Belaúnde, however, their advanced age made the prospects of future reelection unlikely. Peru's 1979 constitution was suspended on 5 April 1992 by President Alberto Fujimori. A new constitution was approved in a plebiscite in October 1993. The new constitution allows for immediate presidential reelection.

7. Some Things Fall Apart, Some Don't

1. UN Economic Commission for Latin America and the Caribbean, *Economic Survey of Latin America and the Caribbean, 1983* (Santiago: United Nations, 1985), 557–59, and *Economic Survey of Latin America and the Caribbean, 1986* (Santiago: United Nations, 1989), 371.

2. UN Economic Commission, *Economic Survey, 1983,* 557. Selected economic indicators for 1983 can be seen in our table 4, in chapter 5.

3. Webb, *Stabilisation and Adjustment Policies,* 25.

4. UN Economic Commission, *Economic Survey, 1984,* 556.

5. Webb, *Stabilisation and Adjustment Policies,* 22.

6. León Febres Cordero, interview, Guayaquil, 28 July 1989. The quotation in the next paragraph is also from this interview.

7. See Walter Spurrier, ''A Muscled Presidency,'' *Weekly Analysis of Ecuadorean Issues,* no. 25, 4 July 1985; Osvaldo Hurtado, *La dictadura civil* (Quito: FESO, 1988). For a further discussion of the authoritarian style of the government, see Gonzalo Ortiz Crespo, ''Neoliberalismo autoritario y encrucijada social,'' *Economía y Desarrollo* 7, no. 9 (July 1985): 1–20.

8. For a complete account of these events, see Gonzalo Ortiz Crespo, *La hora del General* (Quito: Editorial El Conejo, 1986).

9. From the declaration read by Wilfredo Lucero, ''Manifiesto de la Democracia Popular pidiendo el voto NO en la consulta popular,'' in Osvaldo Hurtado, *El voto del no: Crónica de un plebiscito* (Quito: FESO, 1986), 243.

10. Febres Cordero, interview, Guayaquil, 28 July 1989.

11. The official history of the public works program is presented in four volumes: see Secretaría Nacional de Información Pública (SENDIP), *Pensamiento y obra: Gobierno constitucional del ingeniero León Febres-Cordero Ribadeneyra* (Quito: SENDIP, 1988). For critiques from the right of Febres Cordero's spending policies, see Manuel Maldonado Posso, ''An Entrepreneur Discredited the Free Enterprise System in Ecuador,'' *Journal of Economic Growth,* no. 2 (November 1988): 19–28.

12. See *New York Times,* 10 June 1983. The rating figures are taken from a DATUM poll cited by Luis Pásara, ''La libanización en democracia,'' in Pásara and Parodi, *Democracia, sociedad, y gobierno,* 26.

13. For further examination of the development of Sendero Luminoso, see Susan C. Bourque and Kay B. Warren, ''Democracy Without Peace: The Cultural Politics of Terror in Peru,'' *Latin American Research Review* 24, no. 1 (1989): 7–34; Cynthia McClintock, ''Peru's Sendero Luminoso: Origins and Trajectory,'' in *Power and Popular Protest:*

Latin American Social Movements, ed. Susan Eckstein (Berkeley: University of California Press, 1989), 61–101; Carlos Iván Degregori, *El surgimiento de Sendero Luminoso* (Lima: Instituto de Estudios Peruanos, 1990). For a recent collection of essays analyzing Sendero, see David Scott Palmer, ed., *The Shining Path of Peru* (New York: St. Martin's Press, 1992).

14. These totals include the deaths of suspected *senderistas,* civilians, civilian authorities, armed forces, and police personnel. They are calculated from figures given by Gustavo Gorriti, ''Democracia, narcotráfico, y la insurrección de Sendero Luminoso,'' in Pásara and Parodi, *Democracia, sociedad, y gobierno,* 207.

15. Febres Cordero, interview, Guayaquil, 28 July 1989.

16. For insights into the ascendance of economics and how economists use their expertise in the policy-making process, see John Markoff and Veronica Montecinos, ''The Irresistible Rise of Economists'' (unpublished paper, University of Pittsburgh, May 1990).

17. For further discussion of the powers of Congress, see Hernán Salgado, *Instituciones políticas y constitución del Ecuador* (Quito: ILDIS, 1987).

18. Cordero cited in *El Universo,* 21 September 1986. Peñaherrera cited in *Weekly Analysis of Ecuadorean Issues* 16, no. 38, 29 September 1986.

19. *Hoy,* 19 September 1986. As head of the Central Bank, Emanuel could not be interpellated by Congress.

20. Interview, Quito, 5 February 1987. After the resignation, the administration held a special salute to Dahik. For Febres Cordero's speech on the occasion, see ''Homenaje al señor economista Alberto Dahik Garzozi,'' in SENDIP, *Pensamiento y obra,* 2:149–52.

21. For such characterizations of the measures, see Swett, ''Vuelta a medias,'' 29. Also see the remarks by the Central Bank president, ''Entrevista realizada al Dr. Carlos Julio Emanuel, Quito, 26 de agosto de 1986,'' in *Política económica frente a la crisis: Discursos y entrevistas* (Quito: Banco Central del Ecuador, 1987), 2:104–5. Also see the discussion in ''Interest Rates, Currency Are Floated,'' *Weekly Analysis of Ecuadorean Issues* 16, no. 32, 15 August 1986.

22. Febres Cordero, interview, Guayaquil, 28 July 1989.

23. Pachano, ''Políticas económicas comparadas,'' 236.

24. *El Comercio,* 24 February 1988.

25. *Hoy,* 24 March 1988; *El Comercio,* 26 March 1988.

26. Febres Cordero, interview, Guayaquil, 28 July 1989.

27. The founding members were ADEX, Cámara Peruana de Construcción, Confederación de Cámaras de Comercio y Producción del Perú, Confederación Nacional de Comerciantes, SNI, Sociedad Nacional de Minería y Petróleo, and Sociedad Nacional de Pesquería.

28. For a discussion of the defensive behavior of firms, see Webb, ''Internal Debt and Financial Adjustment,'' 55–74. For a discussion and estimations of capital flight in this peirod, see Anaya, *Los grupos de poder económico,* 146–54.

29. Figures are from Manuel Pastor and Carol Wise, ''Peruvian Economic Policy in the 1980s: From Orthodoxy to Heterodoxy and Back,'' *Latin American Research Review* 27, no. 2 (1992): 88. Webb, ''Internal Debt and Financial Adjustment,'' 74.

30. O'Donnell and Schmitter note the role that fortuna plays in the process of political transition. See Guillermo O'Donnell and Philippe C. Schmitter, *Transitions from Authori-*

tarian Rule: Tentative Conclusions About Uncertain Democracies (Baltimore, Md.: Johns Hopkins University Press, 1986), 5.

31. Carlos Julio Emanuel, interview, Quito, 5 February 1987.

32. Juan Antonio Morales, ''Bolivia's Post-Stabilization Problems'' (Documento de trabajo no. 08/90, Instituto de Investigaciones Socioeconómicas, Universidad Católica Boliviana, June 1990), 2.

33. Morales and Sachs, ''Bolivia's Economic Crisis,'' 240.

34. Figures are from Cariaga, ''Bolivia,'' 44.

35. In 1983, the real monthly minimum wage stood at 8,416 pesos. All the figures cited are from *Economic Survey of Latin America and the Caribbean 1988,* 172.

36. There is, for example, a massive literature on this question concerning U.S. presidents. Some of the standard works exploring leadership and the presidency include Thomas Cronin, *The State of the Presidency* (Boston: Little, Brown, 1980); Barbara Kellerman, *The Political Presidency: Practice of Leadership* (New York: Oxford University Press, 1984); Richard Neudstadt, *Presidential Power: The Politics of Leadership* (New York: Wiley, 1960); James David Barber, *The Presidential Character* (Englewood Cliffs, N.J.: Prentice-Hall, 1985).

37. For a discussion of the conflict with the COB in this period, see Malloy, *Bolivia,* 297–302.

38. Gonzalo Sánchez de Lozada, interview, La Paz, 22 February 1986.

39. This point was made by Juan Antonio Morales in a Woodrow Wilson Center program on the politics of economic adjustment, 14 September 1990. An edited transcript of the proceedings was published as ''Politics, Policymaking, and Democratization: Focus on the Andes'' (Working paper no. 196, Latin American Program, Woodrow Wilson Center for International Scholars, Washington, D.C.).

40. For a more detailed discussion of the role of Jeffrey Sachs, see Catherine M. Conaghan, ''Reconsidering Jeffrey Sachs and the Bolivian Economic Experiment,'' in *Money Doctors, Foreign Debt, and Economic Reform in Latin America, 1890s–1990s,* ed. Paul Drake (Wilmington, Del.: Scholarly Resources, 1994).

41. For a look at the demands of the civic committees, see *Informe ''R''* 6, no. 119 (October 1986).

42. Sánchez de Lozada, interview, La Paz, 22 February 1986.

43. Guillermo Bedregal, interview, La Paz, 22 February 1986.

44. The results are taken from *Informe ''R''* 8, no. 141 (January 1988).

45. *Informe ''R''* 7, no. 140 (December 1987).

46. Eduardo Gamarra, ''Bolivia,'' in *Latin American and Caribbean Contemporary Record, 1987–1988,* ed. James M. Malloy and Eduardo A. Gamarra (New York: Holmes and Meier, 1990), 7:B-31–48.

47. Ibid, B-42.

48. For a review of the events surrounding the cabinet crisis, see *Informe ''R''* 7, no. 125 (April 1987).

49. The forum, held in the Hotel La Paz on 22 March, received massive media coverage. For a further description of the event, see *Informe ''R''* 9, no. 169 (April 1989); Raúl Rivadeneira, *Agresión política: El proceso electoral 1989* (La Paz: Librería Editorial ''Juventud,'' 1989), 64–68.

50. See, for example, "Cronología de violencia," *Informe "R"* 6, no. 114 (April 1986).

51. For a detailed account of the events, see "¡Por la vida y la paz! Los caminantes de la patria," *Informe "R"* 6 (separata), no. 118 (September 1986); June Nash, "Interpreting Social Movements: Bolivian Resistance to Economic Conditions Imposed by the IMF," *American Ethnologist* 19 (May 1992): 275–93.

52. For July 1987, see "Petroleros: La histórica se repite," *Informe "R"* 7, no. 132 (August 1987). For a summary of labor conflicts in 1987, see "Aumentarón los conflictos sociales," ibid., no. 140 (December 1987). For March 1988, see "Petroleros: Una lucha sectorial," *Informe "R"* 8, no. 145 (March 1988).

53. Cited in *Informe "R"* 6, no. 116 (June 1986), 19.

54. For a chronology of the hunger strike, see "La huelga contra el hambre," *Informe "R"* 7, no. 125 (April 1987). For a summary of the *Pliego,* see ibid., no. 137 (November 1987).

55. Sachs developed a formal model illustrating how debt relief could be conceptualized as the rational and the best choice for creditors and debtors. For the model, see his "Debt Overhang of Developing Countries," in *Debt, Stabilization, and Development: Essays in Memory of Carlos Díaz-Alejandro,* ed. Guillermo Calvo et al. (Oxford: Basil Blackwell, 1989), 91–95. For another look at Sachs's arguments regarding debt relief, see "How to Save the Third World," *The New Republic,* 28 October 1985.

56. FSE, "Estadísticas básicas." For a recent evaluation of the effects of the program, see Carol Graham, "The Politics of Protecting the Poor During Adjustment: Bolivia's Social Emergency Fund," *World Development* 92, no. 9 (1992): 1233–51.

57. Figures on employment are from Flavio Machicado, "Coca Production in Bolivia," in *Drug Policy in the Americas,* ed. Peter Smith (Boulder, Colo.: Westview, 1992), 91.

58. These figures are taken from Mario De Franco and Ricardo Godoy, "The Economic Consequences of Cocaine Production in Bolivia: Historical, Local, and Macroeconomic Perspectives," *Journal of Latin American Studies* 24, no. 2 (May 1992): 375–406.

59. Economist Intelligence Unit, *Bolivia: Country Report 1991–92* (London: Business International Limited, 1991), 13.

60. Stepan, "State Power," 317–46.

61. Oscar Ugarteche, *El estado deudor: Economía política de la deuda, Perú y Bolivia 1968–1984* (Lima: Instituto de Estudios Peruanos, 1986); Mortimore, "The State and Transnational Banks," 143–48. Figures are from Morales and Sachs, "Bolivia's Economic Crisis" 2:213.

62. Interview, Cochabamba, 23 August 1991.

63. For a discussion of the reactivation decree, see Müller y Machicado Asociados, *Evaluación económica 1987* (La Paz: Bolivia Dos Mil, 1987), 127–75. Also see "¿Reactivación económica por decreto?" *Informe "R"* 7 (separata), no. 131, 1 August 1987.

64. Flavio Machicado, *Sistema financiero y reactivación* (La Paz: ILDIS, 1989), 45.

65. Figures are cited in "¿Por qué no hay mas inversión en Bolivia?" *Epoca,* no. 27 (August 1991): 7.

66. The notion of "reinventing Bolivia" is one that has been used frequently by Gonzalo Sánchez de Lozada. For an analysis of NPE policies in the subsequent govern-

ment of Jaime Paz Zamora, see Eduardo Gamarra, ''Market-Oriented Reforms and Democratization in Bolivia,'' in *A Precarious Balance: Democratic Consolidation and Economic Reform in Latin America and Eastern Europe,* ed. Joan Nelson and Marcelo Cavarozzi (Washington, D.C.: International Center for Economic Growth, forthcoming), 21–196.

8. *Conclusion*

1. Francis Fukuyama is cited from ''The End of History?'' *The National Interest* (Summer 1989): 3–18. For celebratory press accounts of the recent changes, see ''After the Cold War: Views from Latin America,'' *New York Times,* 30 May 1992; B. E. Babbit, ''The New and Improved South America,'' *World Monitor* 4 (February 1991); ''Latin America: The Big Move to Free Markets,'' *Business Week,* 15 June 1992. For accounts by economists see, for example, John Williamson's discussion of Latin America's acceptance of the ''Washington consensus'' on policy reforms, ''What Washington Means by Policy Reforms,'' in *Latin American Adjustment: How Much Has Happened?* ed. John Williamson (Washington, D.C.: Institute for International Economics, 1990), 7–35. For analyses of the failures of populist economic policies, see the case studies in Rudiger Dornbusch and Sebastian Edwards, eds., *The Macroeconomics of Populism in Latin America* (Chicago: National Bureau of Economic Research, University of Chicago Press, 1991).

2. See the editors' introduction in *Issues in Democratic Consolidation: The New South American Democracies in Comparative Perspective,* ed. Scott Mainwaring, Guillermo O'Donnell, and J. Samuel Valenzuela (Notre Dame: University of Notre Dame Press, 1992), 1–16.

3. Theodore J. Lowi, ''The State in Political Science: How We Become What We Study,'' *American Political Science Review* 86, no. 1 (March 1992): 5.

4. Alexis de Tocqueville, *Democracy in America,* trans. George Lawrence, ed. J. P. Mayer (New York: Harper and Row, 1966). For further discussion of Tocqueville's work, see Jean-Claude Lamberti, *Tocqueville and the Two Democracies,* trans. Arthur Goldhammer (Cambridge: Harvard University Press, 1989). Also see James T. Schleifer, *The Making of Tocqueville's Democracy in America* (Chapel Hill, N.C.: University of North Carolina Press, 1980).

5. For these arguments, see Przeworski, *Capitalism and Social Democracy,* 171–203.

6. Adam Przeworski, ''Some Problems in the Study of Transitions to Democracy,'' in *Transitions from Authoritarian Rule: Comparative Perspectives,* ed. Guillermo O'Donnell, Philippe Schmitter, and Laurence Whitehead (Baltimore, Md.: Johns Hopkins University Press, 1986), 58–61.

7. For a valuable overview of the literature on presidentialism in Latin America, see Scott Mainwaring, ''Presidentialism in Latin America,'' *Latin American Research Review* 25, no. 1 (1990): 157–79. Also see the essays in Juan J. Linz and Arturo Valenzuela, eds., *The Failure of Presidential Democracy* (Baltimore, Md.: John Hopkins University Press, 1994).

8. For a discussion of the traditional functions of political parties, see Leon D. Epstein, *Political Parties in Western Democracies* (New York: Praeger, 1967), 289–314.

9. Ruth Berins Collier and David Collier, *Shaping the Political Arena: Critical Junctures, the Labor Movement, and Regime Dynamics in Latin America* (Princeton, N.J.: Princeton University Press, 1991), 470–83.

10. For a discussion of developments in Latin American party systems, see the essays in Scott Mainwaring and Timothy Scully, eds., *Building Democratic Institutions: Parties amd Party Systems in Latin America* (Stanford University Press, forthcoming).

11. Data on Ecuador is taken from Simón Pachano, *Los diputados: Una elite política* (Quito: Corporación Editora Nacional, 1991), 114. The data on Peru was calculated from Enrique Bernales, *Parlamento y democracia* (Lima: Instituto de Estudios Constitucionales y Sociales, 1990), 303.

12. McClintock, "Velasco, Officers, and Citizens," 275–308.

13. The definition of governance is taken from Lester M. Salamon and Alan J. Abramson, "Governance," in *The Reagan Record,* ed. John L. Palmer and Isabel Sawhill (Washington, D.C.: The Urban Institute, 1984), 32.

14. Thomas Ferguson and Joel Rogers, *Right Turn: The Decline of the Democrats and the Future of American Politics* (New York: Hill and Wang, 1986). The political mobilization of American business is described in Vogel, *Fluctuating Fortunes.* For further discussion of mobilization by corporations, see Jerome L. Himmelstein, *To the Right: The Transformation of American Conservatism* (Berkeley: University of California Press, 1990).

15. This argument is developed at great length by Thomas Byrne Edsall and Mary D. Edsall, *Chain Reaction: The Impact of Race, Rights, and Taxes on American Politics* (New York: W. W. Norton, 1991).

16. Gonzalo Sánchez de Lozada, interview, La Paz, 29 May 1988.

17. For a discussion of how linkages between the state and the private sector affect economic policy, see Peter Evans, "The State as Problem and Solution: Predation, Embedded Autonomy, and Structural Change," in *The Politics of Economic Adjustment: International Constraints, Distributive Conflicts, and the State,* ed. Stephan Haggard and Robert R. Kaufman (Princeton, N.J.: Princeton University Press, 1992), 139–81. For country cases that illustrate the central role of both formal and informal policy networks, see Haggard, *Pathways from the Periphery;* Robert Wade, *Governing the Market: Economic Theory and the Role of Government in East Asian Industrialization* (Princeton, N.J.: Princeton University Press, 1990); Peter J. Katzenstein, *Small States in World Markets.*

18. All quotations are from Tocqueville, *Democracy,* 693.

19. Recent works that discuss the malaise in American politics include William Greider, *Who Will Tell the People: The Betrayal of American Democracy* (New York: Simon and Schuster, 1992); E. J. Dionne, Jr., *Why Americans Hate Politics* (New York: Simon and Schuster, 1991); Benjamin Ginsberg and Martin Shefter, *Politics by Other Means: The Declining Importance of Elections in America* (New York: Basic Books, 1990); Robert M. Entman, *Democracy Without Citizens: Media and the Decay of American Politics* (Oxford University Press, 1989).

20. This term was coined by Arthur Schlesinger, Jr., *The Imperial Presidency* (New York: Popular Library, 1974).

21. For further elaboration on the development of the plebiscitary presidency in the United States, see Theodore J. Lowi, *The Personal President: Power Invested, Promise Unfulfilled* (Ithaca, N.Y.: Cornell University Press, 1985).

22. Lowi, "The State," 6. Also see Theodore Lowi, "Knowledge, Power, and the Congress," in *Knowledge, Power, and the Congress,* ed. William H. Robinson and H. Wellborn Clay (Washington, D.C.: Congressional Quarterly, 1991).

23. Kevin Phillips, "Down and Out: Can the Middle Class Rise Again?" *New York Times Magazine,* 10 January 1993, 20.

24. Greider, *Who Will Tell the People,* 16.

25. This point is taken from Robert Bellah et al., *Habits of the Heart: Individualism and Commitment in American Life* (Berkeley: University of California Press, 1985).

26. For a discussion of the role of secondary associations in compensating for failing political parties, see the essays in Kay Lawson and Peter Merkl, eds., *When Parties Fail: Emerging Alternative Organizations* (Princeton, N.J.: Princeton University Press, 1988).

27. See Bellah et al., *Habits of the Heart.* This dark view is part of an intellectual tradition that extends back to C. Wright Mills. See his chilling portrait of American society, *The Power Elite* (Oxford: Oxford University Press, 1956).

28. For further discussion, see Kevin Phillips, *The Politics of Rich and Poor: Wealth and the American Electorate in the Reagan Aftermath* (New York: Random House, 1990). For a discussion of the depth of racial divisions in American life, see Andrew Hacker, *Two Nations: Black and White, Separate, Hostile, Unequal* (New York: Scribner's, 1992)

29. The classic work reflecting on the connection between the development of modern professions and techniques of social control is by Michel Foucault, *Discipline and Punish: The Birth of the Prison* (New York: Pantheon Books, 1977).

30. For a discussion of this phenomenon in reference to Chile, see Garretón, "Chile: In Search of Lost Democracy," 197–216.

31. For a discussion of the various crises associated with late capitalism, see Habermas, *Legitimation Crisis,* 45–94.

32. For a discussion of contemporary social movements in Latin America, see the essays in Arturo Escobar and Sonia Alvarez, eds., *The Making of Social Movements in Latin America: Identity, Strategy, and Democracy* (Boulder, Colo.: Westview, 1992).

BIBLIOGRAPHY

Articles, Books, and Documents

Abril Ojeda, Galo. *Política monetaria y desarrollo industrial en el Ecuador (1970–1983).* Quito: Banco Central del Ecuador, Instituto de Estudios Latinoamericanos, monografía no. 11.

Abugattás, Luis. "Crisis económica y programas de estabilización en los países andinos: Una visión comparativa." Paper delivered at the Séminario sobre el Grupo Andino: Nuevos Enfoques para el Desarrollo y la Integración Subregional, September 1985. Junta del Acuerdo de Cartagena, Lima, Peru.

———. "Una década de estabilización: Perú 1975–1985." Paper delivered at the Séminario sobre el Grupo Andino: Nuevos Enfoques para el Desarrollo y la Integración Subregional, September 1985. Junta del Acuerdo de Cartagena, Lima, Peru.

"After the Cold War: Views from Latin America." *New York Times,* 30 May 1992.

Alberti, Giorgio. "Estado, clase empresarial, y comunidad industrial." In *Estado y clase: La comunidad industrial en el Perú,* ed. Giorgio Alberti et al. Lima: Instituto de Estudios Peruanos, 1977.

Alexander, Robert J. *The Bolivian National Revolution.* New Brunswick, N.J.: Rutgers University Press, 1958.

Ali Ayub, Mahmood, and Hideo Hashimoto. *The Economics of Tin Mining in Bolivia.* Washington, D.C.: World Bank, 1985.

Ames, Barry. *Political Survival: Politicians and Public Policy in Latin America.* Berkeley: University of California Press, 1987.

Anaya, Eduardo. *Los grupos de poder económico: Un análisis de la oligarquía financiera.* Lima: Editorial Horizonte, 1990.

"Apuntando al' 84." *Vistazo,* 6 August 1982.

Arauco, María Isabel. "Los trabajadores del estado y del Banco Central de Bolivia (1982–85)." In *Crisis del sindicalismo en Bolivia,* ed. FLACSO-ILDIS. La Paz: FLACSO-ILDIS, 1987.

Arboleda, María, et al. *Los placeres del poder: El segundo año del gobierno de León Febres Cordero, 1985–86*. Quito: Editorial El Conejo, 1986.

Arrieta, Mario, et al. *Agricultura en Santa Cruz: De la encomienda colonial a la empresa modernizada (1559–1985)*. La Paz: ILDIS, 1990.

Astiz, Carlos. *Pressure Groups and Power Elites in Peruvian Politics*. Ithaca, N.Y.: Cornell University Press, 1969.

Ayres, Robert L. *Banking on the Poor: The World Bank and World Poverty*. Cambridge, Mass.: MIT Press, 1984.

Baer, Werner, and John H. Welch, eds. ''The Resurgence of Inflation in Latin America.'' *World Development* 15, no. 8 (August 1987), special issue.

Banco Central del Ecuador. ''Entrevista realizada al Dr. Carlos Julio Emanuel, Quito, 26 de agosto de 1986.'' In *Política económica frente a la crisis: Discursos y entrevistas*. Volume 2. Quito: Banco Central del Ecuador, 1987.

Banco de Guayaquil, comp. *Guayaquil frente al futuro*. Guayaquil: Banco de Guayaquil, 1973.

Babbit, B. E. ''The New and Improved South America.'' *World Monitor* 4 (February 1991).

Barber, James David. *The Presidential Character*. Englewood Cliffs, N.J.: Prentice-Hall, 1985.

Barksy, Osvaldo. *La reforma agraria ecuatoriana*. Quito: Corporación Editora Nacional/FLACSO, 1984.

Baudoín, Luis F. ''Capacidad de generación de empleo de la industria manufacturera.'' In *La Industria: Problemas y perspectivas*. La Paz: ILDIS, 1990.

Becker, David. *The New Bourgeoisie and the Limits of Dependency: Mining, Class, and Power in ''Revolutionary'' Peru*. Princeton, N.J.: Princeton University Press, 1983.

———. ''Business Associations in Latin America: The Venezuelan Case.'' *Comparative Political Studies* 23, no. 1 (April 1990): 114–38.

Bellah, Robert, et al. *Habits of the Heart: Individualism and Commitment in American Life*. Berkeley: University of California Press, 1985.

Bermeo, Nancy, ed. *Liberalization and Democratization: Change in the Soviet Union and Eastern Europe*. Baltimore, Md.: Johns Hopkins University Press, 1992.

Bernales, Enrique. *Crisis política: ¿Solución electoral? Analisis de los resultados de las elecciones para la Asamblea Constituyente de 1978*. Lima: DESCO, 1980.

———. *El parlamento por dentro*. Lima: DESCO, 1984.

———. *Parlamento y democracia*. Lima: Instituto de Estudios Constitucionales y Sociales, 1990.

Bethell, Leslie, and Ian Roxborough. ''Latin America Between the Second World War and the Cold War: Some Reflections on the 1945–48 Conjuncture.'' *Journal of Latin American Studies* 20, no. 1 (May 1988): 167–89.

Bienen, Henry, and Mark Gersovitz. ''Economic Stabilization, Conditionality, and Political Stability.'' *International Organization* 39, no. 4 (Autumn 1985): 729–54.

———. ''Consumer Subsidy Cuts, Violence, and Political Stability.'' *Comparative Politics* 19, no. 1 (October 1986): 25–44.

Blanes Jiménez, José. ''Cocaine, Informality, and the Urban Economy in La Paz, Bolivia.'' In *The Informal Economy: Studies in Advanced and Less Developed Coun-*

tries, ed. Alejandro Portes et al. Baltimore, Md.: Johns Hopkins University Press, 1989.

Blanksten, George I. *Ecuador: Constitutions and Caudillos.* New York: Russell and Russell, 1964.

Bojanic, Alan. "Evaluación de la estructura agraria en el area integrada de Santa Cruz." In *Tenencia y uso de la tierra en Santa Cruz,* ed. Talleres CEDLA. La Paz: CEDLA, 1988.

Bonilla, Heraclio. "Peru and Bolivia from Independence to the War of the Pacific." In *The Cambridge History of Latin America,* vol. 3, ed. Leslie Bethell. Cambridge: Cambridge University Press, 1985.

Bourque, Susan C., and Kay B. Warren. "Democracy Without Peace: The Cultural Politics of Terror in Peru." *Latin American Research Review* 24, no. 1 (1989): 7–34.

Bromley, R. J. *Development Planning in Ecuador.* Sussex: Latin American Publications Fund, 1977.

Calla Ortega, Ricardo. "La encrucijada de la COB: Temas del movimiento obrero boliviano en la coyuntura democrática." In *Crisis, democracia, y conflicto social,* ed. Roberto Laserna. La Paz: CERES, 1985.

Cámara de Industriales de Pichincha. *Cincuenta años de la Cámara de Pichincha, 1932–86.* Quito: Cámara de Industriales de Pichincha, 1986.

Cámara de Industria y Comercio de Santa Cruz–Bolivia. *El estado empresarial 1970–1980: Fracaso de un modelo.* Santa Cruz: Cámara de Industria y Comercio de Santa Cruz–Bolivia, July 1982.

Cameron, David. "Distributional Coalitions and Other Sources of Economic Stagnation: On Olson's *Rise and Decline of Nations.*" *International Organization* 42, no. 4 (Autumn 1988): 561–604.

Campero, Luis Fernando, et al. "Costo social de la crisis y el ajuste." In *Costo social de la crisis y del ajuste,* ed. Taller de Investigaciones Socio-económicas. La Paz: ILDIS, n.d.

Canitrot, Adolfo. "Discipline as a Central Objective of Economic Policy: An Essay on the Economic Programme of the Argentine Government Since 1976," *World Development* 8, no. 11 (1980): 913–28.

Caravedo Molinari, Baltazar. *Burguesía e industria en el Peru (1933–1945).* Lima: Instituto de Estudios Peruanos, 1976.

Carbo, Luis Alberto. *Historia monetaria y cambiaria del Ecuador.* Quito: Banco Central del Ecuador, 1978.

Cariaga, Juan L. "Bolivia." In *Latin American Adjustment: How Much Has Happened?* ed. John Williamson. Washington, D.C.: Institute for International Economics, 1990.

———. "How Stabilization Was Achieved in Bolivia." In *Bolivia After Hyperinflation,* ed. J. R. Ladman and Juan Antonio Morales. Tempe, Arizona: Center for L.A. Studies, Arizona State University, forthcoming.

Carmagnani, Marcello. *Estado y sociedad en América Latina, 1850–1930.* Barcelona: Editorial Crítica, 1984.

Carnoy, Martin. *The State in Political Theory.* Princeton, N.J.: Princeton University Press, 1984.

Carranza Fernández, Gontrán. *El proceso histórico de la planificación*. La Paz: Editorial de la Universidad Mayor de San Andrés, n.d.

Carrasco Veintimilla, Adrián. ''Los límites del reformismo: La política económica de Roldós-Hurtado y Hurtado-Roldós.'' In *El estado y la economía: Políticas económicas y clases sociales en el Ecuador y América Latina,* ed. Luis Pacheco. Quito: Instituto de Investigaciones Económicas, Pontificia Universidad Católica del Ecuador, 1983.

Cavarozzi, Marcelo. ''Elementos para una caracterización del capitalismo oligárquico.'' Documento CEDES/G.E. CLACSO no. 12. CEDES, 1979.

———. ''Beyond Transitions to Democracy in Latin America.'' *Journal of Latin American Studies* 24, no. 3 (October 1992): 665–84.

CEDATOS. ''Estudios y datos de la realidad ecuatoriana, 1979–84.'' Photocopy.

Centro de Estudios y Difusión Social (CEDIS). *Cronología: Hechos políticos, sociales, y económicos en el gobierno de Osvaldo Hurtado*. Quito: CEDIS, 1984.

———. *La política económica del gobierno de Febres Cordero*. Quito: CEDIS, 1986.

Chiriboga, Manuel. ''Política agropecuaria: La búsqueda del imperio del mercado.'' In *Los placeres del poder: El segundo año del gobierno de León Febres Cordero, 1985–86,* ed. María Arboleda et al., 166–80. Quito: Editorial El Conejo, 1986.

Chuquimia, Víctor, and Emilio Tórrez. ''Productividad y competividad de la pequeña y mediana industria.'' In *La Industria: Problemas y perspectivas*. La Paz: ILDIS, 1990.

Cleaves, Peter S., and Henry Pease García. ''State Autonomy and Military Policymaking.'' In *The Peruvian Experiment Reconsidered,* ed. Cynthia McClintock and Abraham F. Lowenthal. Princeton, N.J.: Princeton University Press, 1983.

Cleaves, Peter S., and Martin J. Scurrah. *Agriculture, Bureaucracy, and Military Government in Peru*. Ithaca, N.Y.: Cornell University Press, 1980.

Collier, David, ed. *The New Authoritarianism in Latin America*. Princeton, N.J.: Princeton University Press, 1979.

Collier, Ruth Berins, and David Collier. *Shaping the Political Arena: Critical Junctures, the Labor Movement, and Regime Dynamics in Latin America*. Princeton, N.J.: Princeton University Press, 1991.

Conaghan, Catherine M. ''Party Politics and Democratization in Ecuador.'' In *Authoritarians and Democrats: Regime Transition in Latin America,* ed. James M. Malloy and Mitchell Seligson. Pittsburgh, Pa.: University of Pittsburgh Press, 1986.

———. *Restructuring Domination: Industrialists and the State in Ecuador*. Pittsburgh, Pa.: University of Pittsburgh Press, 1988.

———. ''Reconsidering Jeffrey Sachs and the Bolivian Economic Experiment.'' In *Money Doctors, Foreign Debt, and Economic Reform in Latin America, 1890s–1990s* (Wilmington, Del.: Scholarly Resources, 1994).

Conaghan, Catherine, and Rosario Espinal. ''Unlikely Transitions to Uncertain Regimes? Democracy Without Compromise in the Dominican Republic and Ecuador.'' *Journal of Latin American Studies* 22 (October 1990): 553–74.

Conaghan, Catherine, James M. Malloy, and Luis A. Abugattás. ''Business and the 'Boys': The Politics of Neoliberalism in the Central Andes.'' *Latin American Research Review* 25, no. 2 (1990): 3–30.

Confederación de Empresarios Privados de Bolivia (CEPB). *Pensamiento de la empresa privada.* La Paz: CEPB, 1981.

———. *Pensamiento y acción de la empresa privada, 1982–1985.* La Paz: CEPB, 1985.

Constitución política del Perú. Lima: Editorial S.A., 1980.

Contreras, Manuel E., and Mario Napoleon Pacheco. *Medio siglo de minería mediana en Bolivia, 1939–1989.* La Paz: Biblioteca Minera Boliviana, 1989.

Corbo, Vittorio, and Jaime de Melo. "Lessons from the Southern Cone and Policy Reforms." *World Bank Research Observer* 2, no. 2 (July 1987): 111–42.

———, ed. "Liberalization with Stabilization in the Southern Cone of Latin America." *World Development* 13, no.8 (August 1985), special issue.

Corporación de Estudios para el Desarrollo (CORDES), comp. *Democracia y crisis: Diálogos del Presidente Osvaldo Hurtado con la prensa, 1981–1984.* Vol. B. Quito: CORDES, 1984.

Cotler, Julio. "A Structural-Historical Approach to the Breakdown of Democratic Institutions: Peru." In *The Breakdown of Democratic Regimes: Latin America,* ed. Juan J. Linz and Alfred Stepan. Baltimore, Md.: Johns Hopkins University Press, 1978.

———. *Clases, estado, y nación en el Perú.* Lima: Instituto de Estudios Peruanos, 1978.

———. "Military Interventions and the 'Transfer of Power to Civilians' in Peru." In *Transitions from Authoritarian Rule: Latin America,* ed. Guillermo O'Donnell, Philippe Schmitter, and Laurence Whitehead. Baltimore, Md.: Johns Hopkins University Press, 1986.

Cronin, Thomas. *The State of the Presidency.* Boston: Little, Brown, 1980.

Crozier, Michel, Samuel Huntington, and Joji Watanaki. *The Crisis of Democracy: Report on the Governability of Democracies to the Trilateral Commission.* New York: New York University Press, 1975.

Cuddington, John T. "Capital Flight: Estimates, Issues, and Explanations." *Princeton Studies in International Finance,* no. 58, December 1986.

Cueva, Agustín. *El proceso de dominación política en el Ecuador.* Quito: Ediciones Solitierra, n.d.

Degregori, Carlos Iván. *El surgimiento de Sendero Luminoso.* Lima: Instituto de Estudios Peruanos, 1990.

De Franco, Mario, and Richard Godoy. "The Economic Consequences of Cocaine Production in Bolivia: Historical, Local, and Macroeconomic Perspectives." *Journal of Latin American Studies* 24, no. 2 (May 1992): 375–406.

De Onis, Juan, and Jerome Levinson. *The Alliance That Lost Its Way.* Chicago: Quadrangle Books, 1970.

Devlin, Robert. *Debt and Crisis in Latin America: The Supply Side of the Story.* Princeton, N.J.: Princeton University Press, 1989.

Dionne, E. J, Jr. *Why Americans Hate Politics.* New York: Simon and Schuster, 1991.

di Tella, Guido. "Rents, Quasi-Rents, Normal Profits, and Growth: Argentina and the Areas of Recent Settlement." In *Argentina, Australia, and Canada: Studies in Comparative Development, 1870–1965,* ed. D. C. M. Platt and Guido di Tella. London: Macmillan, 1985.

Diz, Adolfo C. "Economic Performance Under Three Stand-By Arrangements: Peru,

1977–80.'' In *IMF Conditionality,* ed. John Williamson. Washington. D.C.: Institute for International Economics, 1983.

Doria Medina, Samuel. *La quimera de la reactivación: Balance y perspectiva de la economía boliviana.* La Paz: Edobol, 1987.

Dornbusch, Rudiger, and Sebastian Edwards, eds. *The Macroeconomics of Populism in Latin America.* Chicago: National Bureau of Economic Research, University of Chicago Press, 1991.

Drake, Paul W. ''Debt and Democracy in Latin America, 1920s–1980s.'' In *Debt and Democracy in Latin America,* ed. Barbara Stallings and Robert Kaufman. Boulder, Colo.: Westview, 1989.

———. *The Money Doctor in the Andes: The Kemmerer Missions, 1923–33.* Durham, N.C.: Duke University Press, 1989.

Dunkerley, James. *Rebellion in the Veins: Political Struggle in Bolivia, 1952–82.* London: Verso, 1984.

Durand, J. Francisco. *Los industriales, el liberalismo, y la democracia.* Lima: Fundación Friedrich Ebert, DESCO, 1984.

———. ''Mario Vargas Llosa y la nueva derecha peruana.'' Paper presented to the Fifteenth Congress of the Latin American Studies Association, 4–6 December 1989, Miami, Florida.

———. ''The National Bourgeoisie and the Peruvian State: Coalition and Conflict in the 1980s.'' Ph.D. diss., University of California, Berkeley, 1990.

Eaton, Jonathan. ''Public Debt Guarantees and Private Capital Flight.'' *World Bank Economic Review* 1, no. 3 (May 1987): 377–95.

Eckstein, Susan, and Frances Hagopian. ''The Limits of Industrialization in the Less Developed World: Bolivia.'' *Economic Development and Cultural Change* 32, no. 1 (October 1983): 81–82.

Economist Intelligence Unit. *Bolivia: County Report 1991–92.* London: Business International Limited, 1991.

Edér, George Jackson. *Inflation and Development in Latin America: A Case History of Inflation and Stabilization in Bolivia.* Ann Arbor: Bureau of Business Research, Graduate School of Business Administration, University of Michigan, 1968.

Edsall, Thomas Byrne, and Mary D. Edsall. *Chain Reaction: The Impact of Race, Rights, and Taxes on American Politics.* New York: W. W. Norton, 1991.

Edwards, Sebastian, and Alejandra Cox Edwards. *Monetarism and Liberalization: The Chilean Experiment.* Cambridge, Mass.: Ballinger, 1987.

Entman, Robert M. *Democracy Without Citizens: Media and the Decay of American Politics.* Oxford University Press, 1989.

Epstein, Edward C. ''What Difference Does Regime Type Make? Economic Austerity Programs in Argentina.'' In *Paying the Costs of Austerity in Latin America,* ed. Howard Handelman and Werner Baer. Boulder, Colo.: Westview, 1989.

Epstein, Leon D. *Political Parties in Western Democracies.* New York: Praeger, 1967.

Escobar, Arturo, and Sonia Alvarez, eds. *The Making of Social Movements in Latin America: Identity, Strategy, and Democracy.* Boulder, Colo.: Westview, 1992.

Evans, Peter B. ''The State as Problem and Solution: Predation, Embedded Autonomy, and Structural Change.'' In *The Politics of Economic Adjustment: International*

Constraints, Distributive Conflicts, and the State, ed. Stephan Haggard and Robert R. Kaufman. Princeton, N.J.: Princeton University Press, 1992.

Evans, Peter B., Dietrich Rueschemeyer, and Theda Skocpol, eds. *Bringing the State Back In.* Cambridge: Cambridge University Press, 1985.

''Exposición del presidente de la CEPB Licenciado Carlos Iturralde con motivo del XVII aniversario de la Federación de Empresarios Privados de Cochabamba.'' CEPB, 29 August 1986. Photocopy.

''Febres Cordero: La gente dice que mi imagen ha crecido.'' *Impacto* 44 (1983).

Febres Cordero, León. ''Guayaquil frente al futuro en el campo desarrollo industrial.'' In *Guayaquil frente al futuro,* comp. Banco de Guayaquil. Guayaquil: Banco de Guayaquil, 1973.

Felix, David. ''Income Distribution and the Quality of Life in Latin America: Patterns, Trends, and Policy Implications.'' *Latin American Research Review* 18, no. 2 (1983): 3–33.

Ferguson, Thomas. ''From Normalcy to the New Deal: Industrial Structure, Party Competition, and American Public Policy in the Great Depression.'' *International Organization* 38, no. 1 (Winter 1984): 41–94.

Ferguson, Thomas, and Joel Rogers. *Right Turn: The Decline of the Democrats and the Future of American Politics.* New York: Hill and Wang, 1986.

Fernandes, Florestan. *Reflections on the Brazilian Counter-Revolution: Essays by Florestan Fernandes.* Edited by Warren Dean, translated by Michel Vale and Patrick M. Hughes. Armonk, N.Y.: M. E. Sharpe 1981.

Fernández Moscoso, Miguel. ''La empresa privada y la reactivación: Apuntes para el debate.'' In *El rol de la empresa privada en el desarrollo,* ed. Taller de Investigaciones Socio-económicos (La Paz: Instituto de Investigaciones Sociales, n.d.).

Ferner, Anthony. *La burguesía industrial en el desarrollo peruano.* Lima: Editorial Esan, 1982.

Ferrand Inurritegui, Alfredo, and Arturo Salazar Larraín. *La década perdida.* Lima: Sociedad de Industrias, 1980.

Fierro Carrión, Luis. *Los grupos financieros en el Ecuador.* Quito: Centro de Educación Popular, 1991.

Figueroa, Alfredo, and Richard Weisskoff, ''Viewing Social Pyramids: Income Distribution in Latin America.'' In *Consumption and Income Distribution in Latin America,* ed. Robert Ferber. Washington, D.C.: Organization of American States, 1980.

Finegold, Kenneth, and Theda Skocpol. ''State, Party, and Industry: From Business Recovery to the Wagner Act in America's New Deal.'' In *Statemaking and Social Movements,* ed. Charles Bright and Susan Harding. Ann Arbor: University of Michigan Press, 1984.

Fitch, John S. *The Military Coup d'Etat as a Political Process: Ecuador 1948–1966.* Baltimore, Md.: Johns Hopkins University Press, 1977.

Fitzgerald, E. V. K. *The Political Economy of Peru 1956–78: Economic Development and the Restructuring of Capital.* Cambridge: Cambridge University Press, 1979.

FLACSO (Facultad Latinoamericana de Ciencias Sociales), ed. *Elecciones en el Ecuador, 1979–1980.* Quito: Editorial Oveja Negra, n.d.

FLACSO–ILDIS. *Empresas Públicas.* La Paz: FLACSO–ILDIS, 1986.

———. *Crisis del sindicalismo en Bolivia.* La Paz: FLACSO–ILDIS, 1987.

Fondo Social de Emergencia (FSE). ''Estadísticas básicas.'' La Paz, 18 April 1988. Photocopy.

Foucault, Michel. *Discipline and Punish: The Birth of the Prison.* New York: Pantheon Books, 1977.

Foxley, Alejandro. *Latin American Experiments in Neoconservative Economics.* Berkeley: University of California Press, 1983.

Foxley, Alejandro, Michael MacPherson, and Guillermo O'Donnell, eds. *Development, Democracy, and the Art of Trespassing: Essays in Honor of Albert O. Hirschman.* Notre Dame: University of Notre Dame Press, 1986.

Franco, Carlos, ed. *El Perú de Velasco.* 3 volumes. Lima: Centro de Estudios para el Desarrollo y la Participación, 1986.

Frieden, Jeffry A. ''Classes, Sectors, and the Foreign Debt in Latin America.'' *Comparative Politics* 21, no. 1 (October 1988): 1–20.

———. *Debt, Development, and Democracy: Modern Political Economy and Latin America.* Princeton, N.J.: Princeton University Press, 1991.

Fukuyama, Francis. ''The End of History?'' *National Interest* (Summer 1989): 3–18.

Gallo, Carmenza. *Taxes and State Power: Political Instability in Bolivia, 1900–1950.* Philadelphia, Pa.: Temple University Press, 1991.

Gamarra, Eduardo. ''Between Constitutional and Traditional Coups: The Bolivian Elections of 1985.'' Florida International University, 1985. Photocopy.

———. ''Political Stability, Democratization, and the Bolivian National Congress.'' Ph.D. diss., University of Pittsburgh, 1987.

———. ''Bolivia.'' In *Latin American and Caribbean Contemporary Record, 1987–1988,* vol. 7, ed. James M. Malloy and Eduardo A. Gamarra. New York: Holmes and Meier, 1990.

———. ''Market-Oriented Reforms and Democratization in Bolivia.'' In *A Precarious Balance: Democratic Consolidation and Economic Reform in Latin America and Eastern Europe,* ed. Joan Nelson and Marcelo Cavarozzi, 21–196. Washington, D.C.: International Center for Economic Growth, 1994.

García Belaúnde, Víctor Andrés. *Los ministros de Belaúnde, 1963–68, 1980–85.* Lima: Editorial Minerva, 1988.

García-Rodríguez, Enrique. ''Structural Change and Development Policy in Bolivia.'' In *Modern-Day Bolivia: Legacy of the Revolution and Prospects for the Future,* ed. Jerry R. Ladman. Tempe: Center for Latin American Studies, Arizona State University Press, 1982.

Garretón, Manuel Antonio. ''Chile: In Search of Lost Democracy.'' In *Latin American Political Economy: Financial Crisis and Political Change,* ed. Jonathan Hartlyn and Samuel A. Morley (Boulder, Colo.: Westview, 1986): 197–216.

Gautsi, Laura. ''The Peruvian Military Government and International Corporations.'' In *The Peruvian Experiment Reconsidered,* ed. Cynthia McClintock and Abraham F. Lowenthal. Princeton, N.J.: Princeton University Press, 1983.

Gelb, Alan, and Associates, eds. *Oil Windfalls: Blessing or Curse?* New York: Oxford University Press, published for the World Bank, 1988.

Gereffi, Gary, and Donald Wyman, eds. *Manufacturing Miracles: Paths of Industrializa-*

tion in Latin America and East Asia. Princeton, N.J.: Princeton University Press, 1990.

Gerschenkron, Alexander. *Economic Backwardness in Historical Perspective*. Cambridge, Mass.: Harvard University Press, 1962.

Gilbert, Dennis. *The Oligarchy and the Old Regime in Peru*. Ithaca, N.Y.: Latin American Program Dissertation Series, Cornell University, 1977.

Gillis, Malcolm. "The Structure of Bolivian Mining Taxes." In *Taxation and Mining: Nonfuel Minerals in Bolivia and Other Countries,* ed. Malcolm Gillis. Cambridge, Mass.: Ballinger, 1978.

Ginsberg, Benjamin, and Martin Shefter. *Politics by Other Means: The Declining Importance of Elections in America*. New York: Basic Books, 1990.

Goldethorpe, John. "Problems of Political Economy After the Postwar Period." In *Changing Boundaries of the Political: Essays on the Evolving Balance Between the State and Society, Public and Private in Europe,* ed. Charles Maier. Cambridge: Cambridge University Press, 1987.

Gonzales, Michael J. "Planters and Politics in Peru, 1895–1919." *Journal of Latin American Studies* 23, no. 3 (October 1991): 515–41.

Gootenberg, Paul. "Beleaguered Liberals: The Failed First Generation of Free Traders in Bolivia." In *Guiding the Invisible Hand: Economic Liberalism and the State in Latin American History,* ed. Joseph L. Love and Nils Jacobsen. New York: Praeger, 1988.

———. *Between Silver and Guano: Commercial Policy and the State in Postindependence Peru*. Princeton, N.J.: Princeton University Press, 1989.

Gorriti, Gustavo. "Democracia, narcotráfico, y la insurrección de Sendero Luminoso." In *Democracia, sociedad, y gobierno en el Perú,* ed. Luis Pásara and Jorge Parodi. Lima: CEDYS, 1988.

Gourevitch, Peter. *Politics in Hard Times: Comparative Responses to International Economic Crises*. Ithaca, N.Y.: Cornell University Press, 1986.

———. "Keynesian Politics: The Political Sources of Economic Policy Choices." In *The Political Power of Economic Ideas: Keynesianism Across Nations,* ed. Peter Hall. Princeton, N.J.: Princeton University Press, 1989.

Graham, Carol. "The Politics of Protecting the Poor During Adjustment: Bolivia's Emergency Social Fund." *World Development* 20, no. 9 (1992): 1233–51.

Greaves, Thomas, and W. Culver, eds. *Miners and Mining in the Americas*. Manchester: Manchester University Press, 1985.

Grebe López, Horst. "Innovaciones de las políticas económico-sociales en la Bolivia postdictatorial." Documento de trabajo no. 17, Programa FLASCO–Bolivia, La Paz, 1988.

Grebe López, Ronald, et al. *¿Qué ofrecen los candidatos? Elecciones 1985*. La Paz: Educación Radiofónica de Bolivia, 1985.

Greider, William. *Who Will Tell the People: The Betrayal of American Democracy*. New York: Simon and Schuster, 1992.

Grupo de Estudios Andrés Ibáñez. *Tierra, estructura productiva, y poder en Santa Cruz*. La Paz: Universidad Boliviana, 1983.

Guerrero, Andrés. *Los oligarcas del cacao*. Quito: Editorial El Conejo, 1980.

Habermas, Jürgen. *Legitimation Crisis*. Translated by Thomas McCarthy. Boston: Beacon Press, 1975.

Hacker, Andrew. *Two Nations: Black and White, Separate, Hostile, Unequal*. New York: Scribener's, 1992.

Haggard, Stephan. "The Politics of Adjustment: Lessons from the IMF's Extended Fund Facility." In *The Politics of International Debt,* ed. Miles Kahler. Ithaca, N.Y.: Cornell University Press, 1986.

———. *Pathways from the Periphery: The Politics of Growth in Newly Industrializing Countries*. Ithaca, N.Y.: Cornell University Press, 1990.

Haggard, Stephan, and Robert Kaufman. "Economic Adjustment and the Prospects for Democracy." In *The Politics of Economic Adjustment: International Constraints, Distributive Conflicts, and the State,* ed. Stephan Haggard and Robert R. Kaufman. Princeton, N.J.: Princeton University Press, 1992.

Hall, Peter A. "Policy Innovation and the Structure of the State: The Politics-Administration Nexus in France and Britain." In *Annals of the American Academy of Political and Social Science* 466 (March 1983): 43–59.

———. *Governing the Economy*. Cambridge, Mass.: Harvard University Press, 1986.

———. "Economic Planning and the State: The Evolution of Economic Challenge and Political Response." In *Political Power and Social Theory,* vol. 3, ed. G. Esping-Anderson and R. Friedland. Greenwich, Conn.: Jai Press, 1987.

———, ed. *The Political Power of Economic Ideas: Keynesianism Across Nations*. Princeton, N.J.: Princeton University Press, 1989.

Handelman, Howard, and Thomas Sanders, eds. *Military Government and the Movement Toward Democracy in South America*. Bloomington: Indiana University Press, 1981.

Hargrove, C. Erwin, and Samuel A. Morley. *The President and the Council of Economic Advisors: Interviews with CES Chairmen*. Boulder, Colo.: Westview, 1984.

Hartlyn, Jonathan, and Samuel A. Morley, eds. *Latin American Political Economy: Financial Crisis and Political Change*. Boulder, Colo.: Westview, 1986.

Held, David. *Models of Democracy*. Cambridge: Polity Press, 1987.

Hillman, John. "The Emergence of the Tin Industry in Bolivia." In *Journal of Latin American Studies* 16, no. 2 (November 1984): 403–37.

Himmelstein, Jerome L. *To the Right: The Transformation of American Conservatism*. Berkeley: University of California Press, 1990.

Hirschman, Albert O. *Exit, Voice, and Loyalty: Responses to Decline in Firms, Organizations, and States*. Cambridge, Mass.: Harvard University Press, 1970.

———. *Shifting Involvements: Private Interests and Public Action*. Princeton, N.J.: Princeton University Press, 1979.

Hurtado, Osvaldo. *Political Power in Ecuador*. Translated by Nick D. Mills. Albuquerque: University of New Mexico Press, 1980.

———. *El voto del no: Crónica de un plebiscito*. Quito: FESO, 1986.

———. *La dictadura civil*. Quito: FESO, 1988.

———. *Política democrática II: Testimonios: 1964–1989*. Quito: FESO, Corporación Editora Nacional, 1990.

Iglesias, Enrique. ''Development and Equity: The Challenge of the 1980s,'' *CEPAL Review* 15 (December 1981): 7–46.

Iguíñiz, Javier, and Noemí Montes. *Proyecto nacional: Empresarios y crisis, 1970–1987.* Lima: DESCO, 1990.

Ikenberry, John G. ''The Irony of State Strength: Comparative Responses to the Oil Shocks in the 1970s.'' *International Organization* 40, no. 1 (Winter 1986): 105–37.

———. ''Conclusion: An Institutional Approach to American Foreign Economic Policy,'' *International Organization* 42, no. 1 (Winter 1988): 219–43.

''Informe anual presentado por el Presidente de la Cámara de Industrias de Guayaquil.'' *Revista de la Cámara de Industrias de Guayaquil* 9, no. 38 (1978).

Instituto de Investigaciones Económicas y Políticas. *El capitalismo ecuatoriano: Su funcionamiento.* Guayaquil: Facultad de Ciencias Económicas, n.d.

Instituto Libertad y Democracia (ILD). *Democracia e economía de mercado: Ponencias y debates de un simposio.* Lima: ILD, n.d.

Instituto Nacional de Planificación. *Plan nacional de desarrollo 1971–75: Plan global.* Lima: Instituto Nacional de Planificación, 1971.

Instituto Peruano de Administración de Empresas (IPAE). *CADE 79: Anales de la XVIII Conferencia Anual de Ejecutivos, 1979.* Lima: IPAE, 1979.

Irvin, George. *Planning Investment in Bolivia: The Changing Role of the Public Sector.* The Hague: Institute of Social Studies, Research Report Series no. 6, 1979.

Jameson, Kenneth. ''Dollarization and Dedollarization in Bolivia.'' Unpublished paper, Department of Economics, University of Notre Dame, Notre Dame, Indiana, 1986. Photocopy.

Jaworski, Helan. ''Democracia y socialización en los medios de comunicación.'' In *El Perú de Velasco,* vol. 3., ed. Carlos Franco. Lima: Centro de Estudios para el Desarrollo y la Participación, 1983.

Jessop, Bob. ''Capitalism and Democracy: The Best Possible Political Shell?'' In *States and Societies,* ed. David Held et al. New York: New York University Press, 1983.

Junta Nacional de Planificación y Coordinación Económica (JUNAPLA). *Bases y directivas para programar el desarrollo económico del Ecuador.* Quito: JUNAPLA, 1958.

———. *Plan integral de transformación y desarrollo 1973–77: Resumen general.* Quito: JUNAPLA, n.d.

Kahler, Miles. ''Orthodoxy and Its Alternatives: Explaining Approaches to Stabilization and Adjustment.'' In *Economic Crisis and Policy Choice: The Politics of Adjustment in the Third World,* ed. Joan Nelson. Princeton, N.J.: Princeton University Press, 1990.

Karl, Terry L. ''Petroleum and Political Pacts: The Transition to Democracy in Venezuela,'' in *Transitions from Authoritarian Rule: Latin America,* ed. Guillermo O'Donnell, Philippe Schmitter, and Laurence Whitehead. Baltimore, Md.: Johns Hopkins University Press, 1986.

———. ''Dilemmas of Democratization in Latin America.'' In *Comparative Politics* 23, no. 1 (October 1990): 1–21.

Katzenstein, Peter J. ''Conclusion: Domestic Structures and Strategies of Foreign Economic Policy.'' In *Between Power and Plenty: Foreign Economic Policies of Advanced Industrial States,* ed. Peter J. Katzenstein. Madison: University of Wisconsin Press, 1978.

———. *Corporatism and Change: Austria, Switzerland, and the Politics of Industry.* Ithaca, N.Y.: Cornell University Press, 1984.

———. *Small States in World Markets: Industrial Policy in Europe.* Ithaca, N.Y.: Cornell University Press, 1985.

Kaufman, Robert. ''Democratic and Authoritarian Responses to the Debt Issue: Argentina, Brazil, Mexico.'' In *The Politics of International Debt,* ed. Miles Kahler. Ithaca, N.Y.: Cornell University Press, 1986.

———. ''Economic Orthodoxy and Political Change in Mexico: The Stabilization and Adjustment Policies of the de la Madrid Administration.'' In *Debt and Democracy in Latin America,* ed. Robert Kaufman and Barbara Stallings. Boulder, Colo.: Westview, 1989.

Keech, William R., Robert H. Bates, and Peter Lange. ''Political Economy Within Nations.'' In *Political Science: Looking to the Future,* ed. William Crotty. Evanston, Il.: Northwestern University Press, 1991.

Kellerman, Barbara. *The Political Presidency: Practice of Leadership.* New York: Oxford University Press, 1984.

Kelley, Jonathan, and Herbert S. Klein. *Revolution and the Rebirth of Inequality: A Theory Applied to the National Revolution in Bolivia.* Berkeley: University of California Press, 1981.

Kennedy, Paul. ''Preparing for the Twenty-First Century: Winners and Losers.'' *New York Review of Books* 40, no. 4 (11 February 1993): 36.

Kertzer, David I. *Ritual, Politics, and Power.* New Haven, Conn.: Yale University Press, 1988.

Klaren, Peter E. ''The Origins of Modern Peru, 1880–1930.'' In *The Cambridge History of Latin America,* vol. 5, ed. Leslie Bethell. Cambridge: Cambridge University Press, 1986.

Klein, Herbert S. *Parties and Political Change in Bolivia, 1880–1952.* Cambridge: Cambridge University Press, 1969.

———. *Bolivia: The Evolution of a Multi-Ethnic Society.* New York: Oxford University Press, 1982.

———. ''Bolivia from the War of the Pacific to the Chaco War, 1880–1932.'' In *The Cambridge History of Latin America,* vol. 5, ed. Leslie Bethell. Cambridge: Cambridge University Press, 1986.

Knight, Peter T. ''New Forms of Economic Organization in Peru: Toward Workers' Self-Management.'' In *The Peruvian Experiment Reconsidered,* ed. Cynthia McClintock and Abraham F. Lowenthal. Princeton, N.J.: Princeton University Press, 1983.

Kuczynski, Pedro Pablo. *Peruvian Democracy Under Economic Stress: An Account of the Belaúnde Administration, 1963–1968.* Princeton, N.J.: Princeton University Press, 1977.

Ladman, Jerry R. ''The Political Economy of the 'Economic Miracle' of the Banzer Regime.'' In *Modern-Day Bolivia: Legacy of the Revolution and Prospects for the*

Future, ed. Jerry R. Ladman. Tempe: Center for Latin American Studies, Arizona State University Press, 1982.

Ladman, Jerry R., and Ronald L. Tennermeir. "The Political Economy of Agricultural Credit: The Case of Bolivia." In *American Journal of Agricultural Economics* 63 (February 1981): 66–72.

Lamberti, Jean-Claude. *Tocqueville and the Two Democracies.* Translated by Arthur Goldhammer. Cambridge: Harvard University Press, 1989.

Langer, Erik D. "Andean Banditry and Peasant Communal Organization, 1882–1930." In *Bandidos,* ed. Richard Slatta. Westport, Conn.: Greenwood Press, 1987.

———. *Economic Change and Rural Resistance in Southern Bolivia, 1880–1930.* Stanford: Stanford University Press, 1989.

Larrea, Carlos, ed. *El banano en el Ecuador: Transnacionales, modernización, y subdesarrollo.* Quito: Corporación Editora Nacional, 1987.

———. "The Mirage of Development: Oil, Employment, and Poverty in Ecuador." Ph.D. diss., York University, 1992.

Larson, Magali Sarfatti, and Alma E. Bergman. *Social Stratification in Peru.* Berkeley: Institute of International Studies, University of California, 1969.

Laserna, Roberto. "La insurrección de la democracia." In *La acción colectiva en Bolivia: 1982–1985,* ed. Roberto Laserna. Cochabamba: CERES, 1985.

———. "Democratization and the New Dependency: A View from Bolivia." Paper presented to the Fifteenth Congress of the Latin American Studies Association, 4–6 December 1989, Miami, Florida.

———, ed. *Crisis, democracia, y conflicto social: La acción colectiva en Bolivia: 1982–85.* Cochabamba: CERES, 1985.

"Latin America: The Big Move to Free Markets." *Business Week,* 15 June 1992.

Lawson, Kay, and Peter Merkl, eds. *When Parties Fail: Emerging Alternative Organizations.* Princeton, N.J.: Princeton University Press, 1988.

Lazarte, Jorge. *Movimiento obrero y procesos políticos en Bolivia: Historia de la COB, 1952–1987.* La Paz: ILDIS, 1988.

Leff, Nathaniel. "Industrial Organization and Entrepreneurship in Developing Countries: The Economic Groups." In *Economic Development and Cultural Change* 26, no. 4 (July 1978): 661–75.

León, Jorge, and Juan Pablo Pérez Sáinz. "Crisis y movimiento sindical en Ecuador: Las huelgas nacionales del FUT (1981–1983)." In *Movimientos sociales en el Ecuador,* ed. Manuel Chiriboga et al. Quito: CLACSO, 1986.

Lessard, Donald R., and John Williamson, eds. *Capital Flight and Third World Debt.* Washington, D.C.: Institute for International Economics, 1987.

Levine, Daniel H. "Venezuela Since 1958: The Consolidation of Democratic Politics." In *The Breakdown of Democratic Regimes: Latin America,* ed. Juan J. Linz and Alfred Stepan. Baltimore, Md.: Johns Hopkins University Press, 1978.

Libro blanco de las realizaciones del gobierno de las fuerzas armadas: Bolivia, 1971–78. La Paz, 1978.

Lindblom, Charles. *Politics and Markets: The World's Political-Economic Systems.* New York: Basic Books, 1977.

———. "The Market as Prison." In *The Political Economy: Readings in the Politics and Economics of American Public Policy,* ed. Thomas Ferguson and Joel Rogers. Armonk, N.Y.: M. E. Sharpe, 1984.

Linz, Juan J., and Arturo Valenzuela, eds. *The Failure of Presidential Democracy.* Baltimore, Md.: Johns Hopkins University Press, 1994.

Lofstram, William L. "Attitudes of an Industrial Pressure Group in Latin America: The Asociación de Industriales Mineros de Bolivia, 1925–1935." M.A. thesis, Cornell University, 1968.

Lomnitz, Larissa Adler, and Marisol Pérez-Lizaur. *A Mexican Elite Family, 1820–1980.* Princeton, N.J.: Princeton University Press, 1988.

Love, Joseph L., and Nils Jacobsen, eds. *Guiding the Invisible Hand: Economic Liberalism and the State in Latin American History.* New York: Praeger, 1988.

Lowenthal, Abraham F., ed. *The Peruvian Experiment: Continuity and Change Under Military Rule.* Princeton, N.J.: Princeton University Press, 1975.

Lowi, Theodore J. *The Personal President: Power Invested, Promise Unfulfilled.* Ithaca, N.Y.: Cornell University Press, 1985.

———. "Knowledge, Power, and the Congress." In *Knowledge, Power, and the Congress,* ed. William H. Robinson and H. Wellborn Clay. Washington, D.C.: Congressional Quarterly, 1991.

———. "The State in Political Science: How We Become What We Study." *American Political Science Review* 86, no. 1 (March 1992): 1–7.

McClintock, Cynthia. *Peasant Cooperatives and Political Change in Peru.* Princeton, N.J.: Princeton University Press, 1981.

———. "Velasco, Officers, and Citizens: The Politics of Stealth." In *The Peruvian Experiment Reconsidered,* ed. Cynthia McClintock and Abraham F. Lowenthal. Princeton, N.J.: Princeton University Press, 1983.

———. "Peru's Sendero Luminoso: Origins and Trajectory." In *Power and Popular Protest: Latin American Social Movements,* ed. Susan Eckstein. Berkeley: University of California Press, 1989.

McGraw, Thomas. "Business and Government: The Origins of the Adversary Relationships." *California Management Review* (Winter 1984): 33–52.

Machicado, Flavio. *Sistema financiero y reactivación.* La Paz: ILDIS, 1989.

———. "Coca Production in Bolivia." In *Drug Policy in the Americas,* ed. Peter Smith (Boulder, Colo.: Westview, 1992).

Maier, Charles. *In Search of Stability: Explorations in Historical Political Economy.* Cambridge, Mass.: Cambridge University Press, 1987.

Mainwaring, Scott. "Presidentialism in Latin America." *Latin American Research Review* 25, no. 1 (1990): 157–79.

Mainwaring, Scott, and Timothy Scully, eds. *Building Democratic Institutions: Parties and Party Systems in Latin America.* Stanford University Press, forthcoming.

Mainwaring, Scott, Guillermo O'Donnell, and J. Samuel Valenzuela, eds. *Issues in Democratic Consolidation: The New South American Democracies in Comparative Perspective.* Notre Dame: University of Notre Dame Press, 1992.

Maldonado Posso, Manuel. "An Entrepreneur Discredited the Free Enterprise System in Ecuador." *Journal of Economic Growth,* no. 2 (November 1988): 19–28.

Mallon, Florencia E. *The Defense of the Community in Peru's Central Highlands: Peasant Struggle and Capitalist Transition, 1860–1940*. Princeton, N.J.: Princeton University Press, 1983.

———. "Indian Communities, Political Cultures, and the State in Latin America, 1780–1990." *Journal of Latin American Studies* 24 (Quincentenary supplement, 1992): 35–54.

Malloy, James M. *Bolivia: The Uncompleted Revolution*. Pittsburgh, Pa.: University of Pittsburgh Press, 1970.

Malloy, James M., and Eduardo Gamarra. *Revolution and Reaction: Bolivia 1964–1985*. New Brunswick, N.J.: Transaction, 1988.

Malloy, James M., and Richard S. Thorn, eds. *Beyond the Revolution: Bolivia Since 1952*. Pittsburgh, Pa.: University of Pittsburgh Press, 1971.

Malloy, James M., and Silvia Borzutsky. "The Praetorianization of the Revolution." In *Modern-Day Bolivia: Legacy of the Revolution and Prospects for the Future,* ed. Jerry R. Ladman. Tempe: Center for Latin American Studies, Arizona State University, 1982.

Malpica, Carlos. *El poder económico en el Perú*. Lima: Mosca Azul Editores, 1989.

Manzetti, Luigi, and Marco Dell'Aquila. "Economic Stabilization in Argentina: The Austral Plan." *Journal of Latin American Studies* 20, part 1 (May 1988): 1–26.

March, James, and Johan Olsen. "The New Institutionalism: Organizational Factors in Political Life." *American Political Science Review* 78, no. 3 (September 1984): 734–49.

Markoff, John, and Veronica Montecinos. "The Irresistible Rise of Economists." Unpublished paper, University of Pittsburgh, May 1990. Photocopy.

Marshall-Silva, Jorge. "Ecuador: Windfalls of a New Exporter." In *Oil Windfalls: Blessing or Curse?* ed. Alan Gelb and Associates. New York: Oxford University Press, published for the World Bank, 1988.

Martz, John D. *Ecuador: Conflicting Political Culture and the Quest for Progress*. Boston: Allyn and Bacon, 1972.

———. "Populist Leadership and the CFP." *Studies in Comparative International Development* 3 (Fall 1983): 22–50.

———. *Politics and Petroleum in Ecuador*. New Brunswick, N.J.: Transaction Books, 1987.

Mayorga, René A., ed. *Democracia a la deriva: Dilemas de la participación y concertación social en Bolivia*. La Paz: Ediciones CERES, 1987.

Meller, Patricio, ed. *The Latin American Development Debate: New Structuralism, Neomonetarism and Adjustment Processes*. Boulder, Colo.: Westview, 1991.

Menéndez-Carrión, Amparo. *La conquista del voto: De Velasco a Roldós*. Quito: Corporación Editora Nacional, 1986.

Migdal, Joel. *Strong Societies, Weak States: State Capacity in the Third World*. Princeton, N.J.: Princeton University Press, 1988.

Miliband, Ralph. *The State in Capitalist Society*. London: Weidenfeld and Nicolson, 1969.

———. "Reply to Nicos Poulantzas." *New Left Review* 59 (January–February 1970): 53–60.

———. "Poulantzas and the Capitalist State." *New Left Review* 82 (November–December 1973): 83–92.

Mills, C. Wright. *The Power Elite*. Oxford: Oxford University Press, 1956.

Mills, Nick D. *Crisis, conflicto, y consenso: Ecuador, 1979–1984*. Quito: Corporación Editora Nacional, 1984.

Mitchell, Christopher. *The Legacy of Populism in Bolivia: From the MNR to Military Rule*. New York: Praeger, 1977.

Moncayo, Patricio. *Ecuador: Grietas en la dominación*. Quito: Escuela de Ciencias de la Información de la Universidad Central del Ecuador, 1977.

Montero, Nely, ed. *Cronología: Hechos políticos, sociales, y económicos en el gobierno de Osvaldo Hurtado*. Quito: CEDYS, 1984.

Morales, Juan Antonio. ''Estabilización y nueva política económica en Bolivia.'' In *El Trimestre Económico* 54 (September 1987): 179–211.

———. ''Inflation Stabilization in Bolivia.'' In *Inflation Stabilization: The Experience of Israel, Argentina, Brazil, Bolivia, and Mexico,* ed. Michael Bruno et al. Cambridge, Mass.: MIT Press, 1988.

———. ''Las políticas de estabilización en Bolivia, 1982–89.'' Paper presented to the Fifteenth Congress of the Latin American Studies Association, 4–6 December 1989, Miami, Florida.

———. ''Bolivia's Post-Stabilization Problems.'' Documento de trabajo no. 08/90. Instituto de Investigaciones Socioeconómicas, Universidad Católica Boliviana, June 1990.

———. ''The Transition from Stabilization to Sustained Growth.'' In *Lessons of Economic Stabilization and Its Aftermath,* ed. Michael Bruno et al. Cambridge, Mass.: MIT, 1991.

Morales, Juan Antonio, and Jeffrey D. Sachs. ''Bolivia's Economic Crisis.'' In *Developing Country Debt and Economic Performance,* vol. 2, ed. Jeffrey D. Sachs. Chicago: University of Chicago Press, 1990.

Morner, Magnus. *The Andean Past: Land, Societies, and Conflict*. New York: Columbia University Press, 1985.

Mortimore, Michael D. ''The State and Transnational Banks: Lessons from the Bolivian Crisis of External Public Indebtedness.'' *CEPAL Review* 14 (August 1981): 143–48.

Müller y Machicado Asociados, ed. *El diálogo para la democracia*. La Paz: Müller y Machicado, 1986.

———. *Evaluación económica, 1987*. La Paz: Bolivia Dos Mil, 1987.

Musgrave, Richard A. *Fiscal Reform in Bolivia: Final Report of the Bolivian Mission on Tax Reform*. Cambridge, Mass.: International Tax Program, Harvard Law School, Harvard University, 1981.

Nash, June. ''Interpreting Social Movements: Bolivian Resistance to Economic Conditions Imposed by the IMF.'' *American Ethnologist* 19, no. 2 (May 1992): 275–93.

National Association of Medium Miners (ANMM). *Annual Report July 1977–June 1978*. La Paz: ANMM, 1978.

Navarro, Guillermo. *La concentración de capitales en el Ecuador*. Quito: Ediciones Solitierra, 1976.

Needell, Jeffrey. *A Tropical Belle Epoque: Elite Culture in Turn-of-the-Century Rio de Janeiro*. Cambridge: Cambridge University Press, 1987.

Nelson, Joan M. ''The Political Economy of Stabilization: Commitment, Capacity, and Public Response.'' In *World Development* 12, no. 10 (October 1984): 983–1006.

———. ''The Diplomacy of Policy-Based Lending.'' In *Between Two Worlds: The World Bank's Next Decade,* ed. Richard Feinberg and Valeriana Kalb. Washington, D.C.: Overseas Development Council, 1986.

———, ed. *Economic Crisis and Policy Choice: The Politics of Adjustment in the Third World.* Princeton, N.J.: Princeton University Press, 1990.

Nelson, Robert. ''The Economics Profession and the Making of Economic Policy.'' *Journal of Economic Literature* 25, no. 1 (March 1987): 49–90.

Neudstadt, Richard. *Presidential Power: The Politics of Leadership.* New York: Wiley, 1960.

Nicklesburg, Gerald. ''Inflation, Expectations, and Qualitative Government Policy in Ecuador.'' *World Development* 15, no. 8 (August 1987): 1077–85.

Novoa Peña, Alfredo. ''Acción empresarial.'' In IPAE, *CADE 79: Anales de la XVIII Conferencia Anual de Ejecutivos, 1979.* Lima: IPAE, 1979.

Núñez del Prado, Arturo. ''Bolivia: Inflación y democracia.'' *Pensamiento Iberoamericano* 9 (2d semestre, 1986): 249–76.

O'Connor, James. *The Fiscal Crisis of the State.* New York: St. Martin's Press, 1973.

O'Donnell, Guillermo. *Modernization and Bureaucratic Authoritarianism: Studies in South American Politics.* Berkeley: Institute of International Studies, University of California Press, 1973.

———. ''Corporatism and the Question of the State.'' In *Authoritarianism and Corporatism in Latin America,* ed. James Malloy. Pittsburgh, Pa.: University of Pittsburgh Press, 1977.

———. ''Reflections on the Patterns of Change in the Bureaucratic-Authoritarian State.'' *Latin American Research Review* 12, no.1 (Winter 1979): 3–38.

———. ''On the Fruitful Convergences of Hirschman's Exit, Voice, and Loyalty and Shifting Involvements: Reflections from the Recent Argentine Experience.'' In *Development, Democracy, and the Art of Trespassing: Essays in Honor of Albert O. Hirschman,* ed. Alejandro Foxley, Michael MacPherson, and Guillermo O'Donnell. Notre Dame: University of Notre Dame Press, 1986.

———. *Bureaucratic Authoritarianism: Argentina 1966–76 in Comparative Perspective.* Translated by James McGuire. Berkeley: University of California Press, 1988.

———. ''Argentina: De Novo.'' *Novos Estudos CEBRAP,* no. 24 (July 1989).

———. ''On the State, Democratization, and Some Conceptual Problems: A Latin American View with Glances at Some Postcommunist Countries.'' *World Development* 21, no. 8 (August 1989): 1355–69.

O'Donnell, Guillermo, and Philippe C. Schmitter. *Transitions from Authoritarian Rule: Tentative Conclusions About Uncertain Democracies.* Baltimore, Md.: Johns Hopkins University Press, 1986.

Olson, Mancur. *The Rise and Decline of Nations.* New Haven, Conn.: Yale University Press, 1982.

Ortiz de Zevallos, Felipe. ''Peru: An Insider's View.'' In *State Shrinking: A Comparative Inquiry into Privatization,* ed. William P. Glade. Austin: University of Texas at Austin, Institute of Latin American Studies, Office for Public Sector Studies, 1986.

———. *The Peruvian Puzzle: A Twentieth Century Fund Paper*. New York: Priority Press Publications, 1989.

Ortiz Crespo, Gonzalo. "Neoliberalismo autoritario y encrucijada social." *Economía y Desarrollo* 7, no. 9 (July 1985): 1–20.

———. *La hora del General*. Quito: Editorial El Conejo, 1986.

Ozlak, Oscar. "The Historical Formation of the State in Latin America: Some Theoretical and Methodological Guidelines for Its Study." *Latin American Research Review* 16, no. 2 (1982): 3–32.

Pachano, Abelardo. "Políticas económicas comparadas: Ecuador 1981–1987." In *Neoliberalismo y políticas económicas alternativas,* ed. CORDES. Quito: CORDES, 1987.

Pachano, Simón. *Los diputados: Una elite política*. Quito: Corporación Editora Nacional, 1991.

Paige, Jeffrey. *Agrarian Revolution: Social Movements and Export Agriculture in the Underdeveloped World*. New York: Free Press, 1975.

Palmer, David Scott, ed. *The Shining Path of Peru*. New York: St. Martin's Press, 1992.

Parodi, Carlos. "State Growth in Bolivia, Ecuador, and Peru, 1970–78." Unpublished paper, University of Pittsburgh, 1989. Photocopy.

Parodi, Jorge. "Desmovilización del sindicalismo industrial peruano en el segundo Belaundismo." In *Movimientos sociales y crisis: El caso peruano,* ed. Eduardo Ballón. Lima: DESCO, 1986.

———. *Ser obrero es algo relativo*. Lima: DESCO, 1986.

———. "Los sindicatos en la democracia vacia." *Democracia, sociedad, y gobierno en el Perú,* ed. Luis Pásara and Jorge Parodi. Lima: CEDYS, 1988.

Partido Popular Cristiano (PPC). *Programa de gobierno*. Lima, May 1980. Photocopy.

Pásara, Luis. "La libanización en democracia." In *Democracia, sociedad, y gobierno en el Perú,* ed. Luis Pásara and Jorge Parodi. Lima: CEDYS, 1988.

Pásara, Luis, and Jorge Parodi, eds. *Democracia, sociedad, y gobierno en el Perú*. Lima: CEDYS, 1988.

Pastor, Manuel, and Carol Wise. "Peruvian Economic Policy in the 1980s: From Orthodoxy to Heterodoxy and Back." *Latin American Research Review* 27, no. 2 (1992): 83–117.

Pease García, Henry. *Los caminos del poder: Tres años de crisis en la escena política*. Lima: DESCO, 1981.

Pechman, Joseph. "Making Economic Policy: The Role of the Economist." *Handbook of Political Science,* vol. 6, ed. Fred Greenstein and Nelson Polsby. Reading, Mass.: Addison-Wesley, 1975.

Peñaherrera Padilla, Blasco. *El viernes negro: Antes y después de Taura*. Quito: Editorial El Conejo, 1988.

Pérez Sáinz, Juan Pablo. *Clase obrera y democracia en el Ecuador*. Quito: Editorial El Conejo, 1985.

———. "Crisis y conflictos sociales en Ecuador: Algunas hipóteses." *Economía y Desarrollo* 8, no. 11 (noviembre 1986): 23–47.

Phillips, Kevin. *The Politics of Rich and Poor: Wealth and the American Electorate in the Reagan Aftermath*. New York: Random House, 1990.

———. ''Down and Out: Can the Middle Class Rise Again?'' *New York Times Magazine,* 10 January 1993.

Pineo, Ronn F. ''The Economic and Social Transformation of Guayaquil, Ecuador, 1870–1925.'' Ph.D. diss, University of California, Irvine, 1987.

———. ''Reinterpreting Labor Militancy: The Collapse of the Cacao Economy and the General Strike of 1922 in Guayaquil, Ecuador.'' *Hispanic American Historical Review* 68, no. 4 (November 1988): 707–36.

Pion-Berlin, David. *The Ideology of State Terror: Economic Doctrine and Political Repression in Argentina and Peru.* Boulder, Colo.: Lynne Rienner, 1989.

''Politics, Policymaking, and Democratization: Focus on the Andes.'' Working papers no. 196, Latin American Program, Woodrow Wilson Center for International Scholars, Washington, D.C.

Portes, Alejandro. ''Latin American Class Structures: Their Composition and Change During the Last Decade.'' *Latin American Research Review* 20, no. 3 (1985): 7–39.

Portocarrero, Felipe, Arlette S. Beltrán, and Alex N. Zimmerman. *Inversiones públicas en el Perú (1900–1968): Una aproximación cuantitativa.* Lima: Centro de Investigación, Universidad del Pacífico, 1988.

Portocarrero Maisch, Gonzalo. ''Empresarios, Sociedad Nacional de Industrias, y proceso político, 1950–1968.'' Informe preliminar, Departamento de Ciencias Sociales, Pontífica Universidad Católica del Perú, Lima, January 1978.

———. *De Bustamante a Odría: El fracaso del Frente Democrático Nacional, 1945–50.* Lima: Mosca Azul Editores, 1983.

Poulantzas, Nicos. *Political Power and Social Classes.* Translated by Timothy O'Hagan. London: New Left Books, 1973.

———. ''The Capitalist State: A Reply to Miliband and Laclau.'' In *New Left Review* 95 (January–February 1976): 63–83.

PREALC. *Beyond the Crisis.* Geneva: International Labour Organization, 1985.

Przeworski, Adam. *Capitalism and Social Democracy.* Cambridge: Cambridge University Press, 1985.

———. ''Some Problems in the Study of Transitions to Democracy.'' In *Transitions from Authoritarian Rule: Comparative Perspectives,* ed. Guillermo O'Donnell, Philippe Schmitter, and Laurence Whitehead. Baltimore, Md.: Johns Hopkins University Press, 1986.

———. *Democracy and the Market: Political and Economic Reforms in Eastern Europe and Latin America.* Cambridge: Cambridge University Press, 1991.

Przeworski, Adam, and Henry Teune. *The Logic of Comparative Social Inquiry.* New York: Wiley, 1969.

Quijano, Aníbal. *Nationalism and Capitalism in Peru: A Study in Neo-Imperialism.* Translated by Helen R. Lane. New York: Monthly Review Press, 1971.

Quintero, Rafael. *El mito del populismo en el Ecuador: Análisis de los fundamentos socioeconómicos del surgimiento del Velasquismo, 1895–1934.* Quito: FLACSO, 1980.

Quiroz, Alfonso S. ''Financial Leadership and the Formation of Peruvian Elite Groups, 1884–1930.'' *Journal of Latin American Studies* 20, part 1 (May 1988): 49–81.

Ramírez Soruco, Alejandra. ''Empresarialismo regional, 1985–89.'' Tesis de licenciatura,

Sociología, Facultad de Ciencias Económicas y Sociología, Universidad Mayor de San Simón, Cochabamba, 1992.

Ramos, Joseph. *Neoconservative Economics in the Southern Cone of Latin America*. Baltimore, Md.: Johns Hopkins University Press, 1986.

"Reflexión política." *Carta Industrial* 34. Cámara de Industriales de Pichincha, September 1978.

Reaño, Germán, and Enrique Vásquez. *El Grupo Romero: Del algodón a la banca*. Lima: Centro de Investigación, Universidad del Pacífico, 1988.

Reisman, David. *The Political Economy of James Buchanan*. London: Macmillan, 1990.

Remmer, Karen L. "Exclusionary Democracy," *Studies in International Comparative Development* 20, no. 4 (Winter 1985–86): 64–85.

———. "The Politics of Economic Stabilization: IMF Standby Programs in Latin America, 1954–1984." *Comparative Politics* 19, no. 1 (October 1986): 1–24.

República de Bolivia. *Plan de desarrollo económico y social, 1976–80*. La Paz, 1976.

Rivadeneira, Raúl. *Agresión política: El proceso electoral 1989*. La Paz: Librería Editorial "Juventud," 1989.

Rivera, Ramiro. *El pensamiento de León Febres Cordero*. Quito: Ediciones Culturales, 1986.

Rivera, Silvia. *'Oprimidos pero no vencidos': Lucha del campesinado aymara y quechua, 1900–1980*. La Paz: Hisbol, 1986.

Roca, José Luis. *Fisionomía del regionalismo boliviano*. La Paz: Editorial Los Amigos del Libro, 1980.

Roca, Ovidio. *Problemas y perspectivas de la industrialización en Santa Cruz*. Santa Cruz: Centro de Información y Documentación Santa Cruz, 1983.

Rodríguez, Linda Alexander. *The Search for Public Policy: Regional Politics and Government Finances in Ecuador, 1830–1940*. Berkeley: University of California Press, 1985.

Rojas Samanez, Alvaro. *Partidos políticos en el Perú: Desde 1872 a nuestros días*. 4th ed. Lima: Ediciones F & A, 1985.

Roldós Aguilera, Jaime, et al. "*¡Viva la Patria!*" Quito: Editorial El Conejo, 1981.

Roldós Aguilera, León. *El abuso del poder: Los decretos-leyes económicos urgentes aprobados por el gobierno del Ing. León Febres Cordero*. Quito: Editorial El Conejo, 1986.

Rose, Richard, and B. Guy Peters. *Can Government Go Bankrupt?* New York: Basic Books, 1978.

Rubio, Marcial, and Enrique Bernales. *Perú: Constitución y sociedad política*. Lima: DESCO, 1981.

Rueschemeyer, Dietrich, Evelyne Huber Stephens, and John D. Stephens. *Capitalist Development and Democracy*. Chicago: University of Chicago Press, 1992.

Sachs, Jeffrey D. "The Bolivian Hyperinflation and Stabilization." *American Economic Review* 77, no. 2 (1987): 279–83.

———. "Debt Overhang of Developing Countries." In *Debt, Stabilization, and Development: Essays in Memory of Carlos Díaz-Alejandro,* ed. Guillermo Calvo et al. Oxford: Basil Blackwell, 1989.

———. *Social Conflict and Populist Policies in Latin America*. San Francisco: International Center for Economic Growth, Occasional Papers Series, no. 9, 1990.

———, ed. *Developing Country Debt and the World Economy*. Chicago: National Bureau of Economic Research, University of Chicago Press, 1989.

Salamon, Lester M., and Alan J. Abramson. ''Governance.'' In *The Reagan Record,* ed. John L. Palmer and Isabel Sawhill. Washington D.C.: Urban Institute, 1984.

Salazar Bustamante, Federico. ''Mecanismos del estado.'' In *Proyecto Perú: Hacia un proyecto nacional de desarrollo a mediano y largo plazo,* vol. 2. IESS, Sociedad Nacional de Industrias, Lima, 1987.

Salgado, Germánico. ''Ecuador: Crisis and Adjustment Policies.'' *CEPAL Review* 33 (December 1987): 129–43.

Salgado, Hernán. *Instituciones políticas y constitución del Ecuador*. Quito: ILDIS, 1987.

Sanborn, Cynthia. ''El APRA en un contexto de cambio, 1968–1988.'' In *El APRA: De la ideología a la praxis,* ed. Heraclio Bonilla and Paul Drake. Lima: Editorial y Productora Gráfica ''Nuevo Mundo'' EIRL, 1989.

Sánchez Albavera, F. ''La economía social de mercado: ¿Un modelo para rearmar el capitalismo?'' *Quehacer* 2 (November–December 1979): 26–32.

Sánchez de Lozada, Gonzalo. ''La nueva política económica.'' *Foro Económico* 5 (September 1985): 6.

Schamis, Hector. ''Reconceptualizing Latin American Authoritarianism in the 1970s: From Bureaucratic-Authoritarianism to Neoconservatism.'' *Comparative Politics* 23, no. 2 (January 1991): 201–20.

Scheetz, Thomas. *Peru and the International Monetary Fund*. Pittsburgh, Pa.: University of Pittsburgh Press, 1986.

Schleifer, James T. *The Making of Tocqueville's Democracy in America*. Chapel Hill, N.C.: University of North Carolina Press, 1980.

Schlesinger, Arthur, Jr. *The Imperial Presidency*. New York: Popular Library, 1974.

Schodt, David W. ''The Ecuadorian Public Sector During the Petroleum Period: 1972–83.'' Technical Papers Series no. 52, Office for Public Sector Studies, Institute of Latin American Studies, University of Texas, Austin, 1986.

———. *Ecuador: An Andean Enigma*. Boulder, Colo.: Westview, 1987.

Schodt, Kerry. ''The Rise of Keynesian Economies in Britain, 1940–64.'' *Economy and Society* 11, no. 3 (1982): 292–316.

Schuldt, Jürgen, and Luis Abugattás. ''Neoliberalismo y democracia en el Perú, 1980–1985.'' In *Neoliberalismo y políticas económicas alternativas,* ed. CORDES. Quito: CORDES, 1987.

Schydlowsky, Daniel M. ''The Tragedy of Lost Opportunity in Peru.'' In *Latin American Political Economy: Financial Crisis and Political Change,* ed. Jonathan Hartlyn and Samuel A. Morley. Boulder, Colo.: Westview, 1986.

Schydlowsky, Daniel M., and Juan Wicht. ''The Anatomy of Economic Failure.'' In *The Peruvian Experiment Reconsidered,* ed. Cynthia McClintock and Abraham F. Lowenthal. Princeton, N.J.: Princeton University Press, 1983.

Scott, James C. *Weapons of the Weak: Everyday Forms of Peasant Resistance*. New Haven, Conn.: Yale University Press, 1985.

Scurrah, Martin. ''El estado latinoamericano y las políticas de austeridad: Perú 1980–85.'' *Apuntes* 20 (1987): 15–32.

Secretaría Nacional de Información Pública (SENDIP). *Pensamiento y obra: Gobierno constitucional del ingeniero León Febres-Cordero Ribadeneyra, 1986–87.* Quito: SENDIP, 1988.

Sheahan, John. ''Market-Oriented Economic Policies and Political Repression in Latin America.'' *Economic Development and Cultural Change* 28, no. 2 (January 1980): 267–91.

———. *Patterns of Development in Latin America: Poverty, Repression, and Economic Strategy.* Princeton, N.J.: Princeton University Press, 1987.

Sikkink, Kathryn. *Ideas and Institutions: Developmentalism in Brazil and Argentina.* Ithaca, N.Y.: Cornell University Press, 1991.

Silva Ruete, Javier. *''Yo asumí el activo y el pasivo de la Revolución.''* Lima: Centro de Documentación e Información Andina, 1981.

''Sinopsis de los lineamientos y principios del plan de gobierno de Ing. León Febres Cordero.'' Guayaquil, 1984. Photocopy.

Skocpol, Theda. ''Political Responses to Capitalist Crisis: Neo-Marxist Theories of the State and the Case of the New Deal.'' *Politics and Society* 10, no. 2 (1980): 157–201.

———. ''Bringing the State Back In: Current Research.'' In *Bringing the State Back In,* ed. Peter Evans et al. Cambridge: Cambridge University Press, 1985.

———. *Protecting Soldiers and Mothers: The Political Origins of Social Policy in the United States.* Cambridge, Mass.: Harvard University Press, 1992.

Smith, Tony. ''The Alliance for Progress: The 1960s.'' In *Exporting Democracy: The U.S. and Latin America,* ed. Abraham Lowenthal. Baltimore, Md.: Johns Hopkins University Press, 1991.

Smith, William C. ''Notes on the Political Economy of Alfonsinismo.'' Paper presented to the Fifteenth Congress of the Latin American Studies Association, 4–6 December 1989, Miami, Florida.

———. ''Democracy, Distributional Conflicts, and Macroeconomic Policymaking in Argentina, 1983–1989.'' *Journal of Inter-American Studies and World Affairs* 32, no. 2 (Summer 1990): 1–42.

Sola, Lourdes de. ''The Political Constraints to Heterodox Shocks in Brazil: Técnicos, Politicians, Democracy.'' *Journal of Latin American Studies* 23, no. 1 (February 1991): 163–95.

Soto, Hernando de. *The Other Path: The Invisible Revolution in the Third World.* Trans. June Abbott. New York: Harper & Row, 1989.

Spurrier, Walter. ''A Muscled Presidency.'' *Weekly Analysis of Ecuadorean Issues,* no. 25, 4 July 1985.

Stallings, Barbara. ''International Capitalism and the Peruvian Military Government.'' In *The Peruvian Experiment Reconsidered,* ed. Cynthia McClintock and Abraham F. Lowenthal. Princeton, N.J.: Princeton University Press, 1983.

———. *Banker to the Third World: U.S. Portfolio Investment in Latin America, 1900–1986.* Berkeley: University of California Press, 1987.

———. ''Politics and Economic Crisis: A Comparative Study of Chile, Peru, and Colombia.'' *Economic Crisis and Policy Choice: The Politics of Adjustment in the Third World,* ed. Joan Nelson. Princeton, N.J.: Princeton University Press, 1990.

Stein, Steve. *Populism in Peru: The Emergence of the Masses and the Politics of Social Control.* Madison: University of Wisconsin Press, 1980.

Stepan, Alfred. *The Military in Politics: Changing Patterns in Brazil.* Princeton, N.J.: Princeton University Press, 1971.

———. *The State and Society: Peru in Comparative Perspective.* Princeton, N.J.: Princeton University Press, 1978.

———. ''State Power and the Strength of Civil Society in the Southern Cone of Latin America.'' In *Bringing the State Back In,* ed. Peter Evans et al. Cambridge: Cambridge University Press, 1985.

Stephens, Evelyne Huber. *The Politics of Workers' Participation: The Peruvian Approach in Comparative Perspective.* New York: Academic Press, 1980.

———. ''The Peruvian Government, Labor Mobilization, and the Political Strength of the Left.'' *Latin American Research Review* 18, no. 2 (1983): 57–93.

Swett, Francisco. ''Vuelta a medias: Los vaivenes del liberalismo económico en el Ecuador, 1984–1988.'' Unpublished ms., Guayaquil, 1989. Photocopy.

Tabini, Alejandro. ''Cómo y por qué nació ADEX.'' In *Perú Exporta* 99 (June–July 1983): 4–7.

Thorn, Richard. ''The Economic Transformation.'' In *Beyond the Revolution: Bolivia Since 1952,* ed. James M. Malloy and Richard S. Thorn. Pittsburgh, Pa.: University of Pittsburgh Press, 1971.

Thorp, Rosemary. ''The Stabilisation Crisis in Peru, 1975–78.'' In *Inflation and Stabilisation in Latin America,* ed. Rosemary Thorp and Laurence Whitehead. New York: Holmes and Meier, 1979.

———. ''Peruvian Adjustment Policies, 1978–85: The Effects of Prolonged Crisis.'' In *Latin American Debt and the Adjustment Crisis,* ed. Rosemary Thorp and Laurence Whitehead. London: Macmillan, 1987.

Thorp, Rosemary, and Carlos Londoño. ''The Effect of the Great Depression on the Economies of Peru and Colombia.'' *Latin America in the 1930s: The Role of the Periphery in the World Crisis,* ed. Rosemary Thorp. New York: St. Martin's, 1984.

Thorp, Rosemary, and Geoffrey Bertram. *Peru 1890–1977: Growth and Policy in an Open Economy.* New York: Columbia University Press, 1978.

Tocqueville, Alexis de. *Democracy in America.* Translated by George Lawrence, edited by J. P. Mayer. New York: Harper and Row, 1966.

Torre, Juan Carlos. ''El gobierno de la emergencia en la transición democrática: De Alfonsín a Menem.'' Unpublished paper, Instituto Torcuato di Tella, Buenos Aires, 1990. Photocopy.

Tuesta Soldevilla, Fernando. *El parlamento en el Perú: Un perfil social y político de sus representantes.* Unpublished ms., Lima, 1986. Photocopy.

———. *Perú político en cifras: Elite política y elecciones.* Lima: Fundación Friedrich Ebert, 1987.

Ugarteche, Oscar. *El estado deudor: Economía política de la deuda: Perú y Bolivia, 1968–1984.* Lima: Instituto de Estudios Peruanos, 1986.

United Nations Economic Commission for Latin America and the Caribbean. *Economic Survey of Latin America and the Caribbean, 1978*. Santiago: United Nations, 1980.

———. *1979*. Santiago: United Nations, 1981.

———. *1980*. Santiago: United Nations, 1982.

———. *1983*. Santiago: United Nations, 1985.

———. *1984*. Santiago: United Nations, 1986.

———. *1985*. Santiago: United Nations, 1987.

———. *1986*. Santiago: United Nations, 1989.

United States Operations Mission to Bolivia. *Problems in the Economic Development of Bolivia*. La Paz: U.S. Operations Mission to Bolivia, 1956.

Useem, Bert. "The Workers' Movement and the Bolivian Revolution." *Politics and Society* 9, no. 4 (1980): 447–69.

Valenzuela, Arturo. *The Breakdown of Democratic Regimes: Chile*. Baltimore, Md.: Johns Hopkins University Press, 1978.

Varas, Augusto, and Fernando Bustamante. *Fuerzas armadas y política en Ecuador*. Quito: Ediciones Latinoamerica, 1978.

Vogel, David. "Why Businessmen Distrust Their State: The Political Consciousness of American Corporate Executives." *British Journal of Political Science* 8, no. 1 (January 1978): 169–73.

———. "The Political Power of Business in America: A Reappraisal." *British Journal of Political Science* 13 (1983): 19–43.

———. *National Styles of Regulation: Environmental Policy in Great Britain and the United States*. Ithaca, N.Y.: Cornell University Press, 1986.

———. *Fluctuating Fortunes: The Power of Business in America*. New York: Basic Books, 1989.

Vos, Rob. "Structural Change and Macro Balances in a Small Open Economy." In *Theory and Policy Design for Basic Needs: A Case Study of Ecuador,* ed. Rudolf Teekens. Aldershot: Gower Publishing, 1988.

Wade, Robert. *Governing the Market: Economic Theory and the Role of Government in East Asian Industrialization*. Princeton, N.J.: Princeton University Press, 1990.

Waisman, Carlos. *Reversal of Development in Argentina: Postwar Counterrevolutionary Policies and their Structural Consequences*. Princeton, N.J.: Princeton University Press, 1987.

Webb, Richard. *Government Policy and the Distribution of Income in Peru, 1963–1973*. Cambridge: Harvard University Press, 1977.

———. "Internal Debt and Financial Adjustment in Peru." *CEPAL Review* 32 (August 1987): 55–74.

———. *Stabilisation and Adjustment Policies and Programmes*. Country Study no. 8, Peru. Helsinki: World Institute for Development Economics, Research of the UN University, 1987.

Weeks, John. *Limits to Capitalist Development; The Industrialization of Peru, 1950–1980*. Boulder, Colo.: Westview, 1985.

Weinman, Lois. "Ecuador and Cacao: Domestic Responses to the Boom-Collapse Monoexport Cycle." Ph.D. diss., University of California, Los Angeles, 1970.

Weir, Margaret, and Theda Skocpol. "State Structures and the Possibilities for Keynesian

Responses to the Great Depression in Sweden, Britain, and the U.S.'' In *Bringing the State Back In,* ed. Peter Evans et al. Cambridge: Cambridge University Press, 1985.

Weir, Margaret, Anna Shola Orloff, and Theda Skocpol. *The Politics of Social Policy in the United States*. Princeton, N.J.: Princeton University Press, 1988.

Whitehead, Laurence. ''National Power and Local Power: The Case of Santa Cruz de la Sierra.'' In *Latin American Urban Research,* vol. 3, ed. Francine Rabinovitz and Felicity Trueblood. Beverly Hills: Sage Publications, 1973.

Wiener, Martin. *English Culture and the Decline of the Industrial Spirit, 1850–1980.* Cambridge: Cambridge University Press, 1981.

Wilkie, James W. *The Bolivian Revolution and U.S. Aid Since 1952: Financial Background and Context of Political Decision.* Los Angeles: Latin American Center, University of California, 1969.

———, ed. *Statistical Abstract of Latin America,* vol. 28. Los Angeles: UCLA Latin American Center Publications, University of California Press, 1990.

Williamson, John. ''What Washington Means by Policy Reforms.'' In *Latin American Adjustment: How Much Has Happened?* ed. John Williamson. Washington D.C.: Institute for International Economics, 1990.

———, ed. *IMF Conditionality.* Washington, D.C.: Institute for International Economics, 1983.

Wilson, Graham K. ''Corporate Political Strategies.'' *British Journal of Political Science* 20, no. 2 (April 1990): 281–88.

Wilson, Patricia A., and Carol Wise. ''The Regional Implications of Public Investment in Peru, 1968–83.'' *Latin American Research Review* 21, no. 2 (1986): 93–116.

Wise, Carol. ''Peru in the 1980s: Political Responses to the Debt Crisis.'' Papers on Latin America no. 2, Institute of Latin America and Iberian Studies, Columbia University, 1988.

World Bank. *Ecuador: Development Problems and Prospects.* Washington, D.C.: World Bank, 1979.

———. *Peru: Major Development Policy Issues and Recommendations.* Washington, D.C.: World Bank, 1981.

———. *Bolivia: Structural Constraints and Development Prospects.* Washington, D.C.: World Bank, 1983.

———. *Bolivia: Agricultural Pricing and Investment Policies.* Washington, D.C.: World Bank, 1984.

———. *Ecuador: An Agenda for Recovery and Sustained Growth.* Washington, D.C.: World Bank, 1984.

Woy-Hazelton, Sandra L. ''SINAMOS, Infrastructure of Participation.'' In *Political Participation in Latin America,* ed. John Booth and Mitchell Seligson. New York: Holmes and Meier, 1978.

Zambrano Castillo, Guido. *León Febres-Cordero: Significación histórica.* Guayaquil: Centro de Publicaciones de la Universidad Católica Santiago de Guayaquil, 1987.

Zeitlin, Maurice, and Richard Earl Ratcliff. *Landlords and Capitalists: The Dominant Class of Chile.* Princeton, N.J.: Princeton University Press, 1988.

Zysman, John. *Governments, Markets, and Growth: Financial Systems and the Politics of Industrial Change.* Ithaca, N.Y.: Cornell University Press, 1983.

Periodicals

Business Latin America, 25 July 1988; 3 April 1989.
CEDOIN. *Informe "R,"* 1985, 1986, 1987, 1988, 1989.
DESCO. *Banco de datos bibliográficos.*
DESCO. *Cronología Política,* 1977, 1978, 1979, 1980.
El Comercio (Lima), 1980, 1981.
El Comercio (Quito), 1982, 1984, 1988.
El Diario, 1980, 1981.
El Expreso, 11 May 1984.
El Universo, 1986.
Epoca, 1991.
Ficha de Información Socio-política, 1974, 1975.
Hoy, 1982, 1984, 1986, 1988.
La Prensa, 1980, 1981.
New York Times, 1983.
Oiga, 1981.
Opinion Libre, 1980, 1981.
Weekly Analysis of Ecuadorean Issues, 1985, 1986.

INDEX

Abusada, Roberto, 117, 120, 141, 152, 226
Acción Democrática Nacionalista (ADN) Bolivia, 89–90, 125–29, 147, 189–93, 202, 229
Acción Popular (AP) Peru, 37, 85, 88, 92, 115–19, 141, 146, 153–55, 173, 175–76, 184
Acuerdo Patrótico, 229
Agrarian Reform Law (1969), 61
Agrarian Reform Law (1973), 62
Albán, Hugo, 181
Alianza Democrática (Peru), 34
Alianza Popular Revolucionaria Americana (APRA) Peru, 32–38, 53, 61, 85, 88, 92, 95, 115–19, 173, 185, 206, 210–12, 226
Allende, Salvador, 121, 130, 199
Alliance for Progress, 37, 51
Alva Orlandini, Javier, 78, 154, 185
Alvear, Miguel, 85
Andean Pact, 44, 59, 62, 79
Andrés Pérez, Carlos, 203–04
Angel Mufarech, Miguel, 154
Anticommunism, 130
Antistatism, 20–21, 69–70, 85, 98–119, 125–29, 131, 136–38, 151, 179, 207–08, 216–19. *See also* Statism
Aramayo, Carlos, 25
Araníbar, Antonio, 193
Araníbar, Ernesto, 199
Arequipa, 18
Argentina, 4, 11, 13, 17, 47, 107, 151, 203
Aristocratic Republic (1895–1919), 26, 32–33
Arosemena, Carlos Julio, 39, 134
Arosemena, Otto, 39
Arroyo del Río, Carlos, 33–34
Asamblea Popular (Bolivia), 58
Asociación de Exportadores (ADEX) Peru, 73, 78–79, 84–87, 117, 153–55, 181
Asociación Industrial de Mineros de Bolivia (AIMB), 72, 74
Asociación Nacional de Empresarios (ANDE) Ecuador, 74
Asociación Nacional de Mineros Medianos (ANMM) Bolivia, 74
Austria, 8
Authoritarianism, 4, 6, 11–12, 86, 170, 204, 231; military, 4, 20, 70–71, 49, 82, 90, 97, 114, 220; bureaucratic, 47, 168, 208
Autocoup (*autogolpe*), 53, 58, 66, 125, 206, 226–29
Autonomy (relative), 6–7, 13–14, 23, 155; economic, 13, 31, 220; state, 14, 220

Banco Agrícola de Bolivia (BAB), 42, 57
Banco Central de Reserva (BCR) Peru, 72, 104–05, 120, 139, 175–79
Banco de Santa Cruz, 45
Banco del Pacífico, 132
Banco Industrial (Peru), 72
Bancocracia, 27

Bank of America, 102
Banzer, General Hugo, 49–67, 75, 79–93, 106–07, 126–28, 137, 147, 187–92, 206–08, 229
Banzeristas, 67–68, 126
Barrantes, Alfonso, 173
Barrientos, General René, 44–45, 51, 210
Barthelemy, Fernando, 194–95, 215
Barua Castañeda, Doctor Luis, 102, 104
Becerra Sotero, Alvaro, 176
Bedoya, Luis, 115–19, 225, 251*n13*
Bedregal, Guillermo, 97, 128–29, 190–91, 201
Belaúnde Terry, Fernando, 5, 38, 50–51, 88, 92–95, 105, 115–20, 137–78, 181–89, 196, 199, 202–19, 225–29
Bellah, Robert, 223
Beltrán, Pedro, 36
Bertram, Geoffrey, 35
Benavides, José, 176
Beni, Bolivia, 45, 149
Billinghurst, Guillermo, 32
Blanco, David, 127
Bloque progresista, 136, 147, 168–71
Bohan, Merwin, 41
Bolivian Communist party (PCB), 96, 188
Boloña, Carlos, 227
Borja, Rodrigo, 132, 135–36, 180, 228
Brazil, 11, 13, 17, 47, 203
Bucaram, Abdalá, 180
Bucaram, Assad, 131
Bucaram, Averroes, 169
Buchanan, James, 83
Busch, Germán, 34
Bustamante y Rivero, José Luis, 34–36

CADE. *See* Conferencia Anual de Ejecutivos Peru
CAEM. *See* Centro de Altos Estudios Militares Peru
Calvo, Carlos, 67
Cámara Agropecuaria del Oriente (CAO) Bolivia, 74–75, 156–67
Cámara de Comercio de Guayaquil (Ecuador), 132, 158, 181
Cámara de Industria y Comercio de Santa Cruz (Bolivia), 75, 82
Cámara de Industriales de Pichincha (Ecuador), 76, 136
Cámara Nacional de Industrias (CNI) Bolivia, 156–57
Cambio-90 (Peru), 227
Canada, 151, 197
CAO. *See* Cámara Agropecuaria del Oriente Bolivia
Capitalism, 5, 7, 18–20, 27, 42, 203–06, 218–19, 223; democratic, 8–9, 84; and domestic capitalists, 16–19, 21–22, 27–37, 60–63, 70–71, 80–91, 115–23, 151, 209; and political mobilization, 70–98, 121–24, 150, 169, 230
Cariaga, Juan, 127–29, 144, 189–90
Carmigniani, Eduardo, 134
Cartagena Agreement (1970), 59; and Decision 24, 24, 62–63, 76, 143
Catholic Church, 86, 126, 194–95; and National Conference of Bishops, 126
CBF. *See* Corporación Boliviana de Fomento
Cebrecos, Ruffino, 116
CENDES. *See* Centro de Desarrollo Industrial Ecuador
Central Bank (Bolivia), 72, 112–13, 123, 144, 190
Central Bank (Ecuador), 56, 142, 176, 179–80
Central Obrera Boliviana (COB), 40–41, 58, 89–90, 97, 108–10, 122–26, 149–50, 186–95, 201, 257*n45,* 260*n18*
Centro de Altos Estudios Militares (CAEM) Peru, 38
Centro de Desarrollo Industrial (CENDES) Ecuador, 39, 50
Centro de Ejecutivos (Ecuador), 74
Centro de Formación Profesional, 74
CEPB. *See* Confederación de Empresarios Privados de Bolivia
CEPE. *See* Corporación Estatal Petrolera Ecuatoriana
Cerro de Pasco Corporation, 59
Certificado de Reintegro Tributario a la Exportación (CERTEX), 141, 146, 153, 176
CFN. *See* Corporación Financiera Nacional Ecuador
CFP. *See* Concentración de Fuerzas Populares Ecuador
CGTP. *See* Confederación General de Trabajadores del Péru
Chaco War (1932–35), 33
Chase Manhattan Bank, 59, 102
Chile, 4, 17, 27, 47, 59, 121, 151, 185–88, 197–203

China, 188
Christian Democratic party (PDC) Ecuador, 38, 97, 170
Chuquisaca, Bolivia, 192
Citibank, 102
Clientelism, 15, 66–67, 115–18, 212–13
CNA. *See* Confederación Nacional Agraria Peru
CNI. *See* Cámara Nacional de Industrias Bolivia
CNT. *See* Confederación Nacional de Trabajadores Peru
Coalitions, economic, 43, 99, 136; neoliberal, 115–30, 138, 161, 178–79, 209–10, 218–19, 226; political, 15, 24, 27, 40, 115, 216–19; social, 8, 12, 23, 47, 86; and coalition-building, 121
COAP. *See* Comité de Asesoramiento de la Presidencia Peru
COB. *See See* Central Obrera Boliviana
Cochabamba, Bolivia, 45, 75
COFADENA. *See* Corporación de las Fuerzas Armadas de Desarrollo Nacional Bolivia
Co-gobierno (Bolivia), 40, 122
Colombia, 59, 192, 204
COMIBOL. *See* Corporación Minera de Bolivia
Comité Cívico Pro-Santa Cruz, 75
Comité de Asesoramiento de la Presidencia (COAP) Peru, 64
Commission on Stabilization (Bolivia), 190
Communism, 48, 83, 203
Compañia Minera del Sur S.A. (COMSUR), 45, 127
Compactación Obrera, 32
COMSUR. *See* Compañia Minera del Sur S.A.
Comunidad industrial (CI), 61–62, 77
CONACI. *See* Confederación Nacional de Comunidades Industriales Peru
CONAL. *See* Consejo Nacional Legislativo
CONAPOL. *See* Consejo Nacional Político
Concentración de Fuerzas Populares (CFP) Ecuador, 38, 94, 111, 130–35, 147, 169
Concertación, 174, 184
La Concordancia, (Bolivia), 34
CONEPLAN. *See* Consejo de Economía Planeamiento
Confederación de Empresarios Privados de Bolivia (CEPB), 63, 66–67, 74, 80–97, 108, 121–29, 157, 189–93, 200
Confederación de Trabajadores de la Revolución Peruana (CTRP), 61
Confederación de Trabajadores del Ecuador (CTE), 63
Confederación General de Trabajadores del Péru (CGTP), 61, 78, 148
Confederación Nacional Agraria (CNA) Peru, 65, 78
Confederación Nacional de Comunidades Industriales (CONACI) Peru, 65, 78
Confederación Nacional de Instituciones Empresariales Privadas (CONFIEP) Peru, 74, 181
Confederación Nacional de Trabajadores (CNT) Peru 61
Conferencia Anual de Ejecutivos (CADE) Peru, 74
CONFIEP. *See* Confederación Nacional de Instituciones Empresariales Privadas Peru
Congress of 80, 96–97, 108
Consejo de Economía Planeamiento (CONEPLAN), 190
Consejo Nacional Legislativo (CONAL), 90
Consejo Nacional Político (CONAPOL), 190
Conservatism (fiscal), 102–05, 135
Consulta popular (Bolivia), 194–95
Córdova, Gonzalo, 29
Corporación Boliviana de Fomento (CBF), 50
Corporación Estatal Petrolera Ecuatoriana (CEPE), 56
Corporación Financiera Nacional (CFN) Ecuador, 39, 50
Corporación de las Fuerzas Armadas de Desarrollo Nacional (COFADENA) Bolivia, 64
Corporación Minera de Bolivia (COMIBOL), 40, 50, 63, 122, 140, 144, 151, 186–88, 194–95
Corporatism, 8, 66, 86
CTE. *See* Confederación de Trabajadores del Ecuador
CTRP. *See* Confederación de Trabajadores de la Revolución Peruana
Currency devaluation, 102, 107–13, 132, 164, 196–97, 228

Dahik, Alberto, 132, 176–78, 225–29, 261*n37*
Democracia Popular party (DP) Ecuador, 133, 135–36
Democratic despotism, 21, 205, 223. *See also* Tocqueville, Alexis de
Democratization, 4–5, 13, 20–22, 34, 71, 85–97, 108–16, 124, 152, 203–06, 215–16, 220

Development Bank (Ecuador), 56
Developmentalism, 19–20, 27–28, 35–41, 111; economic, 23, 45, 48, 49, 55, 60, 64, 71; industrial, 55; *desarrollismo,* 36
Dirección de Industrias de Ejército (DINE) Ecuador, 53
Dominican Republic, 97
Drug trade, 204; cocaine, 198; and Operation Blast Furnace, 196
Duhuarte, Raymundo, 65–67, 78, 83
Durán, Juan Carlos, 194, 215
Durán Ballén, Sixto, 91, 130–34, 185, 203, 225–29
Durand, Francisco, 155

Eckstein, Susan, 45, 157
ECLA. *See* United Nations Economic Commission for Latin America
Economia social de mercado, 95, 126
Economic austerity, 3, 11, 17, 88, 100–14, 122, 144, 175–78, 189, 217. *See also* International Monetary Fund
Economic diversification, 26–27, 39, 42–45, 55–58
Economic intervention, 3, 7–8, 19–24, 35, 45–51, 61–62, 85, 99, 114–17, 125, 141–46; infrastructure, 24, 83, 117; state-centric economics, 41–42, 71–79, 98–105, 114, 127–29, 136, 208
Ecuadorean Chambers of Production, 76
El pueblo, 31–33
Emanuel, Carlos Julio, 132, 159, 176–78, 183–84
Emusa S.A., 45
Endeudamiento agresivo (Ecuador), 111
Enríquez, Colonel Alberto, 33
Escuela Superior de Administración de Empresas (ESAN) Peru, 74
Espinoza Bermeo, Rodrigo, 178
Exchange Control Board (Bolivia), 72

Falange Socialista Boliviana (FSB), 53, 66
Falkland Islands–Malvinas War, 112, 162
Febres Cordero, León, 5, 83, 87, 94, 131–52, 158–62, 166–99, 202, 214–19, 225, 228–29, 259*n79*
Federación de Empresarios Privados de Cochabamba (Bolivia), 75
Federación Ecuatoriana de Industrias Exportadores (FEDEXPOR) Ecuador, 73
Federation of Agriculture (Ecuador), 92
Ferrand, Alfredo, 83, 152–53
Finegold, Kenneth, 7, 9
First Bank of Boston, 118
Fitch, John, 39
Fitzgerald, E.V.K., 52, 60
Fondo Social de Emergencia (FSE) Bolivia, 151, 197–98
Frente Amplio de Izquierda (FADI) Ecuador, 135–36
Frente de Reconstrucción Nacional (FRN) Ecuador, 134–36, 147, 168–69, 183, 215
Frente Radical Alfarista (FRA) Ecuador, 134, 147
Frente Revolucionario de Izquierda (FRI) Bolivia, 97
Frente Unitario de Trabajadores (FUT) Ecuador, 112, 149
Frieden, Jeffry, 12
Friedman, Milton, 153–54
FSB. *See* Falange Socialista Boliviana
Fuerza del Cambio (Ecuador), 130
Fuji-golpe, 204, 228–29. *See also* Autocoup
Fujimori, Alberto, 203–04, 225–28, 262*n40*
Fukuyama, Francis, 203
Fundación Boliviana (1981), 85

Gamarra, Eduardo, 122
García, Alan, 185, 226
García Meza, General Luis, 90–96, 107, 199, 210
Garretón, Manuel Antonio, 224
Germany, 23
Gerschenkron, Alexander, 19
Gisbert, Roberto, 129, 189–90
Golpe constitucional (Bolivia), 125
González Alvear, Raúl, 91
González Izquierdo, Jorge, 116–17, 120
Gourevitch, Peter, 7–9, 12
Grados Bertorini, Alfonso, 174
Gradualism, 159–60
Gran Colombia, 18
Great Britain, 9, 23
Great Depression (1930s), 7, 9, 19, 27, 33–35, 99
Grupo consultivo (Bolivia), 127–28
Guayaquileños, 72, 132

Guayaquil, Ecuador, 26, 29–31, 38, 43–44, 56, 74, 87, 94, 130–35, 179, 225
Gueiler, Lidia, 89–93, 100, 107
Guevara Arce, Walter, 89–93, 96
Guzmán, Marco Antonio, 62

Haggard, Stephan, 12
Hagopian, Frances, 45, 157
Halco Mining, 118
Hall, Peter, 7–8
Hartlyn, Jonathan, 12,
Haya de la Torre, Víctor Raúl, 32–33, 118
Hegemony, 9, 28, 84, 203
Heterodoxy, 4, 11, 29, 108–09, 162, 188, 226–28. *See also* Orthodoxy
Hirschman, Albert, 70
Holland, 197
Hoschild, Mauricio, 25
Huerta, Raúl Clemente, 130
Hurtado, Osvaldo, 91, 94, 100, 110–14, 130–35, 142, 149, 163, 170
Hurtado Miller, Juan Carlos, 227
Hyperinflation, 4, 106, 110, 123–27, 143, 185–86, 199–201, 226, 230

ILD. *See* Instituto Libertad y Democracia
IESS. *See* Instituto de Estudios Económicos y Sociales
Illanes, Fernando, 124–25, 127
Industrial Development Bank (Bolivia), 50
Industrial Community Law (1970) Peru, 51, 59, 61–62, 77, 87, 101
Industrial Development Law (1957) Ecuador, 36, 45, 56
Industrial Promotion Law (1959) Peru, 45
Industrialization, 27, 31, 43, 55, 59, 153; import-intensive, 101; import-substitution, 19, 41, 47, 55, 99, 157–59, 218; state-promoted, 36, 44
Instituto de Estudios Económicos y Sociales (IESS), 83. *See also* Sociedad Nacional de Industrias
Instituto Libertad y Democracia (ILD), 85, 118
Instituto Peruano de Administración de Empresas (IPAE), 74
Inter-American Development Bank, 145
International Petroleum Company (IPC), 59
International Monetary Fund (IMF), 3, 11–12, 21, 30, 41, 99, 102–07, 112–13, 122, 139–45, 155, 165–66, 175–76, 184, 196–97, 214–16, 227
Interpellation, 146–47, 160, 177, 192, 210–11
IPAE. *See* Instituto Peruano de Administración de Empresas
IPC. *See* International Petroleum Company
Iran-Contra, 221, 223
ITT Corporation, 59
Iturralde, Carlos, 67, 157
Izquierda Democrática party (ID) Ecuador, 130–36, 171
Izquierda Unida (IU) Peru, 173

Jensen, Brian, 120
Jordan Pando, Roberto, 128
JUNAPLA. *See* Junta Nacional de Planificación y Coordinación Económica Ecuador
Junta Cívica (Ecuador, 1975), 88
Junta Nacional de Planificación y Coordinación Económica (JUNAPLA) Ecuador, 37, 39, 50

Katzenstein, Peter, 7–9, 12–13
Kaufman, Robert, 12
Kennedy administration, 37
Kennedy School, 127
Kemmerer, Edwin, 30, 33–34; and Kemmererian coalition, 30
Keynesian economic policies, 8–9, 13, 28, 34–36, 99, 206
Kohn, Pedro, 136
Korean War, 35
Kuhn, Loeb, 118

Lanata, Gabriel, 79, 83, 116, 251*n13*
Laserna, Roberto, 123
La Paz, Bolivia, 18, 31, 45, 52, 107, 189, 194, 224
Latifundistas, 40
Lechín Oquendo, Juan, 149
Leguía, Augusto, 30–32
Levoyer, General Richelieu, 93–94
Liberalism, 24, 27, 35–37, 69, 83, 94; economic, 25–26, 49, 53, 77, 98, 207. *See also* Neoliberalism
Lima, Peru, 18, 31, 52, 72, 78, 104, 122
Lindblom, Charles, 5, 9, 80
Lowi, Theodore, 204, 222

Machicado, Flavio, 122
MacLean, Ronald, 127
Malloy, James, 122
Management Committee of Creditor Banks, 143
Manta air base, 169
Manufacturers Hanover, 102
Marcha hacia al oriente (Bolivia), 42
Marcha por la vida (Bolivia), 150, 194
Marchán, Miguel, 181
Marcona Mining, 59
María Albuja, Commander General Manuel, 169
Mariátegui, Sandro, 176
Market-oriented economy, 3, 136–38, 144, 174–80, 217; controls on, 5, 108–110, 114, 143, 180; liberalization of, 5, 12, 23, 34–36, 83, 99, 105–06, 128–29, 154–56, 160, 174–87
Marshall-Silva, Jorge, 56
Marx, Karl, 6
Massacre of Toalata (1974), 58
MBL. *See* Movimiento Bolivia Libre
McClintock, Cynthia, 65
Melgarejo, Mariano, 25
Menem, Carlos, 203
Mercado, Mario, 67, 127; family of, 45
Mexico, 29, 110–12, 162, 164, 203
Miliband, Ralph, 7, 11
Mining Law (1950) Peru, 45
MIR. *See* Movimiento de la Izquierda Revolucionaria Bolivia
MNCs. *See* Multinational corporations
MNR. *See* Movimiento Nacionalista Revolucionario Bolivia
Morales Bermúdez, General Francisco, 75, 79, 88, 102–06, 114–18, 148, 197, 206
Moreyra, Manuel, 104–05, 141
Morgan Guaranty, 102
Morley, Samuel, 12
Monetary Board (Ecuador), 65
Movimiento Bolivia Libre (MBL), 193, 230
Movimiento de la Izquierda Revolucionaria (MIR) Bolivia, 96–97, 128, 188, 191–93
Movimiento Nacionalista Revolucionario (MNR) Bolivia, 34, 40–45, 53, 66, 97, 126–27, 147, 161, 187–93, 212, 229–30
Movimiento Nacionalista Revolucionario-Izquierda (Bolivia), 96–97, 126–28
Movimiento Popular Democrático (MPD) Ecuador, 134–36
Multinational corporations (MNCs), 44

National Development Plan (Bolivia), 111
National Finance Corporation (Ecuador), 56, 65
National Federation of Chambers of Commerce (Ecuador), 92
National Federation of Chambers of Industry (Ecuador), 92, 94, 131–33, 158
National Secretariat of Planning and Coordination (Bolivia), 50
National Minimum Wage Commission (Peru), 72
Nationalism, 24, 33, 48, 59
Natusch Busch, Colonel Alberto, 93, 107
Neira, Xavier, 159
Neoliberalism, 5–6, 12, 17–21, 48–49, 98–114, 125–39, 143–52, 157–62, 167–69, 174, 176–79, 185–88, 202, 216–19, 225–27. *See also* Liberalism
"New Bolivia Plan," 66
Noboa Naranjo, Luis, 43, 181
Noboa economic group, 131–32, 158
Nueva politica económica (NPE), 144–45, 157, 185–202

O'Donnell, Guillermo, 4, 13, 47, 124, 158, 208
Odría, Manuel, 35–36
Organization of American States (OAS), 50
Oligarchy, 19–20, 43–44, 68, 84, 130, 133, 170; and politics, 22–40, 46, 72–73, 76, 94, 205
Olson, Mancur, 83
OPIC. *See* Overseas Private Investment Corporation
Orthodox Marxism, 150
Orthodoxy, 162, 165–67, 175, 196–97, 203, 227. *See also* Heterodoxy
Ortiz de Zevallos, Felipe, 83, 85
Ovando, General Alfredo, 51, 58
Overseas Private Investment Corporation (OPIC), 140, 143

Pablo Kuczynski, Pedro, 118, 141
Pacto de Punto Fijo, 118–19
Pacto por la democracia (Bolivia), 128, 147, 191, 202, 229
Pando, Bolivia, 149
Paniagua, Valentín, 176
Paquetazo, 112
Paraguay, 17, 97, 203
Paris Club, 143, 196
Parodi, Jorge, 150

Partido Civilista (Peru), 26, 32, 36
Partido Conservador Ecuatoriano (PCE), 38, 88, 94, 131, 134, 229. *See also* Conservative party
Partido Demócrata (PD) Peru, 26,
Partido Demócrata (PD) Ecuador, 135–36
Partido Demócrata Cristiano (PDC) Peru, 37, 115. *See also* Christian Democratic party
Partido Liberal Radical (PLR) Ecuador, 38, 131, 134. *See also* Liberal party
Partido Nacionalista Revolucionario (PNR) Ecuador, 38, 88, 134. *See also* National Revolutionary party
Partido Popular Cristiano (PPC) Peru, 88, 92, 95, 115–20, 126, 146, 153–54, 174–76, 184, 210
Partido Revolucionario Auténtico (PRA) Bolivia, 96
Partido Roldosista (Ecuador), 180
Partido Social Cristiano (PSC) Ecuador, 38, 130–31, 134, 185, 228–29. *See also* Social Christian party
Partido Socialista (PS) Bolivia, 97
Partido Unidad Republicana (PUR) Ecuador, 228–29
Patiño, Simón, 25
Paz, Rodrigo, 133, 137
Paz Estenssoro, Víctor, 5, 40–41, 50, 106, 125–29, 138–39, 143–63, 187–201, 212–19, 225, 229
Paz Zamora, Jaime, 93, 125, 128, 187, 193, 229–30
PCB. *See* Bolivian Communist party
PCE. *See* Partido Conservador Ecuatoriano
Peñaherrera, Blasco, 134, 177
Peñaranda, General Enrique, 34
Pennano, Guido, 227
Peronism, 29
Persivale, Roberto, 153
Personalism, 81, 126, 170
Petroleum Law (1952) Peru, 45
Piazza, Walter, 104
Pinchincha, Ecuador, 87, 130
Piñeiros, Luis, 169
Pinochet, Augusto, 199, 202
Plan Austral, 226
Plan Túpac Amaru (Peru), 88, 92, 95
Plaza Lasso, Galo, 35
Pliego nacional (Bolivia), 195
PLR. *See* Partido Liberal Radical Ecuador
Pluralismo empresarial, 95
PNR. *See* Partido Nacionalista Revolucionario Ecuador
Ponce, Camilo, 36–37
Poncista party, 88
Populism, 20–36, 46, 119, 131–37, 189, 204, 214, 230
Portes, Alejandro, 42–43, 150
Poulantzas, Nicos, 7, 11
Poveda Burbano, Admiral Alfredo, 56, 75, 79, 88, 91–93, 111, 178
PPC. *See* Partido Popular Cristiano Peru
PRA. *See* Partido Revolucionario Auténtico Bolivia
Prado, Manuel, 35–36
Prebisch, Raúl, 19, 36
Presidentialism, 209–10, 222; and parliamentarism, 210
Professionalism, business, 73–74; in the military, 47, 53; political, 170
Protectionism, 23, 70, 159, 207, 218
Przeworski, Adam, 8, 208; and class compromise, 8
PS. *See* Partido Socialista Bolivia
PS-1. *See* Socialist party-1 Bolivia
PSC. *See* Partido Social Cristiano Ecuador
Puente, Gonzalo de la, 153
PUR. *See* Partido Unidad Republicana Ecuador

Quijano, Aníbal, 55
Quintero, Rafael, 32–33
Quiroga, Jaime, 67
Quito, Ecuador, 52, 72, 94, 132–33, 222

Racism, 18, 24
Reagan, Ronald, 99–100, 217, 221; and Reaganism, 217, 223
Realpolitik, 98
Reactivation, 157, 176, 181, 186, 200–01
Reformism, 23, 82, 133, 207, 212
Remmer, Karen, 12
Rent-seeking, 48, 84, 116, 160, 174, 214, 218
Revel, Jean-François, 85
Revolución Juliana (1925), 29–30
Rivera, Iván, 116, 120
Rodríguez Lara, General Guillermo, 49, 51, 55–56, 62–65, 75–77, 83, 86–88, 91–92, 206–07
Rodríguez Pastor, Carlos, 117, 154–55, 165–66, 173, 175, 185, 197, 226–27

Roldós, Jaime, 56, 91, 94, 111–13, 130–33
Romero, Boris, 153
Romero, Fernando, 128
Rotondo, Roberto, 153

Saavedra, Bautista, 32
Sachs, Jeffrey, 128, 189–92, 196, 202
Sáenz, General Alcibiades, 104
Salinas, Carlos, 203
Sánchez Cerro, Luis Alberto, 32–33
Sánchez de Lozada, Gonzalo, 45, 126–29, 137, 143, 156, 187–202, 218, 225, 229–30
Santa Cruz, Bolivia, 18, 41–42, 45, 57, 74, 157, 187, 192
Schumpeterian innovations, 24
Schydlowsky, Daniel, 117, 154
Schwalb, Fernando, 175
Sendero Luminoso, 173, 226
Servicio Ecuatoriano Capacitación Profesional, 74
Sheahan, John, 12
SI. *See* Sociedad de Industrias Peru
Sierra Ranchers' Association, 92
Siles Reyes, Hernando, 30, 32
Siles Zuazo, Hernán, 41, 93, 96–97, 100, 106–14, 121–28, 149–50, 158, 188–202, 212, 219
Silva Ruete, Javier, 79, 83, 104–05, 116, 141, 251*nn12, 13*
Sistema Nacional de Apoyo a la Movilización Social (SINAMOS) Peru, 61, 63, 65, 78, 206
Skocpol, Theda, 7–9
Smith, William, 13
SNA. *See* Sociedad Nacional Agaria Peru
SNI. *See* Sociedad Nacional de Industrias Peru
SNM. *See* Sociedad Nacional de Minería Peru
Soberón, Luis, 81
Social Christian party (Ecuador), 36
Social Security Board (Bolivia), 72
Socialist party (Peru), 37
Socialist party-1 (PS-1) Bolivia, 97
Sociedad de Industrias (SI) Peru, 77, 82
Sociedad Nacional Agaria (SNA) Peru, 65–66, 72, 77, 84
Sociedad Nacional de Industrias (SNI) Peru, 65–66, 72, 77–80, 84–89, 95, 116–17, 152–55, 181, 250*n40;* export committee of, 78
Sociedad Nacional de Minería (SNM) Peru, 72, 155
Sola, Lourdes de, 13
Soto, Hernando de, 83, 85, 118, 226–27
Stabilization program, 12, 41, 99–109, 112–14, 128–32, 142–44, 148–49, 157, 163, 172, 185–88, 196, 225–230. *See also* International Monetary Fund
Standard Oil, 50
Statism, 24, 45, 47–69, 71, 82–85, 92. *See also* Antistatism
Stein, Steve, 31
Stepan, Alfred, 47, 53, 59, 199
Subsidies, 105–07, 110–12, 125, 141, 143
Supergroup Noboa, 43. *See also* Noboa economic group
Sweden, 9, 151, 197
Switzerland, 151, 197, 220
Swett, Francisco, 132, 142, 148, 159, 166, 176–78

Taiwan, 220
Tarija, Bolivia, 192
Taura air force base, 171
TGC. *See* Tribunal de Garantías Constitucionales Ecuador
Thatcher, Margaret, 99
Thorp, Rosemary, 35, 101
Tocqueville, Alexis de, 21, 204–05, 220, 223–24
Toro, Colonel David, 33
Torre, Juan Carlos, 13
Torrelio, General Celso, 90, 93, 107–08
Torres, General Juan José, 51, 58
Townsend, Andrés, 118
Tribunal de Garantías Constitucionales (TGC) Ecuador, 171, 178
Tribunal Supremo Electoral (Ecuador), 130
Trujillo, Julio César, 87

UCS. *See* Unión Cívica Solidaridad Bolivia
UDP. *See* Unión Democrática Popular Bolivia
UEPP. *See* Unión de Empresarios Privados del Perú
Ugarteche, Oscar, 199
Ulloa, Manuel, 117–20, 137, 139–42, 149, 153–56, 165, 174, 197, 215
Unidades ejecutoras, 172
Unión Cívica Solidaridad (UCS) Bolivia, 230
Unión de Empresarios Privados del Perú (UEPP), 73

Unión Democrática Popular (UDP) Bolivia, 96–97, 122–23, 126
United Nations Economic Commission for Latin America (ECLA), 18–19, 36, 39, 50–55, 105
United States, 9–10, 41, 126, 196–97, 217, 221–23; and Agency for International Development (USAID), 39, 41, 145, 151, 197; Democratic party of, 222; and New Deal (1930), 8–9, 217, 222; Republican party of, 126
Universidad de Lima, 74
Universidad del Pacífico, 74
Uruguay, 4, 47, 203
USAID. *See* United States, and Agency for International Development

Vallejo, Andrés, 171
Vargas Llosa, Mario, 83, 85, 118, 225–27
Vargas Pazzos, General Frank, 169–71
Vega, Jorge, 116
Velasco Alvarado, General Juan, 49–52, 58–66, 75–81, 84, 86–88, 95, 98–106, 115, 152, 206–07
Velasco Ibarra, José María, 33–34, 39, 206
Velasquista party (Ecuador), 38, 60, 88
Venezuela, 59, 118, 192, 203
Vietnam War, 221
Vildoso, General Guido, 90, 93, 97, 108
Villanueva, Armando, 118–19
Villaroel, General Gualberto, 34
Vogel, David, 7, 9–10
Von Hayek, Friedrich, 85

Watergate, 221–23
War of the Pacific (1879–83), 26–27
Webb, Richard, 80, 117, 120, 139, 164–65, 175–76, 182
Weber, Max, 15
Weir, Margaret, 7, 9
Wells Fargo Bank, 102, 118, 120, 154
Wheeler Mission, 145
World Bank, 99, 107–08, 120, 128, 139, 141–45, 151–55, 165–66, 184, 197, 214–16, 227

Yacimientos Petrolíferos Fiscales Bolivianos (YPFB), 50, 194
Yerovi, Clemente, 39

Zondag, Cornelius, 41
Zysman, John, 7, 9–10

PITT LATIN AMERICAN SERIES

James M. Malloy, Editor

ARGENTINA

Argentina: Political Culture and Instability
Susan Calvert and Peter Calvert

Argentina Between the Great Powers, 1936–1946
Guido di Tella and D. Cameron Watt, Editors

Argentina in the Twentieth Century
David Rock, Editor

Argentine Workers: Peronism and Contemporary Class Consciousness
Peter Ranis

Discreet Partners: Argentina and the USSR Since 1917
Aldo César Vacs

The Franco-Perón Alliance: Relations Between Spain and Argentina, 1946–1955
Raanan Rein, translated by Martha Grenzeback

Frondizi and the Politics of Developmentalism in Argentina, 1955–62
Celia Szusterman

Institutions, Parties, and Coalitions in Argentine Politics
Luigi Manzetti

The Life, Music, and Times of Carlos Gardel
Simon Collier

The Political Economy of Argentina, 1946–1983
Guido di Tella and Rudiger Dornbusch, Editors

BRAZIL

The Brazilian Voter: Mass Politics in Democratic Transition, 1974–1986
Kurt von Mettenheim

Capital Markets in the Development Process: The Case of Brazil
John H. Welch

External Constraints on Economic Policy in Brazil, 1899–1930
Winston Fritsch

The Film Industry in Brazil: Culture and the State
Randal Johnson

Kingdoms Come: Religion and Politics in Brazil
Rowan Ireland

The Manipulation of Consent: The State and Working Class Consciousness in Brazil
Youssef Cohen

The Politics of Social Security in Brazil
James M. Malloy

Politics Within the State: Elite Bureaucrats and Industrial Policy in Authoritarian Brazil
Ben Ross Schneider

Unequal Giants: Diplomatic Relations Between the United States and Brazil, 1889–1930
Joseph Smith

CHILE

Chile: The Political Economy of Development and Democracy in the 1990s
David E. Hojman

The Overthrow of Allende and the Politics of Chile, 1964–1976
Paul E. Sigmund

Primary Medical Care in Chile: Accessibility Under Military Rule
Joseph L. Scarpaci

CUBA

Cuba After the Cold War
Carmelo Mesa-Lago, Editor

Cuba Between Empires, 1878–1902
Louis A. Pérez, Jr.

Cuba Under the Platt Amendment, 1902–1934
Louis A. Pérez, Jr.

Cuban Studies, Vols. 16–24
Carmelo Mesa-Lago et al., Editors

The Economics of Cuban Sugar
Jorge F. Pérez-López

Intervention, Revolution, and Politics in Cuba, 1913–1921
Louis A. Pérez, Jr.

Lords of the Mountain: Social Banditry and Peasant Protest in Cuba, 1878–1918
Louis A. Pérez, Jr.

Sport in Cuba: The Diamond in the Rough
Paula J. Pettavino and Geralyn Pye

MEXICO

The Dynamics of Domination: State, Class, and Social Reform in Mexico, 1910–1990
Viviane Brachet-Marquez

The Expulsion of Mexico's Spaniards, 1821–1836
Harold Dana Sims

Mexico Through Russian Eyes, 1806–1940
William Harrison Richardson

Oil and Mexican Foreign Policy
George W. Grayson

The Politics of Mexican Oil
George W. Grayson

Voices, Visions, and a New Reality: Mexican Fiction Since 1970
J. Ann Duncan

NORTHERN AND CENTRAL ANDES

Domestic and Foreign Finance in Modern Peru, 1850–1950: Financing Visions of Development
Alfonso W. Quiroz

Economic Management and Economic Development in Peru and Colombia
Rosemary Thorp

Gaitán of Colombia: A Political Biography
Richard E. Sharpless

Military Rule and Transition in Ecuador: Dancing with the People
Anita Isaacs

The Origins of the Peruvian Labor Movement, 1883–1919
Peter Blanchard

Peru and the International Monetary Fund
Thomas Scheetz

Peru Under García: An Opportunity Lost
John Crabtree

Poverty and Peasantry in Peru's Southern Andes, 1963–90
R. F. Watters

Restructuring Domination: Industrialists and the State in Ecuador
Catherine M. Conaghan

Roads to Reason: Transportation, Administration, and Rationality in Colombia
Richard E. Hartwig

Unsettling Statecraft: Democracy and Neoliberalism in the Central Andes
Catherine M. Conaghan and James M. Malloy

CARIBBEAN

The Last Cacique: Leadership and Politics in a Puerto Rican City
Jorge Heine

The Meaning of Freedom: Economics, Politics, and Culture After Slavery
Frank McGlynn and Seymour Drescher, Editors

A Revolution Aborted: The Lessons of Grenada
Jorge Heine, Editor

“To Hell with Paradise”: A History of the Jamaican Tourist Industry
Frank Fonda Taylor

CENTRAL AMERICA

At the Fall of Somoza
Lawrence Pezzullo and Ralph Pezzullo

Black Labor on a White Canal: Panama, 1904–1981
Michael L. Conniff

The Catholic Church and Politics in Nicaragua and Costa Rica
Philip J. Williams

The Costa Rican Women's Movement: A Reader
Ilse Abshagen Leitinger, Editor and Translator

Perspectives on the Agro-Export Economy in Central America
Wim Pelupessy, Editor

INTERNATIONAL RELATIONS

The Giant's Rival: The USSR and Latin America
Cole Blasier

The Hovering Giant: U.S. Responses to Revolutionary Change in Latin America
Cole Blasier

Illusions of Conflict: Anglo-American Diplomacy Toward Latin America
Joseph Smith

Images and Intervention: U.S. Policies in Latin America
Martha L. Cottam

The United States and Latin America in the 1980s: Contending Perspectives on a Decade of Crisis
Kevin J. Middlebrook and Carlos Rico, Editors

OTHER STUDIES

Adventurers and Proletarians: The Story of Migrants in Latin America
Magnus Mörner, with the collaboration of Harold Sims

Ascent to Bankruptcy: Financing Social Security in Latin America
Carmelo Mesa-Lago

Authoritarianism and Corporatism in Latin America
James M. Malloy, Editor

Authoritarians and Democrats: Regime Transition in Latin America
James M. Malloy and Mitchell A. Seligson, Editors

Business and Democracy in Latin America
Ernest Bartell and Leigh A. Payne, Editors

The Constitution of Tyranny: Regimes of Exception in Spanish America
Brian Loveman

Education and Society in Latin America
Orlando Albornoz

Female and Male in Latin America: Essays
Ann Pescatello, Editor

Latin American Debt and the Adjustment Crisis
Rosemary Thorp and Laurence Whitehead, Editors

Public Policy in Latin America: A Comparative Survey
John W. Sloan

Rebirth of the Paraguayan Republic: The First Colorado Era, 1878–1904
Harris G. Warren

Selected Latin American One-Act Plays
Francesca Colecchia and Julio Matas, Editors and Translators

The Social Documentary in Latin America
Julianne Burton, Editor

The State and Capital Accumulation in Latin America. Vol. 1: Brazil, Chile, Mexico. Vol. 2: Argentina, Bolivia, Colombia, Ecuador, Peru, Uruguay, Venezuela
Christian Anglade and Carlos Fortin, Editors

''They Eat from Their Labor'': Work and Social Change in Colonial Bolivia
Ann Zulawski

Transnational Corporations and the Latin American Automobile Industry
Rhys Jenkins